Bob Dylan and Leonard Cohen

Bob Dylan and Leonard Cohen

Deaths and Entrances

David Boucher and Lucy Boucher

BLOOMSBURY ACADEMIC

NEW YORK · LONDON · OXFORD · NEW DELHI · SYDNEY

BLOOMSBURY ACADEMIC
Bloomsbury Publishing Inc
1385 Broadway, New York, NY 10018, USA
50 Bedford Square, London, WC1B 3DP, UK
29 Earlsfort Terrace, Dublin 2, Ireland

BLOOMSBURY, BLOOMSBURY ACADEMIC and the Diana logo are trademarks of Bloomsbury Publishing Plc

First published in the United States of America 2021

For legal purposes the Acknowledgments on p. 285 constitute an extension of this copyright page.

Cover design by Louise Dugdale
Cover images: Bob Dylan, 1966, Bettmann/Getty Images,Leonard Cohen, 1985,
Photo by Oliver Morris/Getty Images

Library of Congress Cataloging-in-Publication Data

Names: Boucher, David, 1951- author. | Boucher, Lucy, 1988 author.
Title: Bob Dylan and Leonard Cohen : deaths and entrances / David Boucher, Lucy Boucher.
Description: New York : Bloomsbury Academic, 2021. | Includes bibliographical references and index. | Summary:
"Both Dylan and Cohen have been a presence on the music and poetry landscape spanning six decades. This
book begins with a discussion of their contemporary importance, and how they have sustained their enduring
appeal as performers and recording artists. The focus then returns to their ambitions when they first started
out, arguing that they both shared the aspirations of the Beat Generation of Ginsberg, Kerouac and Corso to be
as famous as Dylan Thomas and live the life of his sense of unconditional social irresponsibility. The 'Rimbaud
of Cwmdonkin Drive' took America by storm, demonstrating that the bohemian poet could earn a living
outside the academy. The fame of Dylan and Cohen, while it fluctuated over the decades, was sustained and
was sustainable because they self-consciously adopted different personas, or masks, to distance themselves
from the public self. This necessarily requires an exploration of their relation to religion as avenues to find and
preserve their inner identities. Their lyrics and poetry are explored in the context of the relation between poetry
and song, and of Lorca's concepts of the poetry of inspiration, and the deep dark emotional depths of 'duende.'
Such ideas draw upon the dislocation of the mind, and the liberation of the senses that so struck Dylan and
Cohen when they first read the poetry and letters of Arthur Rimbaud and Federico García Lorca. We see that the
performance and the poetry are integral, and the 'duende,' or passion, of the delivery, is inseparable from the
lyric or poetry, and common to Dylan, Cohen and the Beat Generation – Provided by publisher.
Identifiers: LCCN 2020055211 (print) | LCCN 2020055212 (ebook) | ISBN 9781501345654 (hardcover) | ISBN
9781501345661 (paperback) | ISBN 9781501345678 (epub) | ISBN 9781501345685 (pdf)
Subjects: LCSH: Dylan, Bob, 1941- | Cohen, Leonard, 1934-2016 |
Singers–United States–Biography. | Singers–Canada–Biography.
Classification: LCC ML420.D98 B64 2021 (print) | LCC ML420.D98 (ebook) | DDC 782.42164092/2 [B]–dc23
LC record available at https://lccn.loc.gov/2020055211
LC ebook record available at https://lccn.loc.gov/2020055212

ISBN: HB: 978-1-5013-4565-4
PB: 978-1-5013-4566-1
ePDF: 978-1-5013-4568-5
eBook: 978-1-5013-4567-8

Typeset by Deanta Global Publishing Services, Chennai, India
Printed and bound in the United States of America

To find out more about our authors and books visit www.bloomsbury.com and
sign up for our newsletters.

Contents

Introduction

There are few singer-songwriter music legends whose fame and careers span six decades, having the versatility continuously to adapt to the demands of the music industry, producing high-quality material and able to attract new audiences, while retaining the hard-core support through the good times and the bad. In country music the longevity and durability of the careers of singer/songwriter have been more evident than in other genres of popular music. Dolly Parton, Emmy Lou Harris and Willie Nelson are obvious candidates, while the folk/rock revival of the 1960s gave rise to remarkable talents such as Paul Simon and Neil Young. There are two, however, whose lyrics elevated them to an iconic status because of the unique social and political circumstances that prevailed. Bob Dylan's and Leonard Cohen's success was facilitated by a disaffected, disenfranchised youth, disgruntled with an establishment that hated non-conformity, and vilified and humiliated anyone who pressed against the boundaries of mainstream society. A society that was almost paranoiac about the corrupting influence of all genres of music that was expressive of sexual, political or social upheaval that deviated from the norm.

Yet the fascination of the forbidden, unconventional, daring, darker and seamier side of cultural life generated a voyeurism of immense proportions. While newspaper headlines derided Chuck Berry, Little Richard, Jerry Lee Lewis, Elvis Presley and Bill Haley and the Comets for playing the Devil's music in the 1950s, and for corrupting the morals of the young, poets, artists and authors were ridiculed and demonized for their bohemian, shocking and outrageous life-styles. Dylan Thomas and Brendan Behan were exotic and Celtic, and seemed to break all cultural taboos, cause sensations and leave lasting impressions. Dylan Thomas was the modern-day manifestation of such ultra-bohemians as Arthur Rimbaud, Paul Verlaine and Federico ía Lorca, all of whom indelibly marked the lives of the Beat generation, including Kerouac, Ginsberg, Corso and William Burroughs. The mantra of the era, in whatever cultural genre that pushed against the boundaries of the socially acceptable, was 'Would you let your daughter marry someone like this?' From the Beats, Andy Warhol and the

Rolling Stones, who Dylan references as 'them British bad boys' on *Rough and Rowdy Ways* (2020), to political radicals such as Malcolm X, Eldrige Cleaver and Martin Luther King, all constituted subversive elements in a paranoiac American culture permanently under siege from the dark satanic forces of communism. The spectre has even raised its head in the 2020 presidential election with Biden accused of being the Trojan Horse of socialism.

The America emerging from the McCarthy communist witch-hunts of the 1950s, into the anti-nuclear and pro-civil rights era of the 1960s, unnerved middle America, with the emergence of a consolidated music industry providing an outlet not only for the mainstream but also for the subversive. A music industry that had become devastated by the Great Depression of the 1930s, and alongside of it a burgeoning diversity of independent labels recording and distributing roots and race music from the far-flung corners of America, disappeared overnight. Such records sold in considerable quantities because of their novelty and easy accessibility. The small-time entrepreneurs were responsive to localized demand, and made recordings readily available to buy of your local roots, country and race singers who achieved minor celebrity in their communities. The songs composed exposed the harsh conditions of extreme deprivation of the ordinary working man living in the rural South, and of the deep-rooted racism of a segregated society in the crumbling inner suburbs of the large northern cities and the faltering economies of the Midwest, and told stories of hardship and deprivation articulated through an accessible medium that died with the Depression.

The downtrodden whites and discriminated-against segregated blacks had a muted voice through these independent labels, barely audible above the noise of the dominant culture. The enterprising Harry Smith, a stalwart of the Beat generation, a raconteur and resident of the Chelsea Hotel, rescued hundreds of these Bakelite 78 rpm records and compiled the *Anthology of American Folk Music* (1952), which included everything from roots, blues and country to gospel and Appalachian mountain music. There were eighty-four selections on three long-playing records, with volume 2 devoted to 'social music'. Smith literally invented the American folk tradition by constructing a canon that became the bible for all those who were part of the folk revival of the 1960s. Smith's anthology was quirky not only in its Catholic choice of 'representative' material but also because, unlike standard commercial recordings that clearly identified 'race' and mainstream music, there is no indication of the ethnic identity of the singers. The anthology also served to revive the careers of surviving entertainers of a wide cultural spectrum who had fallen by the wayside and were forgotten after the Depression.

The new generation of folk and blues singers actively sought out entertainers represented by the anthology. Many of them began appearing at the Newport Folk Festival that George Wein, the music producer, and his associate Albert Grossman instituted in 1959 on the back of the success of the Newport Jazz Festival. The aim of the festival was to give a platform to the diversity of the rural American folk music tradition, and urban popular developments. Between 1959 and 1965, for example, such luminaries as Son House, Doc Watson, Doc Boggs, Odetta, Mother Maybelle Carter, Jesse Fuller, Mississippi John Hurt, Mississippi Fred McDowell, Reverend Gary Davis and a host of others performed and imparted their skills to the younger generation, including Joan Baez who appeared for the first time in 1959, and Bob Dylan who appeared in 1963. Cohen's induction was not until 1967.

Harry Smith's enterprise would not have been possible without the music ethnographers, such as Cecil Sharpe, John Lomax, Norman Cazden, Charles Seeger and Moses Asch, who researched and sought to preserve the rich American heritage for posterity. On 31 December 1945, a group of people, including Pete Seeger, Alan Lomax and Lee Hays, founded an organization called People's Songs in New York City whose mission was to encourage the discovery, creation and promotion of songs that represented the labouring American people. People's Songs produced a quarterly Bulletin from 1946 to 1950, which served as the exemplar for *Sing Out!* and *Broadside*, the principal organs of the Folk Movement of the 1960s. This, of course, was the ambience that Bob Dylan lived and breathed when he emerged, not only as the repository of the great American blues and folk heritage but also as the voice of the underprivileged, downtrodden and disenfranchised, whose travails were catalogued and championed in his early topical songs.

The Canadian's emergence into the milieu of the folk revival traverses a very different path that took him, through his poetry and prose writing, via the Greek island of Hydra where he spent most of the early years of the decade, writing and periodically returning to Montreal to promote his work. Yet this familiar story disguises the extent to which Cohen's impetus came from the same source and social concern as Dylan's. At seventeen, before he started his formal writing career, Cohen was a member of the Montreal folk, country and western group the Buckskin Boys, in which he played rhythm guitar. He had been introduced to leftist folk music by seeing Josh White live in 1949, and in 1950 by Irving

Morton, a left-wing agitator and folk singer whom he met at Camp Sunshine, a Jewish community camp. He taught Cohen to play and sing traditional songs from *The People's Songbook*. The lyrics of the songs fascinated Cohen, inspiring him to visit the Harvard Library of Folk music one summer, where he researched and listened to songs compiled by John Jacob Niles, John and Alan Lomax, the Almanac Singers, Pete Seeger and *People's Songbook*. Cohen was deeply moved by that whole tradition. Their passionate commitment to social justice and brotherhood in their lyrics inspired him to write his own lyric poetry. What distinguished his style from Dylan's was the European influence of Spanish flamenco, Portuguese fado singers, particularly Amália Rodrigues, and French chanteuses.

Dylan and Cohen, in their different ways, constituted a bridge between the great heritage of the radical folk tradition, and the new generation of politically disaffected youth who were left-leaning, anti-establishment, pro-civil rights, anti-Vietnam and anti-nuclear. The disaffected found it impossible to have their voices represented in the media, except negatively, and so Dylan and Cohen's sympathies resonated with those who railed against convention, rejected racial injustice and were on the side of ordinary working men and women crushed by the harsh realities of the economic system. The Beat generation, of course, was a sub-culture which influenced both Dylan and Cohen, and prided itself on its subversiveness. The Beats aspired, like the French poet Rimbaud and the Spanish poet Lorca, to write poetry that appealed to the masses. It was the voices of Dylan and Cohen, representing the anger and angst of their generation in their lyric poetry, that gave impetus to the popularity of the writings of the Beats. Whereas the Beats recognized the close correlation between music and poetry, modern free-form jazz with its idiosyncratic rhythms and dissonant melodies was not the medium to carry their poetry to a mass appreciative audience. The folk and folk-rock vehicle proved infinitely more conducive.

This book is not a history of the career trajectories of Dylan and Cohen. There are already many thick and slim volumes that do this, and whose claims to originality are the discovery of a new fact here and there, which are nevertheless always welcome additions to our knowledge of these enigmatic legends. Instead, what we offer is a series of explorations of facets of the careers, personalities and contexts which serve to shed light on how they came to be who they are, and the formative influences on their creative output.

We begin by establishing the formidable success they both enjoyed in the latter part of their careers, and the challenges they faced in maintaining their places on the popular music landscape, not only during their own personal crises but also during the revolutionary changes in the music industry, which transformed not only the recording process but also the manner in which songs are sold, which has placed live performance and 'official merchandise' at the centre of the marketplace. It remains to be seen, of course, how the industry will emerge from the devastation of the Covid-19 Pandemic. We also show how their career paths intersected through mutual acquaintances, mutual admiration and occasional brief encounters. They were never close friends, but certainly respected each other, and followed each other's work with keen interest. In the early years of his career Cohen was hailed, even by John Hammond, as the next Bob Dylan, which inadvertently placed them in competition for the same ground. This initially made them a little wary of each other, but their mutual insecurity soon dissipated.

Both poet/songwriters were, of course, Jewish and this gave them a closer connection than they otherwise would have had. They felt an affinity with each other, having grown up in households that observed customary practices of Judaism. There were, as is well attested, significant periods in their lives when religion eclipsed their art. Bob Dylan when he became a born-again Christian, and Leonard Cohen when he became ordained as a Buddhist monk. These are the spectacles that detract from the fact that both men are defined by a continuous spiritual quest that led them down many paths on the road to enlightenment, but all roads led home to the faith of their forefathers. Their spiritual quests are inseparable from, and integral to, their lyric poetry, and the experiences that are expressed in what they write.

Much has been written about the name of Dylan Thomas and how Bobby Zimmerman appropriated the Welsh poet's Christian name to transform himself into Bob Dylan. After years of obfuscation, Bob Dylan unequivocally admitted that he did indeed take the Welshman's name, but not for the reasons usually proposed. In *Chronicles* (2004), he says he liked both the spelling and the name, but he was not enamoured by his namesake's poetry. After all, Bob Dylan has been accused of plagiarizing numerous poets, authors, playwrights, songwriters and even photographers, but never of plagiarizing Dylan Thomas. We examine the immense cultural phenomenon that Thomas became in America and Canada during the 1950s and into the 1960s. He was famous in his own lifetime, not only for his poetry but also for his uncompromising irresponsibility and indomitable drunken performances. The Beat poets coveted his fame. He proved to them, although in reality for Thomas it was an illusion, that the poet could make a living outside of the academy. Both Cohen and Dylan aspired to such fame and, like the Beats they admired, became casualties of the lifestyle they emulated.

Dylan Thomas first published his poetry in the United States in the August 1938 issue of *Poetry: A Magazine of Verse*. Among the four poems was 'O Make Me a Mask', which pleads for a mask and a wall to hide behind and protect the author from the prying eyes of those who constitute a threat. We argue that Bob Dylan and Leonard Cohen constructed different personas, explicitly adopting the image of a mask to enable them to construct various identities, in attempts to preserve their own against the corrosive gaze of fame. The mask is a pervasive symbol from antiquity to the present and it is adopted to serve three main purposes. First, the mask is used to transform one's image or personality, and may signify a continuous process of self-creation and renewal, often to break free of the constricting images and expectations of the audience which serve to define the performer. Both Dylan and Cohen began with images largely of their own creation, the angry young protest singer and the godfather of gloom, and spent the rest of their careers escaping from them in order to evolve as artists. Second, the mask may function to conceal and disguise: a strategy adopted for protection against the glare of public scrutiny in order to preserve the line between their public and private selves. Third, the mask serves to embolden the wearer and facilitates the telling of truths that are revelatory of the personalities of the characters in songs that Dylan and Cohen inhabit.

The relationship between poetry and song has been a particularly protracted discussion in relation to the work of the American and the Canadian, with each of our authors reluctant to pronounce themselves unequivocally poets or songwriters, and instead treading an ambiguous line by adopting ambivalent responses when directly asked the question. Neither were quite as forceful as Charles Bukowski, who believed poetry lacked the complexity of the work of a novelist, journalist or historian. For him poetry was all about feeling, adding: 'When people call me a poet, it makes me want to vomit. I'm a writer'.[1] Both Dylan and Cohen have proudly adorned the title of poet, and both have eschewed it. When they adopt the title, they do so modestly, at pains to indicate that they are somewhat embarrassed to be identified in the same tradition as the likes of Wordsworth, Browning, Pound, Blake and Coleridge. Both Dylan and Cohen were accused of selling out: Dylan during his most explicit protest days when he adopted the mantle of poet proudly, only to be accused of selling the folk movement down the river for writing more personal poetry, and Cohen by his

---

[1]   Cited in Ben Pleasants, 'Rexroth, Bukowski and the Politics of Literature' (Coventry: The Beat Scene Press, 2007), p. 1.

Canadian counterparts in Montreal for turning to songwriting and prostituting his art. Cohen cleverly sidestepped the issue of designating what he wrote on the page as poetry by suggesting that it is a verdict, a judgement made by others after the event. We want to navigate the terrain between poetry and song, and identify those features that both distinguish and identify them. Poetry and song may be inextricably tied to their performance, and it is this performative element that unites lyric poetry and song. Lorca's concept of *duende*, which attributes the impact of great flamenco to the powerful surge of emotion rising from the darkest caverns of the spirit and expressed in performance. Lawrence Ferlinghetti once commented that Dylan's songs would be nothing without that guitar, and Dylan essentially agreed in his Nobel lecture (2017) in justifying his performative art.

Finally, we turn to the significant sources of inspiration from whom both Dylan and Cohen found their voices, in an attempt to answer the questions as to what they aspired to, and who they were aspiring to emulate in their lyric poetry. This gives us an avenue into distinguishing different lyrics into separate categories, and suggest that our responses to them and the questions we ask of each category have to be appropriate. We suggest that the French poet Rimbaud, the Spanish poet Lorca and the Welsh poet Thomas shared a common vision of a type of poetry which Rimbaud attributed to a derangement of the senses, and Lorca to inspiration, and which Thomas describes as the effort of expressing the terror and fearful expectation unleashed in the beast, the madman and the angel, resident within him. All three poets inspire Dylan and Cohen to blacken their pages, and saturate them with lines that relinquish the idea of resolving and abating mystery, and instead abandoning oneself to its deepest and darkest crevices, that point to nothing outside the poem for its meaning. As Thomas declared, the poem is self-contained. It has its own questions and answers, contradictions and agreements, and travels towards the last line which is its own end. Beyond that the poem does not exist. The rest is 'the problematic stuff of poetry'.[2]

2   Letter from Thomas to Henry Treece, 16 May 1938, Thomas, *Collected Letters,* new edition, ed., Paul Ferris (London: Dent, 2000), p. 344.

1

Dying to get back home

The musical landscape is populated with aging rock stars, spanning the genres of rock and roll, folk, country, folk-rock and blues, with careers casting a shadow over the second part of the twentieth century to the present, most of whom have taken stock of their lives and have passed on or are in the process of putting their affairs in order.

Chuck Berry's final album, *Chuck,* was announced three days after his death on 21 March 2017, and it was released on 16 June 2017. Chuck's daughter, Ingrid Berry, duets with her father on 'Darlin', giving it a strong emotional resonance. It is a father's farewell: 'Darlin', your father's growing older, I fear / Strains of grey are showing bolder each year / Lay your head upon my shoulder, my dear / Time is fading fast away'. Resignation, poignancy and the bitter-sweet taste of imminent death saturate the album. David Bowie died within days of the release of *Blackstar* on 8 January 2016. Bowie wrote and laid down the tracks after being diagnosed with liver cancer, giving impetus to the form and content of the album.

Of those settling accounts, John Mellancamp's *Life, Death, Love and Freedom* (2008), Neil Diamond's *Home Before Dark* (2008) and Paul McCartney's *Memory Almost Full* (2007), written and recorded when he was sixty-four years old, were deemed valedictory homages to the uncertainties, both good and bad, that longevity brings, along with the looming inevitability of death. Although death has not been a stranger to the themes that permeate the albums of both Bob Dylan and Leonard Cohen, their long farewells have been a characteristic part of many of their albums. *Time Out of Mind* (1997) was often portrayed as Dylan's valedictory statement. It had been seven years since he previously released new material. Arising from his enforced confrontation with what he called 'the dread realities of life',[1] *Time Out of Mind* was the result of being snowed-in on an isolated, bitterly cold Minnesota farm, and it precipitated a pervasive sombre

---

[1] Brian Hinton, *The Bob Dylan Complete Discography* (New York: Universe Publishing, 2006), p. 303.

resignation to the realities of his mortality. The funereal 'Tryin' to Get to Heaven'
and 'Not Dark Yet' convinced Dylan devotees that he was settling his earthly
affairs, making peace with the Creator and ignoring the advice of his namesake
to 'Rage, rage against the dying of the light'.[2] 'Not Dark Yet', for example, is
delivered in eerie, sombre, dark tones:

> Every nerve in my body is so vacant and numb
> I can't even remember what it was I came here to get away from
> Don't even hear a murmur of a prayer
> It's not dark yet, but it's getting there.

The assumption was that *Time Out of Mind* was written after a near-fatal attack
of pericarditis in May 1997, which caused an inflammation around the heart,
arising in Dylan's case out of an unusual fungal infection. Dylan insisted, however,
that the album was completed before his illness, and despite speculation to the
contrary, the intolerable pain had not produced any philosophically profound
thoughts, because it wasn't something he had brought on himself, and it wasn't
as if he was desperate for a career break to re-examine his life.[3]

Cohen's *Dear Heather* (2004), in whispered tones, had the air of tired
resignation and farewell about it, with Lord Byron's 'Go No More A-Roving' set
to music, and 'The Faith', which included the lines: 'A cross on every hill / A
star, a minaret / So many graves to fill / O love, aren't you tired yet?' John Lewis,
writing in *Uncut*, commented that the album was 'reflective, puzzled, hushed
and muted', almost 'like a man penning his own eulogy'.[4] It was, however, *Old
Ideas* (2012), co-written with Patrick Leonard, that seemed much more explicit
about his imminent departure, with such songs as 'Going Home' and 'Darkness'.
In 'Darkness' he sings: 'I got no future / I know my days are few / The present's
not that pleasant / just a lot of things to do /I thought the past would last me /
But the darkness got that too'.

When Leonard Cohen, poet, novelist, painter and singer, died at the age
of eighty-two in his modest house, which he shared with his daughter Lorca
and grandchildren, in an unfashionable suburb of Los Angeles, his career had

[2] Dylan Thomas, 'Do Not Go Gentle into That Good Night', *The Collected Poems of Dylan Thomas*, Centenary Edition, ed. John Goodby (London: Widenfeld and Nicolson, 2014), p. 193. 'It Aint Dark Yet' was described as probably the 'most moving song ever written about old age and approaching death'. Philippe Margotin and Jean-Michel, *Bob Dylan All the Songs: The Story Behind Every Track* (New York: Black Dog, 2015), p. 614.
[3] Phil Sutcliffe, 'The Comeback Kid', *Mojo*, September, 2006, p. 71.
[4] *Uncut, The Ultimate Music Guide: Leonard Cohen 1934-2016*, Uncut Ultimate Guide Series, No. 1, 2017, p. 84.

undergone the most remarkable transformation imaginable, which began at the new millennium when he released *Ten New Songs* (2001), marking the beginning of the most prolific period of his life. Around the time of *You Want It Darker* (2016), there were already indications that he was seriously ill, fuelled not least because earlier in the year he had indicated to his erstwhile lover and muse, Marianne, on her death bed, that if she reached out she would find that he was not far behind. It was the last album released during his lifetime and the culmination of the most remarkably successful period in his recording and performing career.

The album he released three weeks before his death, *You Want It Darker* (2016),[5] rehearses his reconciliation with Judaism, which he had never completely renounced even when he became a Buddhist monk. In an interview in the *New Yorker* with David Remnick, on 10 October 2016, he confirmed this reconciliation, saying 'Spiritual things, "*baruch Hashem*" – "thank God" – have fallen into place, for which I am deeply grateful'.[6] The album exudes an intense sense of resistance juxtaposed with resignation: 'I struggled with some demons / they were middle class and tame / Didn't know I had permission to murder and to maim'. The anger gives ways to quiet submission: 'Hineni, hineni. I'm ready, my lord' ('You Want It Darker', 2016). *Hineni* has a number of nuanced meanings. It is the Hebrew word which Abraham used to answer God's call, 'Here I am' (Gen. 22.1). It is not only an indication of where one physically is but also implies a total presence, a full attentiveness and subordination to God's will. It is a reply of surrender, of complete dedication, to place oneself at God's service. If this was not a stark enough signal of Cohen's imminent death, then 'I'm leaving the table' could have left the listener in no doubt: 'I don't need a pardon / There's no one left to blame / I'm leaving the table / I'm out of the game'.

The album was released to critical acclaim. It was Alexis Petridis's album of the week in the *Manchester Guardian*.[7] It was one of Cohen's most commercially successful albums peaking in the charts at No. 1 in Canada, No. 7 in United States and No. 4 in United Kingdom and winning the 2017 Juno Prize. It was a phenomenal success in most European countries. In January 2018, following

---

[5] *Popular Problems* (2014) followed *Old Ideas* and was described as 'a husky valediction, pretty, rueful and very moving'.

[6] David Remnick, 'Leonard Cohen Makes It Darker', *The New Yorker*, 17 October 2016. https://www.newyorker.com/magazine/2016/10/17/leonard-cohen-makes-it-darker. Accessed 23 June 2020.

[7] https://www.theguardian.com/music/2016/oct/20/leonard-cohen-you-want-it-darker-album-review. Accessed 15 June 2020.

on from his Grammy Lifetime Achievement Award of 2010, the title track posthumously received the Grammy Award for Best Rock Performance.[8]

At the press conference launching *You Want It Darker,* Cohen intimated that there might be another album imminently: 'God willing I hope perhaps that another record of songs might emerge, but one never knows'.[9] Three years of painstaking work by Adam Cohen resulted in *Thanks for the Dance*, the fifteenth and final studio album, released on 22 November 2019.[10] It continues the sombre mood of *You Want It Darker* with its acceptance of mortality, but more than that it is a work of self-abnegation pleading with the listener to engage with the world through God's creations in both 'Listen to the Hummingbird' and 'The Goal'.[11] In the former he entreats us to: 'Listen to the mind of God / Which doesn't need to be / Listen to the mind of God / Don't listen to me'. And in the latter, 'No one to follow / And nothing to teach / Except that the goal / Falls short of the reach'.

At the same press conference at which Cohen announced his *You Want It Darker*, he said no one knows it better than Bob Dylan that the songs just come to you, it's not intentional, and no one knows when, or if they will come again. At the age of seventy-nine in March 2020, in the midst of the Covid-19 pandemic that was ravaging the world, Bob Dylan, singer, songwriter, artist and Nobel Poet Laureate, released 'Murder Most Foul', the first original composition to appear from him since September 2012 when the acclaimed album *Tempest* appeared. The title of the new album, *Rough and Rowdy Ways* (2020), alludes to the Jimmy Rodgers 1929 song of the same name and two albums of the late 1990s with identical titles, sub-titled *Early American Rural Music, Badman Ballads and Hellraising Songs* (Yazoo, 1998 and 2000).[12] In 'Key West (The Philosopher's Pirate)' on Dylan's *Rough and Rowdy Ways*, which does not contain the Jimmy Rodgers's classic, Rodgers, Armstrong and Holly – Jimmy, Louis and Buddy – are name-checked by their Christian names, preceded by the surnames of Allen,

---

[8]   It was released by Columbia on 21 October 2016. Both Cohen and his collaborator Pat Leonard heroically completed the album, despite acute illnesses with the encouragement and assistance of Adam Cohen.

[9]   https://www.bing.com/videos/search?q=Leonard+Cohen%2c+Thanks+for+the+Dance&docid=608044232173093590&mid=0F1A0C37E858D03EBE110F1A0C37E858D03EBE11&view=detail&FORM=VIRE. Accessed 16 June 2020.

[10] Will Hermes, 'Leonard Cohen's Profound 'Thanks for the Dance' Is a Posthumous Grace Note', *Rolling Stone*, 22 November 2019. https://www.rollingstone.com/music/music-album-reviews/leonard-thanks-for-the-dance-916417/. Accessed 16 June 2020.

[11] The first is also printed in *The Flame: Poems Notebooks Lyrics Drawings* (New York: Farrar, Strauss and Giroux, 2018), p. 65, and the second in *Book of Longing* (New York: HarperCollins, 2006), p. 153.

[12] It is also the title track on Jimmie Rodgers, *Rough and Rowdy Ways*, RCA Victor.

Gregory and Jack – Ginsberg, Corso and Kerouac – twentieth-century dead American cultural heroes, all born, he claims, on the wrong side of the tracks. The whole album is dark, replete with death, slaughter, threats, edginess and intimidation juxtaposed with references to religion, God, immortality and living legends.

Rough and Rowdy Ways pursues familiar thematic territory as *Tempest* (2012), in that love and mortality are pervasive themes. 'I Contain Multitudes', the second single from the album *Rough and Rowdy Ways,* was accompanied by a picture of Dylan from the late 1980s/early 1990s, in a silver silk shirt, playing a black Fender Stratocaster guitar, defiantly staring down the lens of the camera. The title is the same as the 2016 *Economist* book of the year by microbiologist Ed Yong.[13] It is an angry, even bitter, song reminiscent of the Bob Dylan of the mid-1960s, the young man with attitude – venomous, cutting and dismissive. 'I will sell you down the river, I'll put a price on your head / What more can I tell you? I sleep with life and death in the same bed'. With reference to the latter line, when asked whether he thought about mortality often, Dylan replied that he thinks of the death of humanity, and the long strange evolution of the naked ape: 'Every human being no matter how strong or mighty, is frail when it comes to death. I think about it in general terms, not in a personal way'.[14]

The obsession with death in *Rough and Rowdy Ways* brings us full circle to his first album. The eponymous *Bob Dylan* (1962), thoroughly imbued with the American musical past expressed in the genres of blues, roots, country and folk, was the exemplar of his explanation of a line from 'My Back Pages' in 1964: 'I was so much older then, I'm younger than that now' (*Another Side of Bob Dylan,* 1964), and of what Robert Shelton meant when he referred to the first album as 'the last will and testament of one Dylan, and the birth of a new Dylan'.[15] Since then Dylan has been born again, died and resurrected many times: so many that now he is much older and again he says: 'Can't remember when I was born. And I forgot when I died' ('False Prophet').

The album has elicited extravagant reviews. The *New Musical Express,* for example, suggests that it is Dylan's grandest poetic statement to date.[16] It was

[13] It was sub-titled *The Microbes Within Us and a Grander View of Life* and published by HarperCollins, New York.

[14] Douglas Brinkley, 'Bob Dylan Has a Lot on His Mind', *New York Times*, 12 June 2020. https://www.nytimes.com/2020/06/12/arts/music/bob-dylan-rough-and-rowdy-ways. Accessed 17 June 2020.

[15] Robert Shelton, *No Direction Home: The Life and Music of Bob Dylan* revised and updated edition edited by Elizabeth Thomson and Patrick Humphries (London: Omnibus Press, 2011), p. 90.

[16] https://www.nme.com/en_au/reviews/bob-dylan-rough-and-rowdy-ways-album-review-2688797. Accessed 16 June 2020.

Kitty Empire's album of the week in the *Manchester Guardian*.[17] *Rolling Stone* declared it 'an absolute classic – it has the bleak majesty of latter-day Dylan albums like *Modern Times* and *Tempest*, yet it goes beyond them, tapping even deeper into cosmic American mysteries'.[18] Mojo suggests that it might be viewed as a vaccine against the shrinking expectation of modern culture, or put simply, it is 'great music' which is testimony 'to the vast scope of his vision'.[19] It is Dylan's thirty-ninth studio album, and his ninth UK No. 1, his first since *Shadows in the Night* (2015), a collection of songs that Frank Sinatra made famous from the great American songbook, for example, 'Some Enchanted Evening', 'That Lucky Old Sun' and 'Autumn Leaves'.

Dylan and Cohen

Bob Dylan and Leonard Cohen never became close friends, but they were acquaintances who admired each other's works. Cohen described their friendship over many years as 'intermittent', adding, 'I don't see him very often but we always connect in a very satisfying way'.[20] Dylan was one of the reasons why Cohen harboured the belief that, given he couldn't make an honest living as a poet and novelist, his fortunes may take a turn for the better if he set some of his poems to music, and even composed songs with the intention of recording. By the time Dylan and Cohen met for the first time, the Canadian had released *Songs of Leonard Cohen* (February, 1967) and *Songs From a Room* (April, 1969) to critical acclaim and had gained literary kudos for his poetry and prose that had previously eluded him outside Canada.

It was 1969 and Dylan had emerged from self-exile to frequent some of his old Greenwich Village haunts. He had reached the heights of unimaginable fame, suddenly to become semi-reclusive after an almost-total burnout consequent on the 1966 World Tour, during which the now infamous insult of 'Judas' was hurled

[17] https://www.theguardian.com/music/2020/jun/20/bob-dylan-rough-and-rowdy-ways-review-enthralling-mischievous-and-very-male. Accessed 25 June 2020.
[18] https://www.rollingstone.com/music/music-album-reviews/bob-dylan-rough-rowdy-ways-1015086/. Accessed 26 June 2020.
[19] Review of *Rough and Rowdy Ways* in *Mojo*, August 2020, p. 82.
[20] Nigel Williamson, 'We Are the Marines of the Spiritual World', interview with Leonard Cohen, *Uncut*, 12, 1997, reprinted in *Leonard Cohen 1934-2016, Uncut* Ultimate Guide Series, 2017, issue 1, p. 78.

at him at the Free Trade Hall in Manchester, England.[21] After three albums during which he developed his 'thin, wild mercurial sound',[22] he re-emerged with *John Wesley Harding* (1968). The sound was a completely laid-back, country-blues/roots style and tempo, evoking the imagery of a rural, lawless, American past, in contrast with the cityscape urban sounds of *Bringing It All Back Home* (1965), *Highway 61 Revisited* (1965) and *Blonde on Blonde* (1966).

Dylan's first album *Bob Dylan* (1962) is heavily influenced by the gospel of the generation of bluesmen and women whose careers had undergone a revival with the release of Harry Smith's *Anthology of American Folk Music* (1952) and the increasing popularity of folk and folk-country music which augured the rediscovery of a rural past submerged by the Great Depression. Smith, a self-proclaimed hipster, was a resident at the Chelsea Hotel, where he held court with anyone who would listen including, at different times, Dylan and Cohen. Because of his in-depth knowledge of the breadth of American folk roots culture, he was a magnet to aspiring folksingers.

John Wesley Harding, however, was inspired, not by blues and gospel singers, but by the Bible itself, particularly the Old Testament and rural American history. Dylan makes over sixty allusions to biblical references in the less than forty-five minutes of the album. Fifteen of them occur in 'The Ballad of Frankie Lee and Judas Priest'.[23] Allen Ginsberg, who stayed with Cohen on the Greek island of Hydra in 1961, and who was now a close friend and admirer of Bob Dylan, commented that each line of *John Wesley Harding* meant something and was there not just to rhyme with what went before but to advance the narrative, with each image having a purpose, rather than an ornamental function.

The cover of *John Wesley Harding* makes a concession to the predilection of the day to secrete a message hidden in the sound of the vinyl or the imagery of the album cover itself. When the album cover is turned upside down, the bark on the tree that forms the backdrop to the four principal characters contains small images of the psychedelic Beatles, and of Dylan himself, in his coolest man on the planet days, implying a rejection not only of *St. Pepper's Lonely Hearts Club Band* – on the cover of which he and Dylan Thomas appear – but also of his own former bohemian self. The album was Dylan's biggest seller to date.

[21] For an illuminating and incisive analysis of the incident, see Michael Jones, 'Judas and the Many 'Betrayals' of Bob Dylan', in *The Political Art of Bob Dylan*, ed. David Boucher and Gary Browning, second enlarged edition (Exeter: Imprint Academic, 2009), pp. 75–103.
[22] 'That Thin, That Wild Mercury Sound – Metallic and Bright Gold', *Billboard*, 24 July 1965.
[23] Margotin and Guesdon, *Bob Dylan All the Songs*, p. 276.

Even though the performing Dylan was not visible, his legendary persona continued to be honed and projected despite his self-imposed exile. Because of the expectation that recording artists would release records at the rate of one or two a year with a string of singles to satiate the insatiable and fickle fan base, Columbia released two volumes of Bob Dylan's *Greatest Hits*, a clever marketing ploy in so far as most of the songs had been hits for other people such as Peter, Paul and Mary; The Turtles and The Byrds.

D. A. Pennebaker premiered *Don't Look Back* on 17 May at the Presidio Theatre, San Francisco, 1967, and on 6 September, New York, at 34th Street East Theatre. The film documented the 1965 UK tour. It was deliberately edited to project the hipster image with an acerbic tongue and merciless put-downs, humiliating Donovan and Joan Baez, while holding court at the Savoy Hotel on the Strand in London. The film begins with the promotional footage for 'Subterranean Homesick Blues', with Ginsberg lurking in the background. The deluxe version of 2006 includes a second DVD featuring out-takes which include an alternative promotional film for 'Subterranean Homesick Blues' and a second edit that portrays Dylan in a much softer, less acerbic light and who is attentive to and genuinely engaged with star-struck fans.

In fact, he is more like the person that Michael Iachetta tracked down in May 1968 at Dylan's home outside Woodstock. There, and in the house named 'The Big Pink', the Hawks (soon to become The Band) and Dylan recorded the *Basement Tapes* (belatedly released 1975), the full version of which appeared as the Bootleg Series, vol. 11 (2014). From late winter of 1967, the 'thin, wild, mercury sound' gave way to songs 'derived from old sea shanties, melodic reflections about life's absurdities, hard-rockin' and often hilarious fictitious characters, musical tributes to past heroes which bordered on pastiche . . . devout spirituals and C&W laments, a new take on blues balladry'.[24]

At the time of recording, the tapes' fourteen songs, including 'Too Much of Nothin', 'This Wheel's on Fire', and 'Quinn the Eskimo', were put on to acetate and touted around other recording artists by Albert Grossman, Dylan's enterprising manager. Julie Driscoll, Brian Auger and The Trinity recorded 'This Wheel's on Fire', entering the British charts in 1968, peaking at No. 5, and Manfred Mann, the band which Dylan thought the best interpreter of his music, took 'Quinn the Eskimo', retitled 'Mighty Quinn', to No. 1 in the UK charts.

[24] Bob Dylan and The Band, *The Basement Tapes,* complete. Bootleg Series 11, booklet, p. 4.

In 1969, with the follow-up to *John Wesley Harding* eagerly awaited, Dylan's legendary status was enhanced, rather than diminished, by his mysterious absence. When he heard Cohen's *The Songs of Leonard Cohen* and *Songs from a Room,* Dylan must have been struck by how, as fellow Jews, they drew inspiration from the Bible for the lyrics of their songs. If he were reading the reviews of *The Songs of Leonard Cohen,* Dylan would have noted the frequency with which comparisons were made between the two poets. In discussions of Cohen's lyrics, Dylan's name frequently came up.[25] A less than enthusiastic review in *Rolling Stone* accuses Cohen of pretentiousness, and of making the mistake that poetry easily translates into song: 'Then there is the standard Dylan trick of reversed images ("smoked my eyelids and punched my cigarette"): "I showed my heart to the doctor / He said I'd just have to quit / Then he wrote himself a prescription / And your name was mentioned in it."'[26] The reviewer begrudgingly acknowledged that there were three masterpieces on the album.

The two songwriters had mutual connections in John Hammond, who signed both of them for Columbia, and with Mary Martin, who was Cohen's manager. She was Canadian and incredibly knowledgeable about the music scene. She was ambitious and enterprising, working herself up from a hostess job at the Bitter End in Greenwich Village to become Albert Grossman's executive assistant, then director of A&R at Warner Brothers, before breaking out into management; she persistently pushed the Canadian band the Hawks, which Hammond eventually linked up with Dylan.[27]

Cohen was familiar with Bob Dylan's work and recognized the excellence of the material, its genius and its great lyrical gift. He recognized a certain fellowship between him and Dylan, but after more than a decade of writing his own poetry and prose, Cohen had found his own literary voice, so the admiration was not so much that he wanted to write like Dylan, and more that he wanted be like him. He was captivated by the fame Dylan had attained, and like hundreds of other aspiring men in Montreal with a guitar slung over their shoulders, he wanted to be in Dylan's position.[28]

---

[25] Sylvie Simmons, *I'm Your Man: The Life of Leonard Cohen* (London: Jonathan Cape, 2012), pp. 184–5.

[26] Arthur Schmidt, 'The Songs of Leonard Cohen', *Rolling Stone,* 9 March 1968. https://www.rollingstone.com/music/music-album-reviews/songs-of-leonard-cohen-255565/. Accessed 27 June 2020.

[27] Daryl Saunders, *That Thin, Wild Mercury Sound: Dylan Nashville and the Making of Blonde on Blonde* (Chicago: Chicago Review Press, 2019), p. 23.

[28] Jim Devlin, *Leonard Cohen: In His Own Words* (London: Omnibus, 1998), p. 82. The idea of fame will be explored in chapter four.

Cohen didn't find it easy when he arrived in New York in 1966. Agent after agent declined the invitation to manage him. His appearance was 'square', age was not on his side, and his songs were far too sad. He was the same age as Elvis Presley, and Presley had a decade of success behind him. Eventually a fellow Canadian, Robert Hershorn, introduced him to Mary Martin. Through her contacts she got Cohen the necessary introductions. Judy Collins recorded two of his songs on *In My Life* (1966), her breakthrough album. They were 'Suzanne' and 'Dress Rehearsal Rag'. The album also included Bob Dylan's 'Thom Thumb's Blues' and Brecht's 'Pirate Jenny'. Cohen suddenly had street credibility as a songwriter. Although there are conflicting accounts of Cohen's impressions of New York at that time, on the whole, he was very happy. Things were beginning to work out. It was no longer quite as it had been ten years earlier for Kerouac and Ginsberg, but a 'compatible sensibility' was flourishing, and he was exhilarated by it.[29]

It was Martin who introduced Cohen to Hammond. She got Cohen to record some demos in the bathroom of her flat, and got Garth Hudson, of The Hawks, to write down the lead sheets of music for the purpose of publishing. Martin and her lawyer friend, E. Judith Berger, took the music and demos around personally to Hammond.[30] Hammond was not afraid to take a gamble on the unorthodox. After meeting Cohen for lunch and moving on to the Chelsea Hotel, Hammond said: 'He was not like anything I've ever heard before. I just feel that I always want a true original, if I can find one. . . . the young man set his own rules, and he was a really first-class poet'.[31] The acting chief executive at Columbia, Bill Gallagher, thought Hammond was mad wanting to sign a 32-year-old poet to the label. Cohen was, in Hammond's view, the next Dylan, and the most intelligent artist he had ever wanted to sign so he persisted and persuaded the in-coming president, Clive Davis, to give him permission.

Dylan had returned to New York in January 1968, the month before *Songs of Leonard Cohen* was released, and the month that his own *John Wesley Harding* appeared. He was tentatively ready to face the public again and performed at the Woody Guthrie Memorial Concert. He was backed by The Crackers (The Hawks) and performed at both the afternoon and evening concerts. Their next

[29] Interview with Paul Williams, 'Leonard Cohen: The Romantic in a Ragpicker's Trade', *Crawdaddy*, March 1975. Reprinted in *Leonard Cohen on Leonard Cohen: Interviews and Encounters*, ed. Jeff Burger (Chicago: Chicago Review Press, 2014), p. 91.
[30] Simmons, *I'm Your Man*, p. 157.
[31] Liel Leibovitz, *A Broken Hallelujah: Leonard Cohen's Secret Chord* (Dingwall, Ross-shire: Sandstone Press, 2014), p. 90.

official public appearance was at the 1969 Isle of Wight Festival, in preference to the Woodstock Festival in the United States. Dylan and The Band gave a lacklustre performance, marred by technical sound issues, but it was there that they reprised some of the tracks they had recorded at the Big Pink.

Dylan was curious about the Canadian singer and songwriter, who was older than him by some six years. Dylan invited Cohen to the Kettle of Fish where they met and exchanged pleasantries. They were both admirers of Dylan Thomas who had met their mutual friend Allen Ginsberg at the San Remo in April 1952. Cohen had yet to overcome his fear of touring and Dylan his apprehension about returning to the road. Dylan's *John Wesley Harding* and *Nashville Skyline* (1969) and Cohen's *The Songs of Leonard Cohen* and *Songs From a Room* were all far removed from the acid-fuelled psychedelia, distorted sound effects, surreal imagery and flower power of the Summer of Love (1967), and the revolutionary politics of May 1968. The albums, nevertheless, have hidden depths and darkness, a darkness that continues with Dylan, in a different vein: the desolate landscape he began exploring in 'Hard Rain's a-Gonna Fall'. 'As I Went Out One Morning', off *John Wesley Harding*, inspired Sean Egan to write that it was terrifyingly prescient of a 'terrible fate', with an abrupt ending that leaves unresolved feelings and a haunting 'chill in the air'.[32] The characters who populated the landscape, such as St Augustine and Tom Paine, on the one hand, and, on the other, Judas Priest and the Wicked Messenger, represent the unremitting clash between good and evil, light and darkness.

Cohen's meticulously crafted poems set to music, which owed more to French chanson and the guitar chord progression of Spanish Flamenco than to American roots music, nevertheless projected the darkness and shadowy edginess that were to be indelibly stamped on his projected image, how ever hard he tried to escape it. 'Teachers', for example, is a Kafkaesque nightmare, with an unhinged unreality, stripping the subject of all anchorage and certainty: 'I met a man who lost his mind / In some lost place I had to find / Follow me the wise man said / But he walked behind' (*The Songs of Leonard Cohen*). Or a song that has become definitive of him: 'Like a baby stillborn / Like a beast with his horn / I have torn everyone who reached out for me' ('Bird on the Wire', *Songs From A Room*).

---

[32] Sean Egan, '*John Wesley Harding*', *The Mammoth Book of Bob Dylan*, ed. Sean Egan (London: Robinson, 2011), p. 148.

Because Cohen was often hailed as the new Bob Dylan, even by John Hammond, and with more plausibility than the numerous other contenders, and because they occupied, or competed for, the same space, a certain wariness, or distancing grew between the two performers. Dylan was used to getting his own way, both with his choice of record producers and musicians, and Cohen, it seemed to him, was muscling-in. Bob Johnston, Dylan's record producer, also produced Cohen's *Songs From A Room*, and when Columbia pressurized the Canadian to undertake a major tour to promote his albums, Cohen agreed on the condition that Bob Johnston join him as a member of his backing band for the tour. Cohen also used two of Dylan's regular backing musicians, Ron Cornelius and Charlie Daniels. Both musicians got the impression from Bob Dylan that he wanted them to choose between him and Cohen. They chose to tour with Cohen and subsequently felt that Dylan's pride was hurt. He didn't ask them to work for him again.

In the summer of 1970 Cornelius sensed a tension between Cohen and Dylan. Dylan had deliberately recorded what he believed to be an awful album, *Self-Portrait* (1970), in order to get the fans off his back and shatter the idyllic and iconoclastic vision of him they cherished – the fame and the pressure were just too much for him to bear. It had the desired effect among critics, prompting Greil Marcus to ask rhetorically in his *Rolling Stone* review, 'What is this shit?'. Cohen had come back from Europe, where he had undoubtedly taken Dylan's crown, but in the United States Dylan still reigned supreme. Cohen played Forrest Hills on 25 July. He was burnt-out from substance abuse and faced with a tennis stadium in the rain his mood turned to gloom. His performance reflected his mood. Susan Musmanno, a backing singer with Cohen's Army, confirmed that it was a bad performance.[33] The *Billboard* review by Nancy Erlich on 8 August 1970 was scathing. She described Cohen as a 'nervous uncomfortable man' with 'lifeless delivery' in a humourless, dull voice that had the quality of 'speaking after death'. Dylan took the opportunity to see Cohen perform and to visit him backstage. Security was tight and an overzealous guard initially prevented Dylan from entering the area. Bob Johnston, who was playing in Cohen's band, jokingly claimed he had never seen Dylan before, which went down with Dylan like a lead balloon. When Dylan and Cohen eventually did get to talk, it was at first with a feigned indifference, the conversation was stilted, and both postured

---

[33] https://allanshowalter.com/2019/10/28/leonard-cohen-forest-hills-1970-nervous-uncomfortable
-oppressive-lifeless-in-a-tiff-with-bob-dylan/. Accessed 29 August 2020.

like two cats with their backs up.[34] Cornelius described it as one of the weirdest atmospheres he had ever experienced.[35]

Cohen's career was on the verge of collapse in the United States in 1971. He was a minority taste where audiences were not comfortable with performers wearing their hearts on their sleeves. His most recent album *Songs of Love and Hate* (1971), which took almost a year to record with Bob Johnston in Nashville, was sombre and suicidal. It reflected his mood which was both negative and depressive. Cohen explained that everything seemed to be falling apart for him: 'my spirit, my intentions, my will . . . I began to believe all the negative things people said about my way of singing. I began to hate the sound of my voice.'[36] The album peaked at No. 145 in the American charts and astoundingly it only reached No. 63 in Canada. Elsewhere, there was some redemption. It reached No. 8 in the small Australian market and No. 4 in UK. The album contained what were to become two of his best known and most successful compositions, 'Famous Blue Raincoat' and 'Joan of Arc'.

In the contemporary climate when recording stars had short shelf-lives, CBS began to regard him as something of a liability. He didn't do himself any favours with his reluctance to tour in order to promote sales. Cohen got rid of Mary Martin because he believed he got ripped off when she sold the rights to some of his best songs, including 'Suzanne'.

Marty Machat, Cohen's lawyer, who became his manager, tried to reassure Cohen about the quality of his voice by telling him that none of the guys can sing. If he wanted to hear good singers, he went to the Metropolitan Opera House. Machat persuaded Cohen to do a one-month tour of Europe, promising to include Jerusalem in the schedule. The tour began on 18 March 1972 at the National Stadium in Dublin. Cohen travelled with a small contingent, a skeleton road crew and a band that included Ron Cornelius (guitar), Peter Marshall (bass) and Bob Johnston (organ). His back-up singers were Jennifer Warnes and Donna Washburn.

Machat hired Tony Palmer, the film-maker, to shoot a documentary of the tour, taking the approach of D. A. Pennebaker's 1967 Dylan documentary, *Don't Look Back*, which was filmed *cinema verite*. The Cohen film was to have

---

[34] Howard Sounes, *Down the Highway: The Life of Bob Dylan* (London: Random House, 2001), pp. 252–60.
[35] Simmons, *I'm Your Man*, pp. 220–1.
[36] Cited in Maurice Ratcliffe, *Leonard Cohen: The Music and the Mystique* (London: Omnibus, 2012), p. 24.

no narrator, no interviews and minimum reference to his past career. Despite Machat's hope that the film would help rescue Cohen's career, Cohen rejected the rough edit, complaining that he came across as too confrontational. He also told Palmer that he did not want to be portrayed as a writer of sentimental songs, such as 'Suzanne' and 'So Long Marianne'. He added that 'my songs are political, with a small p. That is what I want to be sure emerges in the film'[37]. It was to be another forty years before the documentary was to see the light of day.

In December 1975, Cohen retreated to Montreal, after an indifferent tour of the United States, as part of a world tour to promote his new album, with a band put together by the producer of *New Skin for the Old Ceremony* (1974), John Lissauer. With excessive drinking and substance abuse, Cohen's moods usually plummeted, and he was feeling predictably low. It was the month that Bob Dylan's Rolling Thunder Revue rolled into town. Dylan immediately thought of adding Cohen to the line-up and asked their mutual acquaintance, Larry 'Ratso' Sloman, to give him a ring. Cohen was reluctant and reticent about getting caught up in the crowd. Sloman assured him that they would get him in through the stage door to avoid the crush. At this point Dylan grabbed the receiver and asked, 'How are you doing Leonard?' 'Can't complain', Cohen replied, 'Well I could, but I won't!' Dylan invited him to the show, and Cohen politely accepted. Dylan then asked him to join the band on stage, and Cohen replied evasively. Later that evening Sloman went around with Sara Dylan to collect a drunken reveling Cohen and his party.

The concert was at the Montreal Forum, and despite repeated pleas from Sloman, Sara Dylan and Joni Mitchell, Cohen resisted. Cohen exclaimed, 'Let it be known that I alone disdained the obvious support. I'm going to sit out there.'[38] When asked why, he said it was just too obvious.[39] It's not clear what he meant, but he was not in the habit, as Dylan was, of repackaging his songs for a carnivalesque spectacle. Sloman speculated that Cohen was too much of a control freak where his music was concerned, wanting to present songs in their proper context, rather than jam with a band.[40] Ian Bell suggests that the Rolling Thunder Revue was a reflection of Dylan's chaotic state of mind in the 1970s and

[37] Andy Greene, 'How Lost Leonard Cohen Doc "Bird on a Wire" Finally Made It to Theatres', *Rolling Stone*, 19 January 2017. https://www.rollingstone.com/movies/movie-features/how-lost-leonard-cohen-doc-bird-on-a-wire-finally-made-it-to-theaters-123707/. Accessed 28 June 2020. A poor re-edited version was released and had a one-night screening in London in 1973, but Cohen hated it.
[38] Larry 'Ratso' Sloman, *On the Road with Bob Dylan* (London: Helter Skelter, 2002), p. 361.
[39] Leibovitz, *A Broken Hallelujah*, pp. 100–103.
[40] Simmons, *I'm Your Man*, p. 278.

'a few, such as Patti Smith and Leonard Cohen, would have the self-possession and the common sense to keep Rolling Thunder at arms length'.[41]

It was while editing his ill-fated film *Renaldo and Clara* that the next recorded meeting between Dylan and Cohen occurred, this time with Ginsberg in tow. Both Cohen and Dylan were struggling to find their places in the rapidly changing landscape of popular music. In 1977 Machat managed both Leonard Cohen and Phil Spector. Machat had negotiated a lucrative contract for Spector with Warner Brothers, which entailed a huge advance, on which Spector failed to deliver. He had begun a collaboration with Cher but had a serious disagreement with her boyfriend David Geffen when he was a little too free with his advice at a recording session. The clash of two super-sized egos wrecked the collaboration.

Geffen was quite an operator and had persuaded Bob Dylan in 1973, by first befriending Robbie Robertson to sign a one-album deal for his new Elecktra/Asylum label, on the expiry of Dylan's Columbia contract the same year. Dylan was angry with Columbia because the company had sacked Clive Davis, the president, and because Albert Grossman's large percentage cut of the deal continued to annoy him. Dylan thought the label was not promoting his work, especially since it had been reluctant to release the soundtrack of *Pat Garret and Billy the Kid*. Columbia appeared to be indifferent to whether he stayed with the label or not, until the single 'Knockin' on Heaven's Door' became an unexpected chart success (US No. 12 and UK No. 14).[42] The gentleman's agreement Dylan reached with Geffen was that he would record one studio album with The Band and embark on a one-month promotional tour, with the possibility of a live album, for which Dylan would gross most of the profits. *Planet Waves* (1974) was the resultant album which immediately went to No.1 in the US charts, but sales quickly slumped. Given the astounding demand for tickets for the comeback tour, Dylan was disappointed at the album sales. He was partly responsible, with his indecisiveness delaying the release until after the tour had started, and then playing only three songs off it in performances, 'Something There Is About You', 'Wedding Song' and 'Forever Young'. By the end of the tour only 'Forever Young' remained on the set-list. Dylan was not completely happy with Geffen and used the success of the tour and partial success of *Planet Waves* to negotiate a more advantageous contract with Columbia.[43]

---

[41] Ian Bell, *Time Out of Mind: The Lives of Bob Dylan* (New York: Pegasus, 2013), p. 108. Cf. p. 27.

[42] Sean Egan, 'Pat Garret and Billy the Kid / Planet Waves / Before the Flood', in *The Mammoth Book of Bob Dylan* (London: Running Press, 2011), pp. 193–205.

[43] Sounes, *Down the Highway*, p. 273.

Warner Brothers was pressing Machat to return the advance, and he knew that if he pressed it Spector would leave the management company, which earned 15 per cent royalties on his back-catalogue – $150,000 a year in the early 1970s. At the same time Machat was getting negative noises from Columbia about Cohen's unimpressive sales in the United States. Machat came up with what he thought was an ingenious idea. Why not get Spector and Cohen to collaborate on a studio album? He could then offer it to Warner and get the company off his back. The problem was that neither Spector nor Cohen was currently appealing to American audiences.

Stephen Machat, Marty's son, was handed the project which he viewed as a 'poisoned chalice' because both Spector and Cohen were 'commercial suicide'.[44] Columbia wanted nothing to do with the project and agreed to release Cohen from his American obligations, making him a free agent in North America. The problem was that Mo Ostin, of Warner Brothers, didn't want anything to do with it either, but was persuaded by Machat junior, who was twenty-one years old, that he was in touch with the spirit of his generation and that the Cohen/Spector collaboration was a marriage made in heaven. What could be more appealing to the younger generation than an album entitled *Death of a Ladies' Man* by two middle-aged men lusting after women? It included tracks such as 'Don't Go Home With Your Hard On' and 'Memories'. The latter has stood the test of time and was occasionally included in his live sets. The sound was a complete departure from his previous albums, and the production distorted the timbre of Cohen's voice by heightening the treble and turning down the bass, while foregrounding the music. 'Memories' is a classic 1950s sound, with a wailing saxophone introduction, in the style of Frankie Lane, whose hit 'Jezebel' is mentioned in the first line. It is a song evocative of the high-school hop, invoking images of Velvet Underground's femme fatale Nico, at the 'dark side of the gym': 'I went up to the tallest and blondest girl / I said you don't know me, but pretty soon you will / Won't you let me see, oh won't you let me see, your naked body'. Introducing the song in a 1980 Tel Aviv concert, Cohen described it as a vulgar ditty that he had written with a fellow Jew in Hollywood. The song contained, he said, 'my most banal and adolescent recollections'.[45]

Bob Dylan and Allen Ginsberg were in Los Angeles at the time of recording 'Don't Go Home with Your Hard On' in June 1976. They both called around the

---

[44] Steven Machat, *Gods, Gangsters and Honour: A Rock 'n' Roll Odyssey* (London: Beautiful Books, 2009), p. 84.

[45] Simmons, *I'm Your Man*, p. 284.

studio on the second day of recording, at 6.00 am, Dylan with two girls on one arm and a bottle of whisky under the other, while Ginsberg brought along his partner Peter Orlovsky, and a host of other revelers. Spector was ecstatic to see them. Dylan was going through an emotionally torrid time with the break-up of his marriage to Sara Lownds, and Ginsberg was on hand to provide emotional support. Dylan had not released a studio album since *Desire* in January 1976. After a good deal of drinking and drug taking, Spector press-ganged Dylan and Ginsberg into providing backing vocals for Cohen. Ginsberg complained, 'Spector was taking a lot of cocaine, and was in a kind of hysterical frenzy, totally Hitlerian and dictatorial and sort of crazed – he started pushing us around, saying "get in there, get on the microphone! – the whole thing was total chaos"'.[46] Devra Robitaille, who is thanked on the album's sleeve 'for coordinating the musicians and for her grave concern in the face of overwhelming odds', when interviewed in 2008 commented: 'When Dylan and Ginsberg came in, there was a kind of magic, I can't explain. . . . They were bombed . . . everyone was bombed. We were on mic singing a backing vocal part. I remember Dylan sliding down the microphone stand and singing from a prone position on the floor'.[47]

Spector was extremely intimidating, surrounding himself with an entourage of thugs and an armoury of weapons, at one point drunkenly holding Cohen's head in an armlock and holding a gun to it, exclaiming, 'I love you Leonard'. To which Cohen replied, 'I hope you do Phil!' He described Spector's madness as having 'a kind of theatrical expression'.[48] Elsewhere, Cohen added, 'my state of mind was only slightly less demented than Spector's at that time'.[49]

Spector took complete control of the recording process, and when Cohen had completed the vocals, he cut Cohen out of the mixing process. Cohen hated the album, describing it as junk, and Spector the worst human being he had ever met. The feeling was mutual with Spector describing Cohen as no better than a member of the Partridge Family, which was the ultimate insult a serious musician could hurl at a fellow musician in the mid-1960s. It was the bubble-gum television programme that spawned David Cassidy.[50]

[46] Cited in Ratcliffe, *Leonard Cohen,* p. 35.
[47] Cited in John Robinson, 'Death of a Ladies' Man', *Leonard Cohen 1934-2016, Uncut* Ultimate Guides Series, 2017, issue 1, p. 41.
[48] Radio interview with Vicki Gabereau, May 1984, printed in, *Leonard Cohen on Leonard Cohen,* ed. Burger, p. 156.
[49] Interview with Jon Wilde, December 1987, printed in *Blitz,* February 1988, and reprinted in *Leonard Cohen on Leonard Cohen,* ed. Jeff Burger (Chicago: Chicago Review Press, 2014), p. 194.
[50] Machat, *Gods, Gangsters and Honour,* p. 85.

Neither Cohen nor Spector were prepared to promote the album, and it was a commercial disaster in the United States. Warner Brothers soon withdrew from promoting it, and it was only with extreme difficulty that Marty Machat persuaded CBS to release it in Europe where it was slightly more successful, reaching No. 35 in the UK album charts. The album was so out of character that even many Cohen fans hated it. Yet music critics were less hostile, and not knowing quite what to make of it, they erred on the side of caution, conceding that it was at once very likely great but greatly flawed. Although ostensibly 'too much of the record sounds like the world's most flamboyant extrovert producing and arranging the world's most fatalistic introvert, such assumptions can be deceiving'.[51] The album has since been rehabilitated, and even Cohen concedes that it contained some of his best lyrics.

Making the album was an ordeal. Spector's assistant and girlfriend, Devra Robitaille, played synthesizer on the album, and she described the whole experience as very tense and uncomfortable. Spector and Cohen just didn't hit it off, there were too many artistic differences, and Spector was just not at his best.[52] Cohen's initial reaction of extreme hostility mellowed over the years to the point where he was prepared to concede some redeeming features, which slightly mitigated the serious character flaws. Cohen commented that Spector often had a sweet nature, which became transformed when he had a crowd to which he could perform. He gestured with the grandeur of the Medici, acting the medieval tyrant, which made things very tricky for those around him. With his usual irony, Cohen maintained that he was very fond of Phil: 'he's one of the great, magnificent figures on the landscape. It's just I don't have much of an appetite for magnificence'.[53] By the time Cohen released the album that re-established him as a major figure on the music scene, *I'm Your Man* (1988), he had concluded it was about time he was more gracious about his debt of gratitude to Spector. He said that the songs they wrote together were very good, and despite the difficulties they had recording together, positive qualities from the experience had begun to surface. 'Aint No Cure for Love', Cohen maintained, owed a great deal to Phil Spector and that he was happy to express his gratitude to him.[54]

[51] Review of *Death of a Ladies' Man* by Paul Nelson, https://www.rollingstone.com/music/music-albu m-reviews/death-of-a-ladies-man-188054/. Accessed 2 July 2020.

[52] Simmons, *I'm Your Man*, p. 290.

[53] Devlin, *Leonard Cohen in His Own Words*, p. 86.

[54] Interview with Albert Manzano, May 1988, *Rockdelux*, reprinted in *Leonard Cohen on Leonard Cohen*, ed., p. 215.

By the end of the 1970s and through most of the 1980s, both Dylan and Cohen struggled to reinvigorate their careers, and both were dissatisfied with their sounds and could not find a connection with new audiences. The year 1978 was bad for Cohen with his mother dying in February and Suzanne Elrod, the mother of his two children, Adam and Lorca, decamping to the house they owned on Hydra, where he had lived with Marianne. Suzanne and the lover she lived there with were arrested for possession of drugs, and Cohen was called upon, at some considerable expense he couldn't afford, to rescue them by getting the charges dropped. She returned to Montreal and then left for Roussillon in France, taking the two children with her. Having disavowed responsibility for *Death of a Ladies' Man*, he was not touring to promote it, which left him more time to establish transatlantic shared parental responsibilities. In 1979 he moved back to Los Angeles from Montreal and began to work with Joni Mitchell's engineer, Henry Lewy, who was not himself a musician and far more empathetic to what musicians themselves wanted to achieve.

Bob Dylan succeeded in disappointing his fans successively in the early 1970s with a string of albums that fell below the expectations of his audience and his label. Dylan justified them, to some extent, by comparing himself with Dostoyevsky who wrote stories to placate his creditors. Dylan suggested that just like him, in the early 1970s 'I wrote albums to ward off mine'.[55]

When Dylan arrived on the scene in New York, he wanted to emulate what Picasso had done in cracking the art world wide open, and indeed Cohen once described Dylan as the 'Picasso of song'.[56] He wanted to be revolutionary. In 1975, however, the horizons of his mind and vision underwent a metamorphosis. His eye for detail and ear for narrative became transformed, manifesting themselves in a heightened awareness of the structure of a song and the palate of colours that brought it to life. He had chanced upon art classes given at Carnegie Hall and decided to drop in, and he stayed for two months. The teacher was a charismatic 73-year-old artist whose name was Norman Raeburn. Dylan believed that his magic was more powerful than any sorcerer, because he taught him to see things differently and more intensely by prolonged and detailed observation, which didn't so much teach him to paint, but perfectly to co-ordinate his mind, head and eye, enabling the composition of much more richly textured art, but also songs.

[55] Dylan, *Chronicles: Volume one*, pp. 38–9.
[56] Devlin, *Leonard Cohen: In His Own Words*, p. 82. Dylan, *Chronicles: Volume one*, p. 55.

The result was *Blood on the Tracks* (1975) and *Desire* (1976), which exhibited a progression of his writing style and the sound he wanted to achieve. *Street Legal* (1978), however, was badly produced, rushed out ahead of a tour upon which he and his band was about to embark, and although Dylan himself thought it the culmination of the process of self-consciously crafting the songs, the critics were unforgiving. Needless to say, his personal circumstances made for a very difficult time that wasn't conducive to sustained and serious work.

Following the last concert of the Rolling Thunder Revue, the comradery, communion and fraternity that developed, or perhaps the longing for certainty emerging from a chaotic period of revelry, debauchery and unreality, turned many of the motley crew to remorse and left them desperate for redemption. Among fifteen or so of their number who became Christian fundamentalists were T-Bone Burnett, David Mansfield, Roger McGuinn and Stephen Soles. C. S. Lewis's *Mere Christianity* seems to have been doing the rounds among the musicians.[57] Lewis argued rhetorically that either Jesus was who he said he was, the son of God, or he was a raving lunatic. This point hit home to most of them.

Dylan did not immediately follow suit, but he become very preoccupied and upset by Elvis Presley's death, at the relatively young age of forty-two in August 1977, and by the extent to which Elvis had degenerated into a parody of himself. Cohen was a few months older than Elvis and published his first book of poems, *Let Us Compare Mythologies*, in the same year as Elvis recorded 'Heartbreak Hotel' in 1956.

Elvis had become a recluse, obese and grotesque. It led to a re-examination by Dylan of his own life, which he described as something of a breakdown during which he was unable to talk to anyone for a week. His own career, he believed, would not have been possible if it was not for Elvis and Hank Williams. Williams had died at the even younger age of twenty-nine from a heart attack, and like Elvis he was heavily involved in substance abuse.

Dylan was thirty-six and began to see himself as an aging rock star, living a life that had lost its meaning for him, especially after his divorce from Sara Lownds. Helena Springs, who co-wrote some songs with Dylan and was a back-up singer with his band from 1978 to 1980, was the impetus for change. He discussed his problems with her, and she suggested that he turn to prayer. Prayer became of intense interest to him as he explored every facet of the concept, just as he had

---

[57] C. S. Lewis, *Mere Christianity* (London: Collins, 2014).

when he devoted himself to art in 1975 under the tutelage of Raeburn.[58] Larry Myers, one of the pastors of the church Dylan visited at home in Brentwood, California, was struck by the intensity of his thirst for knowledge of the truth the Bible taught.[59]

Dylan's girlfriend at the time of his conversion, Mary Alice Artes, was important in the process of immersion in the Bible. She was a member of a religious group called the Vineyard Fellowship in Tarzana, California, and Dylan became baptized into its community, where a number of Rolling Thunder Revue musicians also worshipped. This period of total immersion in the obsessive search for knowledge found expression in his songs. Two songs were written in gratitude to Artes for bringing Jesus into his heart. These were 'Precious Angel' and 'Covenant Woman', which appeared on *Slow Train Coming* in May 1979. This, along with *Saved* (1980), and the more sceptical *Shot of Love* (1981), constitute his so-called gospel period. What they have in common, according to Michael Karwowski, is that the songs, with the exception of 'Every Grain of Sand', do not emanate from his soul and are a return to his finger-pointing days.[60]

The difference is, however, that his finger-pointing songs rarely gave his audience the answers. They diagnosed the structural causes of such social ills as racism, nuclear and conventional war, attributing collective responsibility, while leaving it open to the individual to think carefully about what he or she must do. For example, he put the spotlight on the sport of boxing by exposing the hypocrisy of all those involved who refused to acknowledge any responsibility for Moore's death in the ring, from his opponent to the audience, his manager and referee ('Who Killed Davey Moore', *The Bootleg Series, vol 6: Bob Dylan Live 1964*). Most of his finger-pointing songs are diagnostic and analytic rather than prescriptive, which is what distinguished Dylan from the array of protest singers contemporary with him. In his gospel phase, however, he was certain of the answers – it is God who leads us on the path to redemption – and Dylan was never tired of reminding his audience.

There can be no doubt that Dylan experienced a new presence in his life, a direct communication with Jesus. He felt that he had been called to follow and that he had found the meaning to his life that had so long escaped him. Before the

---

[58] Helena Springs, interviewed by Chris Cooper, reprinted in *Wanted Man*, ed. Bauldie, p. 126.
[59] Scott M. Marshall with Marcia Ford, *Restless Pilgrim: The Spiritual Journey of Bob Dylan* (Lake Mary, FL: Relevant Books, 2002), p. 27.
[60] Michael Karwowski, *Bob Dylan: What the Songs Mean* (Kibworth Beauchamp, Leicestershire, 2019), p. 334.

total destruction of the human race, Dylan believed, Christ would return to save us. Dylan had become convinced, after a close study of the book of Revelations, that ever since the time Adam and Eve were expelled from the Garden of Eden things had gone downhill and that the human race is destined for Armageddon. His belief in Christ the Saviour was not, in his view, incompatible with his Jewish heritage and was consistent with sects within Judaism who described themselves as Messianic Jews.

When news of Dylan's conversion reached Cohen, Jennifer Warnes, who was living with Leonard Cohen at the time, told Howard Sounes that Cohen was incandescent, walking around the house saying: 'I don't get it. I just don't get this. Why would he go for Jesus at a late time like this? I don't get the Jesus part'.[61] Warnes remarked that Cohen was so very Jewish and felt a close affinity with Dylan, that 'I think it rocked his world to see Bob go [Christian]'.[62] He may have initially been taken off balance, but he later had a more considered view, suggesting to Martin Grossman that he was never devastated by the news because he didn't regard it as a conversion. It was, instead, simply the figure of Jesus touching Dylan very movingly. On another occasion, he defended Dylan against critics who pronounced his career finished. The songs that came from Dylan's gospel years, in Cohen's view, 'were some of the most beautiful songs that ever entered the whole landscape of gospel music'.[63]

Although *Shot of Love* was badly received, as his two previous albums had been, it did contain a classic song that ranks among Dylan's very best. The song was inspired by William Blake's 'Auguries of Innocence', which begins with the lines: 'To see a World in a Grain of Sand / And a Heaven in a Wild Flower / Hold Infinity in the palm of your hand / and Eternity in an hour'. Dylan's 'Every Grain of Sand' was written in a flow of consciousness in which he felt he was the instrument of another mind from which the words emanated. So pleased was he with the result that he phoned Jennifer Warnes to come over to his house to hear it. To her surprise, they recorded it together that evening. This version, recorded in September 1980, appeared on *The Bootleg Series, volumes 1–3* (1991). After meeting up with Dylan in a Paris café in February 1990, Cohen was interviewed by the journalist Tom Chaffin and told him that the reaction to Dylan's gospel music was very unfair. He was particularly incensed by a recent review of Dylan's career that criticized *Shot of Love* (1981), for containing only one masterpiece,

---

[61] Sounes, *Down the Highway*, p. 336.
[62] Sounes, *Down the Highway*, p. 337.
[63] Scott M. Marshall, *Bob Dylan: The Spiritual Life* (Washington, DC: WND Books, 2017), p. 78.

'Shot of Love'. Cohen exclaimed: 'My God, only one masterpiece? Does this guy have any idea what it takes to produce a single masterpiece?'[64] As far as Cohen was concerned, anything that Dylan did deserved serious attention.

Dylan also felt an affinity with Cohen, both as a poet and a deeply religious man. Jennifer Warnes told Roscoe Beck a story about a dinner party she and Leonard Cohen were at to honour Bob Dylan. Elizabeth Taylor was also there and Dylan took her by the hand and said, 'Let me introduce you to Leonard Cohen, he's "a real poet"'.[65] Dylan was deeply impressed by 'Hallelujah', and thought many of Cohen's songs were like prayers. 'That song "Hallelujah" has resonance for me,' Dylan said. 'There again, it's a beautifully constructed melody that steps up, evolves, and slips back, all in quick time. But this song has a connective chorus, which when it comes in has a power all of its own. The '"secret chord"' and the point-blank I-know-you-better-than-you-know-yourself aspect of the song has plenty of resonance for me'.[66]

Four years after 'Hallelujah' was released, Dylan's Never Ending Tour came to Montreal's Forum de Montreal in 1988. Knowing it was Cohen's hometown, Dylan honoured him by singing 'Hallelujah'. Dylan sang it again the following month at the Greek Theatre in Los Angeles. The song was still relatively unknown, and it would be three years before John Cale reinterpreted it for the piano and kickstarted the 'Hallelujah' craze.[67] It was just after this in 1990 that Cohen and Dylan arranged to meet in a café in Paris. Dylan asked Cohen how long it had taken him to write 'Hallelujah'. Knowing that Dylan was a notoriously rapid songwriter, often able to compose beautiful songs and melodies in very short periods of time, Cohen understated and said two years. It had actually taken five years. He asked Dylan how long it had taken to write 'I and I' (*Infidels*, 1983), one of his favourite recent songs, and Dylan answered, 'fifteen minutes'.[68]

'Hallelujah' was Cohen's most commercially successful song, covered over 500 times, and has a variety of alternative verses, with only the most sanitized making the final cut on most versions. Alexandra Burke's cover (2008) achieved

[64] Cited in Marshall, *The Spiritual Life*, p. 112.
[65] Michael Bonner, 'A Year on the Road with Leonard Cohen by His Band Mates', *Uncut*, 11 October 2012. https://www.uncut.co.uk/features/hallelujah-leonard-cohen-meets-uncut-29455/2/. Accessed 4 July 2020.
[66] Interview with David Remnick, 'Leonard Cohen Makes It Darker', *The New Yorker*, 10 October 2016, https://www.newyorker.com/magazine/2016/10/17/leonard-cohen-makes-it-darker. Accessed 15 June 2020.
[67] Andy Green, 'Bob Dylan Covers Leonard Cohen's 'Hallelujah'', *Rolling Stone*, 13 October 2016. https://www.rollingstone.com/music/music-news/flashback-bob-dylan-covers-leonard-cohens-hallelujah-121224/. Accessed 4 July 2020.
[68] Williamson, 'We Are the Marines of the Spiritual World', p. 7.

a European sales record, 105,000 digital downloads in one day. The song sold 576,000 copies in one week, and second in the charts was Jeff Buckley's version with Cohen's original reaching No. 36 at the same time. It was Cohen's only top 40 UK single in the whole of his career.

Following the release of Jennifer Warnes's *Famous Blue Raincoat* (1987), including covers and new material, with a guest appearance from Cohen on 'Joan of Arc', interest in the aging hipster from his fan base was regenerated. Cohen was generous in attributing much of the credit to Warnes for the revival of interest in him, especially since it was a considerable risk to her own career, recording a complete album of songs by the 'Godfather of Gloom'. Unexpectedly her album was a modest success, No. 72 in the United States and No. 33 in the British album charts. Close on its heels Cohen capitalized by releasing his own *I'm Your Man* (1988). He promoted this album, which projected a completely different electronic sound from *Various Positions*, which Columbia had refused to release on its label in the United States, and exuded a greater musical confidence than any of his previous albums, with a twenty-five date tour, punctuated with a generous four-month intermission. Never one to be pushed into releasing an album, or publishing a book, until they met his high standards of completion, Cohen devotees had to wait until 1992 until he released his next studio album, *The Future*, an acclaimed collection that was both musically and lyrically ambitious. He was now almost sixty and thinking about financial security for himself and his family. With Kelley Lynch, his manager since Marty Machat died in 1988, an ambitious itinerary was agreed with twenty-six dates in Europe quickly followed by thirty-seven dates in two months around North America.

Whereas Dylan had gone into exile in 1966, Cohen went into exile in the Buddhist monastery on Mount Baldy, following the exhausting schedule of his 1993 career-affirming tour to promote *The Future* (1992). He was burnt-out and wracked with self-loathing after months of heavy drinking, smoking and the usual debauchery, despite his hair having turned grey and aching in the places where he used to play. His engagement to Rebecca de Mornay was over, which Cohen brushed aside, explaining 'she got wise to me!' Cohen had never been a great enthusiast for touring, but it was a necessity in order to increase his album sales and repay the renewed faith Columbia invested in him.

He had frequently gone into retreat at the Buddhist monastery just outside Los Angeles, but this time it was prolonged and required serious dedication, although when he re-emerged he was once again evasive about the significance of Buddhism to his spiritual development, confessing that going into the monastery was an admission of failure, an inability to cope with life, and abandoning the monastery, despite being ordained a monk, was an even greater failure for him. His prolonged flirtation with Buddhism served further to accentuate his always ambivalent, but profound antagonistic and agonistic, relationship with the religion of his forefathers, which he never renounced. He frequently outraged the Jewish community from which he hailed by, for example, naming a collection of poems *Flowers for Hitler* (1964) and placing a comic Hitler centre stage in a scene from his novel *Beautiful Losers* (1966). The hallmark of his writing was the entangling of the sacred and profane, worshipping the human form and encapsulating the act of making love as a righteous religious experience.

Conclusion

In this chapter we began by highlighting the phenomenal contemporary success that the two iconic poets and songwriters of the 1960s currently enjoy. Sadly, Cohen died in 2016, but his posthumous album *Thanks for the Dance*, comprises material for which he had recorded the voice, but without the backing, just before he died. Dylan's *Rough and Rowdy Ways* has once again confounded critics in constituting yet another renaissance in a long and fluctuating career of success. We showed how initially, despite a great deal of mutual respect, they were wary of each other as rivals for what the musical press saw as the same potential market. Each struggled to maintain their careers through periods of audience indifference, when only the most devoted fans stuck with them. Whereas Dylan struggled with maintaining the poetic quality of songs, and seemed at times simply to go through the motions, filling in the gaps by releasing albums of covers of classic blues, folk and Christmas songs, with a late flourish of great American songbook albums, Cohen rarely compromised the quality of his lyrics, and the quality of production of some of his albums, particularly *Death of a Ladies' Man*, was not congruent with someone so conscious of maintaining commercial success. They both endured self-imposed periods of exile, Dylan at the beginning and Cohen almost at the end, of their careers and re-emerged reinvigorated.

2

The road back

I'm a mystery only to those who haven't felt the same things I have.

– Bob Dylan[1]

I love talking about the various ways in which I am unappreciated.

– Leonard Cohen[2]

Introduction

The two decades of the new millennium were prolific for both Dylan and Cohen. The public gaze was focused on them from almost every conceivable angle. Their presence ranged from conventional studio albums, live recordings and videos to books, art exhibitions, extensive touring and, in Dylan's case, a series of radio shows, 'Theme Time Radio Hour', as well as the endorsement of commercial products such as Victoria's Secret lingerie. In a 1965 interview, in response to the question which commercial products he might consider endorsing, he answered ladies' garments! In 2004 he was true to his word.

In 2018, with Spirits Investment Partnership, he launched his own brand of whiskies, Heaven's Door, a 'collection of super-premium craft American Whiskeys', and the bottle was labelled with a design from Dylan's wrought ironwork from the Black Buffalo Ironworks.[3] He also lent his name to, among others, iPod, iTunes, Google Instant, IBM, Cadillac, Chrysler and Pepsi. Probably the most unusual of his endorsements was the licensing of *Live at the Gaslight* (1962) in 2005 to Starbuck's on an exclusive eighteen-month deal to distribute the album through the coffee shop chain.

---

[1] Christian Williams, *Bob Dylan in His Own Words* (London: Omnibus, 1993), p. 101.
[2] Jim Devlin, *Leonard Cohen: In His Own Words* (London: Omnibus, 1998), p. 26.
[3] http://www.citypages.com/music/bob-dylan-selling-out-his-8-best-product-endorsements/48135 4261. Accessed 21 July 2020.

Cohen marked his seventieth birthday, in the same year that Dylan endorsed Victoria's Secret, by releasing the album *Dear Heather* (2004). It was a departure from *Ten New Songs* (2001), on which he had collaborated with Sharon Robinson. On *Ten New Songs* all the songs are credited to Cohen and Robinson, but one of them, 'Alexandra Leaving', is based on a poem by the Greek poet C. P. Cavafy, 'The God Forsakes Anthony', the final line of which reads: 'and bid farewell to the Alexandria you are leaving', which, of course, parallels Cohen's 'Say goodbye to Alexandra leaving'.[4] *Dear Heather* was a more varied collaboration than anything he had done previously – more experimental musically – leaning heavily towards jazz and performed almost in a whisper, more like a poetry recital, harkening back to the Beat jazz collaborations, but with the voice subdued rather than angry, deliberately contrived to express an in-depth humility in homage to Roshi, to whom the previous album had been dedicated.

On *Dear Heather*, there are two poems by Lord Byron and Frank Scott set to music; two dedicated to poet friends A. M. Klein and Irving Layton; one to the singer and actor Carl Anderson; and a cover of 'Tennessee Waltz', an old favourite written by Redd Stewart and Pee Wee King, with an additional verse by Cohen. Cohen's lyrics end with: 'And its stronger than drink / And its deeper than sorrow / This darkness she's left in my heart'. The album is dedicated to Jack McClelland, the Canadian publisher of Cohen's poetry books and novels. It has an air of finality, a retirement speech in which friends and colleagues are thanked. Cohen's management is listed as 'Stranger Management', followed by the email address of his then manager Kelley Lynch. Lynch had become his manager in 1988 after the death of Marty Machat, but she was an associate of Cohen' while working for Machat.

According to Steven Machat, both Cohen and Spector, whom his father represented, set up companies 'to avoid taxes, fool authorities and foil enemies'.[5] Stranger Music was one of the companies which, when Marty Machat was seriously ill, Steven helped to get its administration transferred back to Cohen. Steven claims Cohen never paid Machat for their share of the company, even after Lynch sold Stranger Music for a considerable sum of money to Sony. Within a month of Marty Machat dying, Lynch moved to Los Angeles to become Cohen's executive assistant and then manager. Machat, Jr. thought that Lynch was thoroughly untrustworthy and warned Cohen to be wary of being cheated by her, but he also had little regard for Cohen's integrity where money and

[4]   C. P. Cavafy, *The Collected Poems*, trans. Evangelos Sachperoglou (Oxford: Oxford University Press, 2007), p. 35.
[5]   Steven Machat, *Gods, Gangsters and Honour* (London: Beautiful Books, 2010), p. 246.

business were concerned. When Cohen went into the Mount Baldy monastery after *The Future* tour he signed over power of attorney to Lynch, placing her in control of his finances, and she was also responsible for making critical decisions regarding his treatment in extreme medical circumstances.[6]

According to Cohen, she almost completely wiped out his accounts and sold off the song rights. The problem began when Lynch persuaded Cohen to capitalize on his back catalogue by selling the rights of Stranger Music to Sony Music. There were two agreements. The first in 1997 worth $5 million, and the second in 2001 worth $8 million. The proceeds from the first sale were transferred to Neal Greenberg, an investment advisor, in order to avoid excessive tax. The money raised from the second sale was placed in a newly established company, Traditional Holding LLC. Cohen later claimed that he was under the impression that his children, Adam and Lorca, would be the principal owners, whereas in fact 99.5 per cent was in Lynch's name and 0.5 per cent in Cohen's.

After Lorca had been alerted by a friend, at the end of 2004, that her father's money was being rapidly depleted, Cohen checked with the bank and serious anomalies were unearthed. Greenberg claimed to have warned Cohen in a series of emails that were ignored by Cohen. Cohen insisted that he was not warned and, on the contrary, had been reassured in monthly statements that his retirement funds were safe. Greenberg defended his position by contesting that the monies taken out of the investment account by Lynch were deemed loans to be paid back and hence appeared as assets. Greenberg launched a counter law-suit against Lynch for embezzling funds from Cohen's assets and against Cohen and his lawyer Robert Kory for defamation, extortion and conspiracy. This case was dismissed.[7]

Lynch's side of the story differs and attributed Cohen's financial destitution to his attempts to hide his dealings from the tax authorities and which had now come home to roost. Nevertheless, he won $9 million dollars against her in a civil suit, but she ignored the order. So incensed was she by her sense of having suffered a gross injustice that she embarked upon a campaign of harassment, mainly through a torrent of emails, which she copied in to all her friends and acquaintances. She lost everything in her fight to clear her name and was eventually sentenced to imprisonment for eighteen months in 2012, not for fraud or embezzlement, but for harassment.[8]

---

[6] Colin Irwin, *Leonard Cohen: Still the Man* (London: Flame Tree Publishing, 2015), p. 102.
[7] Andy Gill, 'Tell Me It's a Bad Dream', *The Word*, June, 2006, Issue 40, p. 104.
[8] Kelley Lynch was extremely helpful when David Boucher wrote *Dylan and Cohen: Poets of Rock and Roll* (New York: Continuum, 2004). Her lifestyle was certainly not profligate in 2004, when *Dear*

When Steven Machat met Cohen again in 2007, at Cohen's home on Tremaine Avenue, Los Angeles, to persuade him on behalf of a former promoter of Cohen, Flemming Schmidt, to return to touring, Cohen told Machat that he had been right about Lynch. As Machat was leaving Cohen told him, 'I'm going to have to go back to work. Wish me well'.[9]

Cohen had not, however, been idle and had already embarked upon money-making ventures to replenish his pension fund. Cohen's name had been kept to the forefront of public imagination by a series of projects that were already in the process of recouping some of his losses. Hal Willner's 'Came So Far for Beauty: An Evening of Leonard Cohen Songs', performed at the Brighton Dome in 2004 and Sydney Opera House in 2005, was made into a film by Lian Lunson. *Leonard Cohen I'm Your Man* featured tributes from such luminaries as Nick Cave, Martha Wainwright, Rufus Wainwright and Jarvis Cocker. Cohen performed 'Tower of Song' with U2, which was recorded at the Slipper Room, New York. He also collaborated with Anjani Thomas, his long-standing backing singer, and now his girlfriend, on her album, *Blue Alert* (2006), which he produced and co-wrote. When she toured to promote it, Cohen often accompanied her, and occasionally joined her on stage. Any interviews he was asked to do while travelling with her, he made it conditional that she appeared with him. In 2006 Cohen published a new book of poetry, *Book of Longing*.[10]

Before its publication Cohen had begun collaborating with Philip Glass who wanted to use some of Cohen's poems and images as the themes around which to compose a new work, which also included the recorded voice of Leonard Cohen. Its world premiere was 1 June 2007 at the Luminato Festival Toronto, and its European debut was at Cardiff, Wales, on 18 October. Cohen appeared in conversation with Glass at some performances, including the Barbican in London, 20 October, which was devoted to Glass's works, including collaborations with Ginsberg and Patti Smith.

To the songs, prose and poems of Leonard Cohen, an added dimension was revealed in *Book of Longing* (2006). The book is copiously illustrated with images etched, drawn and painted of himself, naked women and symbols inspired by his fascination with the Far East and Zen Buddhism, which, as we will see in

---

Heather was about to be released. She had ceased to manage Adam Cohen and was fairly convinced that Leonard would never tour again because of his fear that he would not have an audience. She was establishing a business in a suburban wooden bungalow with her mother, specializing in Buddhist greetings cards. The author was a recipient of the many emails which Kelley Lynch sent accusing 'Leonard Norman Cohen' of many misdemeanours.

9   Machat, *Gods, Gangsters and Honour*, p. 256.
10 Leonard Cohen, *Book of Longing* (New York: Harper Collins, 2006).

chapter 3, he embraced with fluctuating degrees of commitment, without ever totally abandoning Judaism.

Taking note of the commercially successful 'Drawn Blank' graphics of Bob Dylan's artworks, Cohen decided to reproduce his own in signed numbered editions. As part of the same Luminato Festival, at which Glass's *Book of Longing* was premiered, Cohen, in association with the Richard Goodall Gallery, launched Cohen's art exhibition, *Drawn to Words*, on 27 March 2007. At Manchester, England, the exhibition had its European premiere, *Leonard Cohen: A Private Gaze Art Works*, 8 July 2007. Almost apologetically, in an introductory poem to the catalogue, he says that if there were no paintings and no songs, then his would be very important. Since there are both paintings and songs in the world, his have to get in the queue, almost at the end. He presented his paintings as 'acceptable decorations', not in a pejorative or ironic sense, but as legitimate vehicles of pleasure in which to take delight and which should be accessible to their viewers.[11]

Cohen's personalized prints of originals were influenced by Van Gogh, Chagall, Braque and Japanese illustrative art. He appears as the humble curator of the past, and present prophet of the heart, who bares all in a curious intertwining of the sacred and profane. Among the prints is a series of drawings of the artist chosen from sketches he drew from the mirror every morning for a year. He did not spare the pencil in revealing the deep, haunting, haggard etched lines in an often weary, bleary, face, on top of which a hat was sometimes precariously perched. A sketch of a besuited Cohen, 'it was the hat after all', whose green painted eyes pierce the onlooker like kryptonite, was one of two images used on posters to advertise the artist's work. The other was 'The End of the Day', a Chagall-like painting of a blue and green guitar resting against a suit jacket, and a fedora hat at the foot, on an armchair.

Tony Wilson, the irrepressible impresario of the North of England, and the larger than life subject of the Steve Coogan film, *Twenty Four Hour Party People* (2002), and sadly in the terminal stages of cancer, unveiled the event by reminiscing a few occasions when he and Cohen worked and played together. When Wilson was at Granada Television, he had Cohen play 'Chelsea Hotel #2'. When the song ended, Wilson apologetically whispered that he would have to do it again because the camera crew didn't get it. Cohen sighed: 'They never fucking do Tony. They never fucking do'. The unfazed, red-wine-drinking, chain-smoking Canadian, whose years of retreat on Mount Baldy, and the lifting of his

---

[11] *Leonard Cohen Artworks*, exhibition catalogue (Manchester: Richard Goodall Gallery, 2007), p. 1.

chronic depression had mellowed and tamed, responded gently: 'I've changed since then'.

Cohen had seen little prospect of touring after he reappeared from the Buddhist monastery in 1999 because his last tour in 1993 had wrecked his health through heavy drinking and smoking, and in addition, he was afraid he would not be able to fill the halls. His financial predicament, following his reputed embezzlement by his manager Kelley Lynch, enforced a return to the stage, about which he was extremely nervous, saying, 'must confess to some degree of anxiety. Hope we can sit down together when the tour is done'. (email 29 April 2008). He first played small venues in Canada, starting at Fredericton, the capital of New Brunswick, gradually building to festivals such as Glastonbury. For someone who didn't get out much, he said in an interview backstage at Hamilton Place, Toronto, in 2008, that he was 'now being sent like a postcard from place to place. It's really wonderful'. He was genuinely touched by the loyalty of his fans and grateful to them for sticking with him all those years.

In 2008, the industry had transformed since he was on the road promoting *The Future* in 1992–3. Leonard Cohen's return at a period when touring was of even greater necessity, with the streaming of music considerably diminishing album sales as a source of income, filled him with trepidation. He had done seventy-seven concerts all over the world in 1988 out of necessity to support his children. The only consolation was meeting new people, but apart from that it was for him 'bleak'. In 1993 he completed his red wine fuelled world tour to promote *The Future* believing it to be his final outing.[12]

In the new millennium, touring was now one of the principal sources of income for recording artists, with seats priced much higher and venues much larger, where the aim was not only to boost the diminishing record sales but also to sell large quantities of specially produced merchandise. Cohen had not played his guitar for years and was paralysed by self-doubt. His greatest fear was that he would make a fool of himself and that he would not prove to be a big enough attraction. He was coaxed into taking tentative steps towards rehearsals on the condition that if he felt it wasn't working out well, that he could pull out, and owe nothing to the promoters who financed the venture. Rob Hallet of AEG Live, the London-based promoter, who had suggested this to Cohen, was taking a big

---

[12] Larry Sloman, 'On the Road with Leonard', in Sharon Robinson, *On Tour with Leonard Cohen: Photographs by Sharon Robinson* (New York: Powerhouse Books, 2014), p. 12.

financial risk. Cohen persuaded Roscoe Beck to be his musical director and to put together a band of mostly fresh faces. He didn't really want to be reminded of the traumas and anxieties experienced during the 1992–3 tour, which resulted in the breakdown that precipitated his retreat to Mount Baldy.

He asked Robert Kory, Anjani Thomas's former husband, to take care of business and to take on the responsibility of management. In order to allay some of Cohen's concerns, Kory agreed to organize a low-key pre-tour of small venues in remotely located Canadian towns. Kory said that this was the first tour that would not be fuelled by red wine. It was sustainable by having a closed backstage with no interviews and a heightened level of support.[13] Still very nervous about the prospect of facing an audience again, having played minor roles next to Anjani Thomas and Philip Glass, the pre-tour began to rapturous applause on 11 May 2008.

Cohen was inducted into the Rock and Roll Hall of Fame on 10 March 2008 by Lou Reed, twenty years after Bruce Springsteen inducted Bob Dylan. Cohen was typically modest in his acceptance speech saying that it was not a distinction that he 'coveted or even dared dream about'. While Bob Dylan's Never Ending Tour continued to traverse the globe, Cohen toured from 2008 to 2013, delivering three-hour shows night after night, with supreme professionalism and energy, endearing him to the faithful, the returning wayfarers and a new generation of devotees.

It was fifteen years since he toured. His last concert on the 1993 tour had been in Kitchener, Ontario, on 5 June. The 2008 tour began on 11 May in Fredericton, and he returned to the same venue in Kitchener, The Centre in the Square, on 2 June 2008. A few days previously, on 24 May, he had gone to see Bob Dylan perform on his sixty-seventh birthday at the Mile One Centre, a large arena in St. John's, Newfoundland. This was the day before Cohen began three days in the Holy Heart of Mary High School. The school was founded in 1958 by the Presentation Sisters and the Sisters of Mercy. The venue held about 850 people and was truly reminiscent of the dark side of the gym at the high school prom where Cohen imagined in 'Memories' that he walked up to the tallest and blondest girl. 'Memories', Cohen said in 1979, was based on 'my extremely boring and pathetic life at Westmount High School, Montreal'.[14]

[13] Sylvie Simmons, 'Travelling Light', *Mojo*, October, 2008, p. 94.
[14] Cited in John Robinson, 'Death of a Ladies' Man', *Uncut Ultimate Guide Series*, 2007, issue 1, p. 41.

The Mile One Centre was the latest of the many Dylan concerts Cohen had attended, and it was 'terrific'. Roscoe Beck, Cohen's musical director and bassist, commented that Cohen had known Dylan for a long time, and they had 'a lot of respect for each other'.[15] Cohen had with him a few more members of the band. Rafael Gayol, Cohen's drummer, distributed earplugs in anticipation of the deafening volume. For three months Cohen's band had been rehearsing and playing softly, and suddenly they were confronted by a crescendo of sound. Playing with his back to one half of the audience, and making no attempt to engage with the rest, Dylan was mesmerizing. Some of the songs were difficult to recognize because of the change of arrangements, and the distortion of the sound, but no one seemed to care. As Sharon Robinson said, Dylan just seemed to have a secret code to engage his audience. Cohen suggested the audience was there to celebrate Dylan's genius, which was at once apparent and very clear. His genius had touched people so significantly that all they needed was some symbolic unfolding of the importance of the event. It didn't need to be the songs as such. All it needed to be was the remembrance of a song and what it did for a person. In this respect Dylan's performances are unfathomable.[16]

Cohen and Dylan did not meet on that occasion. Dylan didn't reciprocate by attending Cohen's concert, even though their events were back to back. Dylan had long since given up attending concerts of fellow performers. He believed that his time was better spent visiting other cultural events for inspiration. Had Dylan attended he would not have met up with Cohen because Cohen and his management made a conscious decision to avoid welcoming guests backstage, with the intention, at seventy-three, of conserving his energy for the three-hour performances.

The world tour continued at small venues until the official starting date on 6 June, with four sold-out performances at the Sony Centre, Toronto, a 3,000 seat arena. Success bred success, and he continued to tour the world, with intermittent breaks until 2013, to ecstatic reviews. Larry Sloman described the concerts as breathtaking: 'Leonard's voice was more magisterial than ever, the arrangements were sublime.'[17]

Dylan took a professional interest in listening to recorded music and made a point of keeping up with Cohen's output. When asked in 1986 if he was worried

---

[15] Michael Bonner, 'A Year on the Road with Leonard Cohen by His Band Mates', *Uncut*, 11 October, 2012.

[16] Brian D. Johnson, 'Leonard Cohen Wore Ear Plugs to a Dylan Show', *Maclean's*, 8 June 2008, https://www.macleans.ca/news/canada/cohen-wore-earplugs-to-a-dylan-show/. Accessed 4 July 2020.

[17] Sloman, 'On the Road with Leonard', p. 12.

about his own record sales, Dylan said that it wasn't important to him at that time because of the nature of his contract, but it may be in the future. He said great records don't necessarily sell, using the example of Cohen's *Various Position* (1985), which he thought 'was a brilliant record', which Columbia had refused to distribute in the United States.[18] When interviewed just after Cohen's death in 2016, Dylan showed an informed awareness of Cohen's catalogue. He said,

> I like all of Leonard's songs, early or late. 'Going Home', 'Show Me the Place', 'The Darkness'. These are all great songs, deep and truthful as ever and multidimensional, surprisingly melodic, and they make you think and feel. I like some of his later songs even better than his early ones. Yet there's a simplicity to his early ones that I like, too.[19]

The second decade of the new millennium was probably the most productive for Cohen, during which he released three studio albums in four years: *Old Ideas* (2012), *Popular Problems* (2014) and *You Want It Darker* (2016), weeks before his death in November 2016. *Old Ideas*, for example, was only his twelfth studio album, but it was his most commercially successful, reaching an unprecedented No. 3 on the US *Billboard* charts and No. 1 in Canada.[20]

Dylan's road back

The release of *Infidels* in 1983 had the potential to reinvigorate Dylan's flagging career, with such highlights as 'Jokerman', but instead it marked the beginning of another prolonged period of artistic drought. It moved away from the Christian fundamentalism of the previous three albums, but remained deeply rooted in religion, and had a more pronounced political content. 'License to Kill', for example, questioned whether advances in science had resulted in progress. It was a strong condemnation of the arms race. It was an album that he over-thought, believing that every note in it, like an Eagles' songs, was predictable.

---

[18] Don McLeese, 'Ask Him Something, and a Sincere Dylan Will Tell You the Truth', 26 January, *Chicago Sun-Times*. Reprinted in Jeff Burger, ed., *Dylan on Dylan Interviews and Encounters* (Chicago: Chicago Review Press, 2018), p. 318.

[19] David Remnick, 'Leonard Cohen Makes It Darker', *New Yorker*, 10 October 2016. https://www.new yorker.com/magazine/2016/10/17/leonard-cohen-makes-it-darker. Accessed 20 July 2020.

[20] https://www.newyorker.com/magazine/2016/10/17/leonard-cohen-makes-it-darker. Accessed 15 June 2020.

He decided to re-record some of the vocals, and instead of improving the tracks, the new arrangements detracted from them and made them worse. Dylan himself admitted that a lot of the songs had just got away from him. *Melody Maker* pronounced that it was 'as stimulating as an evening at the launderette', and *Record Mirror* suggested that 'there is a lot to be said for early retirement'.[21] It nevertheless had its supporters. *Rolling Stone* maintained that it was a remarkable return to form – Dylan's best album since *Blood on the Tracks*.[22]

The period 1984 to 1991 saw the release of five studio albums of original compositions, and he toured extensively with Tom Petty and the Heartbreakers and The Grateful Dead. He found the whole process a drudge, and even considered retirement. Dylan's performance on 13 July 1985 at Live Aid was an embarrassment. Already marred by drunkenness, Dylan, Keith Richard and Ronnie Wood could not hear the sound monitors, resulting in a complete lack of co-ordination and chaotic disharmony. Bob Geldof, one of the organizers, was mortified, not only by the performance but also by a comment which undermined the charity benefit's message of global responsibility. Dylan said that 'we should not forget the plight of the American farmers who were also suffering'. Despite its lack of sensitivity in the context, it did highlight a real problem that Willie Nelson, John Mellencamp and Neil Yong picked up, which inspired them to organize the inaugural Farm Aid benefit on 22 September 1985 where Dylan performed 'Maggie's Farm' with Tom Petty.

Dylan maintained a high profile by picking up various accolades, such as induction into the Rock and Roll Hall of Fame in 1988, but he took the gilt off the honour by performing a distinctly uninspiring, lyrically indistinct, version of 'Masters of War'. In 1991, he was awarded the Grammy Lifetime Achievement Award. He also had a starring role in the highly forgettable film *Hearts of Fire*. The theme of the film paralleled Dylan's success and decline as an aging rock star. In it Dylan sang a forgettable version of Shel Silverstein's 'Couple More Years on You', originally recorded by Willie Nelson. The film had a limited release in cinemas and opened to very poor reviews. Dylan himself later wrote it off as a bad project.

One of his more successful commercial ventures was his 1988 collaboration with George Harrison, Tom Petty, Jeff Lynne and Roy Orbison, who together comprised *The Travelling Wilburys*. Their single 'Handle With Care' included on

[21] Cited in Brian Hinton, *Bob Dylan Complete Discography* (New York: Universe, 2006), p. 190.
[22] Christopher Connelly, Review of *Infidels*, 24 November 1983. https://www.rollingstone.com/music/music-album-reviews/infidels-247152/. Accessed 13 July 2020.

and released prior to the first album, *Travelling Wilburys, vol. 1* (1988), peaked at No. 3 in the *Billboard* singles chart and went on to win a Grammy in the 'Best Rock Performance by a Duo or Group with Vocals' category. Jeff Rosen's brainchild of releasing 'official' outtakes and previously unreleased material gave Dylan devotees a rare opportunity to hear previously unreleased material and alternative takes of some of his iconic songs (*Biograph*, 1985), which proved to be a stimulus to the highly successful official bootleg series.

Dylan is remarkably frank about this period in his life, describing it as having left him 'pretty whitewashed and wasted professionally'.[23] Increasingly he had come to think that he was not keeping faith with himself. There was a missing person inside him, and he had to find him. He was at an all-time low going through the motions of touring, to the point where he was about to throw in the towel at the end of the tour in December 1986, if it were not for experiencing a sudden and unexpected metamorphosis at the Piazza Grande in Locarno, Switzerland. Miraculously, he felt that he had become a transformed performer, standing at the edge of a new beginning, facing the prospect of perfecting a new connection with a widening public that he knew would take years to perfect. He acknowledged that he was going through the motions performing at a level just above a club act, but that his fame and reputation was sufficiently powerful to attract audiences in significant numbers. He set about discussing with Eliot Roberts, who had put together the Tom Petty and Grateful Dead tours, the prospect of promoting a large number of shows the coming year, with repeat performances at more or less the same venues the following year.[24]

Dylan suffered a mysterious freak accident on his hand in 1987 which forced him to confront the existential crisis he was experiencing. Having set himself on a path to redeem his career and self-esteem, suddenly his aspirations were cruelly thwarted. His hand mangled, he was faced with the prospect of having to come to terms with a career-ending injury. He had lost his appetite for writing songs and had avoided it for a long time, but confronted with limited options he suddenly set to writing furiously again. The first song he wrote, of about twenty over the next month or so, was 'Political World'.

On the suggestion of Bono from U2, Dylan contacted the Canadian musician and producer Daniel Lanois to sound him out about recording the new material. A confident Lanois, well aware that Dylan's creative star had faded during the

---

[23] Bob Dylan, *Chronicles, volume one* (London: Simon & Schuster, 2004), p. 147.
[24] Dylan, *Chronicles*, p. 154.

1980s, persuaded him that he had it in him to make a great record. Making it was a tortuous process and Lanois forced Dylan to become more hands-on in its creation than he was normally comfortable with. The result was *Oh Mercy* recorded in March 1989 and overdubbed in April. It was critically well received, and in comparison with his recent efforts, for example, the directionless *Empire Burlesque* (1985), the purposeless *Knocked Out and Loaded* (1986) and the uninspiring *Down in the Groove* (1988), exhibited a totally unexpected lyrical sharpness with a razor-like quality and sound. Dylan was modestly pleased with what Lanois had helped him create. It had, for him, a haunting, magical sound that flowed smoothly rather than stumbled. Sean Wilentz attributes Lanois's technical wizardry for creating 'a rich, layered contemporary sound unlike any previous Dylan album', containing some particularly strong songs, including 'Political World' and 'Most of the Time'.[25] 'Political World', for example, has a powerful message which continues many of the themes that characterized Dylan's finger-pointing songs. Out of a deeply religious moral conviction, Dylan portrays a degenerate world of decaying values, with subservient masses, where wisdom is devalued and denigrated, and in which peace, as the ultimate aim among nations, was rejected.

Nigel Williamson, too, praises Lanois's production skills, for allowing Dylan a disciplined free rein, suggesting that 'Man in the Long Black Coat' was one of the best songs, adding that there could be no doubt 'that *Oh Mercy* is a brilliant record, both musically and lyrically'.[26] Michael Gray was not so enthusiastic about Lanois's production, but still described the album as 'near-great'.[27] Testimony to the strength of the album was what Dylan left out 'Series of Dreams', and 'Dignity'. *Oh Mercy* peaked at No. 6 in the British charts and No. 30 in America. Nevertheless, in Dylan's eyes, it was not comparable with the truth, insightfulness and honesty he previously achieved in such songs as 'Masters of War', 'Hard Rain' and 'Gates of Eden', because those songs were written under different circumstances when he felt that he had 'dominion over the spirits'. It now required someone else to come along to reveal things as they are 'with hard words and vicious insight'.[28]

After this Dylan reverted to recording some of the blues and country-blues songs he had absorbed in his youth. In the two albums that followed *Under the*

---

[25] Sean Wilentz, *Bob Dylan in America* (London: Bodley Head, 2010), p. 212.
[26] Nigel Williamson, *The Dead Straight Guide to Bob Dylan* (London: Red Planet, 2015), p. 143.
[27] Michael Gray, *The Bob Dylan Encyclopedia* (New York: Continuum, 2006), p. 397.
[28] Dylan, *Chronicles*, p. 219.

Red Sky, Dylan returned to playing solo acoustic guitar and harmonica. The songs he chose to sing he saw in a heavy political light. He describes each song on *World Gone Wrong*, for example, in a very different way from how Harry Smith described some of the same songs on his *Anthology of American Folk Music*. Describing the song 'Stack A Lee', a Ma Rainey and Mississippi John Hurt classic, Smith, in his usual cryptic manner, says: 'THEFT OF STETSON HAT CAUSES DEADLY DISPUTE. VICTIM IDENTIFIES SELF AS FAMILY MAN'. He explains that the murder happened in Memphis in about 1900 and that Stack Lee was probably a relation of the Lee family who owned a fleet of steamliners on the Mississippi river.[29] 'Stag' Lee Shelton's ferocity is legendary in American folklore. On Christmas Day, 1895, he killed Billy Lyons in Bill Curtis's saloon in St. Louis and then set out on an unrelenting wave of violence.

Contrast Smith's explanation with Dylan's attempt to make the theme more relevant to contemporary times. Dylan maintained in the liner notes to *World Gone Wrong* that the song says

> no man gains immortality thru public acclaim. Truth is shadowy . . . the song says that a man's hat is his crown . . . No rights without duties is the name of the game and fame is a trick. He is not some egotistical degraded existentialist dionysian idiot, neither does he represent any alternative lifestyle scam (give me a thousand acres of tractable land and all the gang members that exist and you'll see the Authentic lifestyle, the Agrarian one).

In fact, all of the songs on the album are chosen not because they represent a traditional musical genre, but because they have continuing relevance. They may have been composed at a certain time, but their relevance is timeless.[30]

On 7 June 1988 at the Concord Pavilion, California, Dylan set foot on stage in pursuit of a new audience, to cast off the myths that surrounded him, in an attempt of self-renewal. Phil Sutcliffe described the adventure: 'So, one of the greatest songwriters ever set off to rediscover his working, creative self with the tank empty and barely even aware he needed to find a gas station'.[31] The first four years of what has come to be dubbed the Never Ending Tour saw Dylan play 364 concerts. Some of the concerts were with a smaller band in intimate venues. In November 1993, the year Cohen entered the monastery, Dylan played

---

[29] Smith describes each song in the handbook that accompanies the set. The collection was re-issued in 1997 on three CDs and included an additional booklet of essays.

[30] Also see David Boucher, *Dylan and Cohen Poets of Rock and Roll* (New York: Continuum, 2004), pp. 173–4.

[31] Peter Sutcliffe, 'The Comeback Kid', *Mojo*, September, 2006, p. 68.

four acoustic sets with his band over two days at the Supper Club, in New York. It was an invited audience with 200 tickets distributed free of charge to fans. Dylan's intention was to make a concert film for television, but it never saw the light of day.[32] Almost a decade later he played Erie County Fair – number 1,440 on the Never Ending Tour – whose significance was that Al Santos, Dylan's then manager, gave a brief resumé of Dylan's career, which was at once tongue-in-cheek, self-deprecating and a satirical sideswipe at Dylan's many critics. The introduction with minor embellishments, such as the addition of 'Columbia recording artist Bob Dylan', persisted for over a decade. Santos's introduction describes Dylan as the poet laureate of rock and roll, the hope and promise of the 1960s counterculture, who forced folk and rock into bed with each other, and during the 1970s adorned himself with make-up, 'disappeared into a haze of substance abuse, who emerged to find Jesus, who was written off as a has-been by the end of the 80s, and who suddenly shifted gears, releasing some of the strongest music of his career beginning in the late '90s'.[33]

The next time Lanois and Dylan collaborated was in 1997 on Dylan's Grammy winning *Time Out of Mind,* on which Jack Frost (alias Bob Dylan) Productions is also credited. As we saw, it was hailed as Dylan's best in a long time and set Dylan on an upward career trajectory into the twenty-first century, following a number of disappointing albums from the early 1990s that did not fulfil the potential of *Oh Mercy.* These were *Under the Red Sky* (1990), *Good As I Been to You* (1992) and *World Gone Wrong* (1993). Don Was, the producer of *Under the Red Sky,* said that the album was produced in a hurry and that the basic vocals were laid down in two days, and then redone and remixed. Lyrics were recorded, and then rewritten, and as far as he knew the songs could have been written the night before. Looking back Don Was thought that it would have been advisable to insist that recording didn't begin until the songs were finished. Singing a line three seconds after it was written wasn't going to have the vocal confidence and nuance that leaving a song while it matured would allow.[34]

On 25 March 2001, at the 73rd Academy Awards, 'Things Have Changed', which Dylan wrote in 1999 for the soundtrack of the film *Wonder Boy,* directed by Curtis Hansen and starring Michael Douglas, was awarded the Oscar for Best Original Song. This was an achievement he valued more highly than the Grammy he won for *Time Out of Mind.* In his view, thousands of performers

---

[32] June Skinner Sawyers, *Bob Dylan: New York* (Berkeley, CA: Roaring Forties, 2011), p. 108.

[33] Cited in Ian Bell, *Time Out of Mind* (New York: Pegasus Books, 2013), p. 439.

[34] Peter Doggett interview with Don Was, 'Dylan Encounters: The 90s', *Mojo,* p. 72.

had won Grammys, but very few had won an Oscar. It really was special for him because it put him on 'a different plateau'.[35]

A month before Cohen released *Ten New Songs*, Dylan released his self-produced album *Love and Theft*, on 11 September 2001, the day of the terrorist attack on the Twin Towers in New York. The album had long been anticipated given the success of *Time Out of Mind*. Despite the inauspicious coincidence, the album was a great commercial success, reaching No. 5 on the US Billboard charts and No. 3 in the UK. It was a complete departure from the previous album, with a change of tempo, style and rhythm in its unusual playfulness. It was firmly rooted in the heritage that Dylan revived in his acoustic efforts of the 1990s, referencing such blues and country icons as Charlie Paton, Blind Willie Johnson, Gus Cannon and The Carter Family. Its stand-out track is 'Mississippi', which he had initially recorded for *Time Out of Mind* and excluded from the final playlist. In 1998 Sheryl Crow recorded it, and Dylan re-recorded it in 2001 for *Love and Theft*. Alan Jackson was over-enthusiastic in describing the album as 'better yet than *Time Out of Mind*', suggesting that it was equal to anything he had written and recorded for the last thirty years or more. It was bound, in his view, to continue Dylan's 'critical and commercial rehabilitation'.[36] Others were not so generous and went to the opposite extreme. Alex Petridis complains that the album was as erratic and cranky as anything 2001 was likely to see. The attempts at jazz-inflected ballads, in the 1940s style, proved for him that Dylan was no crooner. Often the album, he asserts, 'is simply confused and impenetrable', citing 'Tweedle Dee & Tweedle Dum' as an example.[37]

For some inexplicable reason, the allure of the cinema was irresistible, and after sixteen years since his last venture he co-wrote and starred in *Masked and Anonymous* in 2003, a heavily re-edited version, after the first cut was very poorly received in 2002. Despite the A list of Hollywood stars, of the calibre of John Goodman, Jeff Bridges, Penelope Cruz, Val Kilmer and Mickey Rourke, who fell over themselves to be in it, the film was a commercial and critical failure, gaining only limited release before going to DVD. The plot revolves around Jack Fate (Bob Dylan), a has-been folksinger who is sprung from jail to play a benefit concert, that never actually happens, in an America torn apart by war. As the action unfolds it becomes apparent that Fate is the estranged prodigal son of the ailing President. It is the cinematic counterpart to *Love and Theft*, cryptic,

---

[35] Alan Jackson, 'Dylan on Song', *The Times Magazine*, 8 September 2001, p. 18.
[36] Jackson, 'Dylan on Song', p. 18.
[37] Alex Petridis, 'One for the Bobcats', *The Guardian*, 7 September 2001, p. 15.

playful, drawing upon the edginess of William Burroughs's post-apocalyptic collection of short stories, *Interzone* (1954).

Dylan's cinematic collaborations, particularly the two directed by Martin Scorsese, where Dylan is the subject, were much more successful. The first Scorsese documentary was the initiative of Jeff Rosen, Dylan's manager. Rosen was the executive producer of *No Direction Home*, and he had interviews conducted with Dylan, in addition to compiling material over a ten-year period, before bringing in Scorsese to make sense of it all. Scorsese interviewed Dylan in 2005 and the topics for discussion were carefully choreographed and tightly controlled, with certain matters, such as his first marriage and drug abuse, strictly off limits. When Dylan was asked about the documentary in 2009, he gave the impression of benign indifference, implying that he had little to do with the film and had never seen it.[38] A deluxe edition was released in 2016, with nearly three hours of bonus material, including the trailer for the original release, extended interviews with Liam Clancy and Dave van Ronk, and an interview with Scorsese on the making of the film.

The soundtrack formed the basis of vol. 7 of the bootleg series, which is described as a companion to the two-part documentary. The photograph on the front of both the DVD and CD was taken at the Aust Ferry, just outside Bristol, in 1966, as the Severn Crossing Bridge, between England and Wales, was being constructed. He was on his way to a concert in Cardiff, on 11 May. The license plate of the car is superimposed – 1235 RD – an allusion to 'Rainy Day Women #12 and 35'. Johnny Cash was also on tour in the UK and was backstage at the Capital Theatre where he and Dylan, the worse for wear on drink and drugs, played some songs together before the concert, including the Hank Williams standard, 'I'm So Lonesome I Could Cry'.

The second Scorsese documentary, a Netflix original, rescues footage from the 1975 to 1976 Rolling Thunder Revue tour, on which, as we saw, Leonard Cohen politely declined to perform in Montreal. Footage is culled from Dylan's 1978 film, *Renaldo and Clara*, which is a fictional, fantasized characterization of his life. Scorsese's film mixes fact with fiction by using interviews to refer to imaginary events and happenings, such as Sharon Stone's involvement in the tour and with Bob Dylan. Stone would have been seventeen years old at the time, below the age of consent in many states, and about seven years old when she believed Dylan wrote 'Just Like a Woman' about her. The film is an act of

---

[38] Bell, *Time Out of Mind*, pp. 446–7.

re-creation in which Scorsese is a willing accomplice, consistent with Dylan's moto: 'Life isn't about finding yourself or finding anything. It's about creating yourself.'[39]

Dylan's painted face – sometimes a plastic mask – he says, was a tribute to Kiss, a band that only rose to prominence in the mid to late 1970s. The film features a new Dylan, now a Nobel laureate, interviewed about his *ex post facto* recollections of his fellow traveling minstrels, who included legends such as Allen Ginsberg, Ramblin' Jack Elliott, Roger McGuinn, Joan Baez, Scarlet Rivera and Joni Mitchell. Dylan's forceful exposé of the police framing of Hurricane Carter, the middleweight boxer who aspired to be world champion, for a murder he did not commit, provides a solid anchor around which to sculpt the momentum that the song and tour generated in overturning Carter's conviction some ten years later.[40] Both of the Scorsese films bring to fruition Rosen's and Dylan's visions of different eras in the kaleidoscopic personality of Bob Dylan. Both films were hailed as original and masterly loose portrayals of iconic periods in Dylan's career.

The new millennium witnessed an avalanche of official bootlegs following from the 1998 immensely successful *Live at the 'Albert Hall'*, actually recorded at the Manchester Free Trade Hall, at which a member of the audience shouted 'Judas' just before Dylan and the Band struck-up 'Like a Rolling Stone'.[41] The *Rolling Thunder Revue* (2002), volume 5 in the series, was released, with bonus DVD selections of 'Tangled Up in Blue' and 'Isis', with a booklet written by Larry 'Ratso' Sloman, who also authored a full-length book of his time on the road with the Revue.[42] The series takes us through various time passages, disregarding chronology, with the latest, vol. 15, *Travelin' Thru* (2019), featuring Johnny Cash, guiding the listener on the journeys to Nashville which Dylan took between 1967 and 1970. It shows a much more studio focused Dylan who appears to have worked out exactly what he wanted before turning up. The outtakes for *John Wesley Harding* and *Nashville Skyline* differ very slightly from the versions released on the original albums. Volume 13 of the series, *Trouble No More* (2017), had chronicled the years between 1979 and 1981, the period when Dylan wrote

[39] Peter Travers, "Rolling Thunder Revue' Review: Scorsese's Dylan Doc Is Simply Brilliant', https://www.rollingstone.com/movies/movie-reviews/rolling-thunder-revue-movie-review-scorsese-dylan-doc-845141/. Accessed 2 August 2020.

[40] Peter Bradshaw, 'Rolling Thunder Revue: A Bob Dylan Story by Martin Scorsese Review: Passion on Tour'. *The Guardian*, 11 June 2019. https://www.theguardian.com/film/2019/jun/11/rolling-thunder-revue-a-bob-dylan-story-review-martin-scorsese. Accessed 2 August 2018.

[41] See Jones, 'Judas and the Many "Betrayals" of Bob Dylan', pp. 75–103.

[42] Larry 'Ratso' Sloman, *On the Road With Bob Dylan*, with a new introduction by Kinky Friedman (London: Helter Skelter, 2002).

and recorded gospel music, and at live concerts preached to audiences about sin and salvation, restricting his sets to the performance of songs composed between late 1978 and early 1980.

Since Bob Dylan published *Tarantula* in 1966, his autobiography had been anticipated with some trepidation. Would it be as unreadable? Would it lay to rest the misinformation spread about him and by himself? It is certainly readable, and it is in fact beautifully written in a style that flows and rolls with ease. This is certainly not a book of self-analysis, but there is a good deal of self-reflection. It is a book of reminiscences and astute observations and characterizations of people and places and is particularly engaging in conveying the vibrancy of Greenwich Village in the early 1960s. The style is reminiscent of a detective novel, using the typical tricks of the film-noir genre, such as flashbacks and leaps forward, as he chronicled his way through the early years of fulfilling what he believed to be his destiny. He described listening to Ricky Nelson while waiting to be called to sing at Café Wha and then relates how ten years later Nelson was booed off the stage for changing direction. Nelson was a man with whom he could empathize, having gone through the experience many times himself.

Dylan's *Chronicles* is not a history. Bob Dylan is born on page 29, and after gliding through various episodes, including signing for John Hammond at Columbia records, he returns to describe his hometown of Hibbing, Minnesota, on page 229. In between there is a sudden leap to 1987 when he is recuperating from the hand injury we mentioned earlier, and artistically burnt out. He begins *Chronicles* by describing a meeting with Lou Levy, the music publisher at Leeds Music, just after arriving in Greenwich Village and ends the book by telling how Al Grossman, his manager, gave him $1,000 to buy himself out of the deal.

His character sketches of the people he knew are precise and incisive, such as of Tiny Tim, later famous for his hit, sang in a falsetto voice accompanied by his ukulele, 'Tip-Toe through the Tulips'. In describing Bob Neuwirth, who became a close friend, Dylan writes, in Raymond Chandler style: 'Right from the start you could tell that Neuwirth had a taste for provocation and that nothing was going to restrict his freedom. He was in a mad revolt against something. You had to brace yourself when you talked to him'. Neuwirth appears in the Pennebaker film *Don't Look Back*, and these character traits are evident in his treatment of Joan Baez.

There is a good deal of self-justification in the book. Dylan tries to put the record straight on a few mythologies that have surrounded him. He treats in a cursory manner his well-known predilection to fabricate stories about his own background. He explains how when confronted with Billy James, the publicity man for Columbia Records, he felt intimidated by his Ivy League Harvard presence, telling him that he was from Illinois, worked on construction in Detroit, had no family, and had rode into New York on a freight train. He doesn't explain why he lied about his past to his friends, nor does he try to analyse how hurt his parents were at being disowned by him. He is quite bitter in remembering how Joan Baez criticized him for abandoning the folk movement. He vehemently denies having been a spokesman for a generation, but this is disingenuous. He didn't feel comfortable with the responsibility of being hailed as a spokesman, but there is no getting away from the fact that he consciously wrote songs, such as 'Blowing in the Wind', 'Playboys and Playgirls' and 'The Times They Are a-Changin'' in order to appeal to the social conscience of his generation. After Kennedy's assassination, the subject of 2020 'Murder Most Foul', he felt distinctively vulnerable and did not want to become a target himself.

Fans who were won over to Bob Dylan by the strength of his lyrics will be disappointed that he talks only of the process of writing songs, but not of their content. He makes no attempt to explain their meaning nor to analyse their impact. This is not surprising given that when asked about the meaning of his lyrics he always got irritated and dismissed the questions with such curt answers as 'I don't know, man'.

The book is not an act of self-disclosure, the mask is not taken from the face and there is very little sense of the emotional life of the author, except for the period following the accident to his hand. He says very little about intimate relations, except to express his desire to protect his wife and family from the gaze of publicity, but it's not always clear which wife, and to complain of the constant invasion of privacy.

Chronicles, while it does not allow the reader too great an insight into the inner life of the artist, reveals something about his psychology, and how he was still prepared to be economical with the truth on many issues. In fact, he reveals a great deal about his manner of writing when he talks of himself and Bono of U2. He says that they are very alike in that 'We can strengthen any argument by expanding on something either real or not real'.[43] Like so many of his other projects, it too has been subject to accusations of plagiarism, including the use of a 1961 *Time* magazine article to fill out details that had escaped Dylan's memory,

---

[43] Dylan, *Chronicles,* p. 175.

and direct unattributed quotations from Jack London, who was himself not unaccustomed to borrowing phrases from others.[44]

The one constant is that the Never Ending Tour falters, but never ends, as he circumnavigates the globe year after year at once delighting and enraging his following, which spans the generations, with rearrangements of his back catalogue and frequently refusing to acknowledge the audience. What changed from 2009 was that a significant percentage of his musical output consisted in the great American songbook, ranging from the inimitable *Christmas in the Heart* (2009), featuring such classics as 'Here Comes Santa Claus' and 'It Must Be Santa', to three albums, one of them consisting of three CDs, *Triplicate* (2017). The others are *Shadows in the Night* (2015) and *Fallen Angels* (2016). This is the penultimate transformation in his perpetual reinvention. Having croaked his way through *Love and Theft* (2004), featuring 'Mississippi', *Together Through Life* (2009) and *Tempest* (2012), he now crooned his way through Frank Sinatra, Tony Bennett, Bing Crosby, Sarah Vaughan and Ella Fitzgerald standards. The live performances around these albums had a stage set that mimicked the interior of a nightclub. In his *Chronicles* Dylan anticipated his diversion by suggesting that he had nothing against modern pop songs, but they just did not measure up to compositions such as 'Without a Song', 'Old Man River' and 'Stardust'. He says that his favourite of all time was 'Moon River', which perversely doesn't appear on any of the three albums of the great American songbook.[45]

At a time when his literary skills appeared to have deserted him, Bob Dylan was awarded the Nobel Prize for Literature in October 2016. He did not attend the ceremony in December but delivered the Nobel Lecture to the Swedish Academy in Los Angeles on 4 June 2017, within weeks of the deadline expiring, thereby fulfilling the criteria for the $900,000 award. In the lecture Dylan discussed the influence of three books on his artistry: Herman Melville's *Moby Dick*, Erich Maria Remarque's *All Quiet on the Western Front* and Homer's *Odyssey*. The lecture itself was not free of controversy in that his observations on *Moby Dick* bear a remarkable resemblance to the analysis in *SparkNotes*, a guide for students, similar to *Coles Notes* in the UK, which summarizes and provides commentary on classic

---

[44] See Bell, *Time Out of Mind*, pp. 431–6.

[45] Dylan, *Chronicles*, p. 81. Dylan sang the song in memory of Stevie Ray Vaughan in a concert in Merriville, Indiana, 27 August 1990. Vaughan had died hours earlier. https://dylanchords.info/00 _misc/moon_river.htm. Accessed 26 July 2020. He performed the song again for the first time since Merriville at the Johnny Mercer Theatre in Savannah, 10 November 2013. The song was written by Johnny Mercer and Henry Mancini.

novels and plays.[46] What is more interesting about the lecture, however, is that he touches upon some themes of this book. In contradiction to the Academy's judgement, Dylan is emphatic that 'songs are unlike literature. They're meant to be sung, not read on a page'.[47] This is a theme – the relation between songs and poetry – that is addressed in chapter 7. In the lecture Dylan further suggests that if a song moves you, that is all that matters. You don't have to know what it means. He says that his own songs include all sorts of references which mean nothing to him. This theme is pursued in chapters 8 and 9 in relation to both Cohen and Dylan.

Dylan's art lessons with Norman Raeburn transformed his perceptual vision and artistic imagery to levels that would have been unimaginable at the time his child-like primitivist paintings adorned the covers of the Band's *Music From the Big Pink* (1968) and his own *Self Portrait* (1970). As the Never Ending Tour went from town to town between 1989 and 1992, Dylan sketched his visual impressions, as a way to relax and refocus. He put together and published his sketches in a book in 1994. They were works that expressed Dylan's perceptions and observations. *Drawn Blank* comprised interior studies, portraits, expansive landscapes, still life studies, nudes and scenes from the street.

Ingrid Mössinger who was the curator of the Kunstsammlungen Museum, in Chemnitz, Germany, discovered the *Drawn Blank* sketches while in New York in 2006. She was immediately impressed and suggested to Dylan's management that a public exhibition should be staged, to which Dylan agreed. He was encouraged by her to translate the drawings into paintings using watercolours and gouache. These paintings constituted the commercially and artistically successful *The Drawn Blank Series*. Unlike the drawings, the graphics are emotionally expressive and vibrant, and by reproducing them in different colours, as Andy Warhol had done with his artworks, Dylan was able to communicate different perceptual and emotional nuances, a practice familiar to his concert audiences, where the same songs are transformed by different arrangements and delivery techniques. In terms of composition, design and execution, they were a revelation. It transpired, however, that many of them were taken from photographs.

His use of camera obscura to project outlines of photographs on the canvas as the basis of compositions for his artworks, particularly *The Asia Series* and

---

46 Jon Blistein, 'Bob Dylan Accused of Plagiarizing Nobel Lecture from SparksNotes', https://www.rol lingstone.com/music/music-news/bob-dylan-accused-of-plagiarizing-nobel-lecture-from-sparkn otes-198150/. Accessed 23 April 2020. And Andrea Pitzer. 'The Freewheelin' Bob Dylan: Did the Singer-Songwriter Take Portions of His Nobel Lecture from SparksNotes?' https://slate.com/culture /2017/06/did-bob-dylan-take-from-sparknotes-for-his-nobel-lecture.html. Accessed 23 April 2020.
47 Bob Dylan, *The Nobel Lecture* (New York: Simon and Schuster, 2017), p. 23.

The Beaten Path Collection, extends beyond 'sampling' and enters the realms of infringing intellectual property rights.[48] For example, *The Asia Series*, Dylan's third exhibition, claims to be a journal of first-hand depictions of people, places, landscapes and architecture from his 2011, seven concert tour of Japan, China, Vietnam and Korea. A little under six months after the tour finished, an exhibition of Dylan's drawings was announced by the Gagosian Gallery from 20 September to 22 October 2011. Within days of the opening of the exhibition at Madison Avenue Gallery, accusation of plagiarism began pouring out about the origin of the images, some original photographs in the public domain and free to use, and others that were licensed through reputable archives. The images in many instances were over a century old, and the exhibition, far from depicting real life, projected Western stereotypes of oriental cultures and cultural practices. *Opium*, for example, uses a 1915 photograph taken by the photographer Leon Busy. In it a Vietnamese woman is smoking opium. Doubt has even been cast on whether Dylan actually painted the copies. Nevertheless, Dylan's 'originals' sold for over $300,000 each.[49] Serious art critics described them as lifeless, and little more than mediocre. The value of the graphics is in the fact they were signed and authenticated by Bob Dylan.

In a 2012 interview with *Rolling Stone,* Dylan hit out against those who accused him of plagiarism in his songwriting, describing his borrowings as quotations, adding only 'wussies and pussies complain about that stuff. It's an old thing – it's part of the tradition. It goes way back . . . All those evil motherfuckers can rot in hell. . . . It's called songwriting. It has to do with melody and rhythm, and then after that, anything goes. You make everything yours. We all do it.'[50] It is not surprising, then, that if snatches of Dylan's lyrics are run through a plagiarism programme, or if they remind one of something someone has written or sang elsewhere, that numerous matches will arise. These resemblances are, of course, superficial. Dylan has created a new work which is more than the sum of its parts, but such a defense is more difficult to sustain in relation to his artworks.

[48] Adam Sherwin, 'Bob Dylan 'Copied' My Blackpool Pier Photo for Virginia Painting, Blogger Claims'. https://inews.co.uk/culture/arts/bob-dylan-copied-blackpool-pier-photo-virginia-painting-blogger-claims-530299. Accessed 23 April 2020.

[49] Fred Bals, 'Real Life or Something Like It'. https://medium.com/@fredbals/real-life-or-something-like-it-bob-dylan-and-the-asia-series-547a2873f148#:~:text=%E2%80%9CThe%20Asia%20Series%E2%80%9D%20is%20Dylan%E2%80%99s%20third%20art%20exhibition,his%20first%20public%20showing%20in%20the%20United%20States. Accessed 26 July 2020.

[50] Cited in David Kinney, *The Dylanologists: Adventures in the Land of Bob* (New York: Simon and Schuster, 2014), p. 174.

Conclusion

In this chapter we have focused on the latter part of the careers of Dylan and Cohen, identifying and exploring their periods of self-doubt, anxieties and travails. Neither was satisfied to rest contented with trading on their reputations and sought to recreate themselves to appeal to a changing and transformed marketplace. The years 1988–93 saw Cohen re-emerge, re-invigorated with a new sound and image, only to lose his constant battle with depression, and to retreat from public life to the monastery on Mount Baldy. When he re-emerged and began his rehabilitation, intending never to tour again, he discovered that he had been made almost destitute. He was forced to immerse himself and diversify into a variety of projects in order to rebuild his finances. His return to the road in 2008 catapulted his career to previously unimaginable heights, bowing out with the inimitable *You Want It Darker* and the posthumous *Thanks For the Dance*.

Following successful tours with Tom Petty and the Heartbreakers, and the Grateful Dead, Dylan felt unfulfilled and even contemplated retirement, until he experienced a renaissance in his performative style, convincing him that he could transform himself once again and capture a new audience by extensive touring and returning to the same venues on a regular cycle. His inexplicable hand injury almost curtailed his plans, but instead generated a new impetus for songwriting, resulting in the collaboration with Daniel Lanois and the release of *Oh Mercy* in 1989, the year after Cohen's *I'm Your Man*. Although Dylan's trajectory was uneven and undulating throughout the 1990s and the new millennium, it continued to be punctuated with career highs, including the 1997 Grammy winning *Time Out of Mind*, the Oscar winning 'Things Have Changed' in 2001, and the ultimate accolade, the Nobel Prize for Literature in 2016, the year that Cohen died. After his songwriting talents seemed to have deserted him once again, precipitating a retreat into the great American songbook, he re-emerged in 2020 with some of the strongest material of his career on *Rough and Rowdy Ways*.

Redemption men

The notion that we're divine beings is one that's largely been discarded by society, yet there is a crucial kind of nourishment that belief can supply.
— Leonard Cohen[1]

Jesus tapped me on the shoulder, said, 'Bob, why are you resisting me?'
— Bob Dylan[2]

Introduction

Having demonstrated in Chapters 1 and 2 the remarkable facility that Dylan and Cohen had for resurrecting their careers in meticulously orchestrated attempts to reach out to new audiences while retaining their core devotees, we now turn to the central role of religion in sustaining them through their travails.

Religion and spirituality have defined the work and lives of both Bob Dylan and Leonard Cohen. The two artists share many affinities in this regard; both were raised in traditional Jewish households and were profoundly influenced by the observance of Jewish practices and the study of scripture, and both spent their lives seeking to enrich and understand their religious heritage. They were also brought up in majority Catholic areas, and this proximity to Christian iconography and ideas had a lasting effect on their work, as seen in the repeated references to crucifixes, Jesus and biblical imagery in both Dylan's and Cohen's writing. The sacred texts of the Judeo-Christian tradition shape and inform almost every aspect of their work and are a common thread throughout their lives. Despite their devotion to their Jewish faith, both men experienced a spiritual restlessness which led them into an exploration of Eastern and New

---

[1] Radio interview with Kristine McKenna, *Eight Hours to Harry*, KCRW-FM, October 1988, printed, in *Leonard Cohen on Leonard Cohen: Interviews and Encounters*, p. 246.
[2] Bob Dylan onstage at Syracuse Area Landmark Theatre, 5 May 1980.

Age belief systems as they sought to come to an understanding of the God of their original faith.

The two men share many similarities, with each travelling a separate road on their spiritual journeys. Their paths, nevertheless, converged at many points. In this chapter we will explore how Cohen's religious quest sent him to the Mount Baldy Zen Buddhist monastery of Japanese monk Kyozan Joshu Sasaki while Dylan found himself born-again in the evangelical Christian Vineyard Fellowship, and how music played an integral part in these spiritual journeys.

A secret chord that pleased the Lord: Music and divinity

Music and spirituality have been entwined throughout human history. More than any other art form, music has been invested with divine spirituality and has been employed as a principal means to inspire religious devotion. Edward Foley suggests that music is assumed to be a powerful means of connecting listeners to the divine because it is 'an experience of the intangible'.[3] Unlike painting, sculpture or written forms, the experience is not fixed, and 'its elusive but dynamic impermanence evokes images of a divine spirit'.[4] Tribal civilizations have used chanting and music as a means of achieving spiritual fervour and communing with deities. In ancient Greece, Plato saw music as a powerful tool because 'rhythm and harmony find their way into the inward places of the soul'.[5]

The idea that music is a profound expression of divinity is a strong part of the Judeo-Christian tradition, with Jewish psalmodies chanted in the synagogue, and the Christian mass featuring hymns performed by the congregation. The Book of Psalms extolls song as a form of praise, instructing followers to 'sing a song and play the tambourine' (Ps. 81.2) in honour of the Lord, but it is also a means of communication between man and divinity. Psalm 40.3, for example, states, 'he put a new song in my mouth'. The ancient idea that music moves the soul is affirmed by St Augustine who claimed that it was pivotal to his conversion to Christianity.[6]

---

[3]   Edward Foley, 'Music and Spirituality – Introduction', *Religions*, no. 6 (2015), p. 639. DOI: 10.3390/rel6020638. Accessed 18 July 2020.
[4]   Foley, 'Music and Spirituality', p. 639.
[5]   *The Dialogues of Plato: Volume Four: The Republic*, trans. Benjamin Jowett, ed. M. Hare and D. A. Russell (Sphere Books Ltd., 1970), Book III, p. 165.
[6]   Saint Augustine, *Confessions of S. Augustine*, trans. E. B. Pusey (London: Dent, 1907), pp. 234–6.

Plato and Augustine, while acknowledging the divine features of music, were also wary of its powerful influence as an agent of corruption. This idea was particularly evident in the rhetoric surrounding the emerging rock'n'roll genre in the mid-1950s when it was condemned by fundamentalist Christian groups as 'the devil's music'. Jerry Lee Lewis once admitted that he feared he would go to hell playing the piano, telling a reporter that he could not 'picture Jesus Christ . . . doin' a whole lotta shakin'.'[7] Despite this, many rock and pop stars such as Little Richard, Donna Summer, Al Green, Van Morrison, Arlo Guthrie, Richie Furay, Robin Lane and, of course, Bob Dylan have embraced a spiritual path, even embracing fundamentalist Christianity.[8]

Dylan and Cohen were both brought up observing traditional Jewish practices and traditions. Their formative years were spent in the synagogues and ceremonies where they heard the psalmodies and liturgical incantations which imparted a reverence for the power of music as a form of spiritual expression. Both deeply spiritual men, this early instruction shaped their approach to creating music and thoroughly permeated their lyrics. Cohen, for example, believed strongly in the 'sacred function' of music which he saw as 'uniting men, honouring ancestors and placing yourself in a reverent attitude toward the future.'[9]

Hava Negeilah blues: The Jewish roots of Bob Dylan and Leonard Cohen

It is perhaps in their spiritual paths that the two men find most common ground. Both artists were raised in traditional Jewish households, and though their investigations into other religious beliefs led them in different directions, they each retained strong connections to their religious roots. The importance

---

[7] Robert Palmer, 'The Devil and Jerry Lee Lewis', *Rolling Stone* (13 December 1979). https://ww w.rollingstone.com/music/music-news/the-devil-and-jerry-lee-lewis-2-179111/. Accessed 3 August 2020.

[8] Robert Palmer, 'The Pop Life; Rock: No Longer 'Devil's Music'?' *New York Times* (16 September 1981), p. 23. https://www.nytimes.com/1981/09/16/arts/the-pop-life-rock-no-longer-devil-s-musi c.html#:~:text=WHEN%20rock%2Dand%2Droll%20enjoyed,it%20"the%20Devil's%20music. Accessed 3 August 2020.

[9] Leonard Cohen quoted in Karen Lehrman Bloch, 'Healing of the Spirit: The Genius of Leonard Cohen', *Jewish Journal*, 3 July 2019. https://jewishjournal.com/cover_story/301044/healing-of-the-spirit-the-genius-of-leonard-cohen/. Accessed 8 August 2020.

of Judaism to both Dylan's and Cohen's songwriting requires an exploration of
their early lives.

Leonard Cohen was born on 21 September 1934 into a prominent Jewish
family in the affluent Westmount suburb of Montreal, Canada. Westmount was
an enclave for upper-class Jewish and Protestant families who found themselves
grouped together by virtue of not belonging to either Quebec's French-Catholic
majority or the English protestant community.

Judaism defined the Cohen family. The young Leonard was given the Hebrew
name of 'Eliezer' which means 'God is help' and was the name of Abraham's
trusted servant in scripture. The surname Cohen comes from the Hebrew
'Kohen' and marks its bearers as members of the priestly caste who possess both
privileges and obligations in the synagogue. This mantle was taken seriously by
the Cohens and young Leonard was raised to respect and revere the traditions
and achievements of his forbears. In 1994 he told a reporter, 'when they told me
I was a Kohen, I believed it . . . I wanted to be the one who lifted up the Torah'.[10]

The Cohens were an illustrious family. Lazarus Cohen, Leonard's paternal
great-grandfather, emigrated from Russian Poland to Canada in 1860 and
established himself as a luminary of the Montreal Jewish community. He became
president of the Shaar Hashomayim synagogue and established organizations
aiding Jewish immigrants.[11] His son, Lyon Cohen, continued his father's legacy
and was known for being both a formidable business man and a generous
philanthropist, opening a Jewish community centre in Montreal and the
Mount Sinai Sanatorium, alongside raising funds for the victims of the Russian
pogroms.[12] In 1897 he co-founded the *Jewish Times* – Canada's first English
language Jewish newspaper – and was elected president of the Canadian
Jewish Congress in 1919.[13] Despite his wealth and social standing, Lyon Cohen
remained a man of the people and was often found at the docks greeting freshly
arrived Jewish immigrants to the community.[14]

Cohen's mother, Masha Cohen, was the daughter of Rabbi Solomon Klonitzki-
Kline, the noted Talmudic scholar whose works included *Lexicon of Hebrew
Homonyms* and *Ozar Taamei Hazal*, a thesaurus of Talmudical interpretations.

[10] Complete Transcript of Interview Between Leonard Cohen and Arthur Kurzweil (23 November
1993). https://www.leonardcohenfiles.com/arthurkurzweil.pdf. Accessed 31 July 2020. Abbreviated
and edited version published in *The Jewish Book* News in January 1994.
[11] Sylvie Simmons, *I'm Your Man* (London: Jonathan Cape, 2012), p. 7.
[12] Simmons, *I'm Your Man*, p. 7.
[13] Richard Kreitner, 'Lyon Cohen and the Jewish Times', Museum of Jewish Montreal (website). http://
imjm.ca/location/1070. Accessed 28 July 2020.
[14] Kreitner, 'Lyon Cohen and the Jewish Times'.

The scholarly rabbi had a profound influence on his grandson when he moved into the family home on Belmont Avenue, and Cohen often told friends of the older man's impressive ability to place a pin on any page of the Torah and recite every word from memory.[15] Nancy Bacal, who met Cohen during his year in London as a young poet, told Sylvie Simmons, 'Leonard was embedded in religion, deeply connected with the shul through his grandfather'.[16]

Cohen's parents were not fanatical in their religious views, but the practices and rituals of Judaism shaped their everyday lives and they were active participants in the Westmount Jewish community. The expectations of the Jewish community were prominent factors in many of the decisions which shaped Cohen's formative years. At McGill University, Cohen was president of the Jewish fraternity Zeta Beta Tau and even played in the Jewish students' society band.[17] His choice of commerce at McGill and law at Columbia were respectable pursuits for a 'young man from an upper-middle-class Montreal Jewish background'[18] and would please his family more than his ambition to become a writer. Though he explored many other belief systems and religious practices, including Scientology, but most famously Zen Buddhism, he remained rooted in his Jewish faith. Despite this, he was often at odds with the orthodoxy of Jewish thought, especially in his early career where he became the source of much outrage and consternation for the Jewish Canadian establishment. In December 1963, Cohen used an address entitled 'Loneliness and History' at a symposium on the future of Judaism in Canada as an opportunity to attack the crass materialism and business interests that he believed had overtaken the spiritual life of the community. He declared that honour had migrated 'from the scholar to the manufacturer where it hardened into arrogant self-defence'.[19] He claimed that money bred contempt for idealism, and this attitude led to writers being given 'the title of traitor'.[20] Cohen himself had experienced the ire of those within his community who reacted unfavourably to his art, believing it to run contrary to Jewish morals and standards. He defended himself in his lecture, claiming that 'the writers will continue to use the word "Jew" in their poems'[21] and would continue to be bound to the

---

[15] Simmons, *I'm Your Man,* p. 74.
[16] Simmons, *I'm Your Man,* p. 74.
[17] Simmons, *I'm Your Man,* p. 36.
[18] Simmons, *I'm Your Man,* p. 76.
[19] Leonard Cohen's handwritten notes for his December 1963 'Loneliness and History' lecture delivered at the Symposium on the Future of Judaism. Leonard Cohen Papers, Box 9, file 1. Thomas Fisher Library, University of Toronto, p. 3
[20] Cohen, 'Loneliness and History', p. 6.
[21] Cohen, 'Loneliness and History', p. 6.

community, even when the establishment favoured businessmen and bankers over artists. The next night of the symposium was dedicated to tearing an absent Cohen – whose invitation had been conveniently forgotten – 'limb from limb' and engaging in personal attacks that 'identified him with anything in any of his fictional characters that was vulgar'.[22]

His lecture made the front page of the *Canadian Jewish Chronicle* and alienated him from a community which was already affronted by the conflation of the sacred and profane in his poetry and novels. This did not, however, prevent the Jewish National Fund of Canada celebrating the publication of *The Favourite Game* with the planting of a tree in Israel.[23]

While Cohen's ideas and actions may have run counter to the Jewish establishment, Judaism remained a central tenet and guiding principle throughout his life. The influence of the sacred texts of his religion pervades his writing. Cohen's Jewish faith is infused into almost every aspect of his work, from the overt biblical references in his lyrics to the chanted incantations reminiscent of Jewish psalmody found on the 2016 album *You Want It Darker*. He was conscious of the quasi-religious tone of his writing, describing his second novel, *Beautiful Losers*, as 'a prayer . . . a disagreeable religious epic' in a letter to his publishers in 1965.[24] In some instances, the work deliberately attempts to imitate sacred works, such as *Book of Mercy* (1984), which is written in the style of the psalms which features fifty prose-poems that recall the Book of Psalms. He described the poetry collection as a 'book of prayer' and a 'sacred kind of conversation'.[25] In other cases, the scriptural references and allusions are so much a part and texture of Cohen's lexicon and world view that they cannot help but colour his writing. His lyrics and poetry possess a prayer-like quality, even when they are not explicitly religious. In the ostensible 'pop' song 'There Ain't No Cure For Love' (*I'm Your Man*, 1988) the singer finds solace in faith amidst the turmoil of a love affair. The song has echoes of Robert Palmer's 1979 hit 'Bad Case of Loving You' (with its refrain 'No pill's gonna cure my ill / I got a bad case of lovin' you')

---

[22] 'Leonard Cohen Sparks Rumpus: Poet – Novelist Says Judaism Betrayed', *Canadian Jewish Chronicle*, Montreal, 10 January 1964, pp. 1 and 15.

[23] Certificate of tree planting in Israel by Shaar Hashomayim Chapter of Hadassah, Jewish National Fund of Canada, in Thomas Fisher Rare Book Library, University of Toronto, Leonard Cohen Archive.

[24] Leonard Cohen, Letter to McClelland dated August 1965. Leonard Cohen Papers, Fisher Library Toronto.

[25] Interview with Robert Sward, *Malahat Review*, December 1986, reprinted in *Leonard Cohen on Leonard Cohen: Interviews and Encounters*, ed. Jeff Burger (Chicago: Chicago Press, 2014), p. 164.

but is elevated by the almost prayer-like quality of its instrumentation and delivery with female backing singers providing a Gospel choir feel. Indeed, Cohen even turns to his singers, saying, 'ah, tell them angels'. The lyrics are infused with references to sacred spaces, holy texts and appeals to the divine, which are absent from the standard pop love song.

> It's written in the scriptures
> It's written there in blood
> And I even heard the angels declare it from above
> There ain't no cure, there ain't no cure, there ain't no cure for love.

Though Cohen explored various philosophical and religious belief systems throughout his life, it was the Judaic texts and traditions that remained the strongest and most profound force in shaping his work. 'Who By Fire', from 1974's *New Skin For the Old Ceremony*, is a modern interpretation of the ancient Jewish prayer 'Unettaneh Tokef' which is recited on the Jewish holy day of Yom Kippur. The *piyuut* – a liturgical poem that is sung or chanted – cites the various forms in which the Lord will smite sinners on the day of reckoning:

> Who shall perish by water and who by fire,
> Who by sword and who by wild beast,
> Who by famine and who by thirst.[26]

The prayer ends with the optimistic caveat that 'repentance, prayer and righteousness avert the severe decree'.[27] Cohen's version reflects the same liturgical pattern, asking 'who by fire, who by water' and 'who for his greed, who for his hunger', but instead of repentance, he shows defiance as he demands to know who has the authority to make this decree: 'who shall I say is calling?' Cohen, like Dylan, eschewed blindly following orthodoxy and established ideas unless he had examined them thoroughly. This, however, attests Liel Liebovitz, is a central tenet of Judaism, with followers encouraged to scrutinize religious texts and bring their own interpretations to them in a process called *midrash*.[28]

Dylan, like Cohen, was shaped by his Jewish upbringing. Born on Saturday 24 May 1941, in Duluth, Minnesota, Robert Zimmerman was given the Hebrew

---

26 Rabbi Dr Revven Hammer, 'Unetannah Tokef', My Jewish Learning (website). http://myjewishlearning.com/article/unetanahtokef/. Accessed 17 July 2020.

27 Hammer, 'Unetannah Tokef'.

28 Liel Leibovitz, *A Broken Hallelujah* (Dingwall: SAndstone Press, 2014), p. 134.

name 'Shabtai Zisel ben Avraham'. 'Shabtai' is a traditional Hebrew name given to those born on the Sabbath and 'ben Avraham' denotes a son of Abraham. The Zimmermans were descended from a line of Ukrainian Jews who settled in the American Iron Range after fleeing the pogroms of the Russian Revolution in 1905. The family lived in Duluth until Dylan's father, Abram Zimmerman, contracted polio in 1946 and could no longer continue in his work at the Standard Oil company. Physically weakened, the formerly athletic patriarch, moved his family to his wife Beatty's hometown of Hibbing, Minnesota, to be closer to her Lithuanian Jewish parents. The young family lived with Beatty's mother and father when they first arrived in the small town and Dylan observed the rituals and practices of his devout grandfather who studied the Talmud daily and encouraged his grandson to do the same. Dylan and Cohen were both profoundly influenced by their paternal forebears in their study of the Jewish sacred texts, and they shared a fascination with the Book of Isiah which developed under the tutelage of their grandfathers.

Dylan's childhood parallels that of Cohen in its immersion in the Jewish faith and community, but the Zimmermans were less privileged and renowned in Hibbing than the Cohens had been in Montreal. The Jewish community in Hibbing stood in marked contrast to the influential and well-established Jewish community of Cohen's birthplace. The census records for Hibbing in 1948, two years after the Zimmermans arrived, reveal that the town had a Jewish population of only 268,[29] and the small community appears to have been quite conservative with the synagogue retaining separate seating for men and women until 1958.[30] Though the Jewish community was not as strong as that of Westmount, the Zimmerman's played an active part in the Agudas Achim Synagogue and community at large. Beatty served as president of the Zionist charitable organization Hadassah, and Abram was president of a chapter of the Jewish service organization B'nai Birth.[31] In an interview with *Spin* magazine in 1985, Dylan recalled 'there weren't too many Jews in Hibbing, Minnesota. Most of them I was related to. The town didn't have a rabbi'.[32] Despite this, Dylan's bar

[29] Laura Weber, 'Jewish Religious Life on the Iron Range', Mnopedia.org (website). http://mnopedia.org/jewish-religious-life-iron-range. Accessed 19 July 2020.
[30] Weber, 'Jewish Religious Life on the Iron Range'.
[31] Seth Rogovoy, *Bob Dylan: Prophet, Mystic, Poet* (Scribner: New York, 2009). E-book Central.
[32] Scott Cohen, 'Don't Ask Me Nothin' About Nothin', I Might Just Tell You The Truth: Bob Dylan Revisited', *Spin Magazine* (December 1985). https://www.spin.com/featured/bob-dylan-december-1985-cover-story/. Accessed 8 August 2020.

mitzvah was celebrated in style at the Androy Hotel with over 400 guests and was rumoured to have been the biggest of its kind in the town's history.[33]

Much like Westmount, Montreal, Hibbing was a majority Catholic town, with most residents descended from Italian, Slavic and Scandinavian immigrants. Unlike Cohen's hometown, there seems to have been more integration between the Jewish and Hibbing community. The evident discrepancy between the relative strength of Hibbing's and Westmount's Jewish communities is witnessed by the closure of Hibbing's only synagogue in the mid-1980s, where the young Dylan had been bar mitzvahed in 1954.

While Hibbing lacked the strong Jewish community of Westmount, Dylan and Cohen shared similar experiences growing up. Both observed the Sabbath and Jewish holidays and spent their summers at Jewish summer camps. Dylan was even a member of the Jewish Sigma Alpha Mu fraternity at the University of Minnesota and lived in their campus house. Unlike, Cohen, however, Dylan did not flourish within the fraternity system and he was assigned several brothers whose job was to 'shape Zimmerman up'.[34] His non-conformist attitude and unconventional dress did not endear him to the more strait-laced members of his fraternity, but he was permitted to play at a house dance which the master of ceremonies recalls as going 'disastrously'.[35] Dylan's failure to adapt to collegiate life was not a rebellion against his Jewish upbringing, but a demonstration of the general hatred of rules and conventions which the fraternity came to symbolize for him.

Dylan's faith shaped his life and work, though he disassociated himself from specific orthodoxies or doctrines. Even during his 'Gospel' period, he never fully rejected the religion of his birth. For Dylan, his Judaism was an intrinsic part of his personality and did not need to be dictated by an organization. After the death of his father in 1968, Dylan spent three consecutive summers in Israel, even celebrating his thirtieth birthday in May 1971 at the Wailing Wall in Jerusalem and visiting the Mount Zion Yeshiva training centre for Cabala theology.[36]

Dylan has been accused of attempting to obfuscate his Jewish ancestry by changing his name and altering his backstory – particularly in an infamous 1963 *Newsweek* article by Andrea Svedberg which exposed his middle-class

---

[33] Nadine Epstein and Rebecca Frankel, 'Bob Dylan: The Unauthorised Spiritual Biography', Moment (website). https://momentmag.com/bob-dylan-unauthorized-spiritual-biography/). Accessed 8 August 2020.

[34] John Bauldie, 'Bobby Zimmerman in the S.A.M Fraternity', *Wanted Man: In Search of Bob Dylan*, ed. John Bauldie (New York: Citadel Underground Press, 1991), p. 16.

[35] Bauldie, 'Bobby Zimmerman in the S.A.M Fraternity', p. 17.

[36] Scott Marshall and Maria Ford, *Restless Pilgrim: The Spiritual Journey of Bob Dylan* (Florida: Relevant Books, 2002), p. 13.

Jewish roots – yet his religious heritage proves an integral and undeniable foundation to his songwriting. Much like Cohen, Dylan was inspired by the rhythms and cadences of the Book of Isiah that he studied with his grandfather and the apocalyptic imagery of the Book of Revelations. This is evident from his earliest original compositions, such as 1961's 'Talkin' Hava Negeilah Blues' which juxtaposes the folk culture he was absorbing from Woody Guthrie and Alan Lomax with his Hebraic roots. The Hava Negeilah is a traditional Jewish celebration song – often performed at weddings – which wittily segments into a yodel in 'Hava Negeilah Blues'.

The Jewish influence is found at a more profound level in Dylan's lyrics. Seth Rogovoy attests that they demonstrate 'the work of a poetic mind . . . immersed in Jewish texts and engaged in the age-old process of mid-rash: a kind of formal or informal riffing on the texts in order to elucidate or elaborate upon their hidden meaning'.[37] Though Dylan's 'Gospel period' is the most overt declaration of his faith, his music has always been infused with religious imagery. The finger-pointing songs of the early 1960s echoed the texts of the Old Testament in their moral condemnation and fire and brimstone fury and often made direct allusions to scripture. In 'When the Ship Comes In' (1963), Dylan warned that 'the seas will split' and 'like Pharaoh's tribe / They will be drowned in the tide / And like Goliath, they'll be conquered', invoking both Moses's parting of the Red Sea as he led the Israelites in fleeing from Egyptian captivity (Exod. 14.10-22 NIV) and the parable of David defeating the giant Goliath with a slingshot (1 Sam. 17.1–25.7 NIV). *John Wesley Harding* (1967) was described by Dylan as 'the first biblical rock record'[38] and contains numerous allusions to the scriptures, such as 'I Pity the Poor Immigrant', which contains the lyric 'who eats but is not satisfied' echoing Lev. 26.26, 'you shall eat and not be satisfied'. This theme continues in his later work, with 'Not Dark Yet' (1997) opining that 'I was born here and I'll die here against my will', in a refrain of *Ethics of the Fathers* (4:22) 'against your will you are born, against your will you live, against your will you die'.

Dylan's connection to his Jewish heritage is seen beyond his oblique and overt scriptural references. Like Cohen, who explored this theme in *Flowers for Hitler* (1964), Dylan was at once appalled and fascinated by the atrocities perpetrated against his people over the centuries and used his songs to condemn the horrors of the holocaust and those who condoned it, such as in 'With God on Our Side' (1963) where he wonders how the United States can forgive Germany for the

---

[37] Rogovoy, *Bob Dylan: Prophet, Mystic, Poet*, E-book Central.
[38] Neil Hickey, 'Bob Dylan:' . . . A Sailing Ship to the Moon', *Adventures in the Scribblers Trade* (2015) in *Dylan on Dylan: Interviews and Encounters*, p. 217.

'murdered six million' and again in 'Talkin' John Birch Paranoid Blues' where he snarls, 'now we all agree with Hitler / Although he killed six million Jews'. In 1984 he even penned the pro-Israeli anthem 'Neighbourhood Bully' which defends the 'exiled man' who is 'always on trial just for being born'.

Dylan's reverence for his religious heritage and the traditions in which he was raised are evident throughout his work and life, yet he has always remained sceptical of religious dogma, even during his conversion to evangelical Christianity. In a press conference in Travemünde, Germany, on 13 July 1981, he told the assembled journalists 'Jesus is not a religion', and he shared similar sentiments with radio host Bruce Heiman when he said, 'we're not talking about religion . . . Religion is another form of bondage which man invents to get himself to God'.[39]

Dylan and Cohen are alike in their belief that faith and religion are distinguishable entities. Neither man saw a conflict between incorporating ideas and concepts from other belief systems into their own spiritual view of the world. In 1981, when asked about his continued interest in Israel despite his 'born-again Christianity', Dylan answered, 'there's really no difference between any of it in my mind'.[40] Dylan, like Cohen, was reticent about allowing any denomination to claim him as a spokesman. Dylan resented being co-opted by political movements in his early career and canonized as a 'spokesman of his generation', and though he expressed his religious beliefs over the years, he made a point of avoiding affiliating himself publicly with specific organizations. This did not stop these groups fiercely scrutinizing his movements and celebrating his 'return to the fold' – either Judaism or Christianity – when his actions aligned with their world view. The Jewish community was particularly excited when Dylan spent his thirtieth birthday in Israel and when his son, Adam, celebrated his bar mitzvah there. Robert Shelton recalls an American student asking Dylan in 1971 why he was not more open about his faith. Dylan replied, 'I'm a Jew. It touches my poetry, my life . . . Why should I declare something that should be so obvious?'[41]

Both Dylan and Cohen viewed their investigations into philosophical and religious tenets beyond Judaism as an enrichment of the faith into which they were born. Their lives were a spiritual odyssey with no fixed path, but many interesting detours and diversions.

---

[39] Interview with Bruce Heiman, *Tucson Talk* (XMFX Radio) quoted in Clinton Heylin, *Trouble in Mind: Bob Dylan's Gospel Years – What Really Happened* (Pontefract: Route, 2017), pp. 117–18.

[40] Neil Spencer, 'A Diamond Voice Within', *New Musical Express* (15 August 1981), pp. 29–30, quoted in Marshall, *The Spiritual Life*, p. 3.

[41] Robert Shelton, *No Direction Home* revised and updated edition by Elizabeth Thomson and Patrick Humphries (London: Omnibus), p. 413.

Angel-headed hipsters: Spiritual experimentation in the 1960s

The 1960s saw the 'Dawning of the Age of Aquarius' and an influx in New Age spiritual experimentation. Though the counterculture of the era rejected the political apathy and nihilism of the Beat generation, they embraced their popularization of Eastern religions and the expansion of consciousness through psychedelic substances. In the next chapter we will see how Dylan and Cohen were profoundly influenced by the writings of the Beat poets and by the friendships and associations they cultivated with them, particularly Allen Ginsberg, who was a Zen Buddhist.

In 1952, John Clellon Holmes claimed that 'the problem of modern life is essentially a spiritual problem'.[42] The Beats rejected the crass commercialization of post-war America and the staid conformity of the previous generation, instead seeking an authentic way of living a spiritual life outside of the conventional norms of society. Jack Kerouac, born and raised Catholic, became interested in Eastern philosophy in 1954 after reading a discussion by Henry David Thoreau on Hinduism, and he went on to introduce Ginsberg to these ideas. Ginsberg spent time in Maya in 1960 and experimented with the hallucinogenic drug *ayahuasca*. In a letter to William S. Burroughs, he reported that he had experienced 'the ringing sound in all the senses of everything that has ever been Created All the combinations recurring over and over again as before'.[43] This revelation is similar to Nietzsche's concept of the 'eternal recurrence' – the idea that the universe manifests itself in repeated patterns and that 'all events in the world repeat themselves in the same sequence through an eternal series of cycles'[44] – and is central to many Eastern philosophies. It became a cornerstone of Ginsberg's Buddhism and transformed his conception of life.

Dylan and Cohen both associated with Ginsberg and he often impressed upon them his Buddhist beliefs. Though Dylan's involvement with the Greenwich Village folk scene in 1961 led him to reject the 'hungry for kicks' attitude of Kerouac's *On The Road* – a book which had 'been like a Bible'[45] to him – it was to

---

[42] John Clellon Holmes, 'This Is the Beat Generation', *The New York Times* (16 November 1952), p. 10 quoted in Nicholas Campion, *The New Age in the Modern West: Counterculture, Utopia and Prophecy from the Late Eighteenth Century to the Present Day* (London: Bloomsbury, 2016), p. 87.

[43] William S. Burroughs and Allen Ginsberg, *The Yage Letters* (London: Penguin, 1979) quoted in Campion, *The New Age in the Modern West*, p. 66.

[44] Robert Wicks, 'Nietzsche's Life and Works', *The Stanford Encyclopaedia of Philosophy*, ed. Edward N. Zalta (2018). Metaphysics Research Lab, Stanford University (website). https://plato.stanford/edu/archives/fall2018/entries/nietzsche-life-works/. Accessed 27 July 2020.

[45] Bob Dylan, *Chronicles: Volume One* (New York: Simon & Schuster, 2004), pp. 57–8.

the Beats he returned in 1965 when he turned his back on the folk movement's political mobilization and collective action. The Beat vision of individual freedom went beyond its critics' characterization of adolescent hedonism and was instead a path to spiritual transcendence. Various explanations have been given for the generation's 'beat' epithet, but Kerouac described it as coming from 'beato', the Italian word for beatific, 'to be in a state of beatitude, like St. Francis . . . practicing endurance, kindness, cultivating joy of heart',[46] and that 'it never meant juvenile delinquents, it meant characters of a special spirituality'.[47] The Beat ethos is exemplified in Dylan's 'Chimes of Freedom' (1964) which extolls a vision of universal redemption and connection, as he sings

> For the countless, confused, accused, misused, strung out ones at worst,
> And for every hung out person in the whole wide universe,
> We gazed upon the chimes of freedom flashin'.

Though the Beats were the leading proponents in the popularization of Eastern mysticism in America, both Kerouac and Ginsberg, like Dylan and Cohen, remained rooted in the Judeo-Christian frameworks in which they had been raised. When Ginsberg's mother died, there were not enough male attendants at her funeral to perform the traditional Kaddish – a prayer of mourning – and Ginsberg's poem 'Kaddish' sought to remedy this. The Beats also described themselves and others as 'angels'. Kerouac titled his 1965 novel *Desolation Angels* and Ginsberg described his generation as 'angel-headed hipsters' in 'Howl'.

In a 1984 interview, Cohen mentioned how the word 'angel' in beat jargon had impressed him as a young man, 'I always liked . . . [The Beats'] use of the word "angel". I never knew what they meant, except . . . that it affirmed the light in an individual.'[48] Cohen had previously appeared in the 1966 experimental short Canadian movie *Angel* directed by Derek May and featuring a man, woman and dog playing with cloth angel's wings. He also wrote the lyrics for Lewis Furey's 'Angel Eyes' which appeared in the 1984 movie *Night Magic*, which included the lines, 'Falling angel, angel . . . Better stop dreaming, Angel . . . He's just an ordinary man'.

[46] Jack Kerouac, 'Lamb, No Lion', in *Good Blonde & Others*, ed. Donald Allen (San Francisco: Grey Fox Press, 2001), p. 51.
[47] Jack Kerouac, 'The Philosophy of the Beat Generation', *Esquire Magazine* (1 March 1958.) https://classic.esquire.com/article/1958/3/1/the-philosophy-of-the-beat-generation. Accessed 5 August 2020.
[48] Interview with Robert Sward, *Malahat Review* (December 1986) reprinted in *Leonard Cohen on Leonard Cohen: Interviews and Encounters*, p. 165.

The 1960s counterculture generation adopted the ideas of Aldous Huxley's *Doors of Perception*, which advocated psychedelic substances as a means of consciousness expansion. Though neither Dylan nor Cohen embraced the hippie movement, or its philosophy of hallucinatory drug use, they were interested in the Eastern religions and philosophies and embraced alternative spiritual practices. Though Dylan would later deride the hippie culture in a 1978 interview when he declared that the drug use made everything 'irrelevant . . . People were deluded'[49] – he was interested in astrology and palm reading, telling Cynthia Gooding in 1962 that 'I really believe in palm reading, but for a bunch of personal experiences I don't believe too much in the cards'.[50] He would repeat his belief in palm reading in 1977 when he praised Los Angeles-based palm reader Tamara Rand, 'she's for real . . . she's accurate!'[51]

The island of Hydra in Greece where Cohen settled in 1960 attracted artists and writers, including Ginsberg and Gregory Corso, but it also hosted 'the odd shaman', according to British poet Richard Vick, who would 'be into tarot or sandbox play'.[52] Though Cohen had shown an adolescent interest in hypnotism, reportedly using the techniques laid out in *25 Lessons in Hypnotism: How to be an Expert Operator* to undress his family's maid, he was sceptical about the island's fortune-tellers and card-readers. In an unpublished 1965 essay, he wrote, 'we have among us adepts of telepathy, telekinesis, levitation . . . other minor ocular skills which at best assume the importance of parlour games . . . at worst . . . dangerous distraction from higher purposes. I, for one, am rather disposed to the more pessimistic interpretation'.[53]

Despite his scepticism of the shamanic 'parlour tricks' on display, the Bohemian community of Hydra became an important place for Cohen's spiritual development. It was where he would meet his long-time friend Steve Sanfield, the man who would go on to introduce him to his Zen master, Roshi. It was also where Sanfield says both men began to examine 'different spiritual paths like Tibetan Buddhism and the *I Ching*'.[54] Cohen smoked hashish and experimented

[49] Interview with Ron Rosenbaum, *Playboy Magazine* (March 1978) reprinted in *Dylan on Dylan: The Essential Interviews*, ed. Jonathan Cott (London: Hodder & Stoughton, 2007), p. 207.
[50] Radio Interview with Cynthia Gooding, *Folksingers Choice*, WBAI-FM (1962) printed in *Dylan on Dylan: Interviews and Encounters*, ed. Jeff Burger (Chicago: Chicago Review Press, 2018), p. 19.
[51] Interview with Rosenbaum, *Playboy Magazine* (March 1978) reprinted in *Dylan on Dylan: The Essential Interviews*, ed. Cott, p. 222.
[52] Simmons, *I'm Your Man*, p. 105.
[53] Leonard Cohen, 'We Are Getting to Know the Police Better', 1965, pp. 2–3, Leonard Cohen Archive, Fisher Library, Toronto, quoted in Ira B. Nadel, *Various Positions: A Life of Leonard Cohen* (London: Bloomsbury, 1996), p. 132.
[54] Simmons, *I'm Your Man*, p. 84.

with LSD with Sanfield, 'more as a spiritual path than recreational,'[55] and continued the ritual of week-long fasts he had begun in Montreal through which he believed he could achieve spiritual purity, claiming 'it puts you in an extraordinarily perceptive frame of mind so you can listen to the thing that is yourself'.[56] He continued to observe the Sabbath while on Hydra, lighting candles on Friday and refraining from work on Saturdays.[57]

Though Cohen was more sceptical of fortune-tellers and shamans than Dylan, his spiritual path took an interesting detour into the Church of Scientology in 1968. Driving in Los Angeles with Cohen one afternoon, Joni Mitchell noticed the organization's headquarters and asked Cohen what it was for. He told her it was 'some crackpot religion'.[58] A month later, he called Mitchell and told her that he had joined the church and was ready to take over the world.[59]

The Church of Scientology was founded in 1950 by the science-fiction writer L. Ron Hubbard and has attracted numerous celebrities into its fold, such as Tom Cruise, John Travolta and Kirstie Alley. Its followers believe that human beings suffer from spiritual trauma due to past life experiences. Members undergo audits which involve being asked a series of questions intended to reveal the source of this trauma while the electrical impulses in their body are measured by an E-reader. The result of this process – repeated over many sessions – is to overcome the psychological damage of their past lives and 'go clear', a concept that is referenced in Cohen's 'Famous Blue Raincoat' when he asks, 'Did you ever go clear?' Cohen never answered this question himself, though he received the certificate of Senior Dianetic, Grade IV Release, which suggests that he had.[60] He was reluctant to discuss his time in the Church of Scientology, perhaps because of the notorious secrecy surrounding the organization and its hostility to those who abandon it, but in a 1994 interview he admitted, 'it is very interesting, as I continue my studies . . . to see how really good Scientology was . . . their actual knowledge and wisdom writings'.[61] Scientology has been accused of being a cult which extorts money from its followers, and it has been rumoured that Cohen found some difficulty in extricating himself from the church. In interviews and

[55] Simmons, *I'm Your Man*, p. 103
[56] Bruce Lawson, 'A New Religious Age for Leonard Cohen', *The Globe and Mail* (23 July 1966).
[57] Simmons, *I'm Your Man*, p. 81.
[58] Nadel, *Various Positions*, p. 160.
[59] Nadel, *Various Positions*, p. 160.
[60] Simmons, *I'm Your Man*, p. 216.
[61] Interview with Kurzweil, *Jewish Book News*, https://www.leonardcohenfiles.com/arthurkurzweil.pdf.

writing, he was open and honest about his spiritual explorations, but Scientology has been one domain in which he remained tight-lipped.

Cohen, who joked that he had never met a religion he didn't like,[62] admitted that he had been something of a spiritual dilletante before he encountered the Buddhist monk who would go on to shape the course of his life. He claimed, 'I participated in all those investigations that engaged the imagination of my generation . . . I even danced and sang with the Hare Krishnas – no robe'.[63] The 1960s fostered an atmosphere of experimentation where young people sought to reject the traditions of their elders, seeking their own path both politically, socially and spiritually, and both Dylan and Cohen are products of this era.

Cohen's spiritual path led him into an investigation of Eastern religions, though he remained rooted in his Jewish faith throughout. Dylan, though no stranger to esoteric dabbling, found his answers not in the Eastern religions and philosophies he studied, but in the Judeo-Christian tradition in which he had been raised.

Gotta serve somebody: Dylan's born-again years

Dylan has always defied expectations. His conversion to evangelical Christianity in 1979 was perhaps the most difficult volte-face for his original audience to accept, and many boycotted his shows and records. Dylan's 'born-again' era is less shocking than it first appears, however, and was the natural evolution of his religious upbringing, his childhood interest in Gospel and spiritual songs, coupled with the trend towards Christian theology pervading the Los Angeles music scene at the time.

The young Robert Zimmerman often stayed up late at night to listen to the neighbouring towns' radio stations. He recalled that the first time he heard The Staple Singers – the American Gospel group – he was unable to sleep, 'it just went through me like my body was invisible'.[64] Dylan's love for Gospel music would continue throughout his life. He met Mavis Staples, a member of the group, while filming a TV show in New York in the early 1960s and the pair

---

[62] Interview with Mark Lawson, *Front Row*, BBC Radio 4 (26 May 2008).
[63] Simmons, *I'm Your Man*, p. 216.
[64] Robert Love, 'Bob Dylan Uncut', AARP (website). https://www.aarp.org/entertainment/celebrities/
     info-2015/bob-dylan-magazine-interview.html. Accessed 25 August–25 July 2020.

would go on to date, with Dylan even proposing to her.[65] They remained in touch throughout the years and recorded together a version of Dylan's Gospel song 'Gonna Change My Way of Thinking' in 2003.

The Gospel singers whom Dylan listened to on a radio station coming from Shreveport, Louisiana, had a profound influence on both his music and his life.[66] In a 2015 interview with *AARP* magazine, he said that he had always been 'drawn to spiritual songs' and had found a resonance with his own situation in the line 'that saved a wretch like me' in 'Amazing Grace'.[67] This influence is seen early on in Dylan's career. He performed a cover of 'Jesus Met the Woman at the Well' in one of his first performances in the home of Bob and Sid Gleason in 1961, and his debut album in 1962 featured versions of Bukka White's 'Fixin' to Die', which asks the Lord to 'tell Jesus make up my dying bed', and Blind Lemon Jefferson's 'See My Grave Is Kept Clean' with the lyrics 'my heart stopped beating and my hands turned cold / Now I believe what the Bible told'. The well-known spiritual 'Gospel Plow', popularized by Gospel singer Mahalia Jackson, also appeared on the album.

Dylan's mother reported that after her son's motorcycle accident in 1966, there was a 'huge Bible open on a stand in the middle of his study' and despite the vast numbers of books in his Woodstock home, 'that Bible gets the most attention ... as a child, Bob attended *all* the churches around Hibbing; he was very interested in religion, and *all* religions'.[68] The year after the infamous motorcycle accident, Dylan released *John Wesley Harding* – the first self-proclaimed 'biblical rock album'.

While Dylan's lyrics have always contained religious connotations, the 1968 album, as we earlier suggested, is replete with scriptural allusions. 'All Along the Watchtower', later covered by Jimi Hendrix, exemplifies the biblical imagery and themes that dominate the album. The song is a modern-day retelling of the prophecies against profligate nations found in the Book of Isiah. The title alludes to the line 'Day after day, my lord, I stand on the watchtower' and Dylan's imagery reflects the sense of impending doom and damnation found throughout the text. The lyrics 'Business men, they drink my wine / Plowmen dig my earth'

[65] Jude Rogers, 'Mavis Staples: "I Often Think What Would Have Happened If I'd Married Dylan"', *The Guardian* (12 February 2016). https://www.theguardian.com/music/2016/feb/12/mavis-staples-i-often-think-what-would-have-happened-if-id-married-bob-dylan. Accessed 8 August 2020.

[66] Robert Love, 'Bob Dylan History', *AARP* (website). https://www.aarp.org/entertainment/celebrities/info-2015/bob-dylan-magazine-interview-history.html. Accessed 25 July 2020.

[67] Love, 'Bob Dylan History'.

[68] Toby Thompson, *Positively Main Street: Bob Dylan's Minnesota* (Minnesota: University of Minnesota Press, 2008), p. 161.

allude to Isiah 63.3 where the Lord decrees, 'I will never again give your grain to your enemies as food, and foreigners will not drink your wine, which you worked hard to produce'.

Dylan's interest in Christian iconography is evident throughout his work. In 'Sign on the Cross', an unreleased song recorded during the 1967 Basement Sessions, he grapples with the idea that Jesus was the Messiah, a decade before his 'Christian era'.

> Yes, but I know in my head
> That we're all so misled
> And it's that ol' sign on the cross
> That worries me.

This imagery is repeated in 1974's *Renaldo and Clara*. A waitress instructs, 'Just stand and place yourself like the cross'. The film lingers on shots of a cement crucifix in a Catholic grotto and a statue of the Virgin Mary as Allen Ginsberg explains the Stations of the Cross. Jonathan Cott commented on the repeated Christian imagery and the references to Jesus made in the film, prompting Dylan to respond that 'Jesus is a healer . . . he overstepped his duties a little bit'.[69]

Dylan's spiritual quest guided his life and music, but he also rejected dogmas and creeds of any kind. His conversion to evangelical Christianity seemed to contradict everything that Dylan represented to his fans, but it is important to note that Dylan continued to evade definitions and alignments with any one religion or organization. He had always been fascinated by the figure of Jesus and while he had asked whether 'the sign on the cross' might be 'the thing you need most' ('Sign on the Cross') in 1967, by 1979 he was sure of it. His fans were outraged that their counterculture idol was now 'serving somebody', but Dylan was adamant that the only master he served was the Lord and he would not be constrained by any one creed or denomination.

Evangelical Christianity has had a complicated relationship with rock'n'roll. Dylan's boyhood hero, Little Richard, famously quit rock music in 1957 after seeing a blazing fireball appear over an Australian stadium that convinced him he would be going to hell if he continued to play the devil's music. Dylan would go on to echo this sentiment onstage during his Gospel tour, telling audiences that 'if you want rock'n'roll . . . go and see Kiss and you can rock'n'roll all the

69 Jonathan Cott, 'Bob Dylan as Filmmaker: "I'm Sure of My Dream Self. I Live in My Dreams"', *Rolling Stone* (26 January 1978). https://www.rollingstone.com/music/music-news/bob-dylan-as-filmma ker-im-sure-of-my-dream-self-i-live-in-my-dreams-88435/. Accessed 20 August 2020.

way down to the pit'.[70] The trend for Christian conversions continued into the 1970s. John Gilbert, producer and director of the documentary examining Dylan's Gospel years, *Busy Being Born... Again!*, says 'the Christian evangelical movement was "what was happenin' amongst the Los Angeles musician scene in the mid-to-late '70s"'.[71] Though the conversion seemed out of step with the prevailing national climate, Gilbert argues that Dylan's genius lies in his ability to 'experience, feel and describe... what's going on around him. In the early '60s, it was the Civil Rights movement. Now it was "Jesus" in the air'.[72]

The hippies and counterculture youth of the 1960s were beginning to give way to the Jesus People movement, which saw 'a spiritual awakening within hippie culture in the United States, as thousands of young people found themselves on a desperate search to experience God'.[73] T-Bone Burnett, veteran guitarist on Dylan's tours and records, told Howard Sounes that 'beginning in 1976, something happened all across the world... it happened to Bono and The Edge in Ireland. It happened to Michael Hutchence [INXS] in Australia',[74] and touring musicians were known to swap well-read copies of C. S. Lewis's *Mere Christianity*.

The conversion, though startling to his fans, was a 'slow train coming'; the culmination of years of religious study and scholarship, combined with the emotional turmoil of his divorce from Sara Lownds, the critical failure of *Renaldo and Clara,* and the lukewarm reactions to the final leg of the Rolling Thunder Revue. Onstage in 1979, Dylan described his 'Road to Damascus' moment as occurring in San Diego on 17 November 1978. Struggling through a set at the Sports Arena, he recalled that

> someone out in the crowd... knew I wasn't feeling too well... they threw a silver cross on the stage... I brought it with me to the next town... I was feeling even worse... I said, Well I need something tonight. I didn't know what it was... I looked into my pocket and I had this cross.[75]

The next night in a hotel room in Tucson, Arizona, he experienced what he described to Robert Hilburn as 'a truly born-again experience' where he felt a

[70] Bob Dylan onstage in Tempe, Arizona, 26 November 1979, quoted in Clinton Heylin, 'Saved! Bob Dylan's Conversion to Christianity', in *Wanted Man: In Search of Bob Dylan*, ed. Bauldie, p. 130.
[71] Peter Lindbald, 'Go Inside Dylan's "Jesus Years"', *Goldmine* (13 March 2009), p. 41.
[72] Lindbald, 'Go Inside Dylan's "Jesus Years"', p. 41.
[73] 'History and Legacy: Reaching This Generation with the Power of the Gospel', Vineyard.org (website). https://vineyardusa.org/about/history/. Accessed 8 August 2020.
[74] T-Bone Burnett talking to Howard Sounes. Quoted in Marshall and Ford, *Restless Pilgrim*, p. 24.
[75] Bob Dylan onstage at the Golden Hall, San Diego, 27 November 1979. Quoted in Clinton Heylin, *Dylan the Biography: Behind the Shades* (London: Penguin, 1998), p. 327.

'presence' that 'couldn't have been anybody but Jesus'.[76] In this 1980 interview, Dylan would contradict the story about finding Jesus when he was at his lowest ebb. He told Hilburn, 'people think that Jesus comes into a person's life only when they are . . . down and out . . . I was doing fine'.[77]

Several members of Dylan's inner circle had undergone their own conversions to Christianity, such as T-Bone Burnett, David Mansfield and Steven Soles. During the 1978 tour, Dylan was often found engaging them in earnest debates about their newfound faith. Helena Springs, his long-time co-writer and backing singer, remembers that in a moment of emotional turmoil, Dylan turned to her seeking answers to questions that 'no one could possibly help with . . . I just said, Don't you ever pray?'[78]

Christianity seemed to surround Dylan on the 1978 tour, but it was Alice Artes who introduced him to the newly established Vineyard Fellowship in Anaheim, Los Angeles. The church was an evangelical Christian sect which grew from the merging of two Bible studies groups held at the houses of singer/songwriters Larry Norman and Chuck Girard in 1974. The church attracted many musicians because of its associations with the music industry, including members of Dylan's entourage and the American pianist Keith Green. Artes encouraged Dylan to visit the Vineyard where he met with two church pastors, Larry Myers and Paul Edmond, who were also fellow musicians. After the meeting, Dylan was invited to attend an intensive three-month Bible studies course which demanded four full days a week at the Vineyard School of Discipleship. He was reluctant at first, reasoning that he didn't have the time to devote to the endeavour because his touring schedule would be starting again soon, but 'one day I just sat up in bed at seven in the morning and I was compelled to get dressed and drive over to the Bible school. I couldn't believe I was there'.[79]

At the Vineyard, Dylan proved a diligent student. In December 1978 he began pouring over 'The Gospel According to Matthew' which had been written with the intention of convincing the Jews that Jesus was the Messiah. It was an idea that Dylan had struggled with throughout his life, but now it became an obsession.

---

[76] Interview with Robert Hilburn, *The Los Angeles Times* (23 November 1980) reprinted in *Dylan on Dylan*, ed. Cott (London: Hodder & Stoughton, 2006), p. 281.

[77] Interview with Robert Hilburn in *Dylan on Dylan*, ed. Cott, pp. 279–80.

[78] Helena Springs interviewed by Chris Cooper, *Endless Road #7*. Quoted in Heylin, *Behind the Shades*, p. 328.

[79] Interview with Robert Hilburn, *The Los Angeles Times* (23 November 1980) reprinted in *Dylan on Dylan*, ed. Cott, p. 282.

The songs that appear on Dylan's 1979 *Slow Train Coming* album mark the start of what are commonly called his 'Gospel Years' from 1979 to 1981, with the trilogy of *Slow Train*, *Saved* and *Shot of Love*. Though his music was always infused with biblical imagery and moral messages, it now took on an evangelical zeal. The songs were originally written for Carolyn Dennis, another backing singer, to perform because Dylan did not feel ready to invite his fans into his newfound faith. Eventually, however, he embraced the persona of a fire and brimstone preacher and used his 1979 tour to sermonize from the stage, instructing his followers in the lessons he had learnt from the Vineyard.

The Vineyard was an evangelical organization, dedicated to spreading the word of God, but it was not fundamentalist in its interpretation of the Bible, meaning that it saw parts of the Gospels as metaphorical rather than factual. The members did, however, believe fully in the Book of Revelations, which foretells the end of days. This interpretation was influenced by Hal Lindsey's *Late Great Planet Earth* which was circulated widely throughout the Vineyard congregation and colours many of Dylan's statements during the Gospel years. The work was not a hefty theological tome, but a sensationalist blockbuster that the *New York Times* declared the number one bestselling book of the 1970s.[80] Lindsey was a Christian Zionist who believed that the Cold War, the threat of nuclear attack, Chinese communism and war in the Middle East were predicted in the 'Book of Revelations' and that the end of days was approaching. Dylan has never publicly acknowledged reading the book nor watching the accompanying documentary released in 1978, but Larry Myers, a Vineyard pastor and friend, confirmed that Dylan assiduously studied the work.

During the Gospel tours of 1979–81, Dylan preached the Gospel according to Hal Lindsey across America. He announced to his audience in Albuquerque in December 1979:

> You know we're living in the end times. . . . The scriptures say, 'In the last days, perilous times shall be at hand'. . . . Take a look at the Middle East. We're heading for a war. . . . I'm telling you now Jesus is coming back, and He is! And there is no other way of salvation.[81]

---

[80] T. L. Frazier, *A Second Look at the Second Coming: Sorting Through the Speculations* (California: Conciliar Press Ministries Inc., 1999), p. 35.

[81] Bob Dylan onstage at the Convention Centre, Albuquerque, 15 December 1979. Quoted in Heylin, *Trouble in Mind*, p. 334.

His fans were shocked at the 'new' Dylan's explicit sermonizing on damnation and salvation. He had never been loquacious between sets, but fans were not impressed by the vocal singer's new words. They should not have been surprised. Dylan's vision of sin and damnation was not new. His early song-writing displays the same strong moral convictions and a determined sense of what is wrong and right. 'Masters of War' (1963) contained apocalyptic tones and invoked biblical figures 'like Judas of old' to takes swipes at the military-industrial complex and declared that 'even Jesus would never / Forgive what you do'. While Dylan took a more nuanced view on morality and finger-pointing after his rejection of the folk scene, he had always been a man of firm beliefs. What was new, however, was that the man who sang 'don't follow leaders' on 'Subterranean Homesick Blues' (1965) was telling his audience that they had to 'serve somebody'. This message was not contradictory for Dylan. He told Hilburn, 'get in touch with Christ yourself . . . Any preacher who is a real preacher will tell you that: Don't follow me, follow Christ'.[82]

When Dylan began reintroducing his older songs to his set lists in 1981 and stopped sermonizing from the stage, fans breathed a sigh of relief, hoping the Gospel era was over. In March 1981 he rejected an offer to present the 'Gospel Song of the Year' at the National Music Publishers Association Awards in favour of attending his son's bar mitzvah, sparking rumours that he was 'growing restless with his persona as a born-again convert'.[83] By the time *Infidels* was released in 1983, the overt religiosity of his music had faded and many believed his 'Jesus phase' was at an end.

In late 1983, Dylan attended his son Jesse's bar mitzvah in Israel, and upon returning to the United States he began studying at the Chabad-Lubavitch centre in Brooklyn under the tutelage of Rabbi Manis Friedman. When reports of this circulated, many Jewish groups clamoured to reclaim him as one of their own. Throughout the years Dylan would continue to frequent the centre and appeared on several fundraising telethons for the organization. Dylan's apparent immersion in the Chabad movement, however, did not mean a rejection of his belief in Jesus. Across America there was a growing movement of Messianic Jews – such as the '100% Jewish. 100% Christian'[84]

[82] Interview with Robert Hilburn, *The Los Angeles Times* (23 November 1980) reprinted in *Dylan on Dylan: Essential Interviews*, ed. Cott, p. 280.

[83] Geoffrey Himes Review of Bob Dylan at Merriweather Post Pavilion, Columbia, *Washington Post* (June 1981). Quoted in Heylin, *Trouble in Mind*, p. 269.

[84] '100% Jewish. 100% Christian', Jews for Jesus (website). https://www.jewsforjesus.org/100-percent/. Accessed 7 August 2020.

Jews for Jesus movement – who saw a belief in Jesus as compatible with the principles of Judaism. The group was keen to associate itself with Dylan, but he remained characteristically silent. He refused to define himself by his religious affiliations, choosing instead a syncretic version of faith which embraced 'the Jews-for-Jesus movement, Southern Californian New Age, and old fashion fire-and-brimstone millennialism'.[85] Dylan's publicist, Paul Wasserman, has stated that rabbis were an ever-present part of Dylan's entourage, even on the Gospel tours, and he could often be found studying the Torah.[86] Though Dylan has never since publicly displayed the same intensity of devotion to his faith as he did during the Gospel years, he has continued to voice his belief in Jesus. In 1984 he told Kurt Loder of *Rolling Stone* that he believed in the Book of Revelation and that 'there's a world to come'.[87]

A broken Hallelujah: Leonard Cohen and Christianity

Leonard Cohen was shocked by Dylan's conversion to Christianity. He understood and respected Dylan as a deeply spiritual man, but he told Jennifer Warnes, 'I don't get the Jesus part'.[88] Dylan himself claimed, 'it would have been easier . . . if I had become a Buddhist, or a scientologist',[89] perhaps alluding to the relative ease with which fans and press had allowed Cohen to continue his own religious explorations.

Though Cohen was initially stunned by Dylan's turn to Christianity, he would later go on to describe *Slow Train Coming* as an album of 'some of the most beautiful gospel songs that have ever entered the whole landscape of gospel music'.[90] Growing up in French-Catholic Montreal with an Irish Catholic nanny, Cohen was no stranger to Christian iconography and instruction – he often attended church with his nanny and her family and had participated in Christmas plays and choir services at his Westmount High School – and was

[85] Andrew McCaron, 'The Year Bob Dylan Was Born Again: A Timeline', Oxford University Press Blog (website). https://blog.oup.com/2017/01/bob-dylan-christianity/. Accessed 7 August 2020.

[86] Marshall and Ford, *Restless Pilgrim*, p. 67.

[87] Kurt Loder, 'Bob Dylan: Recovering Christian', *Rolling Stone* (21 June 1984). https://www.rollingstone.com/music/music-news/bob-dylan-recovering-christian-87837/. Accessed 7 August 2020.

[88] Sounes, *Down the Highway*. Quoted in Simmons, *I'm Your Man*, p. 300.

[89] Interview with Karen Hughes, *The Dominion* (2 August 1980). https://interferenza.net/bcs/interw/80-may21.htm. Accessed 31 July 2020.

[90] Leonard Cohen, '1985: The Picasso of Song...' printed in *Wanted Man: In Search of Bob Dylan*, ed. Bauldie, p. 142.

no less entranced by it than Dylan. Catholicism pervaded every aspect of life in Montreal for Cohen and its influence was inescapable, as he attests in the poem 'Montreal' from *Death of a Lady's Man*: 'We who belong to this city have never left the Church. The Jews are in the Church as they are in the snow'.[91] He believed that 'every style in Montreal is the style of The Church'[92] and in 1997 he told Bruce Headlam, 'I love Jesus. Always did, even as a kid', though he admitted, 'I didn't stand up in shul and say, "I love Jesus"'.[93]

The affinity for Catholic imagery pervades Cohen's writing. His poetry and lyrics are replete with references to crucifixes, crowns of thorns and other Christian allusions, while – as we will see in our chapter on Cohen's relation to masks – his original stage-persona was that of the martyred saint. In his first poetry collection, *Let Us Compare Mythologies* (1956), he writes in 'Prayer for the Messiah': 'his life in my mouth is less than a man / his death on my breast is harder than stone'. These lines allude to the Catholic concept of transubstantiation in which the communion wafer and wine consumed by the congregation are believed to become the literal body and blood of Christ. The second line denotes the anti-Semitic accusations made by some Christians that the Jewish people are responsible for the death of Christ, and the heavy weight this burden placed upon him. In *Beautiful Losers* (1966), Cohen's narrator is a scholar composing a work on Kateri Tekakwitha, the first North American aboriginal to be canonized as a saint. Born in 1656, Kateri was baptized by the Jesuits and renamed Catherine after the fifteenth-century Italian mystic, Catherine of Siena.[94] She was championed by the church for her rejection of Mohawk values even before her conversion, refusing marriage offers from her tribe members and choosing to remain a virgin. In a scene from the novel, Cohen reimagines Catherine begging to be baptized. The Jesuit father kneels 'as Jesus had kneeled before a naked foot' as he 'forced all her tiny toes into his mouth, his tongue going like a windshield wiper'[95] in a profane parallel of Jesus' washing of the apostles' feet at the Last Supper. Cohen's lyrics are also shaped by Christian imagery. In 'So Long, Marianne' the woman he addresses holds onto

[91]   Leonard Cohen, *Stranger Music* (London: Jonathan Cape, 1993), p. 265.
[92]   Cohen, *Stranger Music*, p. 265.
[93]   Interview with Bruce Headlam, *Saturday Night* (December 1997).
[94]   John Rasmussen, 'Saint Kateri (Kateri Tekakwitha)', The Canadian Encyclopaedia (website), 19 November 2012. Updated by Anne-Marie Pedersen and Maude-Emmanuelle Lambert (4 March 2015). https://www.thecanadianencyclopedia.ca/en/article/tekakwitha-kateri. Accessed 8 August 2020.
[95]   Leonard Cohen, *Beautiful Losers* (London: Jonathan Cape, 1970), p. 87.

him 'like I was a crucifix' and in the 2012 'Show Me the Place', the singer asks to be taken to Jesus' burial site to find the stone rolled away from the tomb and the Messiah has risen:

Help me roll away the stone
Show me the place
I can't move this thing alone
Show me the place
Where the Word became a man

Cohen's final album release before his death in 2016, *You Want It Darker*, grapples with his own mortality and vision of the afterlife. It rejects Christian orthodoxy, most notably in 'Treaty' where the singer watches Jesus turn water into wine, and laments 'I sit at your table every night / I try but I just don't get high with you'. In what is perhaps a reference to the Holy Ghost he sings, 'I'm so sorry for that ghost I made you be / Only one of us was real and that was me'. He then takes a scathing swipe at 'born-again' Christian ideologies, claiming:

I heard the snake was baffled by his sin
He shed his scales to find the snake within
But born again is born without a skin
The poison enters into everything

The snake refers to the temptation of Eve by the serpent in the Garden of Eden. The Genesis story attributes man's fall from grace to Eve's actions when she allows the snake to persuade her to eat the forbidden fruit, indelibly cursing man with original sin. Cohen's lyrics voice scepticism both about the idea that anyone can undergo a religious rebirth where their previous sins and misdeeds are forgotten. This overt rejection of Christianity is reiterated again on 'It Seemed the Better Way' with its chorus of 'sounded like the truth / But it's not the truth today' counterposed with allusions to communion wine in 'this glass of blood' and Jesus' instruction to 'turn the other cheek' culminating in the singer's uneasy acceptance that they must 'hold my tongue' and 'try to say the grace' while unable to reconcile himself to the 'truth' being preached. The instrumentation is complimented by the harmonies of the Shaar Hashomayim Synagogue Choir where Cohen celebrated his bar mitzvah which further affirms his faith in Judaism. The Jewish ceremony conducted when a boy turns thirteen marks the transition from childhood to adulthood and so the inclusion of the synagogue choir is an acceptance of his imminent death and recalls the cyclical nature of the universe taught by the Hindu philosophy that Cohen embraced in his later years.

'I can't even locate a Zen idea': Leonard Cohen and Buddhism

While Dylan was 'busy being born again', Cohen's spiritual journey took him to the top of Mount Baldy to learn the teachings of Japanese Rinzai Zen Buddhist monk Kyozan Joshu Sasaki Roshi. It is interesting to note that both men, while reverent of their Jewish heritage, turned to spiritual systems outside their original faith during periods of emotional turmoil. While Dylan saw Jesus as his saviour, Cohen sought instruction at the feet of Roshi, seeing the discipline and asceticism of Buddhist practice as a way of controlling the 'deep disorder'[96] of his own life. Cohen was aware of Buddhist teachings through his associations with Ginsberg and his reading of the *I Ching*, but it was not until he was introduced to Roshi and his Los Angeles-based meditation centres that he began seriously to study the ancient philosophy.

Buddhism is an Eastern religion, originating in India in sixth-century BCE, and is based on the teachings of Prince Siddhartha Gautama, later known to his followers as 'The Buddha' or 'the enlightened one'. The Prince lived an extravagant life as a young man but when he encountered the suffering of those living outside his palace gates, he renounced his wealth and privilege and became a monk. Through daily meditation he achieved a state of enlightenment and set out to share his newfound understanding with others. The Buddha's teachings are enshrined in the 'Four Noble Truths'. These basic tenets hold that all existence is suffering, that suffering comes from wanting, and suffering ceases when we stop striving for change and focus on acceptance. Buddhism also encourages its followers to overcome the limitations of their own egos and individualistic outlooks, and instead view everything in the universe as interconnected.

The Rinzai Zen studied by Cohen focuses on achieving enlightenment through *kondos* – question and answer sessions with the Zen master – and *koans* – paradoxical riddles set by the master for his students to meditate upon. For Cohen, the teachings of Rinzai Buddhism were secondary to their teacher. He

---

[96] Stina Dabrowski, 'Leonard Cohen interview (2001)'. *YouTube* video, 1:03.57. 5 January 2015. https://www.youtube.com/watch?v=44-xVe_vivs.

told his biographer that, 'if Roshi had been a professor of physics at Heidelberg University, I would have learned German and gone to Heidelberg to study physics'.[97] Indeed, when asked to explain the concepts of the spiritual practice, he replied 'I can't even *locate* a Zen idea . . . I don't really know that much about Zen or Buddhism because I was never really interested in a new religion', and that Roshi's monastery was a 'space for me to kind of dance with the Lord'.[98]

Cohen, like Dylan with Christianity, did not see Buddhism as a replacement for the religion of his birth, but a way to expand and explore his faith. His first encounter with Roshi occurred in 1967 when his friend Steve Sanfield began attending the Zen master's meditation centre in Los Angeles. Sanfield recalls Cohen responding to his own enthusiasm by recounting the tale of Sabbatai Sevi, a seventeenth-century Jew who claimed to be the Messiah. He attracted many followers who believed his claim that he could fly but would not do so in front of them because they were not worthy to witness it, until he converted to Islam to avoid being put to death by the Sultan Mehmed IV if he could not prove his divinity. It was not until Sanfield's wedding in 1969 that Cohen met Roshi for the first time. The ceremony took place at the Rinzai Zen Centre in Los Angeles and was officiated by the monk who would go on to shape the course of Cohen's spiritual life. The two men did not exchange many words on this occasion, but Cohen was taken by the 'Ten Vows of Buddhism' that featured in the ceremony and the impressive amount of sake that Roshi consumed.[99] In 1972, when his gruelling tour schedule and hedonistic lifestyle left him on the verge of collapse, Cohen's thoughts turned again to the softly spoken monk.

As with Dylan and the Vineyard Fellowship, Cohen's interest in Roshi came during a period of personal turmoil and a weariness of the peripatetic touring lifestyle. In the winter of 1972, Sanfield gave Cohen a personal introduction to Roshi who invited him to spend a week at the Mount Baldy Zen Centre – a monastery erected in an 'abandoned boy scouts camp' 6,500 feet on top of the San Gabriel mountains.[100] Cohen underwent what he would later describe as a 'Buddhist bootcamp, grim with all these broken young people trudging through the snow in walking meditation at three o'clock in the morning'.[101] He did not last

---

[97] Simmons, *I'm Your Man*, p. 385.
[98] Interview with Arthur Kurzweil, https://www.leonardcohenfiles.com/arthurkurzweil.pdf.
[99] Simmons, *I'm Your Man*, p. 268.
[100] Simmons, *I'm Your Man*, p. 377.
[101] Simmons, *I'm Your Man*, p. 315.

the week and when he descended the mountain, he hopped straight on a plane heading for the sunnier climes of Acapulco with then partner Suzanne Elrod.

He would spend the next twenty years repeating this pendulous swing from Dionysian revelry, with unlimited drinking, drugs and willing women while on tour, to the asceticism and restraint of Mount Baldy. It was a characteristic established from the outset, evidenced from a quote in an early unpublished novel where he admits, 'I change between glutton and renunciation',[102] but it was in Roshi's monastery that Cohen learnt to recalibrate.

Though he was fascinated by Roshi and his teaching, he remained a devout and committed Jew. When the Yom Kippur War broke out in October 1973, Cohen was on the first flight to Israel to offer his support, performing several times a day for Israeli troops – despite voicing his concerns about the morale-boosting effect of his music.[103] He told *Zig-Zag* magazine, 'I've never disguised the fact that I'm Jewish and in any crisis in Israel I would be there'.[104] For Cohen, there was no conflict between his Zionism and his studies with Roshi. He began composing his 1974 album, *New Skin for the Old Ceremony*, in the Israeli desert and as we have seen the lyrics are profoundly influenced by his Jewish heritage, yet he invited Roshi to attend the recording sessions. The Zen master's contribution was characteristically succinct but essential when he instructed his pupil to sing 'more sad'.[105]

Though Cohen continued his studies with Roshi, spending weeks and months at Mount Baldy in between touring commitments, he found his depression deepening. The critical and commercial success of *I'm Your Man* (1988) and *The Future* (1992) and his burgeoning romance with beautiful young actress Rebecca De Mornay were not enough to fill the spiritual void in his life. In 1993 he returned to Mount Baldy to undergo the cleansing asceticism of Roshi's gruelling regime and spent the next five and a half years with him.

A typical day began at 3.00 am with silent tea before Roshi's students gathered in the small wooden hall for an hour of chanted meditation. The participants then performed the first of six-hour-long *zazen* sessions of silent and seated meditation. Monks bearing sticks would patrol the room, rapping on the shoulders of anyone who appeared to have fallen asleep. After this the

[102] Quote from unpublished novel, Leonard Cohen Archives, in Nadel, *Various Positions*, p. 14.
[103] Simmons, *I'm Your Man*, p. 322.
[104] Interview with Robin Pike, *Zig-Zag Magazine* (October 1974).
[105] Simmons, *I'm Your Man*, p. 267.

group would take part in a walking meditation over the mountainous terrain. Throughout the day they would perform menial tasks such as 'chopping wood, banging nails, and fixing toilets'.[106] Cohen was assigned the role of Roshi's personal chef – the monk's favourite dish being salmon teriyaki.[107] Cohen resided in a spartan wood cabin, living an austere life at the centre. His room contained a single metal-framed bed with no television or stereo, though he was afforded the luxury of a coffee machine and his keyboard. His biographer, Sylvie Simmons, also reported that a menorah had pride of place on top of his dresser.[108] The monastic life was gruelling and in a 1995 interview he claimed that Rinzai monks were 'the marines of the spiritual world'.[109] He was, however, afforded periodic respite from Roshi's regime to descend the mountain into Los Angeles to take care of his business affairs. While away from the monastery, he would grab a Filet-o-Fish from McDonald's and a bottle of good red wine and return to his apartment to watch episodes of the *Jerry Springer Show*. After a few days he would return to Roshi's side, ready to submit himself to monastic life again.

In 1996 he was ordained as a Buddhist monk and given the name Jikan, meaning 'ordinary silence'.[110] Roshi's advancing years had prompted Cohen's extended stay at the monastery – the monk was approaching ninety at the time, though he would go on to live to 107 – but he also saw it as a place of spiritual rehabilitation where 'people who have been traumatised, hurt, destroyed, maimed by daily life'[111] could come to recover. Zen Buddhism was never a religion for Cohen. He claimed his ordination was for 'tax purposes'[112] and that he had never thought of Roshi as 'my spiritual leader . . . I was never interested in Buddhism'.[113] At the monastery, Cohen continued to light candles on Friday evenings in preparation for the Sabbath[114] and in 1997 he wrote the poem 'not

---

[106] Simmons, *I'm Your Man*, p. 380. A Menorah is a sacred candelabrum, having seven branches associated with the ancient temple in Jerusalem.

[107] 'A Resonance Between Two Models – Leonard Cohen and Ramesh Balsekar', Jane Adams Art (website). https://janeadamsart.wordpress.com/2014/09/28/a-resonance-between-two-models-leonard-cohen-ramesh-balsekar/. Accessed 20 July 2020. First published in Ramana Maharshi Foundation UK Journal Self Inquiry (Summer 1999).

[108] Simmons, *I'm Your Man*, p. 380.

[109] Interview with Robert Hilburn, *Los Angeles Times*, 24 September 1995.

[110] Simmons, *I'm Your Man*, p. 488.

[111] Simmons, *I'm Your Man*, p. 385.

[112] Pico Iyer, 'Leonard Cohen: Several Lifetimes Already', *Lion's Roar Magazine*, 1 September 1998. https://www.lionsroar.com/leonard-cohen-several-lifetimes-already/. Accessed 10 August 2020.

[113] Radio Interview with Shelagh Rogers, *Sounds Like Canada*, CBC, 7 February 2006. printed in *Leonard Cohen on Leonard Cohen: Interviews and Encounters*, ed. Burger, p. 516.

[114] John Leland, 'The Prince of Prurience and Loss', *GQ Magazine*, November 2001. reprinted in *Leonard Cohen on Leonard Cohen: Interviews and Encounters*, ed. Burger, p. 497.

a Jew',[115] which declared 'anyone who says / I'm not a Jew / is not a Jew' before signing off with his Hebrew name, 'Eliezar, son of Nissan'.

Despite the moments of peace that Cohen had found at the monastery, he found himself in perhaps the darkest depression of his life in the winter of 1998. In January 1999, he informed Roshi that he had 'come to the end of the road' at Mount Baldy.[116] His master accepted Cohen's resignation of his robes with characteristic grace, only requesting that he cook him one final meal. A week after leaving Roshi, he flew to Mumbai to meet another spiritual adviser – the comparatively youthful 81-year-old Ramesh S. Balsekar. At the monastery, Cohen had studied a series of conversations between Balsekar and one of his students published in the 1992 work *Consciousness Speaks* and saw a resonance between Hindu philosophy and Zen Buddhism.

The Mumbai-based spiritual practitioner taught that the supreme source of the universe was 'Brahman' and that all creatures and things are simply a manifestation of his will. He told his pupils that there is no 'I' or 'me' but a single consciousness in which we are all connected. Balsekar wrote that 'the human mind of subject-object divides what is naturally indivisible and therefore gets into trouble'.[117] He advocated the practice of *Sadhana* which involved ritual fasting, meditation, prayer and charity work to rid oneself of ego-attachment and advance on the path to enlightenment – ideas which echoed Cohen's own spiritual practices. Cohen intended to spend just a week in Mumbai but was so entranced by Balsekar's teachings that he stayed several months.

The self-discipline learnt at Mount Baldy kept Cohen on a strict schedule while in Mumbai. Each morning he would attend *satsangs* in Balsekar's small apartment in which followers sat and listened to the guru speak and were invited to ask questions. Many of the attendees were from Israel and it is interesting to note the attraction that Eastern philosophy had for many practising Jews.[118] Leaving Balsekar's sessions, he often stopped for chai (tea) at a roadside stall and discussed the morning's session with fellow students before visiting the exclusive private members Breach Candy Club for an afternoon swim. He would then

---

[115] Later published in 2006's *Book of Longing* without the epistolary sign off.
[116] Simmons, *I'm Your Man*, p. 395.
[117] Ramesh S. Balsekar, *Consciousness Speaks: Conversations with Ramesh S. Balsekar*, ed. Wayne Liquorman (Redondo Beach, CA: Advaita Press, 1992), p. 14.
[118] Simmons, *I'm Your Man*, pp. 399–400.

retire to his Kemps Corner hotel room to sketch, write, read and meditate, in keeping with the simplicity of life that he had enjoyed on Mount Baldy.[119]

In a recorded conversation between Balsekar and Cohen, the singer told the guru that 'it was the resonance between the two models, yours and my teacher's that led me to study your books with some diligence' and that the Zen tradition encouraged learning from other masters.[120] He explained that his disaffection with monastery life had come from a 'greed' for peace.[121] In the meditation hall he sought with an ego-driven intensity that went against Buddhist principles for the 'interesting experiences' that came from 'sleeplessness and protein deficiency'[122] and the monastery's gruelling work schedule. This 'greed' for an altered state and his inability to capture it led to growing dissatisfaction. It was the dissatisfaction that had haunted Cohen throughout his life, the need for negation that he had sought through both *la petit mort* of his sexual encounters and the asceticism of monastery life. In 'The Night Comes On' (*Various Positions*, 1984), he aptly defines the apparent contradiction in his yearning for absence: 'I needed so much to have nothing to touch / I've always been greedy that way.'

While Cohen learnt much from Roshi, it was at the feet of Balsekar that Cohen refined and reframed the lessons instilled in him through years of Buddhist study. He realized that there was no free will, no individual self and no need to worry. The universe had a plan for everyone. Balsekar told him, 'there is no "best spiritual path". There is only a particular spiritual path for you . . . the Source will send this bodymind organism to that Guru who is appropriate for him or her at the time.'[123] There is a resonance with the teachings of Balsekar and the founder of Cohen's school of Buddhism, the ninth-century monk Rinzai Gigen, who warned 'there is no Buddha, no Dharma . . . rather than attaching yourself to my words, better calm down and seek nothing further.'[124]

The rejection of free will and an acceptance of a divine plan finds expression in the sentiments of Cohen's 1984 song 'If It Be Your Will' (*Various Positions*) in which he addresses his Creator, 'if it be your will / that I speak no more / and my voice be still / as it was before / I will speak no more'. The lyrics, however, still

[119] Ratnesh Mathur, 'Bird on a Wire: How Bombay Helped Leonard Cohen Find His Voice Again', Scroll.in (website). https://scroll.in/article/821415/bird-on-a-wire-how-bombay-help-leonard-cohen-find-his-voice-again. Accessed 30 July 2020.
[120] 'A Resonance Between Two Models'.
[121] 'A Resonance Between Two Models'.
[122] 'A Resonance Between Two Models'.
[123] 'A Resonance Between Two Models'.
[124] *The Zen Teaching of Rinzai*, trans. Irmgard Schloegl (Berkeley, 1976), p. 38.

contain an element of choice, the singer choosing to abide by the Lord's wishes for him, rather than understanding that it is not up to him to acquiesce.

Returning to 'civilian' life, Cohen found 'with a sense of relief that I had no gift for the spiritual life . . . I didn't have to seek for anything. And with the search, the anxieties attendant on that search ended.'[125] The dark veil of depression lifted with the end of his constant yearning for a spiritual solution. This did not prevent him from continuing his studies with Roshi and Ramesh, and being devoted to his Jewish faith. For Cohen, his Judaism remained the guiding principle of his life and work, but he no longer grappled with uncertainty or doubt. He was content to allow his faith to guide him, while applying the techniques and lessons learnt from Hinduism and Buddhism to allow him to accept whatever path God chose for him.

'Every breath we drew was hallelujah': The sacred and profane

In 1969, Ira Mothner declared that Leonard Cohen's songs were about 'piety and genital pleasure'.[126] This statement introduces a tension between the spiritual and carnal that is absent from Cohen's own mind. The fusion of sacred and erotic is a defining feature of his lyrics, as he searches for a 'female beloved' who is also 'the object of his spiritual passion'.[127] For Cohen, spirituality was entwined with sensuality and the two could not be separated. He declared, 'if God is left out of sex, it becomes pornographic; if sex is left out of God, it becomes pious and self-righteous'.[128] The language he used to describe his relationship with religion is telling – in a November 1998 interview he called it 'deep and voluptuous' and regarded it as akin only to the pleasure of 'courting'.[129]

The sexual act, for Cohen, was a spiritual one in which the union of two bodies created the ultimate act of self-negation. In popular vernacular the phrase *la petit mort* is used to describe the transcendence of consciousness experienced during orgasm, but it was originally posited by Roland Barthes as the chief objective of great literature. In subsuming ourselves in the literary moment, the reader

[125] Leland, 'The Prince of Prurience and Loss', p. 499.
[126] Ira Mothner, 'Songs Sacred and Profane', *Look* (10 June 1969).
[127] Eliot R. Wolfson, 'New Jerusalem Glowing: Songs and Poems of Leonard Cohen in a Kabbalistic Key', p. 150. https://www.academia.edu/3331347/New_Jerusalem_Glowing_Songs_and_Poems_of _Leonard_Cohen_in_a_Kabbalistic_Key. Pdf. Accessed 31 August 2020.
[128] Brian Cullman, 'Sincerely, L. Cohen', *Details for Men*, January 1993.
[129] Eleana Cornelli, 'The Virtueless Monk', *La Nazione*, 25 November 1998.

experiences a loss of ego and self-awareness as his or her identity is negated by the text. The 'greed' Cohen experienced for this self-negation, both in Roshi's meditation hall and in his pursuit of sexual gratification, is also enshrined in his songwriting. Wolfson attests that 'the inscription of poems and songs has been a spiritual practice, a sacramental ritual'.[130]

The separation of sex and the sacred began with the puritans, but the early Christian and Jewish mystics and saints did not create such strict demarcations. The sexual union between man and woman in early Judeo-Christian writings was seen as a celebration of the divine and a form of communion with the Lord, though this act was, of course, only sanctioned in the marriage bed. The Old Testament book 'Song of Solomon' contains deeply erotic imagery when describing the union of a bride and groom, and its influence can be seen in Cohen's lyrics and poetry. Verses celebrate the delight bride and groom take in one another after their marriage has been blessed by God and focus on the sensuous pleasure they derive from one another. The groom tells his bride, 'your rounded thighs are like jewels' (Song of Solomon, 7.1) and 'your stature is like a palm tree, and your breasts are like its clusters / I say I will climb the palm tree, and lay hold of its fruit.' (Song of Solomon, 7.7-8.) The erotic imagery of Solomon is a feature of Cohen's own work, as he tells his lover in 'Beneath My Hands', 'your small breasts / are the upturned bellies / of breathing falling sparrows' (*The Spice Box of Earth*, 1961), echoing Song of Solomon, 7.3, 'your two breasts are like two fawns, twins of a gazelle'.

For Cohen, God and sex were inextricably entwined and the sexual act was a form of divine communication. There was nothing profane in his conflation of the erotic and the sacred, as he saw the union of man and woman as the highest form of celebration of the Lord. The most profound expression of this idea can be found in the additional lyrics to Cohen's 'Hallelujah' (*Various Positions*) where he declares the sexual act to be the merging of two spirits in a celebration of the divine: 'and remember when I moved in you / The holy dove was moving too / And every breath we drew was Hallelujah'.

The idea that the spiritual and the carnal were inseparable was not shared by many of Cohen's detractors. His first poetry collection, for example, received an unfavourable review in *The Fiddlehead* for its liberal juxtaposition of sacred, sexual and violent imagery.[131] This reproach, as we saw, was often levelled against

[130] Wolfson, 'New Jerusalem Glowing', p. 151.
[131] Allan Donaldson, 'Review of *Let Us Compare Mythologies*', *The Fiddlehead*, 30 November 1956, pp. 30–1.

him by the Jewish community, but defiantly, speaking through the voice of his narrator in *Beautiful Losers* he advises: 'find a little saint and fuck her over and over in some pleasant part of heaven'.[132] In 1966 Cohen told a reporter, 'we HAVE to be divine . . . We're not different from the universe. We are the word made flesh'.[133] The celebration of the flesh was essential to Cohen's spiritual quest. The spirit and body should not be divided, but used in praise of the Lord, and for Cohen the apogee of this was in sexual union.

The relationship between sex and spirituality is less explicit for Dylan. For Dylan, the divide between the sacred and the sensual is firmly demarcated and his views are more in line with the Church's puritanical teachings. Michael Gray has argued that Dylan's spiritual quest 'has always been a struggle within him between the ideas of the flesh and the spirit, between love and a kind of religious asceticism'.[134] Gray argues that we find in Dylan's songs the idea of a woman's love as the path to redemption. In *Nashville Skyline*'s 'I Threw It All Away' he sings 'love is all there is / It makes the world go round', and more explicitly in 'Wedding Song' (*Planet Waves*) in which romantic love is couched in biblical imagery conflating it with spiritual salvation, 'what's lost is lost, we can't regain / what went down in the flood / but happiness to me is you / and I love you more than blood'. The evolution away from Dylan's belief that earthly love 'is all there is' occurs on both *Blood on the Tracks* (1975) and *Desire* (1976). On these albums, Dylan attempts to reconcile romantic love with religious yearning, epitomized in the lyric 'if only I could turn back the clock to when God and her were born' ('Shelter from the Storm'). The song 'Isis' creates a compelling narrative depicting Dylan's struggle between sensuous pleasure and spiritual salvation, personified in the Hebrew goddess Isis. The song's narrator leaves his beloved to search for gold and diamonds and 'the world's biggest necklace', but when his companion dies and his search is fruitless, he says 'a quick prayer and I felt satisfied / Then I rode back to find Isis just to tell her I love her'. Finding 'the casket empty' of jewels, he rejects the material world and finds redemption in the arms of Isis who is both woman and divinity. After his difficult divorce from Sara Lownds, however, Dylan rejected this dichotomy and sought his salvation in Jesus. Dylan's trajectory is metaphorically a 'slow train' from the belief in love as a religion to a spirituality which rejects the flesh and values only the spirit.

---

[132] Cohen, *Beautiful Losers*, p. 12.
[133] Lawson, 'A New Religious Age for Leonard Cohen'.
[134] Michael Gray, *Song and Dance Man III* (London and New York: Cassell, 2000), p. 208.

Dylan, unlike Cohen, has never been a sensual writer. His lyrics express romantic love in terms of spirit and salvation, not pleasure and gratification, but for Cohen these ideas were not contradictory. Dylan has always been more of a moralist than his Canadian contemporary, and these views are reflected in many of his attitudes. In 1984 he told *Rolling Stone* that 'the problem is not abortion . . . Abortion is the end result of going out and screwing somebody. . . Casual sex'.[135] While sex and spirituality were inextricable to Cohen, Dylan believed that 'male and female are not here to have sex . . . that's not the purpose'.[136] In the struggle between flesh and spirit, the spirit was ultimately the higher calling, and romantic love was often a distraction from the true 'purpose'.

'These rabbis really had something going on':[137] The return to Judaism

As we have seen, Dylan and Cohen were both equally fascinated by religion in a variety of its incarnations and extensively explored their respective spiritual paths, but never unequivocally rejected the Judaism of their birth. While Dylan made certain comments that could be interpreted as distancing himself from his Jewishness – telling *Rolling Stone* in 1978 'listen I don't know how Jewish I am, because I've got blue eyes'[138] – neither artist saw a conflict between his faith and the study of other religions and thought systems.

Leonard Cohen remained a devout and observant Jew throughout his life. During his time in Mumbai he visited the Keneseth Eliyahoo Synagogue and he continued to observe the Jewish Sabbath and holy days at Roshi's monastery. In an interview with the *Jewish Book News* in 1994, he affirmed that 'there are Jewish practitioners in the Zen movement . . . there is no conflict because there is no prayerful worship and there is no discussion of a deity'.[139] He went on to express his frustration with an article in the *Hollywood Reporter* in which he was

[135] Loder, 'Bob Dylan: Recovering Christian'.
[136] Interview with Robert Shelton, from *No Direction Home*, (March 1966) reprinted in *Dylan on Dylan* ed. Cott (London: Hodder & Stoughton, 2007), p. 87.
[137] Interview with Jonathan Cott, *Rolling Stone* (26 January 1978) in *Bob Dylan: The Essential Interviews*, ed. Johnathan Cott (London: Simon & Schuster, 2017), p. 202.
[138] Jonathan Cott, 'Bob Dylan: The Rolling Stone Interview, Part Two', *Rolling Stone* (26 November 1978). https://www.rollingstone.com/music/music-news/bob-dylan-the-rolling-stone-interview-part-2-173545/. Accessed 8 August 2020.
[139] Interview with Arthur Kurzweil. https://www.leonardcohenfiles.com/arthurkurzweil.pdf.

described as a Buddhist. He told his interviewer that he had written a letter to the magazine to correct the mistake, declaring 'I am a Jew'.[140]

Cohen's *Book of Mercy* is a positive affirmation of his Judaism in its fifty psalm-poems. The front cover features the emblem for Cohen's 'Order of the Unified Heart' – a hexagram and Star of David, united by two interlocked hearts. He described the symbol as 'a version of the yin and yang' which tried to 'reconcile the differences'.[141] This encapsulates the book's intentions as he sought to reconcile his Jewish faith with Eastern philosophy. The collection is dedicated to his teacher, Roshi, and conflates his studies with the Zen master and his continued exploration of Judaism. The project came about after Cohen 'wrecked his knees'[142] and was unable to practice the seated meditation that was a feature of monastic life. Unable to partake in the *zazen* sessions, he decided to 'do what I had never done before which was to observe the [Jewish] calendar in a very diligent way, to lay *tefillin* every day and to study the Talmud'.[143] The psalms in *Book of Mercy* offer a beautiful meditation on the nature of faith, religion and the human condition and led Rabbi Mordecai Finley – the former provost and president of the Academy for Jewish Religion – to declare him 'the greatest liturgist alive'.[144] In 2006 Finley met Cohen along with then partner Anjani Thomas when he officiated a mutual friends' wedding. After engaging the rabbi in deep theological discussion, Cohen and Thomas became regular attendees at his Ohr HaTorah Synagogue and active participants in the Monday night 'Jewish spiritual psychology dharma talks' led by Finley.[145] The two men cultivated a deep friendship built on mutual respect. 'He was a devoted Jew', Finley attests. 'He had candles lit every Shabbat. I received photos of candles lit on the tours'.[146]

Despite Cohen's continued assertion that he had never strayed from Judaism, many struggled to reconcile the two facets of his Jewish faith and Buddhist philosophy. Finley recalls an anecdote told to him by Cohen. Several men from the Chabad-Lubavitch Hasidic sect – the same group that Dylan studied with in Brooklyn – trekked up Mount Baldy during Chanukah with the intention

---

[140] Interview with Kurzweil.

[141] Simmons, *I'm Your Man*, p. 314.

[142] Simmons, *I'm Your Man*, p. 315.

[143] Interview with Bruce Headlam, *Saturday Night* (December 1997). A Tefillin is one of two small animal hide cases which house small scrolls inscribed with particular scriptural passages. One fastened to the forehead and the other to the arm to observe weekday morning prayer.

[144] Simmons, *I'm Your Man*, p. 315.

[145] Rabbi Mordecai Finley, 'Being Leonard Cohen's Rabbi', *Jewish Journal* (16 November 2016). https://jewishjournal.com/judaism/212745. Accessed 31 July 2020.

[146] Finley, 'Being Leonard Cohen's Rabbi'.

of returning the wayward monk to the fold. When they arrived, they found the singer in his black robes lighting his Chanukah candles. He invited the men into his little cabin and spent the night drinking whisky, dancing, debating and singing with them.[147] They left convinced that he was no prodigal son, but a true 'Kohen'.

Leonard Cohen's final studio album, *You Want It Darker*, released nineteen days before his death in 2016, contains the definitive declaration of his Jewish faith. The album's title track sees Cohen intone 'Hineni, I'm ready my Lord' which means 'here I am' in Hebrew and is the response Abraham gave to God when asked to sacrifice his son Isaac. The song's refrain alludes to the Kaddish, the Jewish mourning prayer. Cohen sings 'magnified, sanctified, be thy Holy name', recalling the prayer he would have heard at his own father's funeral, perhaps anticipating his own. The song is a fitting epitaph for a man who was defined by his deep and unabating faith.

Much like Cohen, Bob Dylan remained in touch with his Jewish roots, despite exploring other spiritual systems. Both men believed faith was not a matter of religious dogma, strict adherence to creeds or denominations, but about a personal connection with an almighty creator. After the overt religiosity of his Gospel years, Dylan continued to tread his own spiritual path, declaring in 1993 that 'a person without faith is like a walking corpse'.[148] In the years following his 'born-again' albums, his involvement with the Chabad organization and trips to Israel sparked rumours that he had renewed his Jewish affiliations. When he attended a Yom Kippur service at the Temple Beth El Synagogue, Florida, in 1995, the *Jewish Journal* declared, 'say what you want about . . . Dylan's late 1970s experience as a born-again Christian . . . [his] real roots are showing'.[149] Three days later Dylan performed 'In the Garden' – a song about Christ's capture by the Roman guards taken from the *Slow Train* album – onstage in Jacksonville, prompting Christian groups to counterclaim him as one of their own. He would also perform this song at the 1997 World Eucharistic Congress for an audience of the pope and his delegates.

His continued observance of Jewish holidays, even during his Gospel era, confounded religious organizations who scrutinized his actions for signs that

---

[147] Finley, 'Being Leonard Cohen's Rabbi'.

[148] Interview with Gary Hill, Reuters News Service (October 1993). Quoted in Ford and Marshall, *Restless Pilgrim*, p. 117.

[149] Scott Benarde, 'Rock for the Ages: Pop Stars Sing Out About Their Judaism', *Jewish Journal*, 27 August 1999. Quoted in Ford and Marshall, *Restless Pilgrim*, p. 122.

he was 'on their side'. His 2009 *Christmas In the Heart* album further defied his audience's expectations, as did the pro-Israeli anthem 'Neighbourhood Bully'. Paul Edmond, a pastor at the Vineyard Fellowship, explains these contradictions by stating that Dylan never 'left his Jewish roots' but 'realized Judaism and Christianity can work very well together because Christ is just Yeshua ha' Meshiah'.[150] Dylan himself has never felt the need to make a public statement about his religious affiliation. Interviewers on the subject have found him intractable and evasive, unwilling to explain himself or reveal how he reconciles the apparent contradictions. Examination of his lyrics reveals the work of a deeply religious mind, well-versed not only in the sacred texts of the Judeo-Christian tradition but also ancient mythologies and Eastern mysticism. *Rough and Rowdy Ways* (2020) is exemplary in this respect. It indicates that his spiritual quest, like his Never Ending Tour, is perpetual. He reveals, for example, he has 'played Gumbo Limbo Spirituals' and knows 'all of the Hindu rituals' ('Key West'). That he studies 'Sanskrit and Arabic to improve' his mind ('My Own Version of You'), feels 'the holy spirit inside' ('Crossing the Rubicon'), and suggests 'all your earthly thoughts be a prayer' ('Black Rider').

Like Cohen, his faith is not limited by adherence to the decrees of an earthly institution but stems from a deep-rooted faith in a divine being. While Dylan may no longer appear onstage as an evangelical preacher, his religious beliefs are still evident in his music. Ever the trickster, he reminds us with the social media hashtag for his whisky brand Heaven's Door that you gotta #servesomebody.

The never-ending quest: Conclusion

It is impossible to appreciate the work of Dylan and Cohen without admitting the debt that both men owe to their religious and spiritual beliefs. The Jewish faith that they were born into provides the framework for both their lyrical and spiritual explorations. Eliot R. Wolfson believes that the influence of Cohen's Jewish esotericism can only be appreciated in the context of his interest in Christianity and Buddhism. He argues that Cohen's Judaism is affirmed against these other traditions. His study of other spiritual systems 'expands and constricts the boundaries of his Judaism' and establishes 'the distinctiveness of his own

---

[150] Paul Edmond quoted in Marshall, *The Spiritual Life*, p. 90.

cultural formation'.[151] This same analysis is equally apt for Dylan. The foundations of their Jewish faith underpinned their continual theological investigations and provided a spiritual home to which each man may return. Faith and religion defined not just their lives, but their writing, and the evolution of their music follows their various spiritual investigations. The quest for spiritual fulfilment was, like Dylan's touring schedule, never-ending, and as each man travelled his own path they both learnt that it was about the journey, not the destination, and that they would always be drawn back home to the religion of their birth.

[151] Wolfson, 'New Jerusalem Glowing', p. 105.

4

Starting out

Bob Dylan, Leonard Cohen, the Beat Generation and Dylan Thomas

Drowned down in New York's White Horse Tavern /
he went not gentle into his good night.

Ferlinghetti[1]

Whereas Mr Dylan is alienated from society and
mad about it, Mr Cohen is alienated and merely sad about it.

Henahan[2]

Dylan blew everybody's mind, except Leonard's.

Ginsberg[3]

Introduction

In the previous chapter we discussed the spiritual journeys that Dylan and Cohen took in their search for meaning in their lived experience and to impose upon the world an order that appeared to each to be absent from their personal lives. In this chapter we will explore their quest for fame that often proved to be the source of their inner turmoil. This requires examining the connections between Bob Dylan, Leonard Cohen, Dylan Thomas and the Beat poets, in order to suggest that what drew them all together was the desperate desire for fame, but which came at a price which they all paid, even with their lives, in the case Dylan Thomas and Jack Kerouac.

[1] Lawrence Ferlinghetti, 'Belated Palinode for Dylan Thomas', in *These Are My Rivers: New and Selected Poems 1955-1993* (New York: James Laughlin, 1993), p. 43.
[2] Donald Henahan cited in Harold Rasky, *The Song of Leonard Cohen* (Niagara Falls: Mosaic Press, 2001), p. 19.
[3] Cited in Paul Zollo interview with Leonard Cohen, 'Leonard Cohen: Inside the Tower of Song', *Song Talk*, April, 1993. Reprinted in *Leonard Cohen on Leonard Cohen*, ed. Jeff Burger (Chicago: Chicago Review Press, 2014), p. 263.

Dylan Thomas achieved within his lifetime unprecedented fame as a poet in America, and his example was something the Beats were hell bent on emulating. Robert Zimmerman's attraction to the Beats coincided with his rejection of his past identity and the assumption of the persona of Bob Dylan. Leonard Cohen was on the periphery of the Beat scene in the mid-1950s, although he came to know many of them personally afterwards, and for him, as for them, the allure of Dylan Thomas's infamous bohemian irresponsibility was dangerously irresistible. Fame proved to be a powerfully destructive force for them all.

The music critic of *The New York Times*, Robert Shelton, whose early article on 29 September 1961 launched Bob Dylan's career, and which is reprinted on the sleeve of his debut album (*Bob Dylan*), had privileged access to research a biography on the by-then world famous troubadour.[4] On a plane from Lincoln, Nebraska, to Denver, Colorado, in early 1966, Bob Dylan talked to Shelton about Michael McClure saying, 'He's good, man, he's good'. He described Allen Ginsberg as the best of the poets, one of the two saintly people he knew. Ginsberg's 'Kaddish' he claimed was better than 'Howl'. It is a masterpiece. McClure and Ginsberg were the leading poets in the 1960s Beat counterculture. During the latter part of 1965, Bob Dylan increasingly gravitated towards them, and they to him, particularly Ginsberg who idolized Dylan. By this time Ginsberg had become friendly with Leonard Cohen. Cohen met Ginsberg by chance in a café in Athens and asked him if he really was Allen Ginsberg. Ginsberg went over to talk to him,[5] and Cohen invited him to stay with him on Hydra, where they became friends. Ginsberg introduced Cohen to Corso and his association with the Beats became much more intimate than it had been when he lived in New York in 1956.

Ginsberg was already famous, and Cohen was a relatively unknown Canadian poet. In a letter to his sister Esther, Cohen describes Ginsberg as a nice, clean-shaven Jewish boy who had fallen under the influence of a bad crowd of beatniks. It was a phase, he believed, out of which Ginsberg would grow, after all: 'How long can you take money, fame and the rest. After a while you want a decent job.'[6] By the time Bob Dylan emerged into the full spotlight of his fame, Cohen had become an accomplished poet and novelist, leading Ginsberg to comment that while everyone was impressed by Dylan, Cohen appeared unimpressed. Cohen,

---

[4] He took many years to complete it and became something of a burden to him. Robert Shelton, *No Direction Home: The Life and Music of Bob Dylan* (New York: Willian Morrow, 1986). A revised and updated version appeared in 2011 edited by Elizabeth Thomson and Patrick Humphries, published by Omnibus Press.

[5] Sylvie Simmons, 'Travelling Light', *Mojo*, December, 2008, p. 91.

[6] Leonard Cohen, Letter to Esther dated, 18 September 1961. Box 11.5, Leonard Cohen Papers, Fisher Library Toronto.

however, confessed that he and Dylan had a mutual interest in each others' songs: 'Everybody's interested in Dylan but it's pleasant to have Dylan interested in me.'[7]

Bob Dylan became so enthralled by the Beat poets that McClure and Ginsberg were at the famous San Francisco Bob Dylan interview of 3 December 1965, and he intended that the three of them would be on the cover of *Blonde on Blonde*, photographed by Larry Keenan, the Beat photographer. Bob Dylan was in the San Francisco area for a series of five concerts and visited the City Lights bookstore on the day that Keenan took the photographs of the 'Last Gathering of the Beats'. Dylan was in the basement while the Beats assembled above him on the steps outside.[8] Lawrence Ferlinghetti was at the first Berkeley concert with Ginsberg on 3 December. Although he later came to express admiration for Bob Dylan, that weekend Ferlinghetti was extremely resentful of the fame Dylan had achieved. Dylan even described himself as 'really, really famous' at this time.[9] The owner of City Lights just couldn't understand it: 'What is that stringy kid doing up there with his electric guitar? I'm a major poet and this kid has thirty-five hundred kids in this hall.'[10]

While talking about Richard Fariña, Mimi Baez's husband, who wrote the novel *Been Down So Long It Seems Like Up to Me*,[11] Bob Dylan described him as the king of the bullshitters, with nothing to say:

> I don't have any respect for his writing. I remember him in the White Horse with his hat and his moustache . . . I used to dig him a lot more when he wasn't so really uptight . . . I was beneath the bleachers, at Newport, when he played in the rain, and I heard . . . him totally go insane.

Then on one of the rare occasions when Bob Dylan spoke of Dylan Thomas he compared him with Fariña. He knew Fariña well because he had been married to Carolyn Hester, before marrying Mimi. Bob Dylan spent a lot of time with the couple in Carmel, California.

In 1957 Fariña was at Cornell University and was steeped in the bohemian quarter known as College Town. His conversation was splattered with

[7] Zollo, 'Leonard Cohen: Inside the Tower of Song', in *Leonard Cohen on Leonard Cohen*, ed. Burger, pp. 263 and 284.

[8] Larry Keenan, *Beat Scene*, No. 27 (no date).

[9] Robert Shelton, *No Direction Home*, revised and updated edition edited by Elizabeth Thomson and Patrick Humphries (London: Omnibus Press, 2011), p. 233.

[10] Shelton, *No Direction Home*, p. 232.

[11] Richard Fariña, *Been Down so Long It Seems Like Up to Me* (Harmondsworth: Penguin Classics, 1996). First published 1966.

quotations from Dylan Thomas, a favourite poet of his. He even wrote a semi-autobiographical essay indebted to the Welshman entitled 'With a Copy of Dylan Under His Arm'. He also appeared in a student production of *Under Milk Wood* in 1959, some six years after Thomas narrated the play himself at the premiere in New York.[12]

It was not fortuitous, then, that Bob Dylan compared his namesake with Fariña: 'He's a kind of writer like Dylan Thomas.' He then, for the first time, since becoming famous was drawn to make a judgement about Dylan Thomas's poetry:

> Dylan Thomas's poetry is for people that aren't really satisfied in their bed, and who dig a masculine romance. Dylan Thomas's poetry is . . . very . . . what can I say? . . . a butterfly . . . no, ah . . . It reminds me of streets, concrete streets with textures of the butterfly. Or else, just plain suicidal romance, and decaying romance . . Somebody who wrote of the decay of his romance . . . Who needs it. He wrote good words . . . They were good words, but they were flowery.[13]

This was also Ginsberg's view of Thomas's poetry around this time: 'on the whole I don't really dig Thomas. He's too romantic'.[14] He did, nevertheless, pay homage to Thomas by visiting his grave, marked by a humble white cross, in Laugharne, Wales, in 1995.

In January 1964 a play called *Dylan*, written by Sidney Michaels, opened on Broadway. Alec Guinness, who won a Tony award for his portrayal of Thomas, and who had seen him at poetry readings dominated by Edith Sitwell, was 'not overwhelmed by his poetry'. He much preferred the Welshman's short stories.[15]

What was it, if it was not merely his poetry, that so magnetically drew North American audiences to Dylan Thomas and, long after his death, to buy recordings of him reading short stories and poems, and to visit the theatre to see a play about the tragic last two years of his life, and what drew the Beats, Leonard Cohen and later Robert Zimmerman to him? Gregory Corso suggests that poems are nothing without the poet. 'Why', he contends, 'are Shelley, Chatterton, Byron, Rimbaud, to name but a few, so beautiful? I'll tell you why, they and their works

[12] David Hajdu, *Positively 4th Street: The Lives and Times of Joan Baez, Bob Dylan, Mimi Baez and Richard Fariña* (London: Bloomsbury, 2001), pp. 42–3.
[13] Robert Shelton Archive, Music Experience Project, Seattle, Tape IX transcript, p. 28.
[14] Ginsberg cited in Louis Simpson, *Studies of Dylan Thomas, Allen Ginsberg, Sylvia Plath and Robert Lowell* (London: Palgrave Macmillan, 1979), p. 37.
[15] John McCarten, 'Strolling Player', *The New Yorker*, 8 February 1964.

are one and the same, the poet and his poems are a whole.'[16] The Beats wrote a great deal of their poetry with the human voice in mind, using the same bardic devices that Dylan Thomas employed. Bruce Cook suggests that these devices included simple rhythmic chant repetitions to rouse their audiences.[17]

When Corso came out of prison in 1951, Dylan Thomas had already completed his first American tour from February to June 1950. Despite the repressive political culture epitomized by Senator Joseph McCarthy, there were nascent stirrings of discontent among a growing number of rebellious young people in the metropolitan areas. It was after Dylan Thomas's second tour from January to May 1952 that John Clellon Holmes wrote for the *New York Times Magazine*, 'This is the Beat Generation' on 16 November 1952, long before any of those who are now emblematic of it became famous. Coinciding with his third tour in April–June 1953, and the American publication of his *Collected Poems*, *Time* magazine was describing Dylan Thomas as 'a chubby, bulb-nosed little Welshman with green eyes, a generally untidy air, and the finest lyrical talent of any poet under 40'.[18]

The Beat generation found it impossible, as generations after them, to separate Dylan Thomas from his writings. Leonard Cohen, whom Peggy Curran described as the 'beat poet of Belmont Avenue' and who Deborah Sprague described as a 'Montreal Beat poet ... with a country music fetish',[19] exemplified the attitude of the young poets of the day. Cohen confessed, 'Dylan Thomas was the great voice of poetry when I was at college. We (all the young poets) were all intrigued with his fame, his genius, his drinking, his unconditional sense of social irresponsibility.'[20]

Dylan Thomas had gained for himself a certain notoriety in North America, and he was tolerated as a loveable Celtic rogue. His relationship with his wife Caitlin was as legendary as the relationship between his fellow Welshman Richard Burton and Elizabeth Taylor was to become. The New York *literati* loved exaggerated Celtic tales, generously mixed with fiction. Dylan Thomas played the part perfectly. Dylan Thomas was adored by Americans for his outrageousness. He could even get away with mercilessly mocking his audience. They were too

---

[16] Gregory Corso, letter to Hans circa May–June 1956, *An Accidental Autobiography: The Selected Letters of Gregory Corso*, ed. Bill Morgan (New York: New Directions Publishing, 2003), p. 3.

[17] Bruce Cook, *The Beat Generation* (New York: Charles Scribner's Sons, 1971), p. 223.

[18] *Time*, Monday, 6 April 1953: Books: Welsh Rare One.

[19] Deborah Sprague, 'Leonard Cohen and the Death of Cool', *Your Flesh,* Spring 1992. Reprinted in *Leonard Cohen on Leonard Cohen,* ed. Burger, p. 250.

[20] Email to the author, Monday 20 September 2004.

easily and undiscriminatingly seduced by fame. He told them that he counted himself among the 'fat poets with slim volumes', the 'lyrical one-night standers' who travelled the length and breadth of the country talking to women's societies, which were equally as enthusiastic about a lecture on ceramics as the 'modern Turkish novel'.[21] A 1953 review of Thomas's *Collected Poems* commented that 'his incredible yarns tumble over each other in a wild Welsh dithyramb in which truth and fact become hopelessly smothered in boozy invention'.[22]

On his fateful fourth trip to the States in 1953 he stayed, as usual, at the Chelsea Hotel. The Chelsea Hotel, on 23rd Street in New York, is synonymous with Dylan Thomas, the Beats, Bob Dylan and Leonard Cohen. Sherill Tippins, a historian of the Chelsea Hotel, which in Dylan Thomas's day was almost a slum, attributes the hotel's enduring bohemian reputation to Dylan Thomas.[23] The Chelsea Hotel, on West 23rd Street in New York, was where the depressed, outrageous and notorious went to live and die. It is where Dylan Thomas returned to fall dying in the arms of his lover, having had his last few drinks at the White Horse around the corner on Hudson Street, before being taken to St. Vincent's Hospital where he died on 9 November.

Time magazine went as far as to describe Thomas as a 'super bohemian'.[24] LeRoi Jones (Amiri Baraka), in defending the bohemianism of the Beats, remarked that there was no bohemianism or intellectual rebellion in the 1940s: 'Poor Dylan Thomas carried the ball all by himself in England, and we all know what happened when eventually he did get to America.'[25] It was the bohemian irresponsibility of the likes of Dylan Thomas that the younger generation of poets and writers found attractive, many of whom, at one time or another were themselves, or were to become, residents at the Chelsea. The legendary tales of drunken revelry in the White Horse Tavern, and the squalor of the Chelsea Hotel, shrouded Thomas with an air of romantic mystery. It was Dylan Thomas's ability to connect with the ordinary and seduce the listener with his melodious voice and fiery imagination that attracted people to him as a personality. Dylan

[21] Dylan Thomas, 'Visit to America' on *Dylan Thomas Reads His Own Poetry*, Alto Take: 2, ALN 1912. Audio cd.
[22] *Time*, Monday, 6 April 1953.
[23] Tom Leonard, 'The World's Most Decadent Hotel, Where Dylan Thomas Drank Himself to Death and Rock Stars Bedded (and Murdered) Their Lovers, Closes after a Century': http://www.dailymail.co.uk/news/article-2028125/Hotel-Chelsea-New-York-closes-Where-Dylan-Thomas-drank-death.html#ixzz1lJun8FcY
[24] *Time*, 2 December 1957, p. 71.
[25] LeRoi Jones, letter to the editor of *Partisan Review*, summer 1958 reprinted in Matt Theado, ed. *The Beats: A Literary Reference* (New York: Carrol and Graf, 2003), p. 82.

Thomas was famous in America, having toured there in 1950, 1952 and twice in 1953. He was one of the first poets to do extensive tours of America and sign recordings of his readings.[26]

Thomas first signed for Caedmon Records in 1952. He pioneered the spoken word recording, which has burgeoned into a $2 billion dollar audio book industry, with his short story 'A Child's Christmas in Wales' and five poems, including 'Do Not Go Gentle into That Good Night' and 'Fern Hill'. After the first decade of its release, the record had sold over half a million copies. His wife Caitlin feared he was prostituting himself for the love of performing and adulation.[27]

His tours were extensive, exhaustive and exhausting, covering vast geographical expanses, climatic variations and gruelling journeys. The first tour, for example, was from February to June 1950 and scheduled thirty-five performances in ninety-seven days, and his second tour scheduled forty-three readings in 116 days. These do not include his propensity to agree to impromptu readings for small groups and the endless round of receptions and meetings with staff and students at the various universities he visited. He travelled 12,000 miles within the United States on the first tour using cars, trains and aeroplanes, all of which made for excessively arduous journeys, especially for an unfit, overweight, excessive drinker. He travelled by train, not the most comfortable mode of transport in the United States, from New York to Chicago, on to South Bend, Indiana, Urbana, Illinois and Iowa City. From there he flew to San Francisco, then by train to Vancouver, back to the United States, taking in Seattle and Washington, before going back to the Los Angeles area for eight days, then back to New York again.[28]

On his third visit, the first of 1953, Thomas wrote from the Hotel Chelsea: 'Two weeks here in this hot hell . . . I've travelled all over this stinking place, even into the Deep South: in 14 days I've given 14 readings.'[29] To accompany them all was the associated endless unrelenting socializing.[30] He could get away with saying and doing almost anything because of his outlandish cavalier rhetoric and bohemian manner. 'Thomas was a literary rebel, a pre-rock rock star with adoring fans. At one university reading, when asked to explain the

---

[26] He was, of course, much more than a poet.

[27] Andrew Lycett, *Dylan Thomas: A New Life* (London: Phoenix, 2003), p. 391.

[28] Martin E. Gingerich, 'Dylan Thomas and America', *Dylan Thomas Remembered* (Swansea: The Dylan Thomas Society Wales Branch, 1978), pp. 26–34.

[29] Dylan Thomas to Caitlin Thomas, 7 May 1953, *Dylan Thomas: The Collected Letters*, New Edition, ed. Paul Ferris (London: J. M. Dent, 2000), p. 989.

[30] Gingerich, 'Dylan Thomas and America', pp. 26–34.

meaning of "The Ballad of the Long-legged Bait", Thomas replied, "It's about a giant fuck."[31] James Parker has written of him: 'He was the last of the rock-star poets, because the minute the *real* rock stars showed up – amps buzzing, drugs twanging – the poets would be shuffled off into inconsequence.'[32] This overlooks the fact, of course, that the two principal characters of this book, Bob Dylan and Leonard Cohen, were both rock stars and poets, inspired first and foremost by Thomas's fame.

Just as Dylan Thomas represented an anarchic bohemianism, threatening yet exciting, the readings of the Beat poets in the coffee houses around Greenwich Village and their chaotic lifestyles and irreverent commentaries on the dominant culture made them attractive to those young people who were experiencing what the anthropologist Margaret Mead called the 'generation gap'.[33] Dylan Thomas's renowned irreverence was something they wished to emulate, and even surpass, but most of all, like him, they wanted to be famous.

Dylan Thomas's poetry, prose and plays, to the Beat generation, demonstrated that the poet could exist outside the classroom and connect with the people. He was someone they all wanted to meet and be like. They went out of their way to track him down and adopt the anarchic lifestyle he exemplified.

In Montreal, Leonard Cohen, the seventeen-year-old student at McGill University, looked on with envy. Cohen, himself during the 1960s, 1970s and 1980s would go on to emulate the Welshman's behaviour. In his first novel, *The Favourite Game*, Cohen says of his alter ego Lawrence Breavman that he could place his hand on a low cut dress without any complaints: 'He was a kind of mild Dylan Thomas, talent and behaviour modified for Canadian tastes.'[34]

In 1952 Dylan Thomas included McGill University in his North American Lecture tour. He wasn't particularly enthusiastic about it. He wrote to John Malcolm Brinnin, who acted as his agent: 'as I don't particularly want to go to Montreal, soak McGill for twice (at least) as much as I get in the States – plus, of course, full expenses *by air*'.[35] Louis Dudek, a prominent Canadian

[31] 'Dylan Thomas's Night in Montreal', *Cosmopolis*, 31 March 2013. https://coolopolis.blogspot.com /2013/03/dylan-thomass-night-in-montreal.html. Accessed 14 May, 2014.

[32] James Parker, 'The Last Rock-Star Poet', *The Atlantic*, December 2014. https://www.theatlantic.com/ magazine/archive/2014/12/the-last-rock-star-poet/382239/. Accessed 14 May 2020.

[33] Margaret Mead, *Culture and Commitment: A Study of the Generation Gap* (London: Bodley Head, 1970).

[34] Leonard Cohen, *The Favourite Game* (Toronto: McClelland and Stewart, 1994), p. 108. It was first published in 1963.

[35] Letter dated 6 January 1952, *Dylan Thomas, The Collected Letters*, new edition, ed., Paul Ferris (London: Dent, 2000), p. 918. John Malcolm Brinnin, *Dylan Thomas in America* (London: Arlington Books, 1988), p. 135.

poet lecturing at McGill, hosted Thomas. Margaret (Molly) Millar, the popular Canadian crime novelist, was eighteen at the time, and along with Cohen was one of Dudek's protégés. Millar says Cohen started out as a poet 'and didn't he know it'.[36]

Thomas spoke to a large audience in Moyse Hall on 28 February 1952,[37] and Millar remembers sitting in the front of the balcony and being spellbound by Thomas's reading, as were other aspiring poets such as Bill Hartley and Malcolm Miller. Miller was one of Cohen's friends at McGill, who went on to live in total obscurity, in spite of his considerable talent. Miller wrote a poem at the time about Dylan Thomas' visit, entitled 'Dylan Thomas in Canada 1952'.[38]

> In the huge silence of Canada his deep
> Bass voice reading poems was much
> Like roaring bonfire on the tundra
> Row after row of winter
> White face gathered around him
> Far from Wales he was making some money.[39]

After his reading at McGill, Thomas was taken for a drink to the Cafe Andre, known as The Shrine, in downtown Victoria St. Thomas, to the surprise of no one, he drank to excess.[40] Dudek took Molly Millar and some other students, including Leonard Cohen, back to his house with Thomas in a taxi, where they 'lounged' and talked poetry. By then Thomas was tired and drunk and mainly talking to Dudek. What Millar remembers most vividly about the evening was 'Cohen lying on his back on the carpet and suddenly saying, very loudly, 'I shall never forget the first woman who raped me.'[41] Such remarks would not have been out of character for the precocious Cohen who deliberately set out to shock. He claims, however, that he didn't attend the Dylan Thomas event:

---

[36] Email to Jeff Towns, the Dylan Thomas scholar and author, 6 June 2011. We are grateful to Jeff for sharing this with us.
[37] *McGill News*, Alumni Quarterly, Winter, 2008, p. 1. https://mcgillnews-archives.mcgill.ca/news-ar chives/2004/spring/epilogue/. Accessed 14 May 2020.
[38] https://coolopolis.blogspot.com/2016/03/celebrated-after-death-poet-malcolm.html. Accessed 14 May 2020.
[39] Malcolm Miller (1930-2014), *Branches That Have Travelled Far from the Trunk*, 1998, self-published.
[40] 'Dylan Thomas's Night in Montreal', *Cosmopolis*, 31 March 2013.
[41] Email to Jeff Towns, the Dylan Thomas scholar and author, 6 June 2011. We are grateful to Jeff for sharing this with us.

'I didn't go to that reading. It was at McGill, I believe. I don't remember why I didn't go.'[42]

The Beat generation was emerging at the time of Dylan Thomas's death. All aspired to, but none had attained the fame of the Welshman. The *raison d'être* of the Beat poets was to be famous and successful. Beat writers such as Jack Kerouac, Allen Ginsberg, Gary Snyder, Michael McClure and Charles Bukowski did, of course, experience the fame they coveted. Ginsberg himself was star-struck. He romanticized about knowing famous writers. His motivation for going to San Francisco was because Patchen and Rexroth were there, and he systematically promoted the work of those he gathered around him, creating the stars in his firmament.[43] When Kerouac despaired of ever becoming famous, Ginsberg, 'knowing his hunger for fame', gave him the resolve to carry on by reminding him that they *were* on the verge of becoming famous, 'maybe even internationally'.[44] Bukowski wrote in one of his early poems: 'If it doesn't come, coax it out with a laxative. get your name in LIGHTS'.[45.]

Leonard Cohen published his first book of poetry in May 1956, *Let Us Compare Mythologies,* and it was the first in a series edited by his teacher and mentor Louis Dudek and funded by McGill University for the purpose of raising the profile of young Canadian poets. It sold 400 copies and was considered a great success. It comprised forty-four poems revolving around the themes of love, loss, mythology, history and sex. Cohen won the McGill Literary Award for the book and attracted the attention of the Canadian Broadcasting Company which invited him to participate in a venture entitled *Six Montreal Poets*, a spoken-word long-playing record, pioneered by Dylan Thomas in 1953. As Bob Dylan, the Beats and Leonard Cohen periodically entered the Chelsea Hotel from 27 October 1964, they were confronted by a plaque dedicated by Thomas's record label, Caedmon Audio, to the poet on what would have been his fiftieth birthday. It read: 'DEDICATED TO THE MEMORY OF DYLAN THOMAS WHO LIVED AND LABORED LAST HERE AT THE CHELSEA HOTEL AND FROM HERE SAILED OUT TO DIE.'

On the Canadian audio, Cohen read eight poems from his 1956 *Let Us Compare Mythologies,* and the poets publicized it in a series of public performances.

---

[42] Email from Leonard Cohen to David Boucher, dated 6 June 2011.
[43] Barry Miles, *Allen Ginsberg Beat Poet* (London: Virgin Books, 2010), p. 208.
[44] See, Joyce Johnson, *Minor Characters: A Beat Memoir* (London: Methuen, 2006), pp. 120–1.
[45] Charles Bukowski, 'O. We Are the Outcasts', in *Rooming House Madrigals: Selected Poems 1946–66* (New York: Harper Collins, Kindle edition, 2009) Loc. 466. In 'Farewell Foolish Objects' Bukowski wrote: 'I will *read* Dylan and D.H. until my eyes fall out of my head. . .' Loc. 1698.

He appeared in distinguished company. The album was studio recorded with Cohen, Irving Layton, Louis Dudek, A. M. Klein, A. J. M. Smith and F. R. Scott. This album was released on the Folkways label in the United States in 1957. Cohen very quickly became the 'golden boy' of Canadian poetry, which he was consciously to disavow with the publication of his third volume of poetry in 1964, *Flowers for Hitler*.

The title itself announced a new politicization and defiance, and renunciation of usual self-effacement. He referred to the process as 'an old snakeskin slipping away', or the shedding 'of a snakeskin that has already served its purpose'.[46] This was Cohen's deliberate attempt to catapult himself from the limited, and financially un-remunerating, fame of a minor Canadian celebrity and associate himself with the wider counterculture of the Beat generation, about which he had been initially ambivalent. When asked if he would rather be known as a good poet, or a good Canadian poet, Cohen answered, 'A cosmic poet'.[47]

Luis Dudek, formerly a great supporter of Cohen, wrote an unkind review in the Entertainment section of the *Montreal Star* on 31 October 1964, in which he remarked that Cohen the poet needed to cure himself before he could cure his poetry. Cohen's response was graciously passive-aggressive in that he considered that his work would never be viewed objectively in Montreal, complaining that he had yet to receive a serious review there. He went on to say, 'after all, such serious poets as Rimbaud and Baudelaire were considered "sick" yet look at how lasting and valuable their work has been'.[48]

In 1963, in a letter addressed to 'Dear People', written in Montreal, Cohen wrote:

> God I've become public. I can't stand the sound of my own voice. I am the voice of my Generation in Canada, and TV stations pay 100 dollars a half hour for any blasphemous nonsense I can dream up. This Sunday I address the Jewish Public Library and I shall become a Rabbi at last. But I love this limited fame in my own city. I was mailing a letter yesterday and a man came up to me and said, 'I bet there's not a decent poem in that envelope'.[49]

---

[46] Letter from Leonard Cohen to Mme Marian McNamara, 29 March 1964. Fisher Library, Cohen papers, 11:15; and, Erica Pomerance, 'A Profile On: Leonard Cohen', *McGill Daily Panorama*, Friday, 6 November 1964.
[47] Pomerance, 'A Profile On: Leonard Cohen'.
[48] Pomerance, 'A Profile On: Leonard Cohen'.
[49] Leonard Cohen, 11 December 1963. Leonard Cohen Papers, Fisher Library, Toronto. Correspondence, Box 11:14.

By 1964 he was tired once again of Canada, and Montreal in particular, although he was compelled to return from his home on the Greek island of Hydra in order to make money by promoting his *Flowers for Hitler* and renew his 'neurotic affiliations'.[50] This was accomplished by undertaking a reading tour of seven universities with Irving Layton, Phyllis Gotlieb and Earle Birney. They all had new books published by McClelland and Stewart on 24 October 1964. Cohen was welcomed back to Canada as a celebrity, and he described the tour as 'fairly triumphant', quoting the *Montreal Star*. He said he was 'given the kind of attention usually accorded visiting politicians'.[51] In the publicity for the tour, Cohen's *Flowers for Hitler* was described as an 'arresting and disturbing collection intended as a study of the totalitarian spirit'.[52] The dedication page has a quotation from Primo Levi: 'If from the inside of the Lager, a message could have seeped out to free men, it would have been this: Take care not to suffer in your own homes what is inflicted on us here'. In Cohen's unpublished papers, an earlier draft of the book called *Opium and Hitler* includes the inscription: 'Take care this does not happen in your homes – A Camp Survivor'. The back cover of *Flowers for Hitler* stated his intention in a boldness characteristic of the Beat generation in the United States: 'This book moves me from the world of the golden boy poet into the dung pile of the front-line writer'.[53]

He nevertheless found intellectual life in Canada, and in Montreal in particular, oppressive, with its policing having fallen into the hands of a Gestapo that made the rules to ensure that when people moved around they said nothing and merely paraded prevailing ideas. Knowledge was being used to beat people over the head and force them into corners. Cohen complained that with his ideas he was treated like some kind of hick but felt that his was a wider view than that of those who hid behind dark glasses. He continued: 'You can already detect the beginnings of an artistic dictatorship in Montreal'.[54]

Simultaneous with Bob Dylan's turning away from the suffocating constraints of the New York Folk Movement and towards a more introspective personal poetry expressed in *Another Side of Bob Dylan*, Cohen had transformed from

[50] McClelland and Stewart publicity material, 'Poets on Campus', Leonard Cohen Papers, Fisher Library, Box 7: 16. It includes a quotation from Jack McClelland: 'If book sales are a fair measure there is more interest in poetry in Canada than anywhere else in the English-speaking world'.
[51] Letter from Leonard Cohen to Mme Marian McNamara, 29 March 1964. Fisher Library, Cohen papers, 11:15.
[52] 'Poets on Campus'.
[53] Leonard Cohen, *Flowers for Hitler* (Toronto: McClelland and Stewart, 1964).
[54] 'Let Us Be Ourselves Is Poet's Advice', *Montreal Gazette*, 17 November 1964. Cohen Papers, 11: 43, 7 Press clippings.

the intensely personal to an almost obsessive preoccupation with the Holocaust and the persecution of the Jews. Even his 1966 novel, *Beautiful Losers* was replete with references to Hitler and atrocities against the Jews.

After completing *Beautiful Losers* in Hydra, his Greek island home, Cohen was mentally and physically exhausted, having forced himself to write for extended periods without sleep and sustained by various concoctions of narcotics and amphetamines. Following its publication, he was back in Canada to a torrent of bad reviews. They were uniformly unfavourable in his native country, and only a little better in the United States. *Macleans Review*, under the heading 'Is Lavatory Scribbling Necessary', suggested that the book explored a familiar theme that we live in tense and disturbing times, and whose sole originality is that it is 'expressed with such relentless insistence in terms of genitals'.[55] Robert Fulford in the *Toronto Daily Star* lamented that the book was the 'most revolting book ever written in Canada. In fact, it requires a stronger stomach than almost any of the black novels published in recent years'.[56]

In an interview with Bruce Lawson of the Toronto *Globe and Mail*, a somewhat dispirited Cohen lamented that he knew there were writers out there saying what he wanted to say, but so very much better. All of his previous work, he believed, had been a period of training for 'initiation into something else', and it was time for him to 'cut loose'. He said that he wanted to write songs that would turn people on and that would have the character of prayers, if prayers hadn't been so 'devaluated', that is 'devaluated by me'.[57] *Beautiful Losers* had been cathartic for him. In it he had let out a lot of pain, and he had learnt from the suffering, and it was time to move on.

He had arrived in New York first in 1956 to enrol as a student at Columbia University, the year in which the Beats began to become a cultural phenomenon. He went to New York to achieve fame as a writer beyond the Canadian *literati* community.[58] The Golden Boy of Canadian literature was no longer the centre of attention. He had heard that there was a community of artists with a great generosity of spirit living in Greenwich Village. He, however, felt that he was given the cold shoulder and was somewhat resentful.[59] Cohen, however, developed his public persona primarily through poetry recitals, often, as we saw,

---

[55] Bannerman on Books, *Maclean's Review*, 14 May 1966.
[56] 26 April 1966.
[57] Lawson, 'A New Religious Age for Leonard Cohen'.
[58] Simmons, *I'm Your Man*, p. 58.
[59] Radio interview with Vin Scelsa, WXRK-FRM (New York), 13 June 1993.Printed in *Leonard Cohen on Leonard Cohen*, ed. Berger, p. 345.

with fellow Canadian poets such as L. Dudek, I. Layton and A. M. Klein. In addition to these, Canadian Broadcasting Channel (CBC) brought together A. J. Smith and F. R. Scott for a film of poetry which gained public recognition in America through Folkways Records – *Six Montreal Poets* (1957). Cohen read eight poems from *Let Us Compare Mythologies*.

He also chanted poetry to the accompaniment of his own guitar improvisation and occasionally to jazz music, known as jazz poetry. His first readings to jazz accompaniment were in 1957 or 1958 in Birdland, an allusion to Charlie Bird, and a poor imitation of the original New York club, above Dunns Restaurant and Emporium in St. Catherine's Street, West Montreal. Cohen would improvise while Bill Barwick's Trio or Maury Kaye and his jazz group played. Cohen also worked with a jazz guitarist from Winnipeg named Lenny Breau, as for example, when they played at Manitoba in 1964.

As Cohen published his first book of poetry, and recorded his first spoken word album with his fellow Montreal poets, Allen Ginsberg was concurrently catapulted to fame on reading extracts from *Howl* for the first time at the Six Gallery in San Francisco on 7 October 1955, which he read in full seven months later in 1956 at Berkeley. Kerouac said after the 1955 reading: 'Ginsberg this poem will make you famous in San Francisco', while Kenneth Rexroth added, 'No, this poem will make you famous from bridge to bridge'.[60] Ann Charters, who was at the second reading, witnessed the transformation of Ginsberg from the quiet bohemian intellectual into an incandescent bardic performer in the manner of Dylan Thomas. She claimed that Thomas, through his readings and recordings, 'revolutionised the way his American audiences thought about poetry'.[61] In a review of Ginsberg's *Collected Poems 1947–1980*, Blake Morrison suggested that without the musical accompaniment and the intonation of his mantric delivery, the poems may fall flat on the page. The power of *Howl*, for example, is its unrelenting rhythmic drive: 'It is as if Eliot's elegiac "They all go into the dark" had been combined with Dylan Thomas's *hwyl* to make a modern prophet book.'[62]

Richard Eberhart wrote of a revolution of consciousness in San Francisco in an article largely devoted to Ginsberg, much to the annoyance of indigenous

---

[60] Cited in Miles, *Allen Ginsberg Beat Poet*, p. 194. The bridges are the San Francisco Golden Gate Bridge and Brooklyn Bridge.

[61] Cited in Jack Foley, 'Howl and the Howlers', *The Raconteur: America*, ed. Dylan More and Gary Raymond, Winter 2011/12, p. 286.

[62] Blake Morrison, 'Bard of Bohemia', *The Observer*, Sunday, 5 May 1985.

West Coast poets such as McClure and Rexroth. The *New York Review of Books* article provided Ginsberg with instant fame. Joyce Johnson comments in her *Minor Characters*: 'Allen Ginsberg had always been legendary, even before he became famous in the *New York Times*.'[63] Ginsberg's hunger for fame impelled him to seek publicity by staging stunts that detracted from his seriousness as a poet. 'The Bard of Bohemia', one critic commented, 'has ended up a sort of emperor's dancing bear'.[64]

Kerouac's *On the Road* was equally as transformative for him. The review in *New York Times* was superlative, predicting that *On the Road* would become the testament of the Beat generation. Joyce Johnson was with Kerouac when they obtained an early edition. She remarked: 'We returned to the apartment to go back to sleep. Jack lay down obscure for the last time in his life. The ringing phone woke him the next morning and he was famous.'[65] In 1957, recounting the Six Gallery reading, Ginsberg acknowledged Kerouac's rise to stardom, describing him as 'now the most celebrated novelist in America'.[66]

Kerouac exemplifies the Beat generation for the singer-songwriters who were its legacy. His new style of poetry was inspired by jazz, particularly 'bebop', but with a firm conviction that their foundation was in the blues, giving the term 'beat' its musical sense. He was, in addition, fascinated with the dispossessed and down and outs giving the term 'beat' its sense of beat-up and worn-down. Finally, his intense immersion in a search for spirituality in combination with the first two aspects gave the term 'beat' the sense of beatific.[67]

The Beats were, nevertheless, ambivalent in their attitudes towards Dylan Thomas's fame: they were not only desperate to be famous but also acutely aware of the price at which it came. Dylan Thomas himself was conscious of the price. In an interview for the *New York Times Book Review*, Thomas remarked that success was bad for him, lamenting 'I should be what I was'.[68] Arthur Miller speculated that Thomas had tortured himself for achieving fame, while the man from whom he inherited his poetic gifts, his father, was a failure and died unknown: 'Thomas was making amends by murdering the gift he had stolen from the man he loved.'[69] Ginsberg paints an unflattering portrait of Thomas

---

[63] Joyce Johnson, *Minor Characters* (London: Methuen, 2006), p. 118.

[64] Morrison, 'Bard of Bohemia'.

[65] Johnson, *Minor Characters*, p, 185.

[66] Allen Ginsberg, *Deliberate Prose: Selected Essays 1952-1995* (London: Penguin Books, 2000), p. 240.

[67] Laurence Coupe, *Beat Sound, Beat Vision: The Beat Spirit and Popular Song* (Manchester: Manchester University Press, 2007), p. 56.

[68] Cited in Andrew Lycett, *Dylan Thomas: A New Life* (London: Pheonix, 2004), p. 331

[69] Cited in Lycett, *Dylan Thomas: A New Life*, p. 444.

exploiting his fame to the full in Greenwich Village, where he met him in late April 1952.[70]

Between the death of Dylan Thomas in 1953 and the emergence of Kerouac's and Ginsberg's fame in 1957, American cultural, economic and political public life had changed. Television, a novelty in the early 1950s, was in seven million homes transforming the reach and demands of fame.[71] The popular cultural heroes, Marlon Brando, James Dean and Elvis Presley, represented an alluring image of the strong, inarticulate rebel with a menacing raw sex appeal. Gregory Corso, who always remained on the fringes of fame, complained that Presley and Dean were the symbols of rebellion for their generation: 'How sad it has to be a Presley or a dead movie actor bringing all this out. It should be the poet. He is the minstrel, the legislator, the eternal rebel . . . it should be the poet.'[72] Even Ginsberg, 'the PR genius of the Beat Generation,'[73] was ambivalent about his own fame, but only momentarily. In a letter to Kerouac, following the publication of *Howl*, he declared: 'Agh, I'm sick of the whole thing, that's all I think about, famous authorship. Like a happy empty dream . . . how beautiful though.'[74] Fame obsessed him to the end. One of his last poems was entitled 'Death and Fame'. In 1955, before Kerouac published *On the Road*, Gary Snyder, Japhy Ryder in *The Dharma Bums*, sensed about him 'a palpable aura of fame and death.'[75] When Kerouac attained the fame that he had been envious of Dylan Thomas, he was more exposed to its destructiveness because of the fully fledged media environment obsessed with a celebrity.

He became an overnight sensation, the first literary figure of the burgeoning media age, interviewed on television talk shows and performing his poetry to jazz accompaniment at the Village Vanguard.[76] As John Leland suggests, Kerouac 'played the holy fool in public, showing up drunk at readings and baring himself unguardedly in interviews, becoming a sexy beast for a celebrity industry that loved sex and monsters.'[77] At the same time as Lawrence Ferlinghetti was working with Kenneth Rexroth presenting jazz and poetry in The Cellar in San Francisco in the mid-1950s, Jack Kerouac fused jazz and poetry in The Circle in the

[70] Allen Ginsberg, *Journal: Early Fifties, Early Sixties* (New York: Grove, 1977), pp. 14–16.
[71] John Leland, *Why Kerouac Matters* (London: Penguin, 2008), p. 188.
[72] Writing to Mr and Mrs Randall Jarrell from Guaymas, New Mexico, early November, 1956. Corso, *An Accidental Biography*, p. 13.
[73] Ann Douglas, 'Introduction: "A Hoop for the Lowly"'; Jack Kerouac, *The Dharma Bums* (London: Penguin, 2006), p. xiii.
[74] Miles, *Allen Ginsberg*, p. 208.
[75] Douglas, Introduction to *The Dharma Bums*, p. v.
[76] Douglas, Introduction to *The Dharma Bums*, p. vi.
[77] Leland, *Why Kerouac Matters*, p. 194.

Square Theatre, Greenwich Village, and read his works at the Village Vanguard, usually drunk on 'Thunderbird'. Jazz, in Kerouac's view was not incidental to the Beat generation, but central. When asked why, Kerouac answered: 'Jazz is very complicated. It's just as complicated as Bach. The chords, the structures, the harmony and everything. And then it has a tremendous beat. You know, tremendous drummers. They can drive it. It has just a tremendous drive. It can drive you right out of yourself.'[78] Coffee shops proliferated and were animated by the sound of chanted poems and scented by the smell of marijuana burning. The Cedar Tavern was a popular congregating point for artists such as Larry Rivers and Robert Rauschenberg whose poetic comrades included Frank O'Hara, Kenneth Koch, John Ashberry and Ted Berrington, later known as the New York School.[79] In the late 1950s public poetry reading sessions were common and the likes of the young Leonard Cohen, while at Columbia University, and Ritchie Havens, as a nineteen-year-old, would go to the cafes and bars to listen to Lawrence Ferlinghetti, Jack Kerouac, Allen Ginsberg and Ted Jones.

Fame, for Kerouac, Joyce Johnson remarked, 'was as foreign a country as Mexico, but with no sealed borders. You could not leave it behind when you had enough. Its temporary excitement corrupted your life and invaded your dreams. It demanded your secrets and whispered insulting innuendoes behind your back'.[80] Kerouac wrote of the destructive character of fame in *Big Sur*.[81] He wrote to Lawrence Ferlinghetti (Lorenz Monsanto in the book) saying, 'I just finished writing my brand new novel about your cabin in Big Sur. . . . My first novel since the Road was published in 1957'.[82] 'Four years of drunken chaos is the cause.' The trip to San Francisco, Kerouac's *alter ego* Jack Duluoz claims, is the first since 'Road' made him famous, so famous that the endless and relentless intrusion for three years drove him mad. Drunk practically all of the time, he needed to get away or die.

---

[78] Interview by Mike Wallace with Jack Kerouac, *New York Post*, 21 January 1958. Reproduced in *The Beats: A Literary Reference*, p. 118.

[79] Robbie Woliver, *Hoot: A Twenty-Five-Year History of the Greenwich Village Music Scene* (New York: St. Martin's Press, 1994), 8. This book was first published in 1986 by Pantheon Books as *Bringing It All Back Home*.

[80] Johnson, *Minor Characters*, pp. 189–90.

[81] Big Sur is a region of the Central Coast of California. It is sparsely populated because of its rugged terrain. The Santa Lucia Mountains rise abruptly from the Pacific Ocean. The name 'Big Sur' is derived from the original Spanish language 'el sur grande', meaning 'the big south', or from 'el país grande del sur', 'the big country of the south'. The book is now a film: *One Fast Move or I'm Gone: Kerouac's Big Sur*.

[82] Letter to Ferlinghetti, November, 1961, in Selected Letters of Jack Kerouac 1957–1969 (London: Viking, 1999) pp. 313–14.

In the book he arranges an incognito meeting with Monsanto in San Francisco where he would be transported to his host's cabin in the Big Sur for six weeks of solitude and writing. Instead he arrives at City Lights where everyone recognizes him and ends up 'roaring drunk in all the famous bars the bloody "King of the Beatniks" is back in town buying drinks for everyone'. In a letter to Allen Ginsberg, Corso comments on Kerouac's *Big Sur*: 'He sees only his worthless skin, his woe his beatnik plight.'[83]

The constant attention and intrusion, the drunkenness, the self-recrimination, maudlin resignation and receding prospects of ever being on the road again were a recurrent nightmare for him. Success, he said, 'is when you can't enjoy your food anymore in peace.'[84] A reviewer said of the book: 'What can a beat do when he is too old to go on the road? He can go on the sauce. In *Big Sur* Jack does.'[85] Kerouac died at the age of forty-seven of an abdominal haemorrhage.

No one exemplifies the ambivalent attitude of the Beats to fame more than Charles Bukowski. Bob Dylan says of Charles Bukowski on the flight to Denver from Lincoln: 'He's a beat drunken poet . . . and I like a few of his stuff. . . . He's an infantile little madman, he's a drunkard.' Bob Dylan added, 'Bukowski is a drunk, neon-light hotel whorehouse poet, man. Who takes pride and reverence in what he does . . . That's all . . . poets usually do this . . . Poets who have gained attention . . . hey I love poets, man.' Robert Shelton asks, 'What about Yevtushenko?', Bob Dylan replies, 'No I don't like him at all'.

Charles Bukowski's reverence for Dylan Thomas is ambivalent. Through the voice of his *alter ego* Henry Chinaski, Bukowski describes the hectic drink-sodden emotional roller-coaster ride of a journey to a poetry reading, followed by the adoration of fans, particularly of young women, from all over America. Revelling in his fame and notoriety, he exclaims: 'This is what killed Dylan Thomas.'[86]

Throughout Bukowski's letters, this theme haunts him. His own excesses were as notorious as those of Dylan Thomas. Acknowledging the genius of Dylan Thomas, Bukowski opines wistfully: 'The most brilliant thing I do is to get drunk – which any fool can do.'[87] He remarks that Thomas didn't drink himself to death

[83] 7 March 1963, Corso, *An Accidental Autobiography*, p. 352.
[84] Leland, *Why Kerouac Matters*, p. 194.
[85] *Time*, 14 September 1962, p. 106.
[86] Charles Bukowski, 'This Is What Killed Dylan Thomas', in *South of No North: Stories of the Buried Life* (New York: Echo, 1973), pp. 129–33.
[87] Charles Bukowski, letter to Jon Webb, 1962 in *Screams from a Balcony: Selected letters 1960-1970*, ed. Seamus Cooney (New York: Harper Collins, 1978), p. 42.

because he felt his talent was waning. He drank, like me, because he loved it, 'it lifted him where he belonged'.[88]

Thomas's fame in the United States did not wane following his death in 1953. Kenneth Rexroth, who knew and admired him, wrote a tribute entitled 'Thou Shalt Not Kill'. When Dylan Thomas visited California during his first American tour, he met Rexroth in San Francisco, who despite finding Dylan Thomas's drinking a problem came to like him: 'He is sure genuine. A vast relief after these nasty English poets. He is Welsh and proletarian to the core.'[89] Five hundred people tried to squeeze into The Cellar in San Francisco, which had a capacity of forty-three, to hear Rexroth read the poem to the accompaniment of saxophonist Bruce Lippincott.[90] The poem was an angry indictment of American commercialism, its exploitation of fame and its propensity to destroy poets. The poem presages Ginsberg's more famous *Howl*, accusatorily indicting New York 'Society', that same society that Dylan Thomas mocked in his story 'Visit to America'.

> Who killed him?
> Who killed the bright-headed bird?
> You did, you son of a bitch.
> You drowned him in your cocktail brain.

Thomas and Charlie Parker were, in Rexroth's view, great titans of the post-war generation, and both of them were his friends, but they deliberately destroyed themselves through their excesses. In poetry and jazz they were great influences on the Beat generation. In 1957 Rexroth recalled the last time he saw them both. Parker in Jimbo's Bop City,[91] who was so far gone and oblivious to the world that he sat on Rexroth before he realized he was there. The last time he saw Dylan Thomas his self-destruction had not only gone beyond the limits of the rational, 'it had assumed the terrifying inertia of inanimate matter. Being with him was like being swept away by a torrent of falling stones.'[92]

Bukowski was also aware of the danger of pursuing fame. Prostituting oneself, 'bellowing to the idol lovers' is what disgusted him about Ginsberg and Corso.

---

[88] Bukowski, letter to Tom McNamara, 25 October 1965 in *Screams from the Balcony*, p. 219.
[89] Lycett, *Dylan Thomas: A New Life*, p. 321.
[90] *Time*, 2 December 1957, p. 71.
[91] Jimbo's Bop City was a club in San Francisco from 1950 to 1965 in Post Street. It was a famous venue hosting, among others, Charlie Parker, Ella Fitzgerald, Billie Holiday, Miles Davis, Dizzy Gillespie, and John Coltrane.
[92] Kenneth Rexroth, 'Disengagement: The Art of the Beat Generation', in *Beat Down to Your Soul*, ed. Ann Charters (London: Penguin, 2001), p. 495.

Despite having clarity of style, 'they've got a little too much the sweet tooth for their own soul (soul importance) and they suck up a lot of bait'.[93] Bukowski thought Corso's star descended rapidly because of his simplicity of purpose and message, whereas Ginsberg's decline had taken a little longer. They both, nevertheless, swallowed the same bait of adulation and fame as Brendan Behan and Dylan Thomas.[94] Bukowski remonstrated, 'anybody can go the way of Dylan Thomas, Ginsberg, Corso, Behan, Leary, Creeley, sliding down that river of shit. The idea is Creation not Adulation; the idea is a man in a room alone hacking at a stone and not sucking at the tits of the crowd'.[95] There is always a young audience there 'sucked into the cesspool: Bukowski, Thomas, [Bob] Dylan, Ginsberg – anything except by going into that lonely room and finding out WHO THEY ARE OR WHO THEY ARE NOT'.[96]

Like Rexroth, Bukowski blamed Thomas's adulators for his untimely demise. In his poem 'O. We Are the Outcasts'. Bukowski wrote:

> and D. Thomas THEY KILLED HIM, of course.
> Thomas didn't want all those free drinks
> all that free pussy-
> they . . . FORCED IT ON HIM.[97]

The Beats responded to the alienation of the nuclear era with deep angst and personal introspection, and experimented not only with hard liquor but also in true Rimbaud style with hard drugs that pushed them to the extremes of experience. They were famous not only for their poetry but also for their lifestyle which was extreme and often self-destructive. Marianne Faithful recalls that when she went to Paris in 1964, Ginsberg, Corso and Ferlinghetti shared the same room in the Hotel Louisiana as her and her new husband. They ranted about buggery, Tangiers, Rimbaud and the Rosenbergs while vomiting on the floor and spilling rosé all over the place. Breakfast for Corso consisted in mixing-up a Brompton cocktail – 50/50 morphine and cocaine – and then passing out on the floor.

Robert Briggs maintains that Dylan Thomas was the star of the 1950s, and he recalls Pony Poindexter playing a jazz accompaniment to 'Love in the Asylum'

---

[93] Bukowski, letter to Kirby Congdon, ca. mid-March, 1966, *Screams from the Balcony*, p. 245.
[94] Bukowski, letter to Tom McNamara, 25 October 1965, *Screams from the Balcony*, p. 219.
[95] Bukowski, letter to Sten Richmon, February 1967, *Screams from the Balcony*, p. 295.
[96] Bukowski, letter to Carl Wiessner, 28 January 1967, *Screams from the Balcony*, p. 293.
[97] Charles Bukowski, 'O, We Are the Outcasts', in *Roominghouse Madrigals*, Kindle edition, Loc, pp. 480–1.

in the Jazz Basement, San Francisco, in 1959.[98] Louis Dudek, as we saw, was teaching at McGill, and took care of Thomas after the reading in 1952. Dylan Thomas continued to figure in correspondence between Leonard Cohen and Dudek. After seeing a production in 1956 of Christopher Fry's play 'The Lady's Not for Burning', in New York, Dudek wrote to Cohen commenting on the similarity between Fry and Thomas, they both used too many words for the matter, in Fry's case 'witty; in Dylan's fiery imaginative'.[99]

Thomas was to continue to figure in Cohen's imagination. When in 1988 his manager Marty Machat died, Kelley Lynch, who had worked for him, was hired by Cohen, first as his personal assistant and then manager until 2005. She had grown up in a household in which Dylan Thomas's 'A Child's Christmas in Wales', had been standard fare. Her mother told her, as a two-year-old in 1959 Kelley would repeatedly ask to have the story read to her every night before bed. She loved Dylan Thomas, especially to hear the words that sounded like slushy snow under foot. On telling Cohen this he advised her to listen to Thomas's 'marvellous' recording.[100] Even the future president of the United States, Jimmy Carter, 'bought all his books and records' and recited the poems to his children until they memorized them.[101] The American poet William Greenway started reading Thomas in about 1960 and commented that Thomas had taken America by storm, 'and it stayed stormed'.[102]

When Robert Zimmerman arrived in Minneapolis in 1959 Dylan Thomas's fame was undiminished. Famous in his own lifetime, he had entered the pantheon of dead writers martyred in the cause of their art, and Bobby Zimmerman's popular culture heroes were soon to join him, James Dean and Hank Williams, not to mention Buddy Holly, Ritchie Valens, and the Big Bopper, the three of whom he saw perform live in Duluth on 31 January 1959 only three days before their fatal plane crash on 3 February.

In Minneapolis Robert Zimmerman discovered Dinkytown, a small bohemian enclave adjacent to the university. It was the Midwestern equivalent of Greenwich Village. The area was full of jazz clubs and coffee houses where musicians and poets gathered to perform and where, in contrast with Hibbing,

---

[98] Robert Briggs, *Poetry and the 1950s: Homage to the Beat Generation*, audio, label, Skysociety, 1999. ASIN B001GLA4L2.

[99] Letter from Louis Dudek to Leonard Cohen, 258 West 22 St. NYC, June 22, 1956. Leonard Cohen papers, #29, Thomas Fisher rare books library, Toronto University.

[100] Email from Kelley Lynch to David Boucher, 10 March 2003.

[101] https://www.bbc.co.uk/news/uk-wales-15661342. Accessed 28 May 2020.

[102] William Greenway, 'Dylan Thomas and a Contemporary American Poet', *The World Winding Home* (Swansea: The Dylan Thomas Society of Great Britain, 1995), p. 45.

a wide variety of intellectual activity filled the night air. It was there he was seriously introduced to the Beat literature of Kenneth Rexroth, Gregory Corso and Lawrence Ferlinghetti, in addition to Kerouac and Ginsberg.[103] Corso and Ginsberg declared that America could now boast poets who 'have taken it upon themselves, with angelic clarions in hand, to announce their discontent, their demands, their hope, their final wondrous unimaginable dream'.[104]

The whole thrust of the Beat generation was anti-conventional, railing against the accepted mores of sex, art and religion. It was a movement that was also anti-intellectual and radically individualist. Kerouac boasted that the Beats 'transferred literature from colleges and academies into the hands of the folk'.[105] The young Bobby Zimmerman was later to confess: 'I came out of the wilderness and just naturally fell in with the Beat Scene. It was Jack Kerouac, Ginsberg, Corso, Ferlinghetti . . . I got in at the tail end and it was magic . . . It had just as big an impression on me as Elvis Presley.'[106]

Bob Dylan, like the Beat poets he encountered in Dinkytown, Minneapolis, was enthralled by the fame, the irreverence, even decadence, of the Welshman who notoriously conjured a world interwoven with fact and fiction, a performer par excellence. In a 1963 interview, Bob Dylan reminisced: 'I'd fell in love with a new kinda people there in Minneapolis. I was going to new kids' parties an' thinkin' new kinda things . . . I read into what I was doing an' saw myself romantically breakin' off all ties with all things of the established order.'[107] Breaking off all ties for Robert Zimmerman meant breaking with his name, his identity and location. But instead of appropriating a name consistent with the idealism of the collectivist vision of the folk hero who Woody Guthrie represented for him, he chose the name of the poet whose fame the Beats coveted. If you were an aspirant poet in America in 1959, looking to change your name and create an air of romantic mystery around you, the mythology and allure the name Dylan conjured could not be ignored.

In 1959 Bob Dylan stood at the crossroads; Kerouac and Guthrie were the signposts representing different visions of the road: both *On the Road* and *Bound for Glory* were the sacred texts he treasured and which remained

[103] June Skinner Sawyers, *Bob Dylan New York* (Berkeley, California: Roaring Forties Press, 2011), p. 8.
[104] Allen Ginsberg and Gregory Corso, 'The Literary Revolution in America'. Abridged in *Allen Ginsberg: Howl*, ed. Barry Miles (New York: Harper, 1986), pp. 165–6. Originally published in *The Litterair Paspoort 100* (Amsterdam), November 1957.
[105] Leland, *Why Kerouac Matters*, p. 197.
[106] Jon Rogers, 'Allen Ginsberg: The Recordings', *Beat Scene*, no. 23 (n.d.), p. 13.
[107] *Dylan Scrapbook*, p. 13.

reference points for him. New York was where Woody Guthrie was confined in Greystone Hospital, Morristown, suffering from the degenerative disease Huntington's Chorea, and many of his friends and acolytes inhabited Greenwich Village, where the embers of the Beat generation still glowed alongside the self-styled highly politicized 'folk movement'. When Bobby Zimmerman went to New York his repertoire consisted not of poems set to music but of an eclectic mix of country, blues, folk and his first tentative compositions.[108]

By the time Bob Dylan reached New York in 1961, on a mission to see his hero Woody Guthrie,[109] there was no trace of Robert Allen Zimmerman. Bob Dylan legally became his name in 1962. Bob Dylan commented:

> Within the first few months that I was in New York I lost my interest in the 'hungry for kicks' hipster vision that Kerouac illustrates so well in his book *On the Road*. That book had been like a bible for me. Not anymore, though. I still loved the breathless, dynamic bop poetry phrases that flowed from Jack's pen, but now, that character Moriarty seemed out of place, purposeless – seemed like a character who inspired idiocy. He goes through life bumping and grinding with a bull on top of him.'[110]

In February 1964, however, at the height of his fame among the folkniks, but tiring of the constraints imposed by the collectivist ethos imposed by the likes of Irwin Silber, the editor of *Broadside*, Bob Dylan embarked on his own road journey with four companions in a station wagon from New York to California, with only four concerts and various detours on the way, including a visit to the veteran poet, author and song collector Carl Sandberg. Shelton remarks, 'beyond the restlessness, curiosity and hunger for experience was Dylan's compulsion to keep in physical and spiritual motion'.[111] The journey was very much a conflation of the roads Guthrie and Kerouac travelled but represented a consolidation of his estrangement from the folkniks and new affinity with the beatniks.

The admiration of Bob Dylan for the Beats was reciprocated. Rexroth admired his political stance, and considered him the product of the generation

---

[108] On 11 March 1962 he did a Radio show, just prior to the release of his first album. Among the songs he sung were 'Lonesome Whistle' by Hank Williams, 'Fixin to Die' by Bukka White, 'Smokestack Lightening' by Howlin Wolf; 'Hard Travelling' by Woody Guthrie; 'Stealin' arranged by the Memphis Jug Band; and 'Baby Please Don't Go' by Big Joe Williams. He did two of his own compositions, 'The Death of Emmet Till' and 'Hard Times in New York Town'. Bob Dylan: Folk Singer's Choice, Left Field Media, LFMCD501 © 2010.
[109] Shelton, *No Direction Home*, updated edition, p. 62.
[110] Bob Dylan, *Chronicles* (London, Simon and Schuster, 2004), p. 58.
[111] Shelton, *No Direction Home*, updated edition, pp. 172–3.

gap articulating 'a cry of anguished moral outrage against the mess the oldies persist in making out of a world in which all men could be guaranteed lives of peace and modest comfort if only the will existed'.[112] In the Martin Scorsese documentary of Bob Dylan, *No Direction Home*, Ginsberg claims to have wept the first time he heard 'A Hard Rain's a-Gonna Fall' (*Freewheelin*, 1963), which anticipated the abstract expressionism of his albums of the mid-1960s. He first heard the track in 1963 and thought, 'Thank God another soul had emerged to carry the torch'.

Ginsberg first met Bob Dylan in November 1963 at a party in aid of Ginsberg and Peter Orlovsky at the bookshop at 32 West Eighth Street on the same day that Dylan made his embarrassing speech in acceptance of the Thomas Paine Award in which he empathized with Lee Harvey Oswald. Ginsberg and Dylan discussed poetry and politics. Dylan invited him to go on tour with him.[113] Ginsberg declined but accompanied him on the 1965 tour instead and appears on both versions of the famous promotional film for 'Subterranean Homesick Blues' shot in London in 1965.

Marianne Faithful was struck by the fact that Ginsberg believed that most of Bob Dylan's songs were about him.[114] The Dylan-Ginsberg relationship is portrayed in the 2007 film *I'm Not There*, with Cate Blanchett playing Bob Dylan and David Cross as Ginsberg.[115] Ginsberg came to idolize Bob Dylan, contending that by creating an art out of the roots of the culture he had almost single-handedly transformed American poetry.[116]

Bob Dylan, as Lawrence Coupe maintained, was 'firmly within the Beat legacy'.[117] Indeed, Ann Charters includes extracts not only from his *Tarantula* but also 'Blowin' in the Wind', 'The Times They Are a-Changin'' and 'A Hard Rain's a-Gonna Fall' in *The Portable Beat Reader* because they exhibit a characteristically Beat 'vivid and apocalyptic vision'.[118] By early 1964 Bob Dylan was already feeling the strain of carrying the weight of fame on his shoulders. New York was becoming oppressive and he increasingly spent

[112] The Bureau of Public Secrets: Rexroth's San Francisco 1965,
  http://www.bopsecrets.org/rexroth/sf/1965.htm
[113] Marianne Faithful says it was 1964. Marianne Faithful, *Faithful: An Autobiography* (New York: Cooper's Square Press, 2000), 42. Sawyers, *Bob Dylan: New York*, p. 75.
[114] Faithful, *Faithful*, p. 48.
[115] Benjamin Wright, 'The Weird and Wonderful Literary World of Bob Dylan', *Highbrow Magazine*, 13 October 2012. http://highbrowmagazine.com/1640-weird-and-wonderful-literary-world-bob-dylan, posted 5 October 2012.
[116] Allen Ginsberg, 'On the New Dylan', *Georgia Straight*, 25 May 1971.
[117] Coupe, *Beat Sound, Beat Vision*, p. 80.
[118] Ann Charters, ed., *The Portable Beat Reader* (London: Penguin, 1992), p. 370.

more time at the home of his manager, Albert Grossman, in Bearsville near Woodstock. He confessed to Nat Hentoff that he found being noticed a burden and that he frequently had to disappear for a while. In an open letter published in *Broadside* on 20 January 1964, Dylan wrote 'I am now famous, it snuck up on me and pulverized me'.[119] As Sawyers maintained, he was 'growing weary of all the masks he had to wear in public, all of the personas he had assumed over the years; he was drained by the demands it placed on him'.[120] When Bob Dylan went electric in 1965, it represented much more than a sell-out to commercialism, of which he was accused by his devoted folk fans. He demonstrably turned his back on the collectivist values of the self-congratulatory folk movement and embraced the radical individualism of the Beat Movement.

In 1965–66 Bob Dylan was the coolest man on the planet and at the height of his fame. However, he was also physically and mentally deteriorating from the hectic schedule of his life and substance abuse. Frequently, friends and journalists commented that he looked terrible, close to death. Ralph Gleason, the American jazz and popular music critic, was alarmed at how ill Dylan looked. He said: 'I was very worried about him. I figured he was in mortal pain. I wanted to ask what was killing him. I was astounded he was still working, because I figured he would have had a breakdown.'[121] The interviews to which we referred at the start of this chapter were conducted at this time, in March 1966. In them he complains that if he had no money, he could be invisible, but now he has money and it costs him to be invisible. The fame and adulation were getting to him. The relentless schedule of his world tour was taking its toll. He told Robert Shelton: 'It takes a lot of medicine to keep up this pace. It's very hard man. A concert tour like this has almost killed me. It's been like this since October. It really drove me out of my mind. I never had it like this before. It's been a really weird time, and it really had me down.'[122]

The last concert on Dylan's tour was in England on 27 May 1966 at the Albert Hall. He returned to the United States exhausted, burnt out from the cocktail of drugs he needed to fuel the intensity of the pace and the casualty of the fame that seduced him and reduced him to a neurotic physical wreck. He went to live in Woodstock to recuperate and, in July, had a motorcycle accident that fractured

[119] Cited in Sawyer, *Bob Dylan: New York*, p. 70.
[120] Sawyer, *Bob Dylan: New York*, p. 71.
[121] Shelton, *No Direction Home*, revised edn, p. 231.
[122] Shelton, *No Direction Home*, revised edn, p. 240.

his neck and saved his life. Dylan described the period around 'Desolation Row' as 'That kind of New York Type period, when all the songs were just "city songs". Sounds like the city.'[123] Eighteen months later he returned with the album *John Wesley Harding*, an almost complete repudiation of everything the three previous albums represented. He stripped back the sound to bass, drums, rhythm and lead guitars. The song structures changed and were narrative based; he had reconnected himself to the American folklore tradition.

As we saw, Cohen had heard Jack Kerouac's readings over jazz music in the Village Vanguard while a student at Columbia University. He met him at a party that Ginsberg organized and then a few times after that. He was a great admirer of Kerouac's writing. Cohen thought that Ginsberg had spun the great American tale. It had a glistening, shining quality that, like a spider, connected every thread. Cohen thought that Kerouac had a great knack for unifying his vision in a sequence of moments. It is a gift that he thought Bob Dylan also had, but it is one that is destructive of the generation that follows, doomed to mediocrity, not writing, but typing.[124]

Cohen had some brass neck to stand up in a seedy night club – where most of the clientele had come to see a girl floor show, the *Tappettes*, in which they undressed to the legally permissible limit – and chant poetry to jazz accompaniment. Maury Kaye's orchestra included six musicians, including, saxophone, guitar, piano, congas and drums. One account relates that early in the evening the band would play more conventional popular tunes in keeping with the floor show, and when the excitement died down, Cohen appeared at midnight, dressed in black, and illuminated by a single spotlight, seeming to most of the customers to be the MC, and to their astonishment, jaws dropping, and utterances of 'What the fuck!', he started reciting poetry.[125] On occasion Cohen was joined by other Montreal poets such as Irving Layton, Louis Dudek and Daryll Hine. Making poetry popular by using jazz accompaniment was never going to work, because by the early 1960s jazz had become too self-indulgent and esoteric. The media through which poetry became accessible and had mass appeal was folk, folk rock, and rock and roll music.[126]

---

[123] Quotation on the back cover of Joachim Markhorst, *Desolation Row: Bob Dylan's Poetic Letter from 1965* (Amazon self-published, 2020).

[124] Radio interview with Vince Scelsa, in *Leonard Cohen on Leonard Cohen*, ed. Burger, pp. 341–2.

[125] Doug Beardsley, 'On First Looking into Leonard Cohen', in *Intricate Preparations*, ed. Stephen Scobie (Toronto: ECW Press, 2000), pp. 6–7.

[126] Cook, *The Beat Generation*, p. 223.

In 1966 after being an accomplished and well-received poet and author in Canada, he still had made little impression further afield. In 1966 when asked by Robert Shelton whether he had heard of Leonard Cohen, Ferlinghetti replied that he didn't really know much about him other than he published a book of poems.[127] Cohen made his way to New York to seek fame where he was befriended by Judy Collins. Cohen became part of the folk culture, which had changed considerably since Dylan's entry into it. Leonard Cohen became part of the Greenwich Village folk scene in autumn 1966. In a photograph from then, Cohen is pictured on the floor of a New York apartment with Joan Baez and her sister Mimi Fariña, whose husband Richard had died in a motorcycle accident on 30 April, Dave van Ronk, Judy Collins and Chad Mitchell.[128] Cohen was back in the Village after ten years, just after Tim Buckley, Jeff Buckley's father, arrived from California for a residency at the Nite Owl Café, Greenwich Village. Cohen got to know him very well and released his debut album the year after Buckley released his.

At the same time Cohen got to know Nico at the Dom Club, and she introduced him to Lou Reed, who many years later inducted him into the Rock and Roll Hall of Fame, in 2008. Reed owned a copy of *Flowers for Hitler* before it was published in the United States and asked Cohen to sign it for him.[129] Cohen also lived at the Chelsea Hotel where he associated with a whole range of counterculture figures' such as Edie Sedgewick. In 1968 he had almost inherited the mantle of Bob Dylan. *The New York Times* said that he was 'a man-child of our time' and on the verge of becoming a 'major spokesman' for his generation.[130] John Rockwell of *The New York Times* recognized that Cohen was unlike all the other folk singers emerging on the scene in the late 1960s. He remarked that Cohen appeared to have emerged out of the folk scene that post-dated Dylan: 'But his way, even bitter sophistication, he really owes as much to chanting Beat poets and Continental Cabaret song as he does to the folkier and blues revivalists.'[131]

While writing *Beautiful Losers* on Hydra, Cohen listened to country music on the Armed Services radio and wrote some early versions of songs he was later to record. It was Nashville that beckoned him, but he became distracted by what was for him a new phenomenon – Bob Dylan and the folk scene of

[127] Shelton interview with Ferlinghetti, March 1966, p. 1.
[128] The photograph is printed in an article by Simmons, 'Travelling Light', *Mojo*, p. 88.
[129] Interview with Robin Pike, 15 September 1974, *ZigZag*, October 1974. Reprinted in *Leonard Cohen on Leonard Cohen*, ed. Burger, p. 68.
[130] Steve Turner, 'Leonard Cohen: The Prophets of Doom', *Q Magazine*, April 1988. Reprinted in *Leonard Cohen on Leonard Cohen: Interviews and Encounters*, ed. Burger, p. 209.
[131] Cited in Rasky, *Song of Leonard Cohen*, p. 18.

which he had been a part in New York. In a self-deprecating and wry way, Cohen described, to a friend, the qualities he possessed that enhanced his chances of success: 'I've got three things going for me. I have a terrible voice, can't even carry a tune. Also I'm very small, emaciated, with a residue of acne. And I'm demonstrably Jewish (Dylan is not). The only thing going against me is that I play the guitar too well.'[132] For a year or so Cohen pursued his musical and poetry reading careers simultaneously. Invitations to his manager Mary Martin flooded in for his appearance at poetry festivals and for his contribution to panels discussing the state of modern poetry even after his musical success. Whereas Cohen had been on the periphery of the Beat generation in 1956, by the time he published *Poems 1956-68*, he was not only well acquainted with its proponents but also praised by Rexroth who was at once an admirer of Dylan Thomas and inspiration to the Beat writers. Rexroth believed that Cohen's poetry constituted a breakthrough pointing the way to the future of poetry. Cohen was 'the voice of a new civilization'.[133]

Cohen associated with Phil Ochs, Pete Seeger and Joan Baez and made his debut at a Judy Collins' anti-Vietnam benefit concert in April 1967. When he met Judy Collins in 1966 to play her his songs, at Mary Martin's instigation, Cohen struck her as 'very shy and nervous', especially about singing in public. He sang at the Newport Folk Festival in 1967.[134] He had been introduced to Collins by Mary Martin, Albert Grossman's Canadian assistant, who was also responsible for getting the Hawks to play back-up for Dylan. Collins immediately thought Cohen's songs beautiful but that there was nothing in his repertoire for her. She asked him to let her know when he had something else in which she might be interested. He went back to Montreal to finish *Parasites of Heaven*, and there put the finishing touches to a song that he had been working on for some time. He knew it was a powerful song, capturing beautifully the mood of the Montreal waterfront and the righteous beauty of Suzanne Vaillancourt.

Cohen's fame as a novelist and poet in Canada worked to his advantage as a singer in so far as he was cut a little slack. He first sang on television on the CBC show *Take Thirty*. The producers had never heard Cohen sing but took the risk in order to get an interview with the poet. He wore an immaculately tailored

[132] Quoted in Ira Mothner, 'Songs Sacred and Profane', *Look*, 10 June 1969.
[133] Cited in Loranne S. Dorman and Clive L. Rawlins, *Leonard Cohen: Prophet of the Heart* (London: Omnibus, 1990), p. 213.
[134] Judy Collins, *Singing Lessons* (New York: Pocket Books, 1998), p. 144.

grey flannel suit and sang a twenty-minute version of 'The Stranger Song', which was considerably shortened for broadcasting.

The songs he wrote brought a degree, if only marginally, of coherence into his life, to be almost immediately dissipated. He described his second album, *Songs from a Room*, as very bleak. The voice projected despair and pain and accurately reflected the state of mind of the singer. In *The Favourite Game* Cohen sensitively characterizes an extremely disturbed child, Martin, who dies at the summer camp where Breavman is working. Cohen felt an affinity with that little boy, unable to communicate with the world, unable to make sense of it. When young he was drawn to the people whom the world disparaged as mad and to the socially aberrant, drug addicts, tramps and alcoholics who draped themselves all over Philips Square and Clark Street in Montreal. The completion of his second novel *Beautiful Losers* made him completely 'flip out'. He considered himself a loser, as a man and lover, morally and financially. He resented his own life and even vowed to fill the pages with black as an alternative to killing himself. When the book was finished, he fasted for ten days and had a breakdown. He was taken to hospital on Hydra, and Cohen contended that the sky was black with storks that rested on the roofs of houses and took flight the next morning along with his depression.[135]

In the 1970–1 tour he, along with the band he came to call The Army, because he felt they were constantly under siege, included in its itinerary a series of unpublicized concerts at mental institutions. The Beat poets always privileged madness over reason. They talked of the manufacture of madness, questioning who had the right to establish the criteria of sanity and insanity.

Cohen was almost comatose in many of his live appearances. LSD, speed and Mandrax were integral to his life. In his 1972 tour of Europe with The Army he acquired the name of Captain Mandrax and had difficulty in finding the pitch of his songs and maintaining their tempo.[136] He is famously said to have collapsed in the street after taking opium with the infamous Scottish Italian Beat novelist and pornographer, and notorious junkie, Alexander Trocchi. The Beats glamorized drugs in a way that neither Bob Dylan nor Leonard Cohen ever did, even though both notoriously experimented with numerous banned substances. Take, for example, Alexander Trocchi, the Glaswegian Beat, who spent time in New York

---

[135] Richard Goldstein, 'Beautiful Creep', *The Village Voice*, 28 December 1967, p. 27. Reprinted in *Leonard Cohen: The Artist and His Critics*, ed., Michael Gnarowski (Toronto: McGraw-Hill, 1967), p. 44.

[136] John Walsh, 'Research, You Understand...Leonard Cohen', *Mojo*, September 1994, p. 60.

and whom Cohen met in Montreal. Trocchi used drugs to reach the limits of consciousness and saw it as his public duty to introduce everyone else to the experience. At the time Cohen met him Trocchi was working in New York with a group of writers and publishers thought by the 'provincials' in Montreal to be at the cutting edge of literature and poetry. Cohen had read *Cain's Book* and was familiar with Trocchi's messianic view of drugs, which was not unusual among the Beat poets and philosophers who thought that this tainted and smudged reality could be penetrated and a more authentic existence apprehended, embraced and lived. Cohen thought him not unlike William Burroughs and Allen Ginsberg who believed that our perceptions of reality had to be radically altered. These were not new ideas and had been thoroughly explored in England for centuries, for example, by De Quincey and in France by Celine and Rimbaud. Cohen's *The Favourite Game* was compared favourably with the prose of the Beats by the Shelley scholar Kenneth H. Cameron. Cohen's novel, he thought, had a subtle strong flow and a solid structure that was deceptive. This set Cohen apart from the Beats such as Kerouac, who generally sporadically wrote well but lacked movement.[137]

Trocchi fixed himself on opium in Cohen's Montreal flat on Mountain Street and gave him the residue that lined the rim of the pot used to dissolve it. Being inexperienced in hard drugs Cohen digested the dangerously high residue dosage. In the middle of traffic he suddenly went blind, panicked and collapsed. On recovering Cohen concurred with what was a general impression that Trocchi's company was high risk. Writing from Quebec in 1961, Cohen expressed relief at just ridding himself of Trocchi on a ship bound for England. He commented that Trocchi was a tremendous responsibility and wanted you to feel it and that was his motivation for fixing himself in public, 'he's a public junky'.[138] Although this was Cohen's private view, he wrote a poem about Trocchi that valorized the author for living on the edge and risking his life convinced of his own mission.

During the waning of his career in the late 1970s and early 1980s, Cohen had a severe breakdown and found himself unable to write. He sought medical advice and was given antidepressants by a psychiatrist. The drug levelled out the bottom of his mood, but it also put a ceiling on the heights of his emotions. He

---

[137] Leonard Cohen, letter to Esther, 17 September 1963. Leonard Cohen Papers, Box 11, file 13. Thomas Fisher Library, University of Toronto,

[138] Leonard Cohen, a letter dated Quebec, 61 and addressed Dear Bob. Box 11, file 4, Cohen Papers, Fisher Library, University of Toronto.

was semi-comatose, cushioned by cotton wool barriers, able to write a little, but frustrated by the rate of progress.

Subsequently Cohen's view of the Beat glamorization of drugs was that it was a dangerous experiment, an experiment in which he fully immersed himself. He believed that it had disastrous consequences, but that for some, in mitigation, it may have served a purpose, for a few who experienced some revelations. He nevertheless thought that Beat poetry had something beatific about it.[139]

Dylan, too, was an admirer of Beat poetry. He had been introduced to it in Minneapolis through one of his teachers, Dave Morton, who sang at the Ten O'Clock Scholar. Dylan looked back on those days with affection when he said that there was a great deal of unrest in the air, reinforced by the recitation of poems by Kerouac, Corso, Ginsberg and Ferlinghetti. Ferlinghetti first became acquainted with Dylan in the early 1960s at the opening of The Bear nightclub in Chicago, when Dylan 'wasn't projecting much then', and then again in 1964 around Greenwich Village. Ferlinghetti believed that on the level of imagination Dylan could compare with anyone. He thought his imagery brilliant and psychedelic but that he still thought he needed that guitar. Even though there seemed to be a worldwide revival of poetry he didn't see any connection between it and Dylan.[140] Lawrence Ferlinghetti read at the band's farewell concert, in which Dylan performed, captured in the Scorsese film *The Last Waltz*.

Ferlinghetti thought that Ginsberg was America's greatest poet since Whitman and that he was obviously attracted to Dylan, and 'Dylan Obviously Looks Up to Ginsberg'.[141] Ginsberg was part of Dylan's entourage in the mid-1960s and performed in the 1975 Rolling Thunder Revue. Ginsberg, although central to the Beat scene, was regarded as something of an anomaly in comparison with the likes of Burroughs, Corso and Trocchi. When Cohen met Ginsberg in Athens in 1961 he thought him a nice, quiet, clean-shaven Jewish boy who had fallen in with bad company, namely the beatniks.[142] Marianne Faithful knew him quite well and thought him genial and out of his depth with the rock 'n' roll circus onto which he had latched. Ginsberg's manner, however, disguised a courageousness that cannot be underestimated. The publication of *Howl* got him caught up in

[139] Interview with Robert Sword, December 1984, Reprinted in *Leonard Cohen on Leonard Cohen: Interviews and Encounters,* ed. Burger (Chicago: Chicago Review Press, 2014), p. 165. Also see: https://allenginsberg.org/2014/09/leonard-cohen/. Accessed 23 May 2020.
[140] Robert Shelton interview with Lawrence Ferlinghetti, San Francisco, March 1966. Robert Shelton Archive, Institute for Popular Music, Liverpool University.
[141] Shelton interview with Ferlinghetti, March 1966, p. 1.
[142] Leonard Cohen, letter to his sister Esther, 18 September 1961. Box, 11, file 5, Cohen Papers, Fisher Library, University of Toronto.

an obscenity trial; for criticizing Castro's denunciation of homosexuality he was deported from Cuba; on being elected May King in Prague he was detained by the authorities; and he tried to halt a train carrying nuclear waste by sitting on a railway track in Colorado. In other words, like Trocchi, Ginsberg was committed and wanted to change the world and used his poetry as an instrument. He was a master of stunts and came to be something of a parody of himself, which he seemed to recognize in his own self-deprecating way, especially in 'Ode to Failure'.[143]

By the time Cohen published *The Energy of Slaves* in 1972, he had achieved rock star status on the strength of three albums, *Songs of Leonard Cohen* (1967), *Songs from a Room* (1969) and *Songs of Love and Hate* (1971) and had headlined at the 1970 Isle of Wight Festival. A restless, tired and weary audience, disgruntled about the long delays in setting up equipment and checking sound levels between acts, witnessed a dishevelled, unshaven wreck of a man take the stage at 4.00 am in battle fatigues with his band The Army, spaced-out, tuned-up for what seemed like an eternity, and started to play. Kris Kristofferson thought the audience would slaughter him: 'Then he did the damnest thing you ever saw: he charmed the beast. A lone sorrowful voice did what some of the best rockers in the world had tried to do for three days and failed.'[144]

Cohen's poem 'the 15-year old girls', recommends the trappings of fame to everyone: lamenting that the fifteen-year-old girls he wanted when he was fifteen now succumb to his charms, which is both pleasant and demonstrates that it is never too late: 'I advise you all / To become rich and famous.'[145] This recommendation belies the torment, anguish and drug-fuelled psychosis his lifestyle had precipitated. The gruelling toll the 1972 world tour took on Cohen is captured in Tony Palmer's documentary *Bird on a Wire*. In it an interviewer asked Cohen to define success. He answered, 'Success is survival.'

Cohen's personal anguish and pain is nowhere more hauntingly and disturbingly captured than in his 1971 album *Songs of Love and Hate*. 'Dress Rehearsal Rag', although written much earlier and recorded by Judy Collins in 1966, like 'The 15 Year Old Girls' betrayed his current state of mind, a manic

---

[143] Allen Ginsberg, *Collected Poems* (London: Viking, 1985).

[144] 'How Was He for You? Famous Fans on Why Leonard Cohen Is Essential Listening', *The Observer Magazine*, 14 October 2001, p. 13.

[145] Leonard Cohen, *The Energy of Slaves* (London: Jonathan Cape, 1972), p. 97.

depressive mind. Cohen subsequently felt embarrassed about these poems. Both poems he 'retired' and neither appears in *Stranger Music.*[146]

> That's right, it's come to this,
> Yes it's come to this,
> And wasn't it a long way down,
> Ah wasn't it a strange way down?

Conclusion

What we have suggested is that Dylan Thomas represented for the Beats, Leonard Cohen and Bob Dylan, after them, the fame to which an ultra-bohemian could, and did, aspire through performance poetry. The poems and the poet were inseparable, demanding a heavy price for the exemplification on every public appearance of the irreverence and unconditional irresponsibility of the hipster. In a recent biography of Bob Dylan, the tragedy of the life of the poet did not go unnoticed. The author argues that if Bob Dylan had nothing else in common with Thomas, 'the art of poetry imposed a price, and paid a price . . . Three years and less of fame: a blur, a delirium, something unstoppable'.[147] None of them were deluded about the ambivalence of fame. They were desperate to have it but were often resentful of the spotlight it shone on them. Dylan and Cohen had their strategies of coping, which often entailed complete indulgence of the senses, leading to remorse and repentance, adopting different personas behind which to hide or through which to project themselves. Like Dylan Thomas, 'the loveliest poet of all our days',[148] who succumbed to the tidal wave of fame, they longed for a mask to shield them from the outside world.

[146] Leonard Cohen, *Stranger Music: selected poems and songs* (London: Jonathan Cape, 1993).
[147] Ian Bell, *Once Upon a Time: The Lives of Bob Dylan* (Edinburgh: Mainstream, 2013), p. 25.
[148] Ferlinghetti, 'Belated Palinode for Dylan Thomas', in *These Are My Rivers*, p. 43.

5

The Masked Crusader – Bob Dylan

O make me a mask and a wall to shut from your spies.[1] *– Thomas*
Fan: You don't know who I am, but I know who you are.
Bob Dylan: Let's keep it that way.[2]

'O Make Me a Mask': Dylan, Thomas, Cohen and the mask of fame

In 1937 Dylan Thomas published his poem 'O Make Me a Mask' in the Chicago publication *Poetry*. The poem was an anguished reaction to the fame that he had achieved for himself, as he pleaded for a 'mask and a wall to shut from your spies / Of the sharp, enamelled eyes and the spectacled claws'.[3] Dylan Thomas's later life was characterized by the ambivalence he felt towards his own success. While he sought the limelight and played up to his self-styled public image as the 'Rimbaud of Cwmdonkin Drive', it was ultimately this persona that led to his untimely death. Thomas wore the mask of the unapologetic bohemian not only to garner publicity for his work but also to shield his true self from the prying eyes of the public. Tragically, the lines between Thomas's public and private lives became increasingly blurred, as Theodore Dalrymple observed, 'when you play a part long enough, it becomes what you actually are . . . in the end, the image was the man and it killed him'.[4] This separation of selves can become problematic, as Dylan Thomas's life exemplifies, when the public persona colonizes the true self, rendering the mask's wearer unable to distinguish between the role and the

---

[1] Dylan Thomas, 'O Make Me a Mask', *The Collected Poems of Dylan Thomas: The Centenary Edition*, ed. John Goodby (London: Weidenfeld and Nicholson, 2014), p. 98.
[2] Cited in David Kinney, *The Dylanologists: Adventures in the Land of Bob* (New York: Simon & Schuster, 2014), p. i.
[3] Thomas, *Collected Poems*, p. 98.
[4] Theodore Dalrymple, 'The Rimbaud of Cwmdonkin Drive', *City Journal*, Winter, 2015. https://www.city-journal.org/html/rimbaud-cwmdonkin-drive-13712.html. Accessed 7 May 2020.

reality. When this occurs, we can see the transformative mask as an agent of self-negation and ego destruction, encapsulated in Peter Sellers's famous quip that 'there used to be a "me" behind the mask, but I had it surgically removed'.[5]

The pressures of fame are well documented, and many artists and performers have found themselves lamenting the intrusion of public attention beyond their work and into their private lives. In the face of the sense of public ownership of famous people by their fans, many celebrities use masks and personas as a form of concealment and disguise to hide their true selves from the potentially destructive demands of their fans. 'O Make Me a Mask' provides an interesting framework for us to examine the use of masks and personae employed by Bob Dylan and Leonard Cohen throughout their careers simultaneously to attract and deflect public interest. Both men are often associated, as we saw in the previous chapter, with the Welsh bard, with, as we saw, Cohen describing the character of Breavmen in his novel *The Favourite Game* as 'a kind of mild Dylan Thomas',[6] and it was Dylan Thomas who provided the inspiration for Bob Dylan's stage name.[7] All three men desired fame but were not unaware that it came at a price.

The mask has been a ubiquitous symbol in all human civilizations throughout history – from the rituals of ancient tribes to the classical Greek and Roman theatrical traditions which used masks or 'personas' to allow audiences to see and hear the actors better in large amphitheatres, to the modern tradition of theatre directors, such as Bertolt Brecht and Jean Genet, who used masks to alienate and startle their audiences. The mask has three essential functions: transformation, concealment and revelation.

The first function of the mask is transformation. Both Dylan and Cohen used transformative masks and personas to define themselves as emerging performers, and later when they sought to break free from the fixed images, their audiences held of them in order to continue to grow and evolve as artists. The latter stages of both Dylan's and Cohen's careers are best characterized through the use of transformative masks intended to reclaim their artistic identities and escape the constraints of the immutable figures of 'Leonard Cohen' and 'Bob Dylan' projected upon them by the public – for Dylan, the counterculture hero, for Cohen, the depressive lothario.

---

[5] Peter Sellers quoted in *Halliwell's Filmgoer's Companion: Ninth Edition,* ed. Leslie Halliwell (London: Grafton, 1988), p. 622.

[6] Leonard Cohen, *The Favourite Game,* First published 1963, p. 108.

[7] Bob Dylan, *Chronicles: Volume One* (New York: Simon & Schuster, 2004), pp. 78–9.

The second function of the mask is concealment and disguise. We will investigate Dylan's and Cohen's use of masks and personas as a way to protect and hide their own private selves from the glare of public scrutiny and the dangers inherent in the increasingly blurred lines between the singers' public and private personas.

The final function of the mask is revelation and truth-telling. When wearing a mask, performers often find they are better able to speak honestly while shielded from the consequences and criticisms that might be levelled at them if they were to step out from behind the protective barrier of the mask. The mask also allows Dylan and Cohen to inhabit the different characters that populate their songs and poetry, allowing them to assume varying perspectives while revealing universal truths.

In the previous chapter we examined the desire of the Beat generation, Bob Dylan and Leonard Cohen to emulate the fame that Dylan Thomas achieved in his own lifetime. They were drawn to the Welsh poet's unconventional lifestyle and the apparent freedom from social constraints his fame afforded him, yet when their own celebrity status outstripped Thomas's, they learnt that the trappings of fame were psychologically perilous. In this chapter we examine Bob Dylan's use of 'masks' to project different personas at various stages of his career, both as a form of creative expression and as a way to negotiate the intrusions into his private life by the burgeoning musical press which catered to the fans' demand for unfettered intrusion into their lives. In Chapter 5 we will explore the same themes in relation to Leonard Cohen.

The identity of 'Bob Dylan' has been in constant flux throughout his career, changing with each new musical shift and continuously defying audience expectations. From his roots as a folk singer, Dylan has successively inhabited the roles of the champion of the downtrodden; beatnik symbolist poet; surrealist rock star; American balladeer; the country crooner living in a rural idyll; a shamanic ringleader of a rock and roll circus; an evangelical Christian preacher of fire and brimstone; the world-weary man haunted by the spectre of his own mortality; and in his later years, 'an everyman, who carries the fate of mankind and our mortality in the persona of the vagrant blues artist, whose continuous touring . . . becomes more and more allegorical of our ontological rootlessness'.[8]

---

[8] Christophe Lebold, 'A Face Like a Mask and a Voice That Croaks: An Integrated Poetics of Bob Dylan's Voice, Personae, and Lyrics', *Oral Tradition*, vol. 22, no. 1 (2007), p. 63.

In exploring Dylan's many masks, we will focus on five of his major transformations: folk singer, rock star, country crooner, Rolling Thunder shaman and blues veteran personas. We will examine his use of costumes, characters, masks, voices and musical styles to create a 'theatre of identities'[9] which encourages his audience to participate in the intertextual construction of the 'Bob Dylan' persona. Dylan's Gospel years – though representing a radical shift in identity – have been explored in our chapter on religion.

The mask as transformation

The word 'mask' comes from the Arabic *maskhahra* which means to 'transform' or 'falsify'. The mask allows its wearer to *become* something, or someone, else in the rituals and religions of ancient civilizations, but it has also been used by performers *pretending* to be someone else in theatrical traditions worldwide. Whatever function the mask provides for its wearer, it is always an agent of change and transformation. Donald Pollock states that in tribal contexts, the mask has functioned in ritual practice as a 'technique for transforming identity . . . through the temporary – and representational – extinction of identity'.[10] In these rites, the mask is used to embody tribal ancestors, deities or spirits. The Hopi tribe of northeastern Arizona channel the ancient Kachinas by wearing masks and performing ceremonial dances which involve the entire tribe in celebrating these spirits and appealing for their assistance. S. D. Gill, in studying this phenomenon, remarked that though the Hopi wearing the mask figuratively 'becomes' the sacred Kachina, it is the man who gives life to the mask – 'he becomes the sacred Kachina, yet he continues to be himself'.[11]

Dylan has been associated with masks and personas since he took the music world by storm in the early 1960s. Stephen Scobie notes that an early review by the influential *New York Times* critic Robert Shelton remarked that the young Dylan bore the mark of originality, but when the review was reprinted on the

---

[9] Lebold, 'A Face Like a Mask and a Voice That Croaks', p. 58.

[10] Donald Pollock, 'Masks and the Semiotics of Identity', *Journal of the Royal Anthropological Institute*, vol. 1, no. 3 (September 1995), pp. 581–97, and 582. https://jstor.org/stable/3034576. Accessed 15 April 2020.

[11] S. D. Gill, 'The Shadow of a Vision Yonder', *Seeing with the Native Eye: Essays on Native American Religion*, ed. W. H. Capps (New York: Harper & Row, 1976), p. 55. Quoted Pollock, 'Masks and the Semiotics of Identity', p. 584. In the mythology of the Pueblo people the Kachina is a deified ancestral spirit.

back cover of Dylan's debut album it was misquoted as 'mask'.[12] This misprint
aptly defines Dylan's performing career. As we saw in the previous chapter, both
Dylan and Cohen intentionally sought fame – with the young Dylan telling his
grandmother, 'Grandma, someday I am going to be very famous'[13] – and the
construction of saleable identities were essential to this quest.

Robert Zimmerman did not truly become 'Bob Dylan' until 1961 when
he arrived in New York's Greenwich Village, but the groundwork for this
transformation was laid in his formative years. Dylan experimented with aliases
and the adoption of masks and personas to transform himself as far back as his
days in Hibbing High School. His high school yearbook declared his ambition to
join Little Richard, beneath a black and white photograph of Robert Zimmerman
coiffured in the bouffant style of the rock 'n' roller – the first instance of the
young artist borrowing an identity that was not his own.[14]

In his hometown of Hibbing, Dylan was already performing under the
pseudonym Elston Gunn, but it was not until Dylan moved to Minneapolis
in September 1959 – ostensibly to attend the university, though his academic
career did not last long – that he perfected the image that would go on to define
him. The rock 'n' roll scene in the late 1950s was in a marked decline, and it was
almost impossible to break into a market with a confluence of established acts.
In an instance of ambition over ideals, Dylan knew that if he wanted to make
it in the music industry he would have to discard the mask of the rock 'n' roller
Elston Gunn for a more marketable one, and it was in Minnesota that Dylan
was introduced to the burgeoning folk and blues revival music scene that would
offer him his opportunity for success. Dylan has always been forthcoming about
his reasons for involving himself in the folk movement. In a 1965 interview, he
remarked 'I became interested in folk music because I had to make it somehow'.[15]
In another interview that same year, when questioned about his transition away
from folk into rock music, he admitted that his passion had always been rock 'n'
roll, but

[12] Robert Shelton, '20-Year Old Singer Is Bright New Face at Gerde's Club', *New York Times*, 29
September 1961. Quoted in Stephen Scobie, *Alias Bob Dylan: Revisited* (Calgary, Canada: Red Deer
Press, 2003), p. 46.
[13] Interview with Abe and Beatty Zimmerman, The Robert Shelton Minnesota Transcripts, May 1968,
printed in *Isis: a Bob Dylan Anthology*, ed. Derek Barker (London: Helter Skelter Publishing, 2001),
p. 18.
[14] Paul Williams, *Bob Dylan: Performing Artist 1960-1973* (London: Omnibus Press, 1994), p. 11.
[15] Interview with Nora Ephron and Susan Edmiston, *Positively Tie Dream* (August 1965), reprinted in
Dylan on Dylan, ed. Jonathan Cott (London: Hodder & Stoughton, 2007), p. 51.

you couldn't make it liveable then with rock'n'roll . . . It cost too much bread to make enough money to buy an electric guitar, and then you had to make more money to have enough people to play the music . . . it wasn't an alone kind of thing.[16]

While Dylan saw folk music as an 'easy' way to 'make it',[17] he always denied that he was driven by mercenary gains. For Dylan, 'making it' meant 'being able to be nice and not hurt anybody'.[18] Quite what Dylan meant by this is unclear, but his desire for fame, as we saw in the previous chapter, was undeniable.

During his time in Minneapolis, Robert Zimmerman underwent radical changes that laid the groundwork for his metamorphosis into 'Bob Dylan'. Paul Nelson and Jon Pankake, founders of *The Little Sandy Review* – a Minneapolis-based folk magazine – claimed that 'every few weeks, Bob would become a different person with a different style'.[19] After a summer spent sleeping on friends' floors and gigging at the Satire Lounge in Denver, Colorado,[20] the nineteen-year-old Dylan returned to Minneapolis transformed. One of his acquaintances from the time recalls, 'Dylan came back [from Colorado] with a difference in accent. He spoke differently'.[21]

At this early stage, Dylan was still trying on different masks to find the perfect fit, even if some of the identities he adopted were already claimed. Bonnie Beecher – the woman who is often considered to be the subject of 'The Girl from the North Country' – knew Dylan during his Minneapolis years and claims that

He went on a trip, then he came back, talking with a real thick Oklahoma accent and wearing a cowboy hat and boots. He was into Woody Guthrie in a big big way, and I thought it was very silly . . . You're a Minnesota boy but you're trying to pretend to be something that you're not. But he really immersed himself in Woody Guthrie – kind of absorbed Woody. When he'd had too much to drink, you'd have to call him Woody to get a response . . . now I see it as allowing a greater Bob Dylan to come about.[22]

---

[16] Interview with Joseph Haas, *Chicago Daily News* (27 November 1965), reprinted in *Dylan on Dylan*, ed. Cott, p . 57.

[17] Interview with Joseph Haas, *Dylan on Dylan*, ed. Cott, p. 56.

[18] Interview with Joseph Haas, *Dylan on Dylan*, ed. Cott, p. 56.

[19] Paul Nelson quoted in Shelton, *No Direction Home*, revised and updated edition, ed. Elizabeth Thomson and Patrick Humphries (London: Omnibus Press, 2011), p. 61.

[20] Mark Sanders, 'Twenty Fabled Moments in Denver Music: #11: Bob Dylan Crashed in the Mile High City, 1960', *Westword*, 14 June 2020. https://www.westword.com/music/twenty-fabled-moments-in-denver-music-11-bob-dylan-crashed-in-the-mile-high-city-1960-5712891. Accessed 18 April 2020.

[21] Williams, *Performing Artist*, p. 13.

[22] Jaharana Romney (formerly known as Bonnie Beecher) interviewed by Markus Wittman, 'The Girl from the North Country', in *Wanted Man: In Search of Bob Dylan*, ed. John Bauldie (New York:

By the time Dylan arrived in New York in late January 1961, he had transformed from a nice, middle-class Jewish boy into a radical protest singer. It was not just his name that had changed but his entire manner; he spoke in an affected Okie drawl and wore the costume of a working-class mid-Westerner – denim jeans and checked shirts. His vocal performance played into the identity that he created for himself, with Robert Shelton describing it as 'a rusty voice, suggesting Guthrie's old recordings' which sounded 'like an old farmhand folk singer'.[23] Lebold has argued that Dylan's personae 'emerge from the lyrics and interact with the public image', and in his initial incarnation we can see Dylan's complete transformation into the role of the strident folk-singer.[24] Subsuming himself into the role, Dylan altered his clothes, his speaking and singing voice and created a fictional backstory – in 'My Life in a Stolen Moment' he claims to have hitch-hiked across the United States and Mexico and rode on freight trains before arriving in New York – to align with the fictional working-class folk-hero figure of 'Bob Dylan'.

Though this metamorphosis can be seen as a cynical exploitation of blue-collar American culture, critics such as Paul Williams and Stephen Scobie view it in a far more favourable light. Williams argues that, through donning the transformative mask of 'Bob Dylan', Robert Zimmerman was able to 'shape his perceived image and the very sound of his voice into something that more accurately reflected and made space for who he felt like inside'.[25] Similarly, Scobie believes that the act of becoming 'Bob Dylan' allowed Zimmerman to recreate himself, jettisoning ties with his past, and provided 'the signature that guaranteed the authenticity of what he had become'.[26] While it seems paradoxical that the folk scene, which prided itself on authenticity, was so ready to embrace a man whose entire identity was an artifice, it is also a testament to the power of Dylan's transformative mask. Williams notes that, 'if he had been trying to pass himself off as a person from a particular space who spoke in a certain way, then the accent would have been restrictive, a mask that always has to be remembered and maintained in place'.[27] Instead, Dylan chose a mask that allowed for a transformation that went beyond play-acting and became a more honest representation of his true self.

Citadel Press, 1991), p. 20.

[23] Shelton, *No Direction Home*, p. 84.
[24] Lebold, 'A Face Like a Mask and a Voice That Croaks', p. 58.
[25] Williams, *Performing Artist*, p. 15.
[26] Scobie, *Alias Bob Dylan: Revisited*, p. 41.
[27] Williams, *Performing Artist*, p. 16.

His new name was integral to this transformation. From his days as Elston Gunn to his final choice of 'Bob Dylan', Dylan has always been fascinated by aliases. Throughout his career he has guested on other artists' recordings under various pseudonyms such as 'Bob Landy', 'Tedham Porterhouse', 'Blind Boy Grunt' and – in an obvious allusion to the Welsh poet he has spent most of his professional life trying to disassociate himself from – 'Robert Milkwood Thomas'.[28] He has also made various forays into cinema exploring the importance of names, appearing in Sam Peckinpah's *Pat Garret and Billy the Kid* as 'Alias', and his own 2003 critical failure, *Masked & Anonymous*.

Dylan's choice of stage name has been the subject of intense speculation throughout his career. It has been linked to everyone and everything from the poet Dylan Thomas, Dillon Road in Hibbing, Marshall Matt Dillon from the T.V. Western *Gunsmoke* and an alleged Uncle Dillon, back in Hibbing, Minnesota, but Dylan has been characteristically evasive about the inspiration behind his name. In 1968 he claimed it 'wasn't Dylan Thomas at all, it just came to me'.[29] Echo Halstrom, a girlfriend back in Hibbing, has given a conflicting account – she told Howard Sounes that in 1958 Dylan told her about his new name, pointing to a copy of Dylan Thomas's poems tucked beneath his arm as the source of his inspiration.[30] Halstrom, however, has contradicted this story by also claiming that she and Dylan never discussed his name change but that she had always assumed it came from the Welsh poet. It is interesting to note that – if Halstrom's first story is accurate – the poetry collection that the young Robert Zimmerman purportedly carried around his hometown would most probably have been the 1953 edition of Thomas's *Collected Poetry* which contained 'O Make Me a Mask'.

The origins of the 'Bob Dylan' pseudonym, though the subject of heated debate and hotly contested conjectures, is less important than what the change itself represented. Dylan claims 'that name changed me. I didn't sit around and think about it too much. That is who I felt I was.'[31] Scobie sees Dylan's name change as 'a far reaching gesture of self-definition, rooting his identity in an archetypal trickster's move of self-disguise'.[32] The legal changing of Robert Zimmerman's name to Bob Dylan on 2 August 1962, however, was more than

---

[28] Daniel Karlin, 'Bob Dylan's Names', in *Do You, Mr Jones? Bob Dylan with the Poets and Professors*, ed. Neil Corcoran (London: Chatto & Windus, 2002), p. 27.
[29] *Bob Dylan in His Own Words*, ed. Williams, p. 15.
[30] Howard Sounes, *Down the Highway: The Life of Bob Dylan* (London: Black Swan, 2002), pp. 59–60.
[31] Interview with Ron Rosenbaum, *Playboy* (March 1978), reprinted in *Dylan on Dylan*, ed. Cott p. 206.
[32] Scobie, *Alias Bob Dylan Revisited*, p. 40.

a mere act of disguise – it was a transformation that allowed the young Dylan to cut ties with his past in Hibbing and recreate himself as a freewheelin' folk troubadour. Robert Zimmerman's transformation into 'Bob Dylan' necessitated a rejection of his personal history and he was reluctant to discuss his name change because it recalled his past and reminded his audience of the spectre of Robert Zimmerman behind the mask. Dylan's girlfriend during his time in Greenwich Village was Suze Rotolo, whom he met in 1961, and she discovered his real name only when the contents of Dylan's wallet – including his draft card – fell out in the flat they shared on West Fourth Street.[33]

Though Dylan's new identity was authenticated by legally changing his name, the success of the 'Bob Dylan' persona was predicated on more than just a name – to make the mask believable, Dylan relied on performance, voice, props and costume. Richard F. Thomas argues that 'Dylan's art works in elemental ways, not just through his words and music, but also through his look and appearance'.[34] Each stage of Dylan's career is defined by an iconic look – from the blue jeans and button-down shirts of his folk days to the dark sunglasses and expensive suits of his mid-1960s rock star years, and the mid-1970s ramshackle bohemian chic of bandanas, turbans and flower adorned hatbands of the Rolling Thunder Revue, to his later years where he sports the look of an old-time Mississippi gambler, replete with pencil moustache and cowboy boots. As we will go on to discuss in Chapter 7, theatricality and performance play an integral role in our reaction to the music, and Dylan's scrupulous attention to the props and costuming of each of his personas is essential in making the music come to life.

While Robert Zimmerman is never entirely negated, when he wears his 'Bob Dylan' mask, he *becomes* the legendary figure. Sam Shephard, discussing the Rolling Thunder concerts of the mid-1970s, compared Dylan's performances to 'ancient ritual[s]'[35] such as the Hopi snake dances. Anne Waldman also commented that she saw 'Dylan in performance as the metaphoric shaman'.[36] These comparisons to tribal ceremonies which involve the embodiment of ancient spirits and deities are no coincidence. On stage, Robert Zimmerman

---

[33] Suze Rotolo, *A Freewheelin' Time* (London: Arum Press, 2008), pp. 104–6.

[34] Richard F. Thomas, *Why Dylan Matters* (London: William Collins, 2017), p. 40.

[35] Sam Shephard, *Rolling Thunder Log Book* (London: Penguin, 1977), pp. 74–5, quoted in John D. Hughes, "'This Time We Shall Escape'": Bob Dylan's Rolling Thunder Years', in *Rock Music Studies*, vol. 3, no. 1, pp. 62–79. 72. http://www.tandfonline.com/doi/full/10.1080/19401159.2015.1129830. Accessed 27 April 2020.

[36] Anne Waldman, 'Bob Dylan and the Beats', in *Highway 61 Revisited: Bob Dylan's Road from Minnesota to the World*, ed. Colleen J. Sheehy and Thomas Swiss (Minneapolis: University of Minnesota Press, 2009), p. 257.

harnesses the power of his masking persona to transform into 'Bob Dylan'. In a 1978 interview with Jonathan Cott, Dylan claimed that 'I didn't create Bob Dylan. Bob Dylan has always been here . . . always was. When I was a child, there was Bob Dylan. And before I was born, there was Bob Dylan'.[37] Dylan's quote, though perhaps facetious, makes the figure of 'Bob Dylan' seem like a supernatural force that must be channelled through the vessel of Robert Zimmerman. In this context, Shepard's and Waldman's allusions to shamanic rites is apt. It is also interesting to note that the Rolling Thunder performances are perhaps some of the most energetic, raw and primal of Dylan's career. As John D. Hughes noted,

> at times the music is painful listening . . . as Dylan the artist and Dylan the man come increasingly into contact . . . Dylan's always combustible ratios of self-rejection and self-renewal, of privacy and publicity, were now approximating to a spiritual demolition derby.[38]

The transformative mask of 'Bob Dylan' was essential to Dylan's rise to fame, but the fixed image of the young counterculture hero of the early 1960s has haunted him throughout his career. Dylan's later transformations – from rock star to evangelical preacher – should be viewed as part of a larger struggle for artistic and individual autonomy. By deconstructing and subverting his original persona, Dylan has attempted to wrest control of the immutable figure fixed in the minds of his audience and critics alike, challenging their expectations and often disappointing his original fanbase – shown by the famous shouts of 'Judas' as Dylan finished his electric set at the Manchester Free Trade Hall in 1966 with 'Like a Rolling Stone' – the song that cemented his transformation from folk protest singer to rock superstar.[39]

Christophe Lebold argues that 'Dylan spent most of his career in a cultural war against his original position of hyper-relevance, trying to obliterate his original persona as "mouthpiece of his generation" and regain a sense of cultural anonymity'.[40] The original 'Bob Dylan' persona was created by Dylan himself, but it soon became an entity beyond his control. When Dylan emerged into

---

[37] Interview with Jonathan Cott, *Rolling Stone* (November 1978), reprinted in *Dylan on Dylan,* ed. Cott, p. 269.

[38] Hughes, '"This Time We Shall Escape"', p. 77.

[39] Colin Fleming, 'Remembering Bob Dylan's Infamous "Judas" Show' (17 May 2016) *Rolling Stone.* https://www.rollingstone.com/music/music-news/remembering-bob-dylans-infamous-judas-show-203760/. Accessed 19 May 2020.

[40] Christophe Lebold, 'The Traitor and the Stowaway: Persona Construction and the Quest for Cultural Anonymity and Cultural Relevance in the Trajectories of Bob Dylan and Leonard Cohen', *Journal of the International Association for the Study of Popular Music,* vol. 1, no. 2 (2011), p. 2. DOI: 10.5429/2079-3871(2010)v12.6en. Accessed 4 May 2020.

the public consciousness in the early 1960s, he transformed himself from a Hibbing rock 'n' roll wannabe into a strident young protest singer, but it was Albert Grossman's management, the mass media, the marketing department of Columbia Records and the 'Folk Movement' that constructed the idea of 'Bob Dylan' as the prophetic voice of a generation. Grossman – who represented many major folk and rock acts such as Joan Baez, Peter, Paul and Mary, and The Band – was essential to Dylan's quest for fame. The expert management of Grossman allowed Dylan to navigate an industry notoriously hostile to its artists, allowing him to experiment creatively, while still advancing his career. Grossman promoted the image of Dylan as a prophet, a genius, a voice of his generation, which allowed him to succeed in a mainstream pop market that thrived on formulaic pop songs and easy listening. Though the relationship between the two men ended in a long-standing and acrimonious legal dispute, Peter Yarrow (of Peter, Paul and Mary) believes that 'personally, artistically, and in a business sense, Albert Grossman was the sole reason Bob Dylan made it'.[41]

The transformative mask of 'prophet' thrust upon an at-first receptive Dylan became an unbearable burden as his developing self-image came into conflict with the image the 'folk movement' demanded he conform to; his audience and the critics alike projected their own idealized fantasies of what 'Bob Dylan' represented onto the canvas of a man who had no intention of bowing to the demands they made of him. Though Dylan had sought fame, he had not anticipated the vast scrutiny that would accompany his every word and action – even leading to a new field of cultural studies known as 'Dylanology'.[42]

In his 2004 autobiography, Dylan claims that by the mid-1960s he had grown 'sick of the way my lyrics had been extrapolated . . . subverted into polemics . . . that I had been anointed as the Big Bubba of Rebellion'.[43] Dylan's career trajectory from 1965 onwards can be seen as a systematic dismantling of this 'Bob Dylan' persona through the use of transformative masks and new personas.

The release of 'Like a Rolling Stone' on 20 July 1965 heralded the entrance of a new Dylan onto the stage. Seeking to break free from the folk movement that he felt had co-opted him, Dylan switched his mask and transformed from strident protest singer to sneering rock star.

[41] Rory O'Conner, 'Albert Grossman's Ghost', *Musician Magazine* (June 1987). https://theband.hiof.no /articles/agg_musician_june_1987.html. Accessed 26 June 2020.
[42] See Kinney, *The Dylanologists*.
[43] Dylan, *Chronicles*, p. 120.

Though shocking, Dylan's transformations have always been evolutions, rather than revolutions. Throughout his career, Dylan has continued to grow as an artist by exploring and experimenting with different musical genres, methods of writing and his own performances. Dylan's metamorphosis into the beatnik rock star made him the antithesis of the folk scene that had once championed him, but the transformation had begun before he plugged in his electric guitar. Dylan's fourth studio album, *Another Side of Bob Dylan*, released in August 1964 highlighted his growing distance from the folk movement. The album showed an emerging ambiguity and complexity that had been absent in his earlier 'message' songs. 'My Back Pages' affirms Dylan's disillusionment with his role as the 'voice of a generation', dismissing his 'self-ordained professor's tongue' and the certainty with which he preached 'lies that life is black and white'. *Another Side of Bob Dylan*, while musically rooted in the folk style, showcased Dylan's growing interest in abstract lyricism, inspired by the French symbolist poets, and his move towards a more personal form of songwriting. The album presaged Dylan's rejection of the folk ethos manifest in *Highway 61 Revisited* as he began to experiment with his newest persona.

Another Side of Bob Dylan was greeted with dismay and disappointment upon its release in November 1964. Political activist and editor Irwin Silber penned an open letter to Dylan in which he accused his new songs of being 'inner-directed'.[44] In his scathing attack, Silber accused Dylan of losing touch with 'reality' and being too distracted by the 'paraphernalia of fame'[45] to connect with his audience at the Newport Folk Festival in 1964. Though many lined up to criticize, there were others who rushed to his defense. Phil Ochs, a stalwart of the folk-music scene, responded to critiques by Silber and Paul Wolfe by writing 'when I grow used to an artist's style I damn well expect him not to disappoint me by switching it radically'.[46] He applauded Dylan for 'being honest to himself' and 'not how his fans would react to the change'.[47] Dylan was hurt that former champions of his music were turning their backs on him and informed his manager, Albert Grossman, that he would no longer allow *Sing Out!* magazine to

[44] Irwin Silber, 'An Open Letter to Bob Dylan', *Sing Out!* (November 1964). http://www.edlis.org/twice /threads/open_letter_to_bob_dylan.html. Accessed 24 June 2020.

[45] Silber, 'An Open Letter to Bob Dylan'.

[46] An Open Letter from Phil Ochs to Irwin Silber, Paul Wolfe and Joseph E. Levine, *Broadside* (20 January 1965). Republished on Phil Ochs Blogspot (website). http://phil-ochs.blogspot.com/2009/ 02/in-defense-of-bob-dylan-1965.html. Accessed 25 June 2020.

[47] An Open Letter from Phil Ochs to Irwin Silber, Paul Wolfe and Joseph E. Levine.

publish his songs.[48] It is also rumoured 'Positively 4th Street' (released as a single in 1965) with the lyric 'I know the reason, that you talked behind my back/I used to be among the crowd you're in with' was inspired by Silber's disavowal of him.

The backlash and fury that Dylan's evolution provoked among fans and former friends did nothing to halt his creative exploration. With the release of 'Like a Rolling Stone', Dylan transfigured not only his music but also himself. Gone were the 'faded khaki army shirt with wilted epaulets [and] blanched blue jeans'[49] worn at the 1963 Newport Folk Festival, which were replaced with an eclectic wardrobe of Carnaby Street suits, polka-dot silk shirts[50] and peg-leg trousers. The acoustic guitar was traded for an electric. His vocal performance used 'nasal, sliding pitches and a speech-like, highly rhythmic declamatory style'[51] and became, as 'Hugh Dunnit' writing for the Dylan fanzine *The Telegraph* termed it, a 'primal demon voice'.[52]

It is hard to tell what incensed the folk movement more – Dylan's electric guitar or his expensive clothes, with one interviewer describing his black motorcycle jacket as a 'sell-out jacket'.[53] Greil Marcus notes that, 'pop music symbolized the destruction of [the folk] community by capitalist mass society',[54] and Dylan's transformation into a dandified popstar made him the antithesis of everything the folk community stood for. In order to escape the image of 'Bob Dylan' that was simultaneously his own creation and one created for him, Dylan had to dismantle his original persona and transform into its opposite. What must have been even more galling for the fraternity of the folk movement was that Dylan's change of style and image represented much more than a sell-out to commercialization. The folk movement had gradually replaced and ridiculed the Beat culture that had dominated Greenwich Village, with its self-indulgent verse, accompanied by jazz that exuded a bohemian elitism, and on

---

[48] Shelton, *No Direction Home*, p. 219.

[49] Shelton, *No Direction Home*, p. 131.

[50] Bob Geldof admits to being so impressed by Dylan's 'words, the voice, the shirt' as a thirteen-year old in Dublin in 1965 that he 'painted spots on my blue shirt collar, on the shoulders, and halfway down the front and didn't take my jacket off', in 'Turn the Bleedin' Noise Down, Bobbo', *Uncut Legends #1: Bob Dylan*, 2003, p. 23.

[51] John Herdman, *Voice Without Restraint: A Study of Bob Dylan's Lyrics and Their Background* (New York: Delilah Books, 1982), p. 14, quoted in Michael Daley, 'Vocal Performance and Speech Intonation: Bob Dylan's "Like a Rolling Stone"', *Oral Tradition*, vol. 22, no. 1 (2007).

[52] 'Hugh Dunnit', in *The Telegraph*, quoted in Williams, *Performing Artist*, p. 153.

[53] Interview with Nora Ephron and Susan Edminston, *Positively Tie Dream* (August 1965) in *Dylan on Dylan*, ed. Jonathan Cott (London: Hodder, 2006), p. 52.

[54] Greil Marcus, *Like a Rolling Stone: Bob Dylan at the Crossroads* (London: Faber & Faber, 2006), p. 179.

the surface, at least, was radically individualistic. Bob Dylan, in openly rejecting the social responsibility and collectivism of the folk movement, openly and ostentatiously associated with the very people it had rejected and the values of social irresponsibility they represented. While having admired the Beats, especially, Kerouac, Corso, and Ginsberg, from his days in Minneapolis, he was now adopted by them.

These dramatic shifts in persona continued throughout his career, but they were never entirely unprecedented. In 1969, Dylan surprised everyone with the release of *Nashville Skyline*, a bucolic album of charming country songs. The mask of the 'country crooner' whose songs included a list of his favourite pie fillings – 'Blueberry, apple, cherry, pumpkin and plum' ('Country Pie') – disconcerted audiences who had grown used to the abstract symbolism and dystopian visions of Dylan's oeuvre since 1965. In a year that saw the Stonewall Riots, the escalation of the Vietnam War and widespread civil unrest, fans were angered at Dylan's escape into rural idyll and 'undemanding' and 'one-dimensional'[55] lyrics. Yet, to anyone paying attention, Dylan's latest musical evolution should not have come as a shock. Dylan had recorded *Blonde on Blonde* and *John Wesley Harding* with country musicians in Nashville before the release of *Nashville Skyline*. Dylan first met the legendary country-singer Johnny Cash at the Newport Folk Festival in 1964 and an enduring friendship and respect was established when Cash presented Dylan with his guitar.[56] Cash later duetted with Dylan on *Nashville Skyline's* 'Girl from the North Country', but he had previously performed country versions of Dylan's songs, such as 'Don't Think Twice It's Alright' in 1965 and 'It Ain't Me Babe' in 1967. The album *John Wesley Harding* intimated what Jann S. Wenner of *Rolling Stone* magazine described as Dylan's 'natural and logical move'[57] into country music, particularly with its last track 'I'll Be Your Baby Tonight'. Just as Dylan had outgrown his folk-hero persona, he now found tha the mask of the jaded rock star no longer suited him as he continued to grow and evolve as an artist.

Perhaps the most startling aspect of Dylan's transformation into 'country crooner' was the radical change in his voice. Like his name change, Dylan was reluctant to discuss the complete shift in his vocal performance from nasal drawl

---

[55] Robert Christagau, 'Obvious Believers', *Village Voice*, May 1969. https://www.robertchristgau.com/xg/bk-aow/dylan.php. Accessed 10 June 2020.

[56] Jann S. Wenner, 'Country Tradition Goes to Heart of Dylan Songs', in *Rolling Stone*, 26 May 1968. https://www.rollingstone.com/music/music-news/country-tradition-goes-to-heart-of-dylan-songs-246091/. Accessed 26 June 2020.

[57] Wenner, 'Country Tradition Goes to Heart of Dylan Songs'.

to a buttery-soft lilt, telling Jann Wenner of *Rolling Stone*, 'stop smoking those cigarettes, and you'll be able to sing like Caruso'.[58] Dylan was also adamant that 'the songs reflect more of the inner me than the songs of the past',[59] just as he declared that the name 'Bob Dylan' was a more accurate reflection of who he truly was. In his review of *Nashville Skyline*, Robert Christagau claimed that 'as always, Dylan insists that the new Dylan is the real one . . . I am certain Dylan is sincere, but I am also certain he was sincere about protest music . . . he is a master image manipulator, but his mastery has always been instinctual'.[60]

While the 'Bob Dylan' of 1969 felt that his 'true self' was a cheerful cowpoke, his country 'mask' did not stay in place for long. Dylan has remained in a constant state of flux, switching masks and personas with each musical shift, with his latest incarnation as an itinerant blues-man, restless and always on the road, unable to settle down. This persona is performed not just in the music, which relies heavily on blues twelve-chord progressions, but in his costume of pencil-thin moustache, Mississippi gambler hats and bolero ties. Dylan's voice, too, reflects this new persona, with Lebold claiming that '[his] more recent broken voice enables him to present a worldview at the sonic surface of the songs – this voice carries us across the landscape of a broken, fallen world'.[61]

Through his constant reinventions and shapeshifting, Dylan has ensured that his only defining feature is indeterminacy. Kat Peddie argues that this inconsistency is essential to his music – 'his shifts in persona are mirrors to his musical shifts, and this need to shift, to create indeterminacy over what "Dylan" himself is and does, is much of the power of his music, and the reason he is still interesting, exciting and relevant'.[62] Indeed, Dylan's shifting personas have a transformative effect not just on his current music but his back catalogue. The new mask transforms the old classics. In performance, Dylan reinvents and reimagines his oeuvre, rearranging music, melody, rhythm and timbre and additionally changing the lyrics to suit his current persona; memorably in 1978 he changed the lyrics of 'Tangled up in Blue' to omit the reference to the Italian poet in favour of a series of biblical citations which changed each night of the tour to coincide with his rebirth as an evangelical Christian. Dylan's

[58] Jann S. Wenner, 'Bob Dylan Talks: A Raw and Extensive First Rolling Stone Interview', *Rolling Stone* (29 November 1969). https://www.rollingstone.com/music/music-news/bob-dylan-talks-a-raw-and-extensive-first-rolling-stone-interview-90618/. Accessed 10 June 2020.
[59] Interview with Hubert Saal, *Newsweek* (14 April 1969).
[60] Christagau, 'Obvious Believers', *Village Voice*.
[61] Lebold, 'A Face Like a Mask and a Voice That Croaks', p. 65.
[62] Kat Peddie, "I Is Somebody Else': Bob Dylan/Arthur Rimbaud', in *Popular Music History*, vol. 8, no. 2 (2013), pp. 169–88, p. 184.

continual confounding of expectations can be seen in light of Scobie's belief that Dylan is an archetypal 'trickster', continually playing games and tricks on his audience, but it is also symptomatic of his continual need to wrest control of the images and personae that have been projected upon him by his public.

The mask as disguise: Protecting the private self from the public gaze

In 1961, after signing with Columbia Records, Dylan informed girlfriend Suze Rotolo, 'this is the beginning of what I have always known. I am going to be big'.[63] While Dylan knew he was destined for fame, he began to resent the sense of public expectation that came with it and the ownership his audience felt over him. In his *Chronicles*, he recalls being angered by Ronnie Gilbert introducing him to the crowd at the Newport Folk Festival by saying, 'take him, you know him, he's yours'.[64] Dylan writes, 'screw that! As far as I knew, I didn't belong to anybody then or now'.[65]

We have seen how Dylan employed the transformative use of masks and personas to both promote and protect his artistry, but the mask has also been essential for Dylan to separate his 'public' and 'private' self from the scrutiny of both fans and critics alike. In this section, we will examine the mask's second function of disguise and concealment and the role it has played in preserving Dylan's sense of self in the media spotlight.

Chris Rojek has argued that celebrities must necessarily create a 'public' and 'private' self to survive the intense pressure of the global gaze. The idea of protecting the private self behind differing masks and personas is not the sole preserve of celebrities. Irving Goffman noted in *The Presentation of Self in Everyday Life* that it is necessary to adopt different masks in different situations to function within society. Quoting George Santayana, he claimed 'living things in contact with the air must acquire a cuticle'.[66] George Herbert Mead argued that everyone within a society has a 'veridical' self ('I') and a self that is observed

---

[63] Rotolo, *A Freewheelin' Time*, p. 158.
[64] Dylan, *Chronicles*, p. 115.
[65] Dylan, *Chronicles*, p. 115.
[66] George Santayana, *Soliloquies in England and Later Soliloquies* (London: Constable, 1922) quoted in Irving Goffman, *The Presentation of Self in Everyday Life* (London: Penguin, 1990) opening quotation.

by others ('me'),[67] a concept echoed in Sartre's conception of 'The Look'. Sartre contended that we become aware of our own objectivity when we are viewed by others. The look of others 'identifies me with my external acts and appearances, with my self-for-others. It threatens, by ignoring my free subjectivity, to reduce me to the status of a thing in the world.'[68] Fame invites a global 'look'. For the celebrity, the separation between private and public self is far more pronounced, perilous and imperative. To survive the continual process of 'Othering' by the global gaze, the celebrity must create what the existentialist philosopher Søren Kierkegaard termed an 'inner sanctum'. Kierkegaard himself wrote under various pseudonyms, maintaining that 'an author certainly must have his private personality as everyone has, but this must be his ἄδυτον [inner sanctum] . . . just as the entrance to a house is barred by stationing two soldiers with crossed bayonets'.[69] This inner sanctum is essential to preserving the integrity of the public figure's self-hood, and both Dylan and Cohen have used the separation of private and public personas through masking and concealment to survive the pressures and pitfalls of fame.

In a 1986 press conference, Dylan declared, 'I'm only Bob Dylan when I have to be', prompting a bemused reporter to question who he was the rest of the time. 'Myself', came the succinct response.[70] This hints that Zimmerman's transformation into 'Bob Dylan' is less complete than we might suppose. The 'Bob Dylan' mask allowed a young middle-class boy from Hibbing, Minnesota, with a population of around 16,000 throughout the 1950s and 1960s,[71] to metamorphose into the rebellious counterculture folk hero whose image and music defined the early 1960s, but it also provided him with a false sense of protection in the face of overwhelming media attention and scrutiny, to which he eventually succumbed when he retreated to Woodstock to re-invent himself. Dylan recalls this time in his *Chronicles*.

> People think that fame and riches translates into power . . . sometimes it doesn't. I found myself stuck in Woodstock [his family home outside New York], vulnerable and with a family to protect. If you looked in the press, though, you

---

[67] George Herbert Mead, *Mind, Self and Society* (Chicago: University of Chicago Press, 1934).
[68] Hazel Barnes, *Meddling Gods: Four Essays on Classical Themes* (Lincoln: University of Nebraska Press, 1974), pp. 93–4. Quoted in Peddie, 'I Is Somebody Else', p. 186.
[69] SKS 8:94/TA 99 quoted in Jamie A. Lorentzen, 'Kierkegaard, Dylan and *Masked and Anonymous* and Neighbour Love', in *Kierkegaard, Literature and the Arts*, ed. Eric Ziolkowski (Illinois: Northwestern University Press, 2018), p. 284. https://www.jstor.org/stable/j.ctv3znxrg.20. Accessed 15 April 2020.
[70] Press Conference, 1986, quoted in Williams, *Bob Dylan in His Own Words*, quoted in Daniel Karlin, 'Bob Dylan's Names', p. 46.
[71] 'Number of Inhabitants: Minnesota', p. 11, www2.Census.gov. Accessed 29 May 2020.

saw me being portrayed as anything but that. It was surprising how thick the smoke had become.[72]

Sven Birkerts has noted that Dylan's career has been a 'procession of masquerades'.[73] He was 'never not posing. Not even in his most "authentic", unwashed, scraggly, "troubadour" days. He was . . . always Robert Zimmerman trick-or-treating, donning the garb of the wanderer, the hard-luck Woody Guthrie, or the lyric surrealist'.[74] Birkerts believes that these poses are a form of self-protection, allowing Dylan a defence against the increasing encroachment of his audience. It is also a way for Dylan to reconcile the conflicting facets of his own personality – as he sings in 'I Contain Multitudes', from his most recent album, *Rough and Rowdy Ways* (2020): 'I'm a man of contradictions, I'm a man of many moods, I contain multitudes'. Perhaps the most dichotomous aspects of Dylan's nature are his ambition and his idealism. As we saw Dylan not only sought fame but he also held idealistic views about art, society and ethics. When Dylan moved away from his early 1960s finger-pointing songs to explore personal and spiritual themes in his music, he was accused of selling out and turning his back on the cause. Birkerts attests that Dylan has used the 'Bob Dylan' disguise to free himself from accountability for these contradictory positions. Dylan, in what Scobie might term his 'trickster' persona, answered these accusations by explaining to Nat Hentoff of *Playboy* magazine that he moved away from folk and into rock music through 'carelessness' and that 'the word "protest" . . . was made up for people undergoing surgery'.[75]

Beyond using his persona as a tactical evasion from difficult questions from the press, the 'Bob Dylan' disguise also serves to protect Dylan from the expectations and pressures that his fame has imposed upon him. When asked by a journalist whether his audience expected heroism from the imagined 'Bob Dylan' persona, Dylan answered tellingly in the third-person, stating that 'Bob Dylan isn't a cat, he doesn't have nine lives, so he can only do what he can do . . . not break under the strain'.[76]

---

[72] Dylan, *Chronicles*, p. 115.

[73] Sven Birkerts, 'The Ghost of Electricity: The Dylan Face', in *Conjunctions*, no. 46: Subversions: Essays on the World at Large (2006), pp. 263–74, and 263. https://jstor.org/stable/24516747. Accessed 15 April 2020.

[74] Birkerts, 'The Ghost of Electricity', p. 264.

[75] Interview with Nat Hentoff, *Playboy Magazine* (March 1966) reprinted in *Dylan on Dylan*, ed. Cott, p. 100.

[76] Interview with Ron Rosenbaum, *Playboy* (March 1978) reprinted in *Dylan on Dylan*, ed. Cott, p. 233.

In 1978, Dylan appeared on the front cover of *Rolling Stone* magazine, glaring out at the reader from behind his by now signature dark sunglasses. The iconic image, taken by Annie Leibovitz, captures what Jonathan Cott later identified as 'the "Bob Dylan" mask'.[77] The series of photographs accompanying the interview reveal the slow removal of this mask; in one shot, Dylan has removed his shades but circles his fingers around his eyes 'like a child making a mask'.[78] The final picture is Dylan, head tilted, glancing shyly up at the camera, suddenly unsure of himself now that he is stripped of his mask. Upon seeing the image again in 2006, Cott remarked 'how she [Leibovitz] got him to do that, I don't know'.[79] Dylan's removal of his mask in this final shot is perhaps a testament to the trust built between photographer and subject, but it also attests to the protective nature of the mask. Stripped of artifice and disguise, Dylan loses his rock star bravado and is unable to face the camera head on, revealing his true self in all its vulnerability.

Throughout his career, Dylan has made use of the mask as a form of concealment and disguise to reject his audience's expectations and the fixed image of 'Bob Dylan' that has become embedded in popular consciousness. This approach has allowed him to continue to evolve as an artist, but it is also essential to the survival of his 'self' on the world stage. By rejecting the notion of a fixed self, both in public and private, Dylan escapes the crisis that many celebrities face in keeping separate the 'veridical' and 'public' self.

The mask of 'Bob Dylan' has always been worn with the knowledge that it can be taken off when the stage lights dim and the audience disperses. While he wears it, Zimmerman is transformed into Dylan, just as the Hopi *becomes* the Kachina, but the self is never truly extinguished behind the mask, simply preserved. Dylan's self, by continually shifting, is never colonized by one identity or disguise, because it is in a constant state of flux. For Dylan, the rejection of a public immutable 'self' is a means of survival.

Dylan has always presented a nebulous conception of his own identity; he refutes the idea that his personality should be contained by narrow definitions and perimetres. Adhering to the Heraclitian adage that no man can step in the same river twice, Dylan has declared that 'I think one thing today . . . another thing tomorrow . . . I wake and I'm one person, and when I go to sleep I'm

---

[77] Anthony De Curtis, 'The Dylan Mask', in *Rolling Stone* (May/June 2006). Accessed 11 May 2020. https://www.rollingstone.com/music/music-news/the-dylan-mask-68281/.

[78] De Curtis, 'The Dylan Mask'.

[79] De Curtis, 'The Dylan Mask'.

someone else. I don't know *who* I am most of the time.'[80] This refusal, both publicly and privately, to align his identity to a conception of his core 'self' has allowed Dylan to survive for decades in the spotlight.

The mask as revelation: The truth from behind the mask

Dylan's disguises are not solely a means to distinguish the man from the myth. Daniel Karlin believes that assuming various personas and disguises allows Dylan to explore the lives of others. He argues, 'this assumed character is the horn of plenty (the father of multitudes) from which the songs pour.'[81] Dylan has used masks and disguises in both his music and his experimentations in film to explore concepts of self and 'Otherhood'. Peter Meineck, a classical scholar, claims that in antiquity masks were a way for the performers to distinguish themselves from their audience – 'the wearer of the mask is immediately separated from the spectators . . . the simple act of donning a mask indicates that a performance is about to take place,' but the mask also 'demands to be watched'.[82] Disguised as his lyrical characters, Dylan has become adept at employing the mask's final function – that of revelation.

The mask's role as an agent of revelation may seem at odds with its uses for transformation and concealment, but these functions work in harmony to become a powerful tool for self-exposure. As Oscar Wilde once said, 'man is least himself when he talks in his own person. Give him a mask, and he will tell you the truth.'[83]

In a 2010 interview with the *Los Angeles Times*, Joni Mitchell launched an unexpected attack on Bob Dylan, claiming that 'Bob is not authentic at all. He's a plagiarist, and his name and voice are fake. Everything about Bob is a deception.'[84] She clarified her statement in a later interview where she stated

[80] Bob Dylan quoted in *Studio A: The Bob Dylan Reader,* ed. Benjamin Hedin (New York: Norton, 2004), p. 236. Quoted in Paul Lulewicz and Peter Vernezze, 'I Got My Bob Dylan Mask On: Bob Dylan and Personal Identity', in *It's Alright Ma (I'm Only Thinking): Bob Dylan and Personal Identity,* ed. Carl J. Porter, Peter Vernezze and William Irvin (Illinois: Open Court, 2011), p. 132.

[81] Karlin, 'Bob Dylan's Names', p. 47.

[82] Peter Meineck, 'The Neuroscience of the Tragic Mask', *Arion: A Journal of Humanities and the Classics,* Third Series, vol. 19, no. 1 (Spring/Summer), p. 121. https://www.jstor.org/stable/41308596. Accessed 17 April 2020.

[83] Oscar Wilde, 'The Critic as Artist', in *Oscar Wilde: The Complete Collection,* ed. M. Mataev (Di Lernia Publishers, 2013), eBook.

[84] Matt Diehl, 'It's a Joni Mitchell Concert, Sans Joni', *Los Angeles Times,* 22 April 2010. https://www.lat imes.com/archives/la-xpm-2010-apr-22-la-et-jonimitchell-20100422-story.html. Accessed 16 April 2020.

that Dylan 'borrowed his voice from old hillbillies' and 'invented a character to deliver his songs'.[85] She admitted that sometimes she wished she had done the same, because the 'Bob Dylan' character is 'a mask of sorts'[86] which allows him to explore beyond his personal experience, examining the lives of others by inhabiting lyrical characters and adopting varying masks and personas.

The folk movement equated integrity with authenticity and was unable to accept Dylan's transformation from 'a youthful proletarian hobo'[87] who spoke for his generation into a self-reflective dandified rock star who consorted with nihilistic and self-indulgent Beatniks. His shift in persona was taken as a betrayal, and many felt they had been deceived into believing in a Dylan that had never existed. In a Judeo-Christian framework, concealment and disguise are synonymous with dishonesty, which is considered immoral. Moral philosophers, however, have debated over the absolute morality of honesty and argued that there are situations and contexts where deceit can serve a greater cause. The Christian philosopher Søren Kierkegaard advocated the idea of 'pious fraud', wherein deliberate deceit or concealment could be considered a moral act if the lie did more good, or less harm, than the truth. In relation to Dylan's use of masks, disguises and personas, we can argue that as an agent of revelation and truth-telling, the mask-wearer commits a 'pious fraud' for a greater cause.

Kierkegaard, however, was sceptical of theatricality and concealment when it was '*unconfessed*'.[88] In his conclusion to *An Unscientific Postscript*, published under the pseudonym 'Johannes Climacus', Kierkegaard steps out from behind the theatrical curtain and announces himself as the text's true author. The work is a critique of the Hegelian concept of theatricality, yet it employs theatrical devices to make its points. Kierkegaard is not attacking theatricality per se, but theatricality that does not disclose itself as such. Indeed, his work anticipates the innovations of the German theatre director Bertolt Brecht. Brecht experimented with various techniques to 'alienate' and 'distance' his audiences, exposing the artifice of the theatre as he did so. His actors would break the fourth wall, wear masks, step out of character or call attention to the staging cues – screaming

---

[85] *CBC Music,* 'Joni Mitchell on Bob Dylan'. *YouTube* video, 04:39. 11 June 2013. https://www.youtube.com/watch?time_continue=275&v=gZY8aDg_dTI&feature=emb_logo.

[86] *CBC Music,* 'Joni Mitchell on Bob Dylan'.

[87] Lebold, 'The Traitor and the Stowaway', p. 3.

[88] Howard Pickett, 'Beyond the Mask: Kierkegaard's Postscript as Antitheatrical, Anti-Hegelian Drama', in *Kierkegaard, Literature and the Arts*, ed. Eric Ziolkowski (Illinois: Northwestern University Press, 2018), p. 111. https://www.jstor.org/stable/j.ctv3znxrg.20. Accessed 15 April 2020.

'cue the angry red spotlight' to the stagehands.[89] This intentional disruption of the audience's suspension of disbelief was intended to expose the emotional manipulation of traditional bourgeois theatre and the dangers that this could pose in the hands of propogandists. Artifice, then, is not always immoral, providing the audience is aware of it.

In the ancient tradition of Japanese 'Noh' theatre, actors wear masks that do not fully veil their faces. Schechner has called this an 'intentionally incomplete transformation'[90] which alerts audiences to the artifice, and in doing so transforms theatre into real life, and real life into theatre. R. L. Grimes has stated that the masking process in its truest form is not one of concealment or transformation, but revelation. When the face and mask are unified,

> one no longer is worn by his mask, no longer merely hides behind his mask, and does not tease himself into believing he can become maskless, but instead takes responsibility for his mask and wears it so his face, society, and gods, are seen through it but not identified with it.[91]

Dylan has always been aware of the importance of masks and disguise in his work. On 31 October 1964, he appeared onstage at the Philharmonic Hall in New York and told a delighted audience that 'it's just Halloween. I have my Bob Dylan mask on. I'm masquerading.' A decade later, on the same date, Dylan took to the stage in Plymouth, Massachusetts, wearing a real mask. Sam Shephard – playwright, director and Dylan collaborator – recalls the event in his *Rolling Thunder Logbook*, writing that 'Dylan appears in a rubber Dylan mask[92] that he'd picked up on 42nd Street. The crowd is stupefied . . . is this some kind of mammoth hoax? An imposter! The voice sounds the same. If it is a replacement, he is doing a good job.'[93] After an unsuccessful attempt to play the harmonica through his mask, Dylan was forced to reveal himself 'to a bewildered audience . . . still wondering if this is actually him or not.'[94] The concert footage was later used

[89] L. M. Bogad, 'The Alienation Effect', Beautifultrouble.org (website). https://beautifultrouble.org/t heory/alienation-effect/. Accessed 25 May 2020.

[90] R. Schechner, 'Towards a Poetics of Performance', in *Essays on Performance Theory*, ed. R. Schechner (New York: Drama Book Specialists, 1977), p. 4. Quoted in Pamela J. Stewart and Andrew J. Strathern, 'How Masks Work, or Masks Work How?' *Journal of Ritual Studies*, vol. 2, no. 1 (Winter 1988), p. 63. https://www.jstor.org/stable/44378364. Accessed 15 April 2020.

[91] R. L. Grimes, 'Masking: Towards a Phenomenology of Exteriority', *Journal of the American Academy of Religion*, vol. 43, no. 3 (1975), p. 516. Quoted in Stewart and Strathern, 'How Masks Work, or Masks Work How?' p. 63.

[92] There is speculation over the mask Dylan wore that night, but the consensus seems to be that it was a Richard Nixon mask, not a Bob Dylan one.

[93] Shephard, *Rolling Thunder Logbook*, p. 114.

[94] Shephard, *Rolling Thunder Logbook*, p. 114.

as the opening scene in Dylan's 1975 film *Renaldo & Clara* which plays with masks, disguises and theatricality as it explores the nebulous concept of selfhood. During an interview given to promote the film, Dylan remarked that 'the mask in this movie isn't used to hide the inner self, it's used to show the inner self. The mask is more real than the face. It isn't hiding anything'.[95] This mirrors Oscar Wilde's belief that masks were an agent of truth. In his essay 'The Critic as Artist', Wilde contends that art reveals the truth because the concealment of the artist behind the mask of his work allows him to speak openly. He illustrates this with the example of William Shakespeare – 'it is because he never speaks of himself in his plays that his plays reveal him to us absolutely'.[96] Wilde's aesthetic theory parallels Dylan's own philosophy of performance. Wilde argued that 'to arrive at what one really believes, one must speak through lips different from one's own'[97] which is what Dylan has always done through his use of both stage personas and the varying narrative voices employed in his lyrics.

The mask that Dylan wears in the opening footage of *Renaldo & Clara* is translucent, allowing his audience a glimpse of the man beneath it, following the Brechtian and Kierkegaardian tradition of revealing the artifice inherent in all performance. In the movie, Ronnie Hawkins plays Bob Dylan, but Bob Dylan also appears as the character Renaldo. In a 1978 interview, Dylan attempted to explain this to a bemused Jonathan Cott, who asked, 'so Bob Dylan . . . may or not be in the film?'[98]

Martin Scorsese took his lead from Dylan's love of masks, disguises and switched identities when he created the Netflix documentary *Rolling Thunder Revue*. While the documentary appears to be a factual account of the 1975 tour, it features interviews with actors who play composite – or in some cases entirely fictional – characters who never attended the concerts. This is only revealed to the sharp-eyed observer when the credits roll and we see a list of 'The Players' crediting Michael Murphy as 'The Politician' – referring to the Michigan representative Jack Tanner who is interviewed in the film and whose name is taken from Robert Altman's satirical mockumentary *Tanner '88*.[99] While

---

[95] 'Interview with Bob Dylan', *Macleans* (March 20, 1978), pp. 4–6. Quoted in Scobie, *Alias Revisited*, p. 51.

[96] Wilde, 'The Critic as Artist'.

[97] Wilde, 'The Critic as Artist'.

[98] 'Interview with Jonathan Cott', *Rolling Stone* (26 January 1978) reprinted in *Dylan on Dylan*, ed. Cott, p. 173.

[99] Ann Powers, 'To Capture Bob Dylan's Rolling Thunder Revue, Martin Scorsese Had to Get Weird', *NPR.org* (10 June 2019, 10:00 pm). https://www.npr.org/2019/06/10/731305441/to-capture-bob -dylans-rolling-thunder-revue-martin-scorsese-had-to-get-weird. Accessed 16 April 2020.

Scorsese's technique stretches the definition of 'documentary', it was also the best way to capture to essence of the Rolling Thunder tour which used theatricality, masks and disguises to reveal truths to its audiences.

Masks 'serve to liberate the wearer from the inhibitions, laws and niceties of a seemingly well-ordered everyday life', allowing the man behind the mask to reveal his true nature and speak openly, but they also serve to remind the spectator that 'chaos and destruction and mutability are always with us'.[100] The chaotic nature of the Rolling Thunder Revue parallels not only the Brechtian technique of audience alienation but also Brecht's contemporary Antonin Artaud who championed the idea of the 'theatre of cruelty'. Artaud shared the same conception of theatre as those in antiquity – it was not a form of entertainment but a process through which religious or numinous experiences were stimulated. Artaud sought to disrupt his audience's senses, rejecting plot, form, characterization and often words, in favour of gestures, noise and irrationality. Subverting the framework of traditional theatre and bourgeois taste, Artaud wanted to shock spectators out of complacency, causing them to engage with an expanded reality and involve them at such a visceral level that their 'whole organism should have been shaken into participation'.[101]

Dylan was familiar with Brecht's work through Suze Rotolo, his girlfriend during his Greenwich Village years, who is photographed alongside him on the album cover of *The Freewheelin' Bob Dylan* (1963).[102] Rotolo was the assistant to the stage manager of The Sheridan Square Playhouse and invited Dylan to sit in on rehearsals for a staging of *Brecht on Brecht*. She notes that he was captivated by the performance of the song 'Pirate Jenny' – 'He sat still and quiet. Didn't even jiggle his leg. Brecht would be part of him now.'[103]

The Rolling Thunder Revue, with its ramshackle gypsy troupe and disorienting carnivalesque atmosphere, draws upon Brecht and Artaud's own ideas of theatricality. The overt theatricality of the performances where Dylan appeared onstage bedecked in silk scarves and turbans, his face smeared with

---

[100] J. Foreman, *Maskwork* (Cambridge: Lutterworth Press, 2000), pp. 27–9. Quoted in David Roy, 'Masks as a Method: Meyerhold to Mnouchkine', *Cogent Arts & Humanities*, vol. 3, no. 1, p. 2. https://doi.org/10.1080/23311983.2016.1236436. Accessed 25 April 2020.

[101] Bettina Knapp, 'Antonin Artaud's Revolutionary Theatre of Cruelty', *Today's Speech*, vol. 17, no. 3 (1969), p. 26. DOI: 10.1080/01463376909368892. Accessed 20 April 2020.

[102] It is also interesting to note that recalling the photoshoot for the album, Rotolo remembered that it had been freezing cold that day in New York and she had chosen to wear a thick sweater. Dylan, 'conscious of being in the process of creating an image for himself, pulled on a thin suede jerkin and shivered'. Quoted in Richard Williams, 'Tomorrow Is a Long Time', *The Guardian*, 16 August 2008. https://www.theguardian.com/books/2008/aug/16/biography.bobdylan. Accessed 15 June 2020.

[103] Rotolo, *A Freewheelin' Time*, p. 235.

white grease paint, stands in sharp contrast to the early 1960s when he appeared on stage with just a guitar, harmonica and a rakishly tilted hat. The illusion of intimacy generated by Dylan's minimalist early performances was shattered by the surreal freak-show anarchy of the Rolling Thunder years. The flamboyant theatricality – both in costume and in performance – created not only an aesthetic distance between the band and its audience but also a more authentic experience by exposing the artifice of performance and doing away with the false intimacy of the pared-down acoustic performances.

The Rolling Thunder Revue was also the first time that Dylan performed the newly written track 'Isis', written during a period of marital breakdown. Announcing the song to the crowd at Plymouth, Massachusetts, Dylan told them, 'this is a true story ... actually they're all true.' Jason Bailey, who was in attendance that night, claims that he had never seen Dylan perform with such intensity and physicality, 'letting himself go, even behind that white greasepaint'.[104] In fact, it was exactly because he was 'behind' the white greasepaint that Dylan was able to let himself go and expose his own raw emotions and, through doing so, reveal the enduring truth of love and heartbreak.

The mask acts as an agent for revelation because it shields the truth-teller from the ramifications of his speech. Masks were used in Ancient Greek theatre to distinguish the actors from their spectators and to augment the player's expressions so that those at the back of the large amphitheatres could see. The masks, however, also protected the performer from 'direct identification with any political ramifications from performances ... allowing the performer and spectator to feel safe and immune from the performance'.[105] Dylan's choice of white face paint for the Rolling Thunder performances is significant in this respect. Commentators have noted the white mask as an inversion of the black face minstrelsy with which Dylan has been fascinated, but it has also been likened to the masks used in the *commedia dell'arte* tradition. This comparison is interesting because the fifteenth-century art form consisted of a troupe of stock characters and basic plots which allowed actors to improvise their dialogue, giving them the liberty to take swipes at the political establishment or comment on social situations, which would have been censored in scripted comedies.[106]

---

[104] Jason Bailey, '"Actually, They're All True": "Isis" and the Slipping of Bob Dylan's Mask', *Flavorwire*, 28 June 2019. https://www.flavorwire.com/617558/actually-theyre-all-true-isis-and-the-slipping-of-bob-dylans-mask. Accessed 11 May 2020.

[105] Roy, 'Masks as Method: Meyerhold to Mnouchkine', p. 4.

[106] Jennifer Meagher, 'Commedia dell'arte', in *Heilbrunn Timelien of Art History* (New York: The Metropolitan Museum of Art, 2000). https://www.metmuseum.org/toah/hd/comm/hd_comm.htm. Accessed 27 April 2020.

The actors wore masks which not only identified their characters but also allowed them to speak with impunity in their character's voices. The white mask was the signifier of the Pederolino character (also known as Pierrot or Pagilaccio) whose white face was sometimes adorned with a single tear drop to represent his melancholy. Pederolino is one of the *zanni* or servant characters who is an equivalent of the Shakespearean fool. Though he appears naïve and ridiculous, he perceives truths that his masters cannot. This is illustrated in Palaprat's *La fille de bon sens* (1692), when Pierrot muses on his elderly employer's unsuccessful wooing of a younger woman:

> And I'm supposed to think he's a great man of learning after that? Ah, mother and father, how grateful I am to you for never having made me learn to read! . . . Science and books make only fools I've never known anything but the proverbs of old people, and yet I think I'm a cat that you don't pick up without mittens.[107]

Though it is doubtful that Dylan had studied Palaprat's text, it provides an interesting parallel with his own stance on over-education and highlights the aptness of his choice of mask. Pederolino is also portrayed as the unsuccessful lover, in competition with fellow servant Harlequin for the affections of the maidservant Columbina, which echoes the difficulties Dylan was experiencing in his marriage to Sara Lownds.

Dylan's predilection for masks as a tool for self-revelation is exemplified by his 2003 movie *Masked and Anonymous* which he co-wrote and in which he starred. The film was a critical failure and is perhaps only worth mentioning, not for its merit, but its self-referential nature. Dylan plays Jack Fate, an imprisoned singer, whose character and life story parallels so perfectly Dylan's that they almost converge. As Mike Marqusee comments, 'for an artist who harps on about his need for privacy and his unknowability, who for decades treated his personal cult with disdain, it's extraordinarily self-referential'.[108] Perhaps, as Wilde believed, the anonymity granted to Dylan through playing the role of a fictional version of himself afforded him the opportunity to investigate and examine his early life and career – albeit an investigation which did not translate into particularly good cinema.

---

[107] Palapret, *La fille de bon sens*, G, 1V, 78. Quoted in Robert F. Storey, *Pierrot: A Critical History of a Mask* (Princeton: Princeton University Press, 2005), p. 317.

[108] Mike Marqusee, *Wicked Messenger: Bob Dylan and the 1960s* (London: Seven Stones Press, 2005), p. 317.

Dylan's songs feature a cast of characters whose personas he adopts like masks, harnessing the three functions of transformation, disguise and revelation, to create music that speaks to its listener on a universal level. In 'I Am a Lonesome Hobo' (*John Wesley Harding*, 1968), Dylan steps into the persona of a derelict man who had everything and lost it all because of his jealousy and mistrust. He warns his audience, 'stay free from petty jealousies / live by no man's code/and hold your judgement for yourself / lest you wind up on this road'.[109] 'The Ballad of Donald White', written in 1962, sees Dylan assume the mask of a man facing the death penalty for murder. He details the bad luck and social disadvantage that led to his imprisonment and poses the accusatory question whether men like himself are 'enemies or victims / of your society'.[110] Wearing the mask of these characters, Dylan generates both empathy and understanding in his listeners in a way that a detached, third-person account of their crimes could not. The mask of another is an agent for truth-telling and the delivery of a moral and universal message.

Suze Rotolo confirmed this idea when asked about her own influence on Dylan's songs, claiming 'you really listen to those songs, they're somewhat like fiction – he's written something coming from his life, but he sets it in a fiction, maybe using another character's voice'.[111] The characters that populate Dylan's lyrical landscapes allow him to not only inhabit the lives of others and reveal generalised truths but also make autobiographical confessions with an ironic distance. The emotional impact and truth of these revelations is no less meaningful for this distance, but it allows Dylan to explore such concepts free from the fear of being too closely affiliated with these sentiments. Lebold argues that Dylan's use of 'I' and 'you' throughout his lyrics creates a narrative persona through which he explores his own truth, while inviting the listener to 'explore his own subjectivity . . . Dylan's personae and masks, are, ultimately, spaces where our identity and that of the artist can meet and coalesce'.[112]

Conclusion

In this chapter we have examined the ways in which Bob Dylan has used varying masks and personas for three specific functions: transformation, concealment

---

[109] Bob Dylan, 'I Am A Lonesome Hobo', in *Lyrics: 1962-1968* (London: Harper Collins, 1994), p. 383.
[110] Bob Dylan, 'The Ballad of Donald White', in *Lyrics: 1962-1968*, p. 50.
[111] Williams, 'Tomorrow Is a Long Time'.
[112] Lebold, 'A Face Like a Mask and a Voice That Croaks', p. 68

and revelation. These three functions have worked in harmony with one another, allowing Dylan to promote and protect his artistry through the use of transformative personas, while maintaining a separate but mutable self from the global figure of 'Bob Dylan' who has allowed him to explore autobiographical and universal truths in his music, movies and prose. In the next chapter we will go on to examine Leonard Cohen's similar use of masks and personas throughout his work and public life while contrasting the career trajectories of both artists.

Dylan himself has become a multimillion-dollar industry with the commercialization of all dimensions of his career, skilfully orchestrated by his manager Jeff Rosen. The official bootleg series, running into fifteen volumes, was designed to capitalize upon what was potentially a lucrative unofficial illegal commercial enterprise from which others profit. The screen portrayals by Pennebaker and Scorsese, as well as Dylan's own acting roles; the commercial reproduction of his art; and the Never Ending Tour ensure that Bob Dylan, at all stages of his career, wearing all his different masks, is instantaneously and ingeniously accessible, without him having to answer to any of them because they are all simultaneously and concurrently in the public sphere.

6

The Lone Ranger – Leonard Cohen

If you want another kind of love
I'll wear a mask for you

– Leonard Cohen[1]

I met Murder on the way –
He had a mask like Castlereagh –
Very smooth he looked, yet grim;
Seven blood-hounds followed him.

– Percy Bysshe Shelley[2]

Introduction

Leonard Cohen, like the Beat poets and Bob Dylan, pursued the fame and public adoration that Dylan Thomas achieved, but like Thomas he longed for a 'mask and a wall'[3] behind which to take refuge from the glare of the public spotlight. In the previous chapter, we investigated Bob Dylan's use of masks and personas both to protect and to promote his art, to separate his personal and public life, and to reveal what he believed to be universal truths. In this chapter, we will explore Cohen's employment of the metaphor of the mask as an agent of transformation, disguise and revelation.

The transformative masks that Cohen wore to establish himself as both a poet and a serious musician can be separated into six distinct personas, each correlating with different phases of his career. We will discuss how Cohen transformed himself from a literary celebrity in his native Canada to rock's poet laureate in his early musical career. We will examine the symbiotic relationship he shared with

---

[1] Leonard Cohen, 'I'm Your Man', *Stranger Music: Selected Poems and Songs* (London: Jonathan Cape, 1993), p. 357.
[2] Shelley, 'The Mask of Anarchy: Written on the Occasion of the Massacre at Manchester'. Written in 1819, the poem was not published during Shelley's lifetime. It first appears in print in 1832.
[3] Dylan Thomas, 'O Make Me a Mask', *The Collected Poems of Dylan Thomas*, ed. John Goodby (London: Weidenfeld and Nicholson, 2014), p. 98.

his mentor Irving Layton and how both men used each other and their public personas to promote their work and themselves to their audiences. Next, we will go on to discuss the distinctive musical personas that defined each era of Cohen's career. When Cohen first broke into the rock music world, he was marketed by his record label as the 'poet of rock and roll'. Later, Cohen transformed himself into the 'Ladies' Man', with songs that focused on sex and seduction consistent with his personal reputation as a womanizer. Struggling with depression and finding his career at an impasse, Cohen's 'Ladies' Man' became an increasingly melancholy lothario, with Cohen effectively 'killing off' his persona with the 1977 album *Death of a Ladies' Man* and the poetry collection *Death of a Lady's Man*. It was not until 1988, with the release of *I'm Your Man*, that Cohen successfully shifted into his next persona, the 'suave crooner', and entered into a period of critical and commercial rehabilitation. Cohen's final transformation coincided with his growing spiritual awakening as he further explored the precepts of Zen Buddhism, which he had first dallied with in the 1970s, and the religious heritage of the Jewish faith into which he was born. Christophe Lebold categorizes this persona as 'High Priest of the Heart',[4] with Cohen fans such as Elton John describing seeing him in concert as a 'religious experience'.[5] His transformations were natural extensions of Cohen's own personality traits, and his experiences and moods manifested themselves in these respective periods. The personas served to augment his music, allowing the lyrics to come to life through each of his characters.

The masks and personas that Cohen wore to promote himself as both poet and pop star were also a means of concealing his inner self from the public gaze. Cohen, like Dylan, denied the idea of a 'fixed self', claiming in a 1988 interview that 'everybody's continually moving into all different kinds of characters and roles'.[6] Here we will explore how Cohen used masks and personas to separate his public and private identity, and the interplay between the Buddhist ideal of self-negation and his own strong sense of self.

Finally, we will examine Cohen's use of the mask's ultimate function: revelation. Cohen is a contradictory figure – at once wearing his heart on his

[4] Christophe Lebold, 'The Traitor and the Stowaway: Personal Construction and the Quest for Cultural Anonymity and Cultural Relevance in the Trajectories of Bob Dylan and Leonard Cohen', *Journal of the Internal Association for the Study of Popular Music*, vol. 1, no. 2 (2010), p. 2.

[5] Andy Greene, 'Elton John Still Wants to Make Hip-Hop Records', *Rolling Stone* (18 March 2014). https://www.rollingstone.com/music/music-news/elton-john-still-wants-to-make-hip-hop-records -190560/. Accessed 4 July 2020.

[6] ScottishTeeVee, 'Leonard Cohen – Kulturen interview Sweden 1988'. *YouTube* video. 0:3.50. 14 February 2020. https://www.youtube.com/watch?time_continue=53&v=X_FvUHENqsQ&feature =emb_logo

sleeve yet remaining guarded in the face of public scrutiny. His songwriting is often described as 'confessional', yet we contend that Cohen's autobiographical lyrics and poetry are voiced through the fictional persona of 'Leonard Cohen', allowing him to reveal both personal and what he believed to be universal truths from behind the screen of his theatrical mask.

The transformative mask: From poet to pop star

As we have discussed, Leonard Cohen rose to prominence in Canada as a poet first and foremost where he achieved a level of literary celebrity that was until that time unprecedented in his homeland. While his early work as a poet may not have sold in vast numbers, he became a public figure on the Canadian stage, frequently appearing on CBC to promote his poetry, novels and himself. Cohen was also the subject of the 1965 documentary *Ladies and Gentlemen . . . Mr Leonard Cohen* which initially focused on a quartet of Canadian poets – Irving Layton, Earle Birney, Phyllis Gotlieb and Cohen – but was edited to feature Cohen exclusively because 'for some technical reason only the parts of the film that dealt with me seem to have been good'.[7] Cohen's characteristic self-deprecation is an implicit acknowledgement that his youth and energy made him a more appealing and charismatic subject than his ageing mentor Irving Layton, whose own success was on the decline as Cohen's was on the ascent. As Cohen's star rose, Layton's fame waned, in part due to his 'too-frequent appearances before the public'.[8] Despite, Layton's media overexposure, Cohen owed much of his literary celebrity to his public relationship with the aging *enfant terrible* of the Canadian poetry scene, who spent as much time on self-promotion and self-aggrandizement as he did on writing.

The two men developed public personas that were exaggerations of their own personalities; Layton the Grand Prophet and Cohen, his acolyte, the martyred saint[9] – also referred to by Michael Ondaatje as the 'pop saint'.[10] The personas were inextricably linked, playing off one another in a poetic and public dialogue.

---

[7] Michael Harris, 'Leonard Cohen: The Poet as Hero: Cohen by Himself', *Saturday Night*, vol. 84, no. 6 (June 1969), p. 28.

[8] Leonard Cohen quoted in Elspeth Cameron, *Irving Layton: A Portrait* (Toronto: Stoddart, 1985), p. 371.

[9] Joel Deshaye, 'Celebrity and the Poetic Dialogue of Irving Layton and Leonard Cohen', *Studies in Canadian Literature*, vol. 34, no. 2 (2006), p. 80. https://journal.lib.unb.ca/index/php/SCL/article/view12703. Accessed 10 May 2020.

[10] Michael Ondaatje, *Leonard Cohen* (Toronto: McClelland & Stewart, 1970), p. 61.

The two men were often invited to speak together at events, on television shows and poetry readings, and in 1961, McClelland & Stewart issued a promotional flyer jointly launching the publication of Cohen's *Spice Box of Earth* and Layton's *The Swinging Flesh*,[11] further entwining the personas of the Prophet and Saint. Their symbiotic search for media attention saw them referencing one another in their work, often antagonistically, both implicitly and explicitly.

Cohen's 'For My Old Layton' sees the protégé launch a scathing attack on his former professor and his delusions of grandeur, as he declaims '[the] town saluted him with garbage / which he interpreted as praise'.[12] In 'Portrait of a Genius', Layton describes Cohen as a captive of his own self-image as he 'crawls under the bed / to stare at himself in the mirror'. He warns that his protégé will soon find his 'boyhood smile' replaced by 'blank terror'.[13] This antagonism characterizes the competitive nature of Layton's and Cohen's relationship, with both men relying on their connected public personas to promote their work, yet fearful of being outdone by the other. In 'My Eyes Are Wide Open' (*The Swinging Flesh*, 1961), Layton writes of a father's fear of being outstripped by his son – a prophetic vision for the global fame that his disciple would achieve, far surpassing his own mediocre celebrity.

The transformative mask of the 'pop saint' was an extension of Cohen's own preoccupations with religion, faith and his conflicted relationship with his Jewish heritage. Cohen's transformative mask of the sacrificial saint augmented the religious themes woven through his work, elevating his audience's interaction and enjoyment with these ideas as they read his poetry through the prism of his saintly persona. As with Dylan Thomas, however, the fame of the fictional 'St Leonard' character – at least in his native Canada – began to outshine his own work, with audiences more likely to watch him on television than purchase a collection of his poems. This was something for which Cohen later went on to criticize his friend Layton, claiming in 1983 that '[he] will never grow, his work or himself. His sense of urgency of the poetic identity is unparalleled'.[14] Cohen saw that his mentor had become trapped in the fixed image he projected of himself to the point of parody and to the detriment of his poetry. We will discuss Cohen's fear that his work would suffer from the public scrutiny of his private

[11] Deshaye, 'Celebrity and the Poetic Dialogue', p. 86.
[12] Leonard Cohen, 'For My Old Layton', *Flowers for Hitler* (London, Jonathan Cape, 1973; first published 1964), p. 41.
[13] Irving Layton, 'Portrait of a Genius', in *The Laughing Rooster* (Toronto: McClelland, 1964).
[14] Leonard Cohen quoted in Cameron, *Irving Layton: A Portrait*, p. 359.

life when we go on to examine Cohen's use of masks as a form of concealment and disguise, but it is interesting to note the sceptical attitude his poetry reveals towards celebrity. In *The Energy of Slaves* (1972), Cohen equates celebrity with slavery and fears losing both himself and his work to the public gaze:

his absolute privacy
violates itself before our eyes
his absolute privacy
forbids the violation[15]

In the same collection, Cohen advises everyone 'to become rich and famous'[16] demonstrating his ambivalent feelings towards his own fame. Despite this, Cohen clearly strove to achieve recognition and acclaim beyond his motherland, and his move into the arena of global pop stardom necessitated another shift in identity as he sought to break into the rock music scene.

The literary stardom Cohen enjoyed in Canada did not translate into immediate acceptance in the music industry. Critics and audiences were sceptical of his 'rock credentials' and were reticent to embrace the poet as they had his contemporary Bob Dylan. This is a sentiment that Cohen himself expressed in a 1975 interview when he lamented the fact that

I seem to be caught in the critical establishment between two critical houses...the literary people are very resentful because I made money in the rock world and on the other side . . . a lot of people in the rock establishment . . . suggest I don't know anything about music . . . that my voice is very thin . . . They apply standards to me that they've never applied to other singers in the field.[17]

During his transition from the rarefied world of literature to the rock scene, Cohen found it necessary to wear the transformative mask of the 'Pop Poet' as he tried to stake his claim to cultural relevance in the fickle marketplace of popular culture.

Songs of Leonard Cohen was released over a decade after Cohen's first poetry collection, *Let Us Compare Mythologies*. Sylvie Simmons notes the contrast between the album's cover image and the poetry volume's author photo. The cover photograph for *Songs of Leonard Cohen* was taken in a New York subway photo booth and shows a sepia-tinged Cohen staring into the camera, 'a solemn

[15] Leonard Cohen, '89', in *The Energy of Slaves* (London: Jonathan Cape, 1972), p. 99.
[16] Cohen, '89', p. 97.
[17] Williams, 'Leonard Cohen: The Romantic in a Ragpicker's Trade', p. 90.

man in a dark jacket and white shirt . . . it might as well have been the photo of
a dead Spanish poet'.[18] Discarding the persona of poetry's martyred saint, Cohen
appears less 'buttoned up' and more 'defiant'[19] behind the transformative mask
of pop's 'melancholy poet'.

When Cohen released his first album, he was sold as the 'poet' of rock 'n'
roll – a chivalrous throwback to a more romantic era. As he struggled to find
himself as a performer during these early years, Cohen made use of props and
theatricality to deflect from his own insecurities and to create the idea of himself
as a romantic hero. For example, he rode a white horse onstage at a music festival
in Aix-en-Provence, in August 1970, much to the bemusement of his audience.
The festival had been poorly organized and oversubscribed, and when Cohen
and his entourage tried to drive along the winding country roads leading to the
festival fields, they found the route entirely gridlocked. Unable to negotiate the
traffic, the band diverted to a local pub and, after several glasses of good French
wine, found a solution. The provincial inn where 'The Army' were stationed had
stables on site which allowed the guests to hire horses for the day. True to their
name, the band decided to ride the horses to the festival, as though they were
part of a cavalry. Emboldened by the wine, Cohen rode his own steed onstage,
'like a knight from some old-fashioned book' ('Bird on a Wire'), living up to the
public perception of 'Leonard Cohen' as romantic throwback. Simmons claims
that 'Leonard was the consummate showman, appearing to be in full control
of both the spontaneity and the artifice' of his performance.[20] The audience did
not agree. Cohen was booed and heckled for this grandiose performance which
seemed so at odds with the ethos of authenticity and simplicity that defined the
folk scene.

As we saw in the previous chapter, Kierkegaard saw the importance of
theatricality in the delivery of important concepts and ideas. His thoughts on
artifice and showmanship are examined in *An Unscientific Postscript*, which
is a critique of the Hegelian concept of theatricality that employs theatrical
devices to emphasize its points. The work was published under the pseudonym
of 'Johannes Climacus', yet in the book's conclusion, Kierkegaard steps from
behind the theatrical curtain and announces himself as the text's true author.
For Kierkegaard, theatricality was only a cause for concern when it was

[18] Sylvie Simmons, *I'm Your Man: The Life of Leonard Cohen* (London: Vintage, 2017), p. 228.
[19] Simmons, *I'm Your Man*, p. 228.
[20] Simmons, *I'm Your Man*, p. 222.

'*unconfessed*'.[21] The use of personas and masks to trick an audience into believing you were someone else would have been abhorrent to Kierkegaard, unless the audience was aware of the ruse. Cohen, riding his white horse onstage, could not fail to disclose to his audience that this was a performance. Performance, of course, is always an artifice – as we have seen through the examination of Bob Dylan's carefully constructed personas – but the folk purists were unwilling to accept such a brazen and overt display of theatricality. For the folkies, the performance was only acceptable when it was rooted in a reality which allowed them to believe in its authenticity.

As we discussed, Bob Dylan faced similar criticism from the folk community as his stage shows and public personas became evermore flamboyant and theatrical and he embraced electric over acoustic sounds. Cohen, conversely, began his pop career with an extravagant and artificial persona, which alienated the folk scene he was attempting to win over. The blatant artifice of his act allowed his audience to see that the mask was not always the man – an unforgivable transgression in the era of authenticity and truth. This led to Cohen being treated with scepticism and distrust by an industry which was reluctant to accept him as a musical artist, but, ironically, it was through the transformative masks and personas that his initial audience rejected that he found the recognition he thought he deserved.

Simon Frith argues that in the 1960s and 1970s, music journalists acted as the gatekeepers of popular culture with the power to define performers' personas and dictate their audiences' reception.[22] Unfortunately for Cohen, the critics didn't 'get' his brand of music. Allan Evans, reviewing Cohen's 1971 album *Songs of Love and Hate*, remarked, 'What a depressing guy this Cohen is!'[23] As we will discuss later, this depressive persona created by the critics became one of Cohen's defining features, whether he accepted the characterization or not.

To reiterate, Cohen's musical career can be divided into four stages which were defined by five separate personas: the poet of rock and roll, the 'Ladies' Man' and the depressive lothario, the suave crooner and the 'high priest of the heart'.[24] In the 1970s, we can see Cohen's transformative mask of the 'Ladies' Man' begin to slip, as he became a 'depressive lothario', with his lyrics and songs focusing on sex and death in equal measure, epitomized by *Songs of Love and*

---

[21] Pickett, 'Beyond the Mask: Kierkegaard's Postscript as Antitheatrical, Anti-Hegelian Drama', p. 111.
[22] Simon Frith, *The Sociology of Rock* (London: Constable, 1978), p. 10.
[23] Allan Evans, 'Leonard Cohen: Songs of Love and Hate', *New Musical Express* (22 May 1971) quoted Lebold, 'The Traitor and the Stowaway', p. 9.
[24] Lebold, 'The Traitor and the Stowaway', p. 9.

Hate. The 1971 album contains the track 'Last Year's Man' which signifies Cohen's own feelings towards himself during this era. Unable to achieve commercial or critical success, Cohen struggled with the depression that had plagued him throughout his life, the 'avalanche that covered up my soul' (*Songs of Love and Hate*, 'Avalanche'). Cohen's previous transformative masks of 'poetry's martyred saint' and 'pop's melancholy poet' were extensions of Cohen's own personality, but the public mask of the 'depressive lothario' or 'ladies' man' was strikingly close to Cohen's own private identity and threatened to eclipse his inner self. The 1970s marked a period of declining mental health and drug and alcohol abuse, perhaps precipitated by what we have termed the colonization of the 'veridical' self by the 'public' self. Indeed, reflecting on the years before he 'killed off' this problematic persona in both his poetry collection *Death of a Lady's Man* and his album *Death of a Ladies' Man*, Cohen admitted 'the personality that I'd been maintaining was in the process of collapsing, so I had to revise my work until it became the only possible song I could sing'.[25]

While he was initially marketed as the 'poet of rock and roll', in the face of declining album sales and poor critical reception, Cohen 'de-poeticized his stage persona'[26] and embraced the rock ethos. The result of this was the Phil Spector produced *Death of a Ladies' Man*, released in 1976 to negative reactions from both critics and fans alike. The main issue seemed to be the tension between Spector's elaborate melodies and Cohen's sophisticated lyrics – perhaps encapsulated in a behind-the-scenes article about the recording sessions for the album, in which Spector is reported to have screamed 'this isn't punk rock! This is ROCK PUNK!'[27] as Cohen, who we are told was dressed in 'a finely tailored dark blue blazer and well-cut grey slacks,'[28] took his seat in the recording booth. The always sartorially elegant son of a Canadian clothing manufacturer could not have been more at odds with the safety pins and ripped jeans of the emerging punk scene.

Cohen attempted to wear the transformative mask of the anarchic rock star, but the mask was so at odds with his authentic self that it seemed more of a shoddy disguise which failed to fool his critics. This scepticism over Cohen's new 'rock persona' can be seen in the December 1977 cover of French magazine *Rock & Folk* which shows a drawing of an awkward Cohen attempting an Elvis Presley

[25] Radio Interview with Kristine McKenna, *Eight Hours to Harry*, KCRW-FM (October 1988), printed in *Leonard Cohen on Leonard Cohen*, ed. Burger, p. 244.
[26] Lebold, 'The Traitor and the Stowaway', p. 10.
[27] Harvey Kubernik, 'What Happened When Phil Spector Met Leonard Cohen?' *The Los Angeles Phonograph* (January 1978), reprinted in *Leonard Cohen on Leonard Cohen*, ed. Burger, p. 114.
[28] Kubernik, 'What Happened When Phil Spector Met Leonard Cohen', p. 113.

stance, electric guitar slung over his shoulder, beside the dubious headline 'Leonard Cohen, Rocker?' Even Cohen himself seemed wearied by the pretence – his 1976 single 'Do I Have to Dance All Night' containing the lyrics which expressed the exhaustion he felt at trying to keep up with the current trends, 'I'm forty-one, the moon is full . . . I like you Mademoiselle / But do I have to dance all night?'

Cohen's voice had been used to great effect on his previous records. His habit of standing close to the microphone created an intimate whisper which harmonized with the simple instrumentation to make the listener feel as though Cohen was speaking to them alone. Indeed, acclaimed rock critic Robert Christagau once declared that Cohen's voice may have been 'monotonous, but it is also the most miraculous vehicle for intimacy the new pop has yet produced'.[29] On *Death of a Ladies' Man*, Spector's overproduced arrangements clashed with Cohen's measured delivery and saw him struggle to keep pace with the upbeat tempo. This is particularly noticeable in 'Don't Go Home with Your Hard On', where Cohen's voice strains over Spector's 'rock punk' production, yelping his lyrics with uncharacteristic effort.

It was not until 1988 when he released *I'm Your Man* that Cohen began to find himself again as an artist and entered into a period of 'critical and commercial rehabilitation',[30] very much facilitated by Jennifer Warnes's album of Cohen covers, *Famous Blue Raincoat*, which Cohen jokingly suggested to her that she titled 'Jenny sings Lenny'. His construction of a new persona to accompany his new sound – the suave, somewhat menacing crooner – is reflected in the promotional videos of the time. The moody black and white video for 'First We Take Manhattan' mirrors the eerie and threatening atmosphere of the song as Cohen stalks a wind-swept beach in his long black coat. The song itself has been described by Lebold as a 'revenge tragedy that will have him humiliate the industry that . . . rejected him'.[31] In 1984, Walter Yetnikof, the president of Columbia Records, had told Cohen, 'we know you're great, but we don't know if you're any good'.[32] In the face of audience disinterest and scathing critical reviews in the music press, Columbia was uncertain about Cohen's future as a recording artist and decided not to distribute his subsequent records in the United States.

[29] Robert Christagau, 'Esquire Column', *Esquire* (June 1968). https://www.robertchristgau.com/xg/bk-aow/column4.php. Accessed 22 June 2020.
[30] Lebold, 'The Traitor and the Stowaway', p. 11.
[31] Lebold, 'The Traitor and the Stowaway', p. 11.
[32] Ira Nadel, *Various Positions: A Life of Leonard Cohen* (London: Bloomsbury, 1996), p. 238.

The lyrics of 'First We Take Manhattan' address Cohen's sense of cultural marginalization as he declares 'they sentenced me to twenty years of boredom / for trying to change the system from within', referencing his 'melancholy poet' persona and his attempts to bring poetry into pop music.

I'm Your Man saw Cohen adopt the transformative mask of the 'suave crooner'. He appeared on the record's front cover styled in mafia-chic: dark sunglasses, a white T-shirt beneath a pin-striped blazer, and a menacing expression. The implicit threat in the black and white image is undercut by the bright yellow banana he holds in place of the mobster's handgun. The imagery is a playful invocation of the 'ladies'' man' persona that Cohen killed off on his previous album, the phallic imagery of the banana consumed by the 'professed seducer . . . symbolically eating his own weapon'.[33] Musically, it was a departure from his earlier records, embracing the synthesizers and drum-beats of the 1980s, but the deceptively simple arrangements allowed space and pace for Cohen's voice to dominate. Cohen's voice, grown deeper with cigarettes, wine and age, is at once menacing, defiant, grave, tender and seductive, playing into the persona of the ultra-cool crooner.

The transformative mask of this persona was successful because it mirrored the self that Cohen had become. When he let go of the idea of trying to become what his audience wanted, he was able to create music that they could truly connect with. Indeed, on the album's title track, Cohen sings 'I'll wear a mask for you', which is essentially what he had to do throughout his career to convince audiences of his authenticity.

Despite this late career resurgence, Cohen only released one album of new material during the 1990s. *The Future* (1992) was a commercial success, going platinum in his native Canada and gaining plaudits from the critics he had worked so hard to win over. In an interview at the time, he remarked, 'my phone calls are rapidly answered. Limousines receive me at the airport. There are flowers in my hotel. So I know something's going on, and it's quite agreeable.'[34] The adoration and acclaim that Cohen longed for may have been 'agreeable', but it was perhaps emptier than he'd expected. As we saw in Chapter 3, in 1994, he turned his back on the limelight and ascended to the Mount Baldy Rinzai Zen Monastery, located in the San Gabriel mountains, to study at the feet of his

---

[33] Lebold, 'The Traitor and the Stowaway', p. 12.
[34] David Browne, 'Leonard Cohen at Home in 1992: Singer-Songwriter on Pop Success, New Love', *Rolling Stone* (11 November 2016). https://www.rollingstone.com/music/music-features/leonard-cohen-at-home-in-1992-singer-songwriter-on-pop-success-new-love-125889/. Accessed 6 July 2020.

friend and master, Roshi. In early January 1999, Cohen descended the mountain and returned to the studio.

Ten New Songs (2001) saw the unveiling of Cohen's final transformative mask, termed by Lebold as 'The High Priest of the Heart'. Religion and spirituality were always constant themes in his poetry and lyrics, with sacred imagery juxtaposed with the profane, but something had changed for Cohen. His last persona was both a return to and a rejection of the 'Pop Saint' persona he had cultivated as a Montreal poet. The depression that had blighted his life had lifted and Cohen enjoyed a newfound perspective. His songs still meditated on themes of mortality, death, yearning and spiritual fulfilment, but there was a new 'zen' like quality to the work, a quiet acceptance of a flawed reality, hard won after years of following Roshi's gruelling schedule at the monastery. His voice, too, had undergone a change up in the mountains of San Gabriel. It was deeper, more resonant, echoing 'the spiritual realities of exile, brokenness and fall'.[35]

When Cohen resumed touring in 2008, his audiences welcomed him with ecstatic fervour. The High Priest of Heartbreak, now in his seventy-sixth year, impressed the crowds with his showmanship and theatricality. His long-time collaborator and backing singer, Sharon Robinson, who accompanied him on tour, recalls being 'surprised by the showmanship aspect of it . . . He believed in the most committed delivery of a song that he could do . . . the fact that he was older and starting to look kind of frail, that became part of the story'.[36] Cohen's age only added to his gravity – his deep and haunting voice, his iconic tailored suits and fedora made him seem like a 'rat pack Rabbi, God's chosen mobster',[37] and he played upon his advancing years in his stage shows, singing 'I'll wear an old man's mask for you', when he performed 'I'm Your Man'.[38]

The 'religious experience' of Cohen's later shows was enhanced by his 'High Priest of Heartbreak' persona. Each night, Cohen appeared before his devoted followers as a wise spiritual guru, his newfound insights won through years of hardship and shared with his chosen few. In his final transformation, Cohen united aspects of all his previous personas, transforming himself into a poetic priest whose spirituality still embraced the sensual and who remained as suave as ever in his double-breasted suits and fedoras.

[35] Lebold, 'The Traitor and the Stowaway', p. 12.
[36] Andy Greene, 'Sharon Robinson Reflects on Touring with Leonard Cohen', *Rolling Stone* (12 July 2017). https://www.rollingstone.com/music/music-features/sharon-robinson-reflects-on-touring-with-leonard-cohen-194281/. Accessed 20 June 2020.
[37] Simmons, *I'm Your Man*, p. 557.
[38] Simmons, *I'm Your Man*, p. 557.

The enduring appeal of Cohen's transformative masks and personas lay in their implicit invitation to audience participation. Roland Barthes argued that there are 'writerly' (*textes scriptibles*) texts and 'readerly' (*textes lisibles*) texts. The 'readerly' text does not encourage audience interaction. The reader is directed by the author to the conclusion and is not asked to engage his or her critical faculties. Barthes believed that 'readerly texts' made up the enormous mass of literature and culture. The 'writerly' text stands in opposition to passive consumption. 'The writerly text is ourselves writing', he declared, '[it is] the novelistic without the novel, poetry without the poem, the essay without the dissertation, writing without style.'[39] In short, the 'writerly' text is the audience's own interpretation and extrapolation of a text. Celebrity and media personalities are just such 'texts', poured over and interpreted by their admirers, though the depth that these texts provide varies. The transformative masks and personas used by both Dylan and Cohen transmute the two men into 'texts' which can be read in conjunction with their own poetic and song texts, augmenting and enhancing the appreciation of their work. The image of Cohen as a 'Ladies' Man' contributes to our understanding of songs such as 'Chelsea Hotel #2', where the line 'I don't mean to suggest that I loved you the best / I can't keep track of each fallen robin' interplays with his persona as roving lothario. The intertextuality between media-text and song-text propagated by his personas has led to sustained cultural significance and his legacy as the poet of rock and roll.

The mask as disguise

Throughout his career, Cohen used the transformative power of masks to promote himself, but he was also keenly aware of the need to separate his 'private' from his 'public' self. The mask not only transforms its wearer but also disguises him. Though Cohen was an active participant in his own mythologizing, he was wary of allowing too much of his private self to become a part of the public commons, particularly when he made the move from the literary world to the musical stage. In this section, we will examine how Cohen has used masks and personas to keep his public and private selves separate, and the dangers of these selves colliding.

---

[39] Roland Barthes, *S/Z*, translated by Richard Miller (Oxford: Blackwell, 1974), p. 5.

Cohen was accustomed to performing for an audience as a poet, sometimes even with jazz accompaniment, before he released his first album of songs in 1967. Singing in front of a live audience was another matter, however, and he dreaded the 'risks of humiliation'[40] and the artificial intimacy of live music. He had hoped that his songs could function in the same way as his poetry collections and novels, inviting his listeners to enjoy the record as they had done his books, without the need for his physical presence. After the release of his critically acclaimed second album, *Songs from a Room,* his record company Columbia was understandably unhappy with the idea of promoting a performing artist who refused to perform. Cohen had no alternative but to make arrangements for an eight-date European concert tour which began in Amsterdam, on 3 May 1970, and included the legendary performance at the Isle of Wight festival,[41] with a persona very different from the suave turtle neck-top and well-cut suited chansonnier. Dressed in army fatigues, and naming his band 'The Army', his newly adopted 'disguise' reflected his mentality. Always obsessed with military metaphors, he felt as if he was leading his army into combat and under siege at each new encampment.

Cohen, however, still harboured reservations about stepping into the spotlight. Before embarking on the tour, he commissioned his close friend and renowned Canadian artist and sculptor Marty Rosengarten to create a theatrical mask for him to wear on stage. Simmons recounts that the mask was 'of Leonard himself: a live death mask made from a plaster cast of his face, expressionless, with gaps for his mouth and eyes'.[42] Going beyond Dylan Thomas's figurative mask of the poem and Bob Dylan's use of clothes, props and personas to mask his true identity, Cohen wanted a literal mask to hide behind when he faced his audience for the first time. Cohen may, of course, have been aware that Dylan Thomas was immortalized by a death mask made while he lay in the morgue of St. Vincent's Hospital by the sculptor David Slivka. The idea of performing behind a 'Cohen mask' was ultimately abandoned, but Rosengarten believes that the prop was 'useful in deciding his persona onstage',[43] and Cohen valued the piece so highly that he kept it for decades, even asking Rosengarten to create an aluminium cast of it.

---

[40] Harvey Kubernik, 'Interview with Leonard Cohen', *Melody Maker* (1 March 1975). Quoted in Sylvie Simmons, *I'm Your Man*, p. 216.

[41] For footage of the concert, see *Leonard Cohen: Live at the Isle of Wight 1970*, Columbia Legacy records, 2009. Released to capitalize on the resurrected Cohen's world tours.

[42] Simmons, *I'm Your Man*, p. 217.

[43] Simmons, *I'm Your Man*, p. 218.

The mask may not have made it to the stage, but his 'Cohen' persona stood in its place, allowing him to demarcate the man from the image he projected to the world. Though his music has become synonymous with 'confessional' and 'autobiographical' songwriting, Cohen was reluctant to share too much of his true self with his audience and the press. In an interview for *Billboard* magazine in August 1970, Nancy Elrich mused that 'he works hard to achieve that bloodless vocal, that dull, humourless quality of voice speaking after death'.[44] Elrich's words are perhaps more telling than she intended. Just as Bob Dylan adapted his accent to project an image that he felt was truer to his authentic self, Cohen's monotonous intonation deadened the emotion of his words, giving a sardonic edge to every statement. It was impossible to tell whether he was sincere or sarcastic, which allowed him to speak openly, without giving too much away. Indeed, Cohen's 'bloodless' affect is consitent with Derrida's belief that the mask cannot escape its connection with death, foreshadowing as it does the mask we must all ultimately wear – the death mask.

The mask is a negation of its wearer's face, and, as anthropologist Elizabeth Tonkin remarks, 'there is something eerie in the little death of personality which occurs, caused by the replacement of the personality's most immediate *mis-en-scene* the face . . . its immobility is a contradiction to the life of the wearer'.[45] When a man wears a mask for too long, he runs the risk of losing himself to the image he projects. The power, but also the danger, of the mask is seen both in Dylan and Cohen and also the Welsh bard Dylan Thomas with whom we have associated them in this book. Donald Hall, after encountering the poet during an American book tour, wrote that 'Dylan Thomas was an ass playing The Poet. I saw pretense; I saw premeditation, trying to look spontaneous'.[46] When Hall later spent time with Thomas at his boathouse in Laugharne, he caught a glimpse of the vulnerable man behind the public veneer. Thomas's alcoholism and depression, though facets of his personality, were fed by the flames of his own mythology. Thomas was a keen self-promoter, creating elaborate stories about himself to attract public attention and never shied away from playing the part of the 'roaring drunk' and the Welsh Rimbaud. Ultimately, Thomas was unable to separate himself from the public personality he had created and died at the age

---

[44] Nancy Elrich, 'Interview with Leonard Cohen', in *Billboard* magazine (8 August 1970). Quoted in Simmons, *I'm Your Man*, p. 221.

[45] Elizabeth Tonkin, 'Masks and Power', in *MAN*, vol. 24, no. 2 (June 1979), p. 241. https://www.jstor.org/stable/2801565. Accessed 20 April 2020.

[46] Donald Hall, 'Dylan Thomas and Public Suicide', *The American Poetry Review*, vol. 7, no. 2 (January/February 1978), pp. 7–13, p. 7 www.jstor.org/stable/27775802. Accessed 15 April 2020.

of thirty-nine. As Theodore Dalrymple astutely observed, 'he worked hard at his image; and in the end, the image was the man and it killed him'.[47]

Cohen himself sensed the danger that this merging of public and private persona posed for the self, as his poem 'The Price of This Book' testifies – 'I am ashamed to ask for your money . . . but I need it to keep my different lives apart. Otherwise I will be crushed when they join.'[48] As we saw, in the 1970s, Cohen's stage persona and 'private self' came dangerously close to collision, causing a downward spiral of drug and alcohol abuse and a deepening of his depression.

The negation of the mask wearer's personality does not have to result in literal death. One of the tenets of the Buddhist philosophy practised by Cohen is the concept of 'ego death'. While practitioners and enlightenment leaders have contested the exact nature of this self-negation, Deepak Chopra has defined the ego as 'your self-image; it is your social mask; it is the role you are playing'.[49] To achieve ego death, which is itself a form of spiritual rebirth, they must strip themselves of their own self-importance and attachments to worldly markers of success. Paradoxically, while Chopra sees the ego as a mask, it can be through the transformation and negation of the self behind the mask that the wearer finds distance from the material world.

It is interesting to note that Stephen Scobie has also spoken of the negation of self as a theme throughout Cohen's oeuvre. Discussing the 1978 poetry collection *Death of a Lady's Man*, Scobie believes that Cohen's use of double-voicing and the deconstruction of the narrative voice creates a poetic persona that is 'by turns tender, sarcastic, despairing, angry, satiric . . . erotic, pathetic, prosaic, visionary . . . the speaking voice of "Leonard Cohen" assumes too many contradictory positions ever to be assimilated back into any coherent picture of a unified self'.[50] This dissemination of the self is in itself a negation. Wearing the 'Leonard Cohen' mask allowed Cohen to explore a multitude of selves but ultimately led to the repudiation of a stable and core self behind the mask.

For Cohen, however, this loss of self was not to be feared. The 1984 volume of poetry, *Book of Mercy*, contains Cohen's staunchest rejection of ego and

[47] Theodore Dalrymple, 'The Rimbaud of Cwmdonkin Drive', *City Journal* (Winter 2015). Accessed May 7, 2020. https://www.city-journal.org/html/rimbaud-cwmdonkin-drive-13712.html
[48] Leonard Cohen, 'The Price of this Book', in *Stranger Music* (London: Jonathan Cape, 1993), p. 274.
[49] Deepak Chopra, *The Seven Spiritual Laws of Success: A Practical Guide to the Fulfilment of Your Dreams* (London: Bantam, 1996), p. 11.
[50] Stephen Scobie, 'Keynote Address: The Counterfeiter Begs Forgiveness: *Leonard Cohen* and Leonard Cohen', *Canadian Poetry: The Proceedings of the Leonard Cohen Conference*, no. 33 (Fall/Winter 1993), p. 14.

self-hood, dismissing the quest for an immutable identity as a fool's errand. The poem's collective narrative voice tells us, 'we thought we were summoned, the aging head-waiters, the minor singers, the second-rate priests. But we couldn't escape into these self-descriptions'.[51] Though this cast of characters wear the masks of their occupations, their talents, their religious affiliations as stand-ins for their identities, they are never truly transformed. The self remains nebulous and 'only the madman dares himself to be born into the question of who he is'.[52] This rejection of a stable self is essential to the Buddhist ideal of non-attachment and was something which Cohen strove to achieve during his periodic retreats to Mount Baldy, studying at the feet of the Zen master Roshi. Behind the disguise of his stage personas and his narrative voices, Cohen was able to become 'not Leonard Cohen, not any figure of "Leonard Cohen", but the problematic, vacant, discontinuous, non-authorial "author" who . . . has repeatedly emptied himself out in front of us'.[53]

Tonkin has noted that the mask is 'a recreation close to procreation'[54] as it combines two images to create a single being, negating the original in the process. She claims, 'a *persona* is created by suppressing a face . . . the recreation is made by annihilation'.[55] Despite the mask's connection with death – both the literal death mask and the death of the self behind the mask – we can see Cohen's disappearance behind a 'lifeless' mask as an act of self-preservation, shielding him from the intrusions and attacks of his fans and critics. The mask became a protective disguise, and, 'bloodless' though the façade may have been, it was in fact a life-sustaining act rather than a destructive one.

While he may have feared the pitfalls of celebrity, he was not averse to courting publicity. His desire for fame, as we have seen, was evident from his earliest days as a young writer, yet his poetry betrays an uneasy attitude towards success and reveals his fears that public intrusion might prove detrimental to both his personal life and art. 'The Cuckold's Song', from *The Spice Box of Earth*, contains the lines

> but the important thing was to cuckold Leonard Cohen.
> Hell, I might as well address this to the both of you:
> I haven't time to write anything else.[56]

[51] Leonard Cohen, *Book of Mercy* (London: Canongate, 2019), p. 17.
[52] Cohen, *Book of Mercy*, p. 17.
[53] Scobie, 'The Counterfeiter Begs Forgiveness', p. 21.
[54] Tonkin, 'Masks and Power'.
[55] Tonkin, 'Masks and Power', p. 242.
[56] Leonard Cohen, 'The Cuckold's Song', in *Stranger Music* (London: Jonathan Cape, 1993), p. 33.

The poem exposes anxieties about the sense of public ownership over his personal life and relationships that came with his growing fame and the destructive effect celebrity status may have on his art. The second line indicates both the lack of time that Cohen felt he had to dedicate himself to art while he courted publicity, but also the idea that he felt obliged to write for an audience that expected entertainment and sensationalism, which were at odds with the purity he wanted to attain in his work. Later in the poem he admits, 'I like that line because it's got my name in it',[57] revealing that despite the ruinous implications of his newfound fame, he still desired it. Ironically, in refusing to accept Canada's premiere literary prize, The Governor General's Award, in 1968, on the grounds that the world was a cruel place and he wanted none of its gifts, although a petulant gesture, gave him far more publicity than if he had quietly accepted it.[58]

Joel Deshaye describes celebrity, in contrast to other forms of public recognition, as a form of fame that is often intense, sometimes brief, and always commercially exploitable.[59] Deshaye argues that 'to maintain a private life under scrutiny . . . celebrities attempt to shelter behind their chosen personas'.[60] The personas are offered as effigies or decoys to satiate the public need for access and entertainment, while allowing the artist to maintain a private and artistic life. Cohen's strategy to reconcile his inner need for acclaim and recognition with the very real fears that it would interfere with his life and art was to adopt an ironic persona that was an exaggeration and extension of his own personality.

Cohen's conflicted views on celebrity are evident again in his treatment of Janis Joplin in 'Chelsea Hotel #2'. Joplin struggled with fame and ultimately succumbed to its perils when she died of a heroin overdose four years before the song was released on Cohen's *New Skin for the Old Ceremony* album (1974). The lyrics detail a night that Cohen spent with Joplin at the infamous hotel and features the seemingly dismissive line, 'that's all, I don't even think of you that often'. Deshaye believes, however, that given Joplin's resistance to the limelight, the lyric is a fitting tribute to a woman who wished to be forgotten.[61] Paradoxically, the song brought Joplin back to public attention, particularly for fans who saw biographical referents as key to understanding Cohen's lyrics. Unlike Joplin, who

---

[57] Cohen, 'The Cuckold's Song', p. 33.
[58] Nadel, *Various Positions*, p. 174.
[59] Deshaye, 'Celebrity and the Poetic Dialogue', p. 77.
[60] Deshaye, 'Celebrity and the Poetic Dialogue', p. 77.
[61] Joel Deshaye, *The Metaphor of Celebrity: Canadian Poetry and the Public, 1955-1980* (Toronto: Toronto University Press, 2013), p. 114.

never enjoyed her fame, Cohen was conflicted over his own role as both literary celebrity and famous singer – he courted publicity, but he also feared it, but the tension also proved to be an inspiration and driving force for his work.

In a 1972 interview for *Macleans*, Paul Saltzman asked Cohen if he liked himself. Cohen replied that he liked his true self. Saltzman took this to mean that, 'like most of us he had made for himself a number of selves, public facades, heroic images, romantic possibilities but was now in the process of stripping them away to become his true self'.[62] While Bob Dylan is more often associated with aliases, Cohen himself was no stranger to the assumed name. Throughout his career he called himself Field Commander Cohen, L. Cohen and Laughing Lenny, and he was given the Buddhist name Jikan which means 'silence' or the silent one by Roshi. In the poem 'Nancy Lies in London Grass' from *Parasites of Heaven*, Cohen makes a self-referential allusion to his changing personas – 'Leonard hasn't been the same / since he wandered from his name'. To name something is to give it a sense of fixity. The name familiarizes the person and allows us to believe we know who they are and how he or she will behave. By 'wandering from his name', Cohen rejects this fixity and with it the idea that he can be known by anyone – be it fans, critics or lovers. This rejection of the identity conferred upon him by others allows him to form a new sense of self, but without a name it remains formless and mutable, liable to become anything except intractable – an idea which fascinated both Dylan and Cohen throughout their careers.

Cohen's multiple monikers were also an attempt to combat the vast 'array of aliases given to him by the press' which characterized him as 'an artist whose stock-in-trade seemingly consist[ed] of little else than making people feel miserable'[63] – such as 'The Godfather of Gloom', 'The High Priest of Pathos', 'the Mel Brooks of Misery'[64] and 'The Montreal Mope'.[65] The use of aliases allowed Cohen to reclaim his self-image and project a version of himself that he hoped would eclipse the journalistic stereotypes of 'Laughing Lenny'.

This projected image, as we have discussed, also disguised Cohen's private self as he became increasingly involved in publicity, performing and self-promotion. Though his work is self-referential – his L. Cohen signature at the end of 'Famous

---

[62] Paul Saltzman, 'Famous Last Words from Leonard Cohen (The Poet's Final Interview, He Hopes)' *Macleans* (June 1972), reprinted in *Leonard Cohen on Leonard Cohen*, ed. Burger, p. 39.

[63] Agust Magnusson, 'The Existential Cohen', in *Various Positions: Leonard Cohen and Philosophy* edited by Jason Holt (Illinois: Open Court, 2014), p. 15.

[64] Ben Thompson, 'Back to Life with a Blast from the Rocket Man', *The Independent on Sunday* (16 May 1993).

[65] Brad Wheeler, 'Disc of the Week: From Leonard Cohen, Even Old Ideas Are Worthwhile', *The Globe and Mail* (4 February 2012).

Blue Raincoat', the repeated refrain of his name on 'Because Of' *(Dear Heather,* 2004) where women implore 'look at me Leonard' – it is always the 'Leonard Cohen' persona that is referenced, rather than the man himself. In 'Going Home' from *Old Ideas* (2012), Cohen says that he would 'love to speak to Leonard / He's a sportsman and a shepherd'. The longing to speak to his own fictional persona is made more poignant in the chorus, when he sheds this disguise: 'Going home / without my burden / going home / behind the curtain / going home / without this costume / that I wore.' The theatrical imagery augments the idea of 'Leonard Cohen' as a character and disguise as the curtain falls and the singer discards his costume.

The mask as revelation

Throughout his performing career, Cohen used masks and personas both to achieve fame and to distance himself from its ill effects. In this section we will examine Cohen's use of the mask as an agent of revelation. As we saw, the mask has a long-established tradition of allowing its wearer to speak truthfully, shielded from the consequences of their words. In Daphne du Maurier's biography of the Brontë sisters' unfortunate brother Branwell, she informs her readers that the family's father, Reverend Patrick Brontë, would place his children behind a mask when he wished them to tell the truth. Behind the mask and with 'the blessed thrill of anonymity', the sisters were able to 'speak aloud, and yet remain . . . unknown . . . [hidden] behind a hollow face; criticism, mockery, reproof – these things could not touch the wearer of the mask'.[66] For Cohen, his theatrical personas performed a similar function, allowing him to reveal both personal and – what he believed to be – universal truths through his various personas and characters.

Cohen's lyrics and poems have the impressive ability to seem at once intimate and aloof, his audience kept at a distance by the ironic tone of his confessions. Irony functions as a form of not only self-disguise but also self-disclosure. This was a concept practised by the Ancient Greek philosopher Socrates, which Kierkegaard examined in *The Concept of Irony*. Socrates assumed a posture of ironic naivete when instructing the youth of Athens, educating them through his dissembling. Christopher Laeur notes that 'just as Cohen has made a career

---

[66] Daphne du Maurier, *The Infernal World of Branwell Brontë* (London: Virago, 2006), p. 7.

of being simultaneously confessional and reclusive, Socrates always seemed to be hiding something of himself, even when his language sounded straightforward'.[67] This Socratic irony can be detected in Cohen's work. His lyrics often switched between first, second and third person perspective, allowing him to explore various positions from an ironic distance while remaining uncommitted to either point of view. Though he has been accused of overusing the pronoun 'I', his songs and poems are just as likely to feature the collective 'we' or the second person 'you'. In *The Energy of Slaves* (1972), for example, we see this frequent switching of perspectives from 'we' to 'my', to 'your'.

Superficially Cohen has been considered a more straightforward and less evasive figure than Bob Dylan. Cohen did not engage in the same blatant adoption of masks, disguises and tactical manoeuvring with the media that have defined Dylan's performing persona. As Gary Shapiro puts it, Cohen appeared to wear 'his heart on his sleeve or some less clothed part of his body'.[68] Cohen fans cite biographical references as key to understanding his music and it is hard to deny that many of the details in his work draw upon his personal life, what he calls reportage, but this does not mean that the narrative voice in his novels, lyrics and poems is interchangeable with Cohen's own voice. The biographical events that feature in the works may have provided inspiration for Cohen's art, but that does not mean the emotions, reactions and conclusions drawn by Cohen's narrators are the same as those of the man who created them. Like all great artists, Cohen was able to take the personal and make it universal, speaking of shared rather than insular experiences through his assumed personas.

Wieland Schwanebeck uses the concept of the 'lyrical self' employed in literature studies to 'avoid confusion between the historical person who wrote the poem (the author) and the voice that is speaking in the poem'.[69] At a rudimentary level of English Literature education, we are taught that it is a fallacy to confuse the author with the voice they assume in their narrative, but it is one that is often committed. Canadian novelist and critic Michael Ondaatje made the error of seeing the central characters in Cohen's *Beautiful Losers* as nakedly autobiographical, arguing that they were 'powerful extension[s] of several of the

[67] Christopher Laeur, 'Irony as Seduction', in *Various Positions: Leonard Cohen and Philosophy*, ed. Holt, p. 90.

[68] Gary Shapiro, 'The End of the World and Other Times in *The Future*', in *Various Positions: Leonard Cohen and Philosophy*, ed. Holt, p. 39.

[69] Wieland Schwanebeck, 'Why Cohen's Our Man', in *Various Positions: Leonard Cohen and Philosophy*, ed. Holt, p. 28.

traits of Leonard Cohen.[70] He saw the tortured narrator and his rambunctious companion F. as opposing aspects of Cohen's dual nature. This reading, however, neglects the novel's political themes – namely that of the deep divisions between French and English Canadians in the twentieth century. The character of F. is a French nationalist while the narrator is an English-speaking Quebecois. The alternating conflict and intimacy between these two characters represents the tensions that Cohen witnessed between the French and English communities in Montreal, and the examination of this novel through biographical referents is to miss much of its point.

Cohen's first novel, far more than *Beautiful Losers*, lends itself to an autobiographical interpretation, focusing as it does on the struggles of a young poet in Montreal. While the character of Lawrence Breavmen is undoubtedly a cipher for Cohen himself, like all great artists, Cohen transmutes the details of his own life into universal truths. The experiences of Breavmen and Cohen may have been the same, but the novel translates these into art, rather than mere diary entries.

The temptation to take Cohen at his word is more tempting in his songs and poems. The narrative persona that speaks to us as 'Leonard Cohen' misleads us into believing it is the man not the mask that is revealing intimate secrets into the microphone. Stephen Scobie has advocated the approach of reading 'Leonard Cohen' as a text. In a keynote address for *Canadian Poetry's* 1993 conference on the work of Leonard Cohen, Scobie decried the 'facile and dangerous' examination of Cohen's work through an autobiographical lens, advising his audience instead to 'read "Leonard Cohen" – the figure who sits in that Los Angeles bar, or who appears on the *Tonight* show with Jay Leno . . . very much as text, as part of the work, perhaps indeed as the *centre* of the work'.[71] If we take Cohen as a text, we separate the man from the persona, allowing his words to speak to us from behind the 'Leonard Cohen' mask.

Lebold argues that in concert, Cohen 'changes masks from song to song: he is in turn lecherous sinner, wandering Jew, hopeless monk, Zen master, high priest'.[72] The performance of each of these personas is a powerful agent of revelation for his audience who recognize both aspects of Cohen and themselves

---

[70] Ondaatje, *Leonard Cohen*, p. 45. Quoted in Steven Burns, 'Politics in Beautiful Losers', in *Various Positions: Leonard Cohen and Philosophy*, ed. Holt, p. 144.
[71] Scobie, 'The Counterfeiter Begs Forgiveness', pp. 12–13.
[72] Lebold, 'The Traitor and the Stowaway', p. 13.

in each character. The three functions of the mask cannot be activated by the performer alone. The audience must participate in the activation of the mask, believing in its power to transform, conceal and reveal. The mask is controlled by its wearer, but that control is not total. As Nourit Melcer-Padon observes, 'masks can only reflect what is projected onto them: if we do not like what we see, we have only ourselves to blame.'[73] The personas that Cohen adopted onstage and in his poetry, novels and lyrics are extensions of his own personality, but they were also facets of his audience's identities which they both projected onto the figure of Cohen and saw reflected back at them.

Cohen was aware of the importance of showmanship and theatricality in communicating his messages to the crowd. In 1974 he told an interviewer, 'whatever you do, you should be an entertainer first . . . Their imagination has to be engaged and they have to enter into the vortex of imagination and relaxation and suspense that is involved in entertainment.'[74] As we discussed in our chapter on Bob Dylan and masks, authenticity is often seen as an important component of the singer-songwriter's craft. Cohen often struggled to be accepted by the folk movement which prized this authenticity above all else, yet his acknowledgement that the singer must also be an entertainer allowed him to engage audiences while exploring taboo themes such as death, religion, sex and the profane intertwining of all three.

The eighteenth-century French philosopher Jean-Jacques Rousseau shared a similar disdain for theatrics as the folk movement in the early 1960s. In his *Lettre à Monsieur d'Alembert,* Rousseau describes the theatre and its players as inherently corrupt.

> What is the talent of an actor? . . . The art of counterfeit: the art of assuming a personality other than his own, of appearing different from what he is, simulating passion while his feelings are cold, of saying something he does not believe just as naturally as if he really believed it.[75]

Rousseau then goes on to separate the orator – or politician – from the actor, declaring that the orator is authentic and trustworthy because he speaks for

[73] Nourit Melcer-Padon, 'Visual Mask Metaphors in Jean Genet and Maurizzio Cattelan', *Partial Answers: Journal of Literature and the History of Ideas,* vol. 18, no. 1 (January 2020), p. 75. DOI: https://doi.org/10.1353/pan.2020.0003. Accessed 6 May 2020.
[74] Robin Pike, 'September Fifteen 1974', *Zig-Zag magazine* (October 1974). Quoted in Lebold, 'Traitor and the Stowaway', p. 12.
[75] Jean-Jacques Rousseau, *Citoyen de Genève, à Monsieur d'Alembert,* Amsterdam, Rey, 1758, p. 143. Quoted in Maurice Cranston, *The Mask of Politics and Other Essays* (New York: Library Press, 1973), p. 2.

himself, in his own words, with no calculated artifice or carefully prepared mask – 'the man and the *persona* are identical.'[76] This criticism seems charmingly naïve when we consider our modern politicians, stage-managed and media-trained to deliver scripted messages written by professional speech writers. Indeed, in this essence, actors are more honest than the politician because their artifice is already exposed. Actors draw upon their own experiences to portray real emotions, subsuming their identity into their role behind the mask of the character they play onstage. The politician, conversely, must necessarily practice evasion and dishonesty to present an electable image.

Despite the bravery Cohen may have felt behind his theatrical mask, the fear of 'disgrace' and 'humiliation' that he had felt before embarking on his first concert tour continued to haunt him throughout his career. In 1986, he told a reporter that he was 'always struggling with the material, whether it's a concert or a poem or a prayer or a conversation. It's very rarely I find I'm in a condition of grace where there's a kind of flow that is natural.'[77] Just before embarking upon the world tour of 2008, his first tour since 1993, Cohen's anxiety had not abated. Even after months of rehearsal he said: 'Second to last day of rehearsal. Must confess to some degree of anxiety.'[78] This self-consciousness presented a genuine problem for Cohen as a performer, but the adoption of the 'Leonard Cohen' mask allowed him to engage with audiences and speak openly and honestly because any criticism levelled at the performer could be kept separate from the man.

Costume was essential to the presentation of the 'Leonard Cohen' persona. His sartorial choices became a form of self-revelation, signifying both to his audience and himself the sort of man that he was. As the son of a clothing manufacturer, Cohen was always impeccably dressed – and it is perhaps his dedication to elegant dressing that initially kept him from being enthusiastically accepted by the folk scene, as his refinement had kept him just outside the orbit of the Beat generation years earlier. Clothes, for Cohen, were essential in the construction of his personal and performing identity, and, unlike Dylan, he remained faithful to a signature style throughout his lifetime.

Interviews with Cohen rarely failed to mention what he was wearing, with *Rolling Stone* noting his 'conservatively flared tan pants, black shirt and bush

---

[76] Cranston, *The Mask of Politics*, p. 2.
[77] Interview with Robert Sward in *Malahat Review* (December 1986), reprinted in *Leonard Cohen on Leonard Cohen,* ed. Burger, p. 168.
[78] Email from Leonard Cohen to David Boucher, dated 29 April 2008.

jacket'[79] and a reflective piece written by Mikal Gilmore after Cohen's death recalling the chalk-striped double-breasted suit he wore at Carnegie Hall in July 1988. The suit may have made an impression on the journalist because of the attention Cohen himself paid to its presentation:

> At one point he stood up, slipped off his pants and folded them neatly over the back of another chair. It was a sensible thing to do. It was such a hot day; why wrinkle the slacks to a nice suit? Cohen kept on his jacket and tie, his socks, shoes and blue-and-white-lined boxer shorts as he sat back down.[80]

In a piece for the *Globe and Mail*, Natalie Atkinson notes that Cohen's signature sartorial choices were of the 'synergistic' style that marketing executives and stylists would want their artists to wear to align with their 'brand'.[81] For Cohen, however, his clothing was a mask which not only helped him slip into his public persona but also connect with his true self.

> I wear out the old things I've got . . . I can't find any [new] clothes that represent me . . . Clothes are magical, a magical procedure, they really change who you are in a day . . . until I can discover in some clearer way what I am to myself, I'll just keep on wearing my old clothes.[82]

This passion for sartorial elegance rarely waned, but on the 1970–1 tour when he earned for himself the nickname 'Captain Mandrax', he appeared onstage at the Isle of Wight festival, a dishevelled figure in over-sized army fatigues, unshaven, and long unkempt hair, which perhaps added another layer of protection against his 200,000 strong audience. Even after his ordination as a Buddhist monk in 1996, when he wasn't wearing the traditional robe, he often wore Armani suits while he meditated, and as 'he imbued his everyday look with such monastic intention the blazers and trousers may as well have been liturgical vestments.'[83] In 2011, Cohen even collaborated with high fashion brand Comme des Garçons to create a capsule collection featuring his lyrics and drawings. Unlike Bob

[79] Jack Hafferkamp, 'Ladies & Gents, Leonard Cohen', *Rolling Stone* (4 February 1971), reprinted in *Leonard Cohen on Leonard Cohen*, ed. Burger, p. 20.

[80] Mikal Gilmore, 'Leonard Cohen: Remembering the Life and Legacy of the Poet of Brokenness', *Rolling Stone* (30 November 2016). https://www.rollingstone.com/music/music-features/leonard-cohen-remembering-the-life-and-legacy-of-the-poet-of-brokenness-192994/. Accessed 27 May 2020.

[81] Nathalie Atkinson, 'His Spirit and His Clothes', *Globe and Mail* (12 October 2017). https://www.theglobeandmail.com/life/fashion-and-beauty/fashion/singing-the-sartorial-praises-of-leonard-cohen-canadas-moody-mens-wearicon/article36485080/. Accessed 27 May 2020.

[82] Michael Harris, 'An Interview with Leonard Cohen', *Duel* (Winter 1969), reprinted in *Leonard Cohen on Leonard Cohen*, ed. Burger, p. 17.

[83] Harris, 'An Interview with Leonard Cohen', reprinted in *Leonard Cohen on Leonard Cohen*, ed. Burger, p. 17.

Dylan's appearance in car commercials, underwear adverts and various other commercial endeavours which could cause him to be accused of 'selling out', this collaboration aligned with Cohen's essential belief that clothes were an expression of the true self. He believed that the mask of fashion was both a transformative act and a revealing one – allowing the wearer to become who he wanted to be, while simultaneously exposing his authentic self.

Conclusion

We have seen how Cohen adopted the three functions of the mask, less explicitly perhaps than Dylan, but nevertheless evidently so. First as a mode of self-protection, second for self-projection and third as a vehicle of authenticity to inhabit the characters of his songs and reveal their enduring wisdom. Although the mask afforded some degree of protection, it did not protect him from himself. His fragile mental condition, exacerbated by substance abuse, and calmed to some extent by the quest for spiritual healing, did not abate until old age, when he resigned himself to the realization that there was no ultimate reality to find or discover. Throughout the new millennium, the depression having lifted, he became much more effective at protecting himself from the prying public gaze, especially during his world tour of 2008–13 when no one, except in carefully controlled circumstances, got to see the man behind the perfectly orchestrated public performances.

The persona he almost consistently projected as an act of self-disclosure from the release of *Dear Heather* in 2004, which begins with Lord Byron's poem 'Go No More a-Roving', dedicated to his old friend Irving Layton who was suffering from dementia near the end of his life, to the posthumously produced *Thanks for the Dance* (2019) which ends with 'Listen to the Hummingbird', is of self-resignation, self-deprecation and the coming to terms with age and mortality. The quest for spiritual enlightenment, as we saw in Chapter 3, ended in a reconciliation with the religion of his ancestors. There was no raging against the dying of the light in Cohen's resignation and acceptance of his mortality, and he announced to his God, 'I'm ready my Lord' ('You want it Darker') and tells his audience in an act of self-negation: 'Listen to the hummingbird /Whose wings you cannot see / Listen to the Hummingbird / Don't Listen to me' ('Listen to the Hummingbird').

7

Poetry and song

I don't care what people call me, whether you call it folksinging or some people call it a priestly function . . . or poets see it as the popularisation of poetry.

– Leonard Cohen[1]

Poetry is just bullshit.

– Bob Dylan[2]

Introduction

So far we have looked at the enduring careers of Bob Dylan and Leonard Cohen, exploring the different contexts in which they may be located; the undulations in their career trajectories; their ambivalent relationship with religion; their relation to Dylan Thomas, the Beats and the allure of fame; and the motif of the mask in their lives. In this chapter, and the following two, we explore the relationship between poetry and song and consider competing aesthetic considerations for assisting in understanding the artistic creations of the American and Canadian.

Bob Dylan and Leonard Cohen have both been hailed the 'poets' and spokesmen of their generation, yet each has expressed a reticence towards the titles. Bob Dylan has deflected the question of whether his work can be considered poetry with acerbic retorts, telling one interviewer in 1965 that he would rather be known as a 'trapeze artist'.[3] He has spent most of his career since rejecting the folk movement claiming that he never was a spokesman for anyone. Leonard Cohen, though he began his career as a poet, and became evasive about the appellation, putting the responsibility on others to make the judgement,

---

[1] Sandra Djwa, 'After the Wipeout, The Renewal', *The Ubyssey* (3 February 1967) reprinted in *Leonard Cohen on Leonard Cohen: Interviews and Encounters,* ed. Jeff Burger (Chicago: Chicago Review Press, 2014), p. 13.

[2] 'Interview with Paul J. Robbins', *L.A Free Press* (March 1965) reprinted in *Dylan on Dylan: The Essential Interviews,* ed. Jonathan Cott (London: Hodder & Stoughton, 2006), p. 41.

[3] 'Interview with Nora Ephron and Susan Edmiston', *Positively Tie Dream* (August 1965) reprinted in *Dylan on Dylan: The Essential Interviews,* ed. Jonathan Cott (London: Hodder and Stoughton, 2007), p. 49.

became far more well known for his music. While he initially aspired to perform the role of spokesman, he never was a crusader, and eventually self-effacement won through.

The divide between poetry and popular song has proved difficult for literary scholars to conceptualize and bridge. Publication of Richard Goldstein's 1969 *The Poetry of Rock*, which anthologized the lyrics of both Dylan and Cohen, has gone some way to legitimizing the study of the 'pop' lyric as poetry, but there is still a reluctance among the academic community to accept the song lyric alongside the stanza as a legitimate form of high culture. To understand the tension between poetry and song, we must first ask ourselves – 'what is poetry?'

What is poetry?

'Poetry', like the concept of 'freedom', is what the philosopher Maurice Cranston would term a 'hooray word'.[4] To call something 'poetic' is to invoke a positive sense of approval, legitimizing the work with the stamp of 'high culture'. Poetry is an evaluative term. It describes an art form that is readily identified, yet its definition remains contested. The common conception of poetry is that of words on a page, arranged into stanzas which are governed by rhyme, schemes and metres. This description, however, excludes the vast array of works that are judged as poetry while refusing to conform to the idea of how poetry should look and sound.

Literary critics seem unable to agree on a fixed definition of the form, and its classification has remained a site of heated debate, ranging from the literal to the metaphysical. In 1918, the 'Poetry Lovers of New York City' offered a fifty-dollar prize to the public for the best definition of poetry, prompting Petronius Arbiter to write a piece in *The Art World* journal exploring the subject. He deplored the idea that poetry escaped definition and blamed the 'blatant egoists' of the modernist movement who trespassed the 'fundamental laws'[5] that governed the art. For Arbiter, the definition was simple: 'poetry is an expression of thought and emotion, in a written language, of a more or less rhythmical form'.[6] The

---

[4] Maurice Cranston, *Freedom: A New Analysis*, revised third edition (Upper Saddle River, NJ: Prentice Hall, 1967).

[5] Petronius Arbiter, 'What Is Poetry?' *The Crayon*, vol. 3, no. 6 (March 1918), p. 506. https://www.jstor.org/stable/25588388. Accessed 7 March 2020.

[6] Arbiter, 'What Is Poetry?' p. 506.

celebrated philosopher and scientist Hudson Maxim agreed, declaring that poetry 'is no haphazard art . . . it is the child of law, and conforms to law'.[7]

This emphasis on the literal definition of poetry, focusing on language and structure, neglects the metaphysical and spiritual element of poetry that elevates it as an art form. Sir Philip Sydney (1554–86) argued that 'it is not rhyming and versing that maketh a Poet – no more than a long gowne maketh an advocate'.[8] Edgar Lee Masters contended that 'poetry is the orientation of the soul to conditions in life',[9] including, for him, the works of Shakespeare and the books of the Bible.

When we expand the definition of poetry beyond its arrangement on the page, it extends to a wide variety of forms not conventionally considered 'poetic'. Paul Garon has argued that blues music should be considered poetry because 'poetic art necessarily contains within itself elements of revolutionary ferment manifested as the struggle for freedom'.[10] Garon dismisses academia and formal education as a hindrance to achieving this state of freedom, arguing that formal poetry is incapable of expressing original thoughts. This stance, though not articulated as such, is reflective of Bob Dylan's own anti-intellectual assertions. In his early interviews he was keen to reject the confines of the classroom for an education among the working men, believing that folk ballads were more enlightening than the formalized style of T. S. Eliot and Ezra Pound. In his autobiography Dylan expressed his contempt for mainstream culture. He described it as 'lame as hell and a big trick'.[11] In the same book he refers to himself as a 'poet musician'.[12] As far as he was concerned the songs were not just about the words. If that were the case, he asked rhetorically, 'what was Duane Eddy, the great rock-and-roll guitarist, doing recording an album full of instrumental melodies of my songs?'[13]

Despite his ambivalent view of poetry, Dylan was reluctant to draw firm distinctions between poetry and song. In a 1965 interview he said, 'poetry isn't really confined to the printed page' and that his lyrics were 'written as you can

[7] Hudson Maxim, *The Science of Poetry and the Philosophy of Language* (New York: Funk & Wagnalls Company, 1910), p. 54.
[8] Sir Philip Sidney, *An Apology for Poetry or the Defence of Poesy*, ed. R. W. Maslen and Geoffrey Shepherd (Manchester: Manchester University Press, 2002), p. 87.
[9] Edgar Lee Masters, 'What Is Poetry?' *Poetry*, vol. 6, no. 6 (September 1915), p. 307. https://www.jstor.org/stable/20570534. Accessed 7 March 2020.
[10] Paul Garon, *Blues and the Poetic Spirit* (San Francisco: City Lights, 1996), p. 1.
[11] Bob Dylan, *Chronicles volume one* (New York: Simon & Schuster, 2004) p. 35.
[12] Dylan, *Chronicles*, p. 98.
[13] Dylan, *Chronicles,* p. 119.

read it . . . If you take whatever there is to the song away – the beat, the melody – I could still recite it'.[14] Yet, in a characteristic display of self-contradiction, he went on to claim, in the same breath, that 'songs are just songs . . . I don't believe in expecting too much out of any one thing'.[15]

Leonard Cohen, who fraternized with the denizens of the Ivory Tower, such as his Canadian poetry fraternity, Louis Dudek, F. R. Scott, A. M. Klein and Irving Layton, had no interest in pursuing an academic career. He described poetry as a verdict, rather than an intention. The poet cannot declare his work to be poetry; it is an honour that must be conferred upon him by external sources.

While Dylan and Cohen have consistently been championed as lyric poets, the music industry has also been quick to confer this honour on more dubious candidates, packaging the song lyrics of pop stars such as Jim Morrison, Van Morrison, Patti Smith, Joni Mitchell, Shane MacGowan and Bob Geldof into slickly designed volumes of poetry. While pop lyrics may be poetical, they are not intrinsically so. The quality of a lyric is often contingent on its context; many lines from popular songs are unable to function outside of their musical framework, but some soar above others with their poignancy and resonance for the listener. Stephen Troussé has remarked upon the 'tremendous and deep-rooted embarrassment involved in taking the pop lyric seriously', perhaps because of the 'splendid banality' of lyrics such as T. Rex's 'I drive a Rolls Royce / cuz it's good for my voice'.[16] Stephen Scobie, however, contends that conferring the accolade of 'poet' upon a performing artist is a form of academic snobbery which perpetuates the idea that popular music is only valuable when it adheres to the criteria of 'high culture'. For this reason, 'many critics have felt compelled to insist that Dylan is not a poet, but, in a positive sense, a songwriter'.[17]

Historical links between song and poetry

Poetry evades easy classifications, and its ambiguous nature has permitted critics to consider the works of Bob Dylan and Leonard Cohen within a poetical

[14] 'Interview with Paul J. Robbins', *L.A Free Press* (March 1965) reprinted in *Dylan on Dylan*, ed. Cott, p. 37.

[15] 'Interview with Paul J. Robbins', *Dylan on Dylan*, ed. Cott, p. 37.

[16] Stephen Troussé, 'Stupid & Contagious: The Pleasures of the Text', in *The Message: Crossing the Tracks between Poetry and Pop*, ed. Roddy Lumsden and Stephen Troussé (London: The Poetry Society, 1999), p. 41.

[17] Stephen Scobie, *Alias: Bob Dylan, Revisited* (Canada: Red Deer Press, 2004), p. 93.

framework. This is not, as Scobie suggested, entirely an exercise in 'academic snobbery'. Poetry and song may be mutually exclusive categories in modern society, but in antiquity there was no such demarcation. The term 'lyric' comes from the Greek '*lyrikos*' which translates literally to 'singing to the lyre.' In ancient cultures there was a unity between poetry and music that only began to fracture with the introduction of the written word. The combination of the two forms survived the centuries in various iterations, through the bardic tradition and the entertainments of courtiers, until the invention of the printing press created a definitive rift between the two arts. There is, however, no consensus on the exact moment that poetry and song became divided.

Jacques Derrida, French philosopher and founder of the deconstructionist movement, believed that the separation of song from speech occurred at its inception; 'degeneration as separation, severing of voice and song, has always already begun'.[18] Giorgio Agamben dates the breach between poetry and song from the end of the twelfth century when the poem became 'essentially graphic'.[19] James William Johnson believes the metamorphosis in the relationship between poetry and song occurred later, in the fifteenth or sixteenth century, when poets ceased to compose their work for musical presentation and began to write for an audience of readers. This led to poetry becoming a visual rather than a solely auditory medium as the lyric 'found itself bereft of the very element which had been the foundation of its lyricism – music'.[20]

The distinction between poetry and song is also a marker of the divide between 'high' and 'low' culture. In the preface to a nineteenth-century edition of the *Oxford Book of Ballads*, Sir Arthur Quiller Couch wrote that the ballad did not fare well juxtaposed against formalized poetry in other anthologies. 'I have sometimes been forced to reconsider my affection and ask "Are these ballads really beautiful as they have always appeared to me?" . . . the contrast between children and grown folk would be unfair'.[21] This distinction seems to dismiss the ballads as immature and unrefined, yet both Dylan and Cohen have cited the

---

[18] Jacques Derrida, *Of Grammatology*, quoted in Jahan Ramazani, '"Sing to Me Now": Contemporary American Poetry and Song', *Contemporary Literature*, vol. 52, no. 4 (Winter 2011). https://www.jstor.org./stable/41472492. Accessed 1 March 2020.

[19] Giorgio Agamben, *The End of the Poem: Studies in Poetics* (Stanford, CA: Stanford University Press, 1999), p. 33, quoted in Ramazani, 'Sing to Me Now', p. 716.

[20] James William Johnson, 'Lyric', in *The New Princeton Encyclopaedia of Poetry and Poetics* ed. Alex Preminger and T. V. F. Brogan (Princeton, NJ: Princeton University Press, 1993), p. 714, quoted in Ramazani, 'Sing to Me Now', p. 716.

[21] Sir Arthur Quiller Couch, quoted in John Gibbens, *The Nightingale's Code: A Poetic Study of Bob Dylan* (London: Touched Press, 2001), p. 14.

profound influence of folk ballads on their own work. Indeed, Cohen claimed that his early interest in poetry was not inspired by other poets but arose from researching the lyrics of Appalachian folk ballads which 'touched him deeply'.[22]

Despite the arbitrary divide between the song and the poem, the boundaries between the two are not impermeable. Poets have often collaborated with musicians to set their work to music – the Beat poet Allen Ginsberg released a 'folk' album in 1981 entitled *First Blues, Rags, Ballads and Harmonium Songs* and the avant-garde composer Philip Glass created a song cycle which set the poems of Leonard Cohen's *Book of Longing* to orchestral accompaniment.

The fusion of poetry and music, however, has not always been greeted with success. Jacques Roubad has denounced the cross-contamination of the two forms, believing it to be 'an insult to poetry to call it song. It's an insult to song to call it poetry'.[23] The setting of poetry written outside of a musical framework to instrumental accompaniment has not always been well received, and there are doubts as to whether it can be considered song, but there is no denying that the combination of music and lyrics can have poetic effects. Jacques Brel and Serge Gainsbourg, exemplars of the French chanteuse tradition wherein lyrics are given equal prominence with the music, are acclaimed for both their singing styles and powerful lyric poetry. Leonard Cohen, hailing from French-dominated Quebec, was considered a part of this tradition. One reviewer described him as 'singing in the style of the French-Canadian chansonnier'.[24]

While poetry and song have been entwined throughout the ages, the contemporary concept of the 'singer-songwriter' in popular music did not emerge until the early 1960s when artists such as Dylan, Cohen, Patti Smith and Joni Mitchell reconnected the art of poetry with song. In 1968, the *New York Times* critic William Kloman described an up-and-coming Leonard Cohen as 'poet-novelist-composer-singer' and declared it to be 'the age of the hyphenate'.[25] The term 'singer-songwriter' did not enter the popular lexicon until the 1970s and in the meantime 'poet' was applied liberally to this new generation of performing artists, giving the genre the kudos of 'high culture'.

---

[22] Vin Scesla, 'Radio Interview', *Idiots Delight*, WXRK-FM (13 June 1993) reprinted in *Leonard Cohen on Leonard Cohen*, ed. Burger, p. 339.

[23] Jacques Roubad, 'Prelude: Poetry and Orality', quoted in Ramazani, 'Sing to Me Now', p. 726.

[24] *Aspen Magazine*, vol. 1, no. 3, p. 4.

[25] William Kloman, '"I've Been on the Outlaw Scene Since 15": Leonard Cohen', *New York Times* (28 January 1968) D21, quoted in Christa Anne Bentley, '"Poet Composers": Art and Legitimacy in the Singer-Songwriter Movement', in *Routledge Companion to Popular Music Analysis: Expanding Approaches*, ed. Ciro Scotto, Kenneth M. Scott and John Brackett (London: Routledge, 2018), p. 416.

Christa Anne Bentley, in her essay on authenticity in art, is cynical about these claims. She argues that these performers were more mercenaries than *artistes,* using the protective armour of 'poetry' to shield themselves from accusations of commercialism. She points to the language used by reviewer Robert Shelton when he lauded Bob Dylan's abandonment of the left-wing folk movement and overt political messaging for the more confessional and personal approach to song-writing evident on *Another Side of Bob Dylan* (1964), declaring him 'the poet laureate of young America'.[26]

Leonard Cohen, already an established poet and novelist, was essential in legitimizing the claims of this new hyphenate generation of musicians to be taken seriously as poets and artists, rather than pop stars. In 1968, the same year his first album was released, Cohen was honoured with the Canadian governor general's 'Award for English Language Poetry or Drama' for *Selected Poems 1956–1968*, which he declined. Bentley may deem the 'poet-singer' a dubious distinction, dreamt up by record labels to generate sales and gain cultural kudos, but the impact that both Dylan's and Cohen's work had on the landscape of the English language in the twenty-first century is undeniable, with both of them frequently mentioned as worthy nominees for the Nobel Prize for literature, which Dylan, to the astonishment of some critics, was awarded in 2016. Delivering his Nobel lecture in 2017, Bob Dylan told his audience that the award had got him 'wondering how exactly my songs related to literature'.[27] We will now go on to consider this question in relation to both Dylan and Cohen.

Similarities and differences between poetry and song

Roddy Lumsden, in his introduction to *The Message: Crossing the Tracks Between Poetry and Pop*, a collection of essays which examines the link between pop music and poetry, claims that 'poems and lyrics are . . . intrinsically different, though poetry and song are kissing cousins'.[28] Lyrics, stripped of their musical scaffolding, can often fall flat on the page, while poetry set to music tends to lack

---

[26] Robert Shelton, 'Bob Dylan Shows New Maturity in his Program of Folk Songs', *New York Times* (2 November 1964), p. 62, quoted in Bentley, '"Poet Composers": Art and Legitimacy in the Singer-Songwriter Movement', p. 419.

[27] Dylan, *The Nobel Lecture* (London: Simon & Schuster, 2017), p. 1.

[28] Roddy Lumsden, 'Introduction', in *The Message: Crossing the Tracks Between Poetry and Pop*, ed. Roddy Lumsden and Stephen Troussé (London: The Poetry Society, 1999), p. 1.

the affective power of song. There are, however, commonalities between the two forms which have kept them entwined in critical discourse.

Simon Frith believes it is 'aesthetically misleading'[29] to create strict boundaries between 'poetry' and 'song'. Rather than division, there is continuity between the forms, and many have seen both Dylan's and Cohen's work as a continuation of poetry's ancient oral tradition of delivering poetic lyrics to musical accompaniment. This was certainly the view of Henrietta Yurchenco, folk-music broadcaster and champion of Bob Dylan, who likened him to 'a bard – he is a singing poet in an ancient but thoroughly neglected tradition', going so far as to claim that 'he has given poetry a significance and stature which it has never had in American life'.[30] Paul Williams agrees with this assessment. He sees poetry as essentially a performing art with roots that extend beyond the advent of written communication, and though the modern conception of the poet is 'not of someone who walks out into the street with his latest pages . . . That . . . is what writing was like for Dylan'.[31] Fahri Öz echoes the idea of Dylan as a performing poet. He claims that 'poetry in its infancy was a performative art, and the lyric was originally a spectacle delivered by a bard or rhapsode performing in front of an audience'.[32] Richard F. Thomas, professor of Classics at Harvard and the man responsible for establishing a freshman seminar at the university devoted to the study of Bob Dylan, also sees Dylan as a poet in the Homeric sense. He claims that he 'works like a blend of rhapsode (performing artist) and poet on the cusp of oral and literary cultures . . . like Homer he is the original creator and original performer of his narratives and lyrics, the seeds of which may be found in a whole range of texts from the Bible to the blues'.[33]

Leonard Cohen has spoken about the arbitrary distinctions drawn between art forms; 'just because the lines don't come to the end of the page doesn't necessarily qualify it as poetry. Just because they do doesn't make it prose'.[34] The similarities between lyrics and poetry are clear – both are governed by metres and rhyme schemes, and both employ similar rhetorical and imagistic devices

---

[29] Simon Frith, quoted in Scobie, *Alias Revisited*, p. 93.

[30] Henrietta Yurchenco, 'Folk-Rot: In Defence', *Sound and Fury* (April 1966) reprinted in *The Bob Dylan Companion*, ed. Carl Benson (New York: Schirmer Books, 1998), pp. 67 and 69.

[31] Paul Williams, *Bob Dylan: Performing Artist 1960-1973, The Early Years* (London: Omnibus Press, 1994), p. 44.

[32] Fahri Öz, 'Performative Lyric Voice and the Refrain as an Architectonic Element in Bob Dylan', in *Tearing the World Apart: Bob Dylan in the Twenty-First Century*, ed. Nina Goss and Eric Hoffman (Jackson: University of Mississippi, 2017), p. 134.

[33] Richard F. Thomas, 'The Streets of Rome: The Classical Dylan', *Oral Tradition*, vol. 22, no. 1 (2007), pp. 48–9.

[34] Jack Hafferkamp, 'Ladies and Gents, Leonard Cohen', Late 1970 interview, *Rolling Stone*, reprinted in *Leonard Cohen on Leonard Cohen*, ed. Burger, p. 20.

– and Cohen was keen to celebrate the convergence of the two forms. He once claimed that even when he was focused on poetry and novel writing, I 'never wanted my work to get too far away from music. Ezra Pound said something very interesting, "when poetry strays too far from music, it atrophies".'[35]

Öz argues that the lyric shares many commonalities with the popular song, one such being the 'refrain' – the repetition of a key line or concept that characterizes the modern song but has strong roots in poetry. Edgar Allen Poe discussed the importance of this device in his essay 'The Philosophy of Composition', stating that 'the *refrain*, or burden, not only is limited to lyric verse . . . The pleasure is deduced solely from the sense of identity – of repetition.'[36] This sense of familiarity and pleasure in recognition of the repeated phrase is well known to anyone who has listened to Cohen declare 'first we take Manhattan, then we take Berlin' and Dylan's weary utterance of 'I used to care, but things have changed', or awaited the repetition of 'nevermore, quoth the Raven' in Poe's own poem.

Song lyrics can be analysed using the same literary techniques as poetry, as John Gibbens exemplifies in *The Nightingale Code: A Poetic Study of Bob Dylan*. Gibbens undertakes a painstaking analysis of Dylan's body of work using prosodic terms, noting 'the distinctive metrical foot'[37] in Dylan's early songs as an 'anapaest' and his uncommon use of 'dactyls' in the ballad 'The Lonesome Death of Hattie Carroll'. Christopher Ricks, professor of Poetry at Oxford University (2004–9), also takes this approach in *Dylan's Visions of Sin*. Stephen Scobie has commented on the poetic quality of Dylan's 'vivid and bizarre imagery'[38] in lines such as 'the motorcycle black Madonna / Two-wheeled gypsy queen', which are saved from farce by the deployment of poetic devices such as assonance, alliteration and rhyme to provide a counterbalance. Dylan's flamboyant metaphors are undercut by his 'street-slang' delivery, saving him from the accusations of pretentiousness that are levelled at other pop-stars-cum-poets such as Jim Morrison, who lacked both Dylan's and Cohen's irony and wit when employing similar imagery.

Despite Dylan's assertions that much of poetry is 'soft-boiled egg shit',[39] he has experimented with the form on numerous occasions. On April 12, 1963, Dylan

[35] Harvey Kubernik, 'Leonard Cohen: Cohen's New Skin', *Melody Maker* (1 March 1975). https://www.rocksbackpages.com/Library/Article/leonard-cohen-cohens-new-skin. Accessed 8 April 2020.
[36] Edgar Allen Poe, 'The Philosophy of Composition', in *The Raven and The Philosophy of Composition*, Project Gutenberg (website). http://www.gutenberg.org/files/55749/55749-h/55749-h.htm. Accessed 8 April 2020.
[37] Gibbens, *The Nightingale's Code*, p. 206.
[38] Scobie, *Alias Revisited*, p. 98.
[39] 'Interview with Paul J. Robbins', *L.A Free Press* (March 1965) reprinted in *Dylan on Dylan*, ed. Cott (London: Hodder & Stoughton, 2006), p. 39.

read a poem entitled 'Last Thoughts on Woody Guthrie' during a concert in New York City. The oration, performed without musical accompaniment, gained a standing ovation and the loudest applause of the evening. The accompanying programme for the concert contained another poem entitled 'My Life in a Stolen Moment' – a blank verse poem with a subtle and irregular metre, detailing the fictionalized version of his childhood that was being peddled in 1963.[40] 'For Dave Glover', a blank verse prose poem addressed to a friend from Minneapolis, was printed in the 1963 Newport Folk Festival programme and Dylan published his verse on the liner sleeves of some of his early albums, including, for example, *Bringing It All Back Home* (1965). Cohen, of course, began his career as a poet, first and foremost, and included poems and songs in his tour programmes and in the *libretto* of Philip Glass's *Book of Longing* (2007) based on his volume of poetry of the same name.

While poetry and lyrics rely on many of the same techniques, the two forms necessitate differences in approach. Patrick Crotty notes that popular lyrics rely on end-rhymes and internal rhymes for their structure in a way that poetry does not. Half-rhymes cannot be as nuanced on the page as they are when delivered in song as the music and singer's delivery allows approximations of rhymes to become full rhymes. Conversely, when poetry is set to music, the pararhymes and half-rhymes find themselves robbed of their 'subtly dissonantal powers'[41] by their musical accompaniment. Rhyme is also intensely satisfying for the listener or reader; we predict the next rhyme when introduced to the first and find ourselves disappointed if it is not fulfilled. The Victorian poet Algernon Swinburne commented that 'rhyme is the native condition of the lyric verse in English: a rhymeless lyric is a maimed thing',[42] which may explain why, given Dylan's lyrical innovations, he continues to adhere to the convention of rhyming.

Despite their commonalities, the two forms demand differing methods from their creators which mark them as distinct from one another. Cohen illustrates this when he recalled playing Dylan's *Bringing It All Back Home* at a party whose attendees included his old poetry professors Irving Layton and Louis Dudek. 'I

---

[40] There is no fixed number of lines in blank verse poetry. The metre, however, is conventional and often employed in verse drama and lengthy narrative poems.

[41] Patrick Crotty, 'Bob Dylan's Last Words', in *Do You, Mr Jones? Bob Dylan with the Poets and Professors* ed. Neil Corcoran (London: Chatto & Windus, 2002), p. 307.

[42] Algernon Charles Swinburne, quoted in Christopher Ricks, *Dylan's Visions of Sin* (London: Viking, 2003), p. 39.

said, "Fellas, listen to this. This guy's a real poet". I put the record on, and it was greeted with yawns. They said, "That's not a poet".[43]

The poem is a visual art form rather than a solely auditory one. The text contains within it the framework necessary to allow the reader to receive its meaning. Poets experiment with capitalization, the arrangement of stanzas into unusual shapes and patterns, and the use of punctuation, such as strikethroughs and brackets, which only come across on the page. This is what Jahan Ramazani terms the text's 'extravagantly graphic and typographic features'[44] – elements of the poem that are purely visual and inaccessible in song. Examples include Dylan Thomas's 'Vision and Prayer', the lines of which form the shapes of diamonds, and equilateral triangles, apex to apex; and, Gregory Corso's 'Bomb' in the shape of an atomic bomb mushroom cloud.[45] Bob Dylan was particularly impressed by Corso's 'Bomb' which summed-up for him the contemporary spirit better than anything else, 'a wasted world and totally mechanized – a lot of hustle and bustle . . .'[46] Song, too, contains its own unique features which are inaccessible to the written word as we will contend when we go on to explore the Spanish poet Federico Garcìa Lorca's theory of 'duende' which is most notably present in performance.

The centrality of music and its effect on language

There is inevitably a tension between music and language. The critic Lawrence Kramer has described the relationship between words and melodies as 'disintegrative' and 'agonic'.[47] Martin Boykan contends that there is always a 'disjunction between music and text' because music 'obliterates so many of the effects poetry relies on'.[48] Indeed, Ezra Pound was appalled by the disjunction that occurs when formal poetry is set to music, warning that the 'distortion may horrify the poet, who, having built his words into a perfect rhythm and

[43] Brian D. Johnson, 'Cohen Wore Earplugs to a Dylan Show?' Macleans Magazine (12 June 2008) reprinted in *Leonard Cohen on Leonard Cohen*, ed. Burger, p. 544.
[44] Ramazani, 'Sing to Me Now', p. 722.
[45] Thomas, *The Collected Poems*, ed. Goodby, pp. 154–9; Gregory Corso, *Bomb* (San Francisco: City Lights, 1958).
[46] Dylan, *Chronicles*, p. 235.
[47] Lawrence Kramer, *Music and Poetry: The Nineteenth Century and After* (Berkeley: University of California, 1984), p. 129. Quoted in Ramazani, 'Sing to Me Now', p. 723.
[48] Martin Boykan, 'Reflections on Words and Music', *Musical Quarterly*, vol. 84, no. 1 (2000), pp. 123–36. Quoted in Ramazani, 'Sing to Me Now', p. 723.

speech-melody, hears them sung with regard to neither and with outrage to one or both'.[49] This distortion of language set to instrumentation means that the song lyricist cannot approach his craft in the same manner as a poet. Mark Booth, a composer, believes that the vocabulary of song lyrics cannot be as complex, nor loaded with information, as that of the poem. He argues that the song, 'hedged by demands of unity and clarity, must say things that are simplifications'[50] – though one wonders whether he has listened to the compelling narratives, vivid images and intricate wordplay for which both Cohen and Dylan are celebrated.

While the literary merits of the song lyric remain contested, it is impossible to deny that song is a cross-media form, unlike written poetry. Song relies on the subtle interplay of music, words, voice and – as we will later examine further – performance for its meaning, and here, of course, there may be parallels with performance poetry such as that of John Cooper Clarke and Benjamin Zephaniah. Poetry is self-contained. The poet employs rhythm, metre and syntax to determine how the text should be read, dictating its cadence to the reader. The poem can be enhanced by live performance or music, but it can be understood without these 'extras'. Dylan himself has remarked that reading the work of Beat poets Allen Ginsberg and Peter Orlovsky on the page 'would begin some kind of tune in your mind'.[51] Song lyrics do not share this privilege. While the lyrics may be poetic, they often rely on their musical context for their power, as with Dylan's rasping guitars, percussive beats and the singer's snarled delivery, or Cohen's flamenco chord progression, and lugubrious voice, providing an additional framework of understanding to support the audience's interpretation.

Simon Frith has argued that good song lyrics do not make good poems because they do not need to.

> Poems 'score' the performance or reading of the verse in the words themselves... For a lyric to contain its own musical (or performing instructions) is ... to overdetermine its performance, to render it infantile.[52]

Neil Corcoran, in his introduction to *Do You, Mr Jones? Bob Dylan with the Poets and Professors*, warns that, in 'recognising the centrality of the music . . . Dylan

---

[49] Ezra Pound, *Selected Prose, 1909-1965* (New York: New Directions, 1973), p. 37. Quoted in Ramazani, 'Sing to Me Now', p. 724.

[50] Mark Booth, *The Experience of Songs* (New Haven, CT: Yale University Press 1981), p. 13, quoted in Ramazani, 'Sing to Me Now', p. 724.

[51] 'Interview with John Cohen and Happy Traum', *Sing Out!* (October/November 1968) reprinted in *Dylan on Dylan*, ed. Cott, p. 400.

[52] Simon Frith, *Performing Rites: On the Value of Popular Music* (Cambridge: Harvard University Press, 1996), p. 181. Quoted in Scobie, *Alias Bob Dylan Revisited*, p. 93.

cannot be viewed without reserve as a poet'.[53] That is not to say that song lyrics cannot be poetic. Anyone who has been moved by the lyrics of Cohen and Dylan cannot fail to recognize the poetic nature of their words. Songs *can* be poetry, but they are a form of poetry that owe more to the form's ancient oral tradition than the formalized style of modernity.

The song's musical context becomes more essential when considering the synergistic nature of both Dylan's and Cohen's creative processes.

Dylan has been candid in interviews about his approach to songwriting. The words and music are written together, rather than as separate entities joined in the final recording. He claims, 'something will come, like a tune or some kind of wild line . . . If it's a tune on the piano or guitar . . . whatever that brings out in the voice, you'll write those words down.'[54] The exception to Dylan's style of working with music and lyrics simultaneously is the 1967 album *John Wesley Harding*, which contains only two tracks where the music and lyrics were written together. Dylan recalls that 'the rest of the songs were written out on paper, and I found the tunes for them later. I didn't do [that] before, and I haven't done it since'.[55] This change in approach was enforced by Dylan's struggle with writer's block. He claimed, 'one day I was half-stepping and the lights went out . . . It took me a long time to get to do consciously what I used to be able to do unconsciously'.[56] He described the album as 'fearful' because for the first time in his career he was conscious of the effort to find the right words. This album, however, was the exception to Dylan's synergistic creative process, which seems to extend to all his literary efforts, as he told Ralph Gleason in 1965, 'I always sing when I write, even prose'.[57]

Cohen expressed a similar approach to songwriting. Asked in a 1993 interview whether the music or lyrics came first, he declared, 'they're born together, they struggle together, and they influence one another . . . the process is mutual and painstaking and slow'.[58] For Cohen, the process of songwriting was distinct from that of his poetry. He claimed that 'very rarely one crosses

[53] Neil Corcoran, 'Introduction', *Do You, Mr Jones?* p. 12.
[54] 'Interview with John Cohen and Happy Traum', in *Dylan on Dylan*, ed. Cott, p. 113.
[55] Matt Damsker Interview (1978) quoted in Williams, *Performing Artist*, p. 237.
[56] Jonathan Cott, 'The *Rolling Stone* Interview with Bob Dylan', in *Rolling Stone* (16 November 1978) quoted in Williams, *Performing Artist*, p. 237.
[57] Ralph J. Gleason, 'Bob Dylan: The Children's Crusade', *Ramparts Magazine* (March 1966), pp. 27–35, https://recordmecca.com/news/ralph-j-gleason-on-bob-dylanramparts-magazine-march-1966/. Accessed 9 April 2020.
[58] Paul Zollo, 'Leonard Cohen: Inside the Tower of Song', *Songtalk* (April 1993) reprinted in *Leonard Cohen on Leonard Cohen*, ed. Burger, p. 267.

into the other realm'.[59] This is due to the nature of the song lyric, which struggles to accommodate the linguistic complexity or metrical experimentation of the poem. Cohen acknowledged the strictures imposed on the lyric by its musical framework when he told an interviewer that 'the line of music is very influential in determining the length of a line or the density, the syllabic density'.[60]

Cohen was criticized for a 'marked decline in the thematic depth of his poetry' after his decision to pursue a career in popular music.[61] Roy Allan, writing his 1970 MA dissertation on Cohen's poetry, lamented the loss of the lexical density seen in *Spice Box of Earth* (1961) when compared with songs such as 'Bird on the Wire' from Cohen's second studio album, *Songs From a Room* (1969). The contrast, however, is unfair and fails to account for the different vocabularies required for each art form. 'Bird on the Wire' is an affecting work precisely because the simplified language lends pathos to lines such as 'like a bird on the wire / like a drunk in a midnight choir / I have tried in my way to be free'.[62] Indeed, writers such as Philip Larkin have created moving poetry without resorting to verbal acrobatics, as, for example, in the uncomplicated and understated language of 'Aubade' which undercuts the author's contemplation of the eternal to lend a sense of everyday despair to the work.

> I work all day, and get half-drunk at night.
> Waking at four to soundless dark, I stare.
> In time the curtain-edges will grow light.
> Till then I see what's really always there:[63]

The accusation that Cohen's lyrics lack the depth of his poetry fails to acknowledge the important interplay between music and words in popular song. The lyric is enshrined in extralinguistic elements which give it the context and meaning it lacks on the page. Betsy Bowden argues that when we listen to a song, we do not need the same narrative, imagistic or rational links that we require from a written work because the instrumentation and vocal delivery stand in

---

[59] Paul Williams, 'Leonard Cohen: Romantic in a Rag-Picker's Trade', *Crawdaddy!* (March 1975) reprinted in *Leonard Cohen on Leonard Cohen*, ed. Burger, p. 90.

[60] Paul Zollo, 'Leonard Cohen: Inside the Tower of Song', *Songtalk* (April 1993), reprinted in *Leonard Cohen on Leonard Cohen*, ed. Burger, p. 267.

[61] Roy Allen, 'The Worlds of Leonard Cohen: A Study of His Poetry', MA diss., Simon Fraser University, 1970. https://summit.sfu.ca/item/3039. Accessed 8 March 2020.

[62] Leonard Cohen, 'Bird on the Wire', in *Stranger Music Selected Poems and Songs* (London: Jonathan Cape, 1993), p. 144.

[63] Philip Larkin, 'Aubade', *The Complete Poems* edited by Archie Burnett (London: Faber and Faber, 2012), poem #725.

their place.[64] The music gives the lyric a context through its adherence to or divergence from generic conventions such as the twelve-bar progression of the blues, or six-chord progression of flamenco, or the wailing guitar solos of heavy metal. The generic conventions provide an intertextual framework through which the song can be received and understood by its audience. Stephen Troussé believes that the foregrounding of the lyric in critical analysis of popular music is because it is often the easiest element of the song to talk about, but this denies the importance of the lyric's delivery. For Troussé, the genius of 'Like a Rolling Stone' is not in Dylan's words alone, but 'the sheer *weirdness* of the voice, the way the words don't quite fit the metre of the song, the voluptuous swell of the Hammond organ, the ramshackle rhythm.'[65] This is an argument for focusing not just on the 'text' but the 'texture' surrounding it – the music, voice and words all working together to disseminate meaning.

Importance of performance in song

While this idea of 'texture' gives us a critical appreciation of both Dylan's and Cohen's works, the lyric is often the site of pleasure for most listeners and deserves recognition beyond its place as an element within a whole. The emphasis, however, should be placed on the *sung* lyric. Christopher Butler argues, 'Dylan's lyrics carry rhythms and rhymes and emphases which are designed for performance,'[66] and it is in the performance that they truly come alive. As Bob Dylan reminded his audience during his Nobel lecture, 'songs are unlike literature. They are meant to be sung, not read on a page.'[67]

The popular song's performance is imbued with extratextual elements such as the singer's persona, attitude, clothes, body language, inflection, diction, expressiveness and interaction with the crowd, which constitute the experience of the song. Even recorded songs rely on this extratextual information, with album artwork and liner notes informing the listener's reception. Cohen showed a heightened awareness of this aspect of song, especially in its composition. Dylan, he contended is a master of inflection. You can hear in his voice the

---

[64] Betsy Bowden, *Performed Literature: Words and Music by Bob Dylan* (Indiana: Indiana University Press, 1987), p. 74.
[65] Troussé, 'Stupid and Contagious', in *The Message*, p. 46.
[66] Christopher Butler, 'Dylan and the Academics', in *Do You, Mr Jones?* p. 68.
[67] Dylan, *The Nobel Lecture*, p. 23.

tough guy; somebody praying; someone asking, or coming on to you. In the composition of songs, knowing they will occupy an aural space invites the author to embody those inflections. Composing songs to be sung particularly invites irony because 'irony can be conveyed with the voice alone whereas on the page you generally have to have a larger construction around the irony for it to come through'.[68]

Performance poetry readings were popularized by the Welsh poet Dylan Thomas, leading a procession of 'fat poets with slim volumes' to self-crucifixion before rapacious American audiences.[69] His melodic delivery captivated American audiences, on stage, and as a pioneer of audio books on Caedmon gramophone records. Performance, however, is not as essential to the enjoyment of the poetic text as it is to a song. Indeed, Philip Larkin believed that the trend for poetry readings was damaging to the art form and had sprung up from 'a false analogy with music: the text is the "score" that doesn't "come to life" until it's "performed"'. On the contrary, Larkin maintained, 'people can read words, whereas they can't read music'.[70] He believed that the fashion for public readings forced poets to compose their works with performance in mind, degrading the standard of their work. The type of 'poetry' this produced, he lamented, was immediately accessible and understandable, relying on 'easy rhythms, easy emotions, easy syntax'.[71]

Larkin may have disliked poetry readings, but the 1950s and 1960s saw a swell in interest in watching poets perform their work. As we saw in Chapter 4, Allen Ginsberg, Gregory Corso, Kenneth Rexroth, Lawrence Ferlinghetti and Jack Kerouac, to mention a few, performed their poetry to jazz accompaniment, and in doing so, took the poem back to its ancient oral roots. Dylan Thomas stands in the Welsh bardic tradition of oral poetry which emphasized *cynghanedd* – a strict system of alliteration, rhyme and metre governing each line. Allen Ginsberg became renowned for his energetic performances, injecting his poetry with a dynamism and excitement that captivated his audiences, but while the poets' performances enhanced their texts, they were not inextricable from them. The poetic use of metre, rhyme, punctuation and stanzas act almost as a metronome by which the reader is given the pace of the poem on the page. Song

---

[68] Interview with Robert Sward, December 1984, reprinted *Leonard Cohen on Leonard Cohen*, ed. Burger, p. 171.

[69] Dylan Thomas reading 'A Visit to America' *The Caedmon Collection*, 2002, CD5, track 2.

[70] Philip Larkin, 'Paris Review Interview', *The Paris Review* (1982) in *Required Writing* (1982), p. 61. Quoted in Ricks, *Dylan's Visions of Sin*, p. 13.

[71] Ricks, *Dylan's Visions of Sin*, p. 13.

lyrics, however, do not have this encoded framework which is why they often fail to stand on their own.

Songwriting, rather than being judged by the standards of printed poetry, should be considered in the tradition of oral poetry. Cohen and Dylan were both influenced by folk ballads. Dylan, for example, pointed to the evasive qualities of the folk song, telling the truth about life conveyed to us in lies, with which for the most part we feel comfortable. He contended: 'a folk song has over a thousand faces and you must meet them all if you want to play this stuff'.[72]

Dylan and Cohen, as we saw in Chapter 3, were shaped by their Jewish faith and the psalmody of the synagogues they attended as children. Cohen was open about the impact of his early religious instruction upon his music; 'I always loved the music that is called holy, the cantorial music of the church and the synagogue'.[73] Indeed, the principle of '*contrafract*' which has its origins in Jewish psalms is evident in both Dylan's and Cohen's work. *Contrafract* is the use of familiar melodies with new texts to allow the audience a feeling of familiarity, while at the same time carrying an original message. Both Dylan and Cohen, particularly in their early careers, repurposed the music of folk songs and ballads for their own lyrics.

The rich heritage of Jewish oral tradition particularly informed Leonard Cohen's work and has gave him an awareness of the historical links between poetry, song and performance:

> The kind of training I had as a young writer, a young composer, made me very aware of where I stood in a long line of singers or poets, musicians from the Troubadours; even before that, from Homer; and even before that, from Isiah and King David; coming all the way down through the various strains into English literature, into poetry; into folksingers like Pete Seeger, Allan Lomax and Woody Guthrie.[74]

Oral poetry, like song, depends on its performance for its full meaning. Cohen has said 'there's nothing like a song . . . it has an amazing thrust. And a poem, it waits on the page'.[75] We explain this 'amazing thrust' in the following chapter

---

[72] Dylan, *Chronicles*, p. 71.
[73] Alberto Manzano, 'The Future', *El Europeo*, Spring 1993, reprinted in *Leonard Cohen on Leonard Cohen*, ed. Burger p. 325.
[74] Interview with Jim O'Brien, *B-Side Magazine*, August/September 1993, reprinted in *Leonard Cohen on Leonard Cohen*, ed. Burger, p. 361.
[75] Williams, 'Romantic in a Rag-Picker's Trade', *Leonard Cohen on Leonard Cohen*, ed. Burger, p. 90.

by invoking Federico García Lorca's theory of duende which is most overtly observed in performance.

Instrumentation plays a vital role in the power of the popular song lyric, but the singer's voice is also an essential element. Both Dylan and Cohen have faced criticism throughout their careers for their vocal performances, but it is their unique lyrical delivery which has mesmerized so many of their listeners. Dylanologists and Cohen acolytes have commented upon, what Roland Barthes terms, the 'grain' of the singers' voices. The 'grain' is 'the body in the voice as it sings'.[76] Barthes divides the song into two texts. The *pheno-song* encompasses everything within the performance which serves the purpose of communication. The *geno-song* is the level at which the melody works upon the sound signifiers, focusing not on what the singer is saying, but *how* they use their voice and diction to express it. This is an interesting concept when applied to the work of Dylan and Cohen, as many critics point to the performance of both artists' lyrics as essential to their meaning.

Keith Negus reiterates the importance of the voice in understanding the lyrics when he states that 'the grain of the voice of the singer and their words, sung and intoned, are replayed and played with long after the listening event'.[77] It is almost impossible to read Dylan's or Cohen's printed lyrics without automatically hearing their distinctive voices which makes it difficult to read the song-text as a poem because of the extratextual framework it is encumbered with when we approach it having prior knowledge of its performance. This goes some way to explain why the song lyric often feels lacking on the page – once we have experienced the thrill of the performance, the words often seem staid and uninspiring without the passionate delivery of the song.

Simon Frith has argued that the relationship between music and lyrics is defined by conflict and tension. The voice is unique in this respect because it creates meaning in two simultaneous ways – through words and melody. The language of a song can be in direct conflict with the music surrounding it, the intonation of the singer's voice and the melody to which it is sung adds another layer of complexity and meaning to the text. Both Bob Dylan and Leonard Cohen have played with the friction between words and melody within their

---

[76] Roland Barthes, 'The Grain of the Voice', in *Image.Music.Text*, ed. and trans. Stephen Heath (London: Fontana, 1977), p. 189.

[77] Keith Negus quoted in Pete Astor, 'The Poetry of Rock: Song Lyrics Are Not Poems But the Words Still Matter – Another Look at Richard Goldstein's Collection of Rock Lyrics', *Popular Music*, vol. 29, no. 1 (January 2010), p. 148.

songs to create meaning beyond the surface level of the lyrics. Paul Williams agrees that 'performance is essential'.[78] He illustrates this point by noting that before the legendary *The Basement Tapes* were released many of the song lyrics were printed in 1973's anthology of Dylan's lyrics, *Writings and Drawings by Bob Dylan*. Seeing the words on the printed page, without knowing their musical context, Williams was unimpressed. When he finally heard the songs performed, he was overawed by the profundity that they had lacked on the page.

The power of song in performance relies heavily on the vocals. Williams asserts that great singers do not need perfect technique and enunciation, but their voice must speak to him; 'is there an audible complex consciousness present in the enunciation of every noun, verb and pronoun . . . Analyse the words all you want, but remember how those words reached you'.[79]

Dylan is a master of the art of innovative vocal performance, deliberately changing the style, manner, intonation, octave and timbre. Reading his lyrics, one may wonder whether there is a rhyme scheme. Hearing them performed, you are in no doubt that 'skull' is a perfect rhyme for 'capitol'. Allen Ginsberg was so impressed by Dylan's verbal gymnastics on 'Idiot Wind' that he declared it the 'great disillusioned national rhyme'.[80] In 'A Hard Rain's a-Gonna Fall', Dylan manipulates 'mountains' to rhyme with 'highways' and 'forests' with 'oceans' by the rhythm of his intonation. This is a remarkable feat which is only possible in performance. On the page it is almost impossible to imagine how these words could ever be considered rhyming partners, but Dylan achieves the feat with a impressive dexterity and ease which assures his place in the pantheon of song-writing greats.

Ian Hamilton has remarked on what some have called Dylan's 'overreliance' on rhyme, claiming that the unrelenting end rhymes are 'irritating on the page, but sung by him it very often becomes part of the song's point, part of its drama of aggression'.[81] Dylan has spoken about the important role performance plays in his lyrics, claiming that when he has concepts or lines that refuse to be simplified, he will 'take it all – lock, stock and barrel – and figure out how to sing it so it fits the rhyming scheme'.[82]

---

[78] Paul Williams, 'Watching the River Flow', in *Bob Dylan: Watching the River Flow, Observations on His Art in Progress, 1966-1995* (London: Omnibus Press, 1996), p. 46.

[79] Williams, 'Watching the River Flow', p. 46.

[80] Allen Ginsberg, liner notes to *Desire* (1976).

[81] Ian Hamilton, *The Observer* (11 June 1978) quoted in Ricks, *Dylan's Visions of Sin*, p. 33.

[82] Interview with Robert Hilburn, *The Los Angeles Times* (4 April 2004) reprinted in *Dylan on Dylan*, ed. Cott, p. 435.

Bob Dylan's vocal performance does more than just assist the lyric's rhyme scheme. Lavinia Greenlaw has commented on Dylan's use of delay and withholding which creates tension by 'holding a song back from its natural tempo and adds more by tearing the lyric away from its expected cadence'.[83] She argues that much of the power of the ballad 'Girl from the North Country' comes from 'the physical effort' Dylan displays in delaying his syllables and phrases.[84] Lines such as 'if you go when the snowflakes storm / When the rivers freeze and summer ends' are given an additional visceral impact by Dylan's strained delivery. This same technique is deployed in 'Lay Lady Lay', where delay is used to dislocate images, such as 'I long to see you in the / morning / light', creating a melancholic and sombre atmosphere wherein 'everything is caught . . . on the verge of consummation'.[85]

Cohen, perhaps, has endured more criticism of his singing voice. In 2009 *The Telegraph* featured both Dylan and Cohen in their list of 'top ten great singers who can't sing'.[86] In response to the *London Times* declaring Cohen to be Canada's greatest singer in 2008, *Now Toronto* published an article entitled 'Leonard Cohen Cannot Sing', horrified that a man who 'drones' could be considered the best representation of their nation's talents.[87] Cohen himself expressed doubt about his singing voice, saying in a 2016 BBC interview, 'I never thought I could sing'.[88] Cohen tried to explain the appeal of his vocals by saying: 'I think the thing we like about a singer is that he's really singing with his own voice. He's not putting you on. That's why people like me can get away with making records'.[89] Despite the doubts he harboured over his own vocal abilities, Cohen knew the impact his delivery had. He was keenly aware of the difference between his words being read on the page and the lyrics that he sang.

---

[83] Lavinia Greenlaw, 'Big Brass Bed: Bob Dylan and Delay', in *Do You, Mr Jones?* ed. Corcoran, p. 75.

[84] Greenlaw, 'Big Brass Bed', p. 75.

[85] Greenlaw, 'Big Brass Bed', p. 79.

[86] Neil McCormick, 'Top Ten Great Singers Who Can't Sing', in *The Telegraph*, 26 November 2009. https://www.telegraph.co.uk/culture/music/rockandpoDylanpmusic/6654478/Top-ten-great-singers-who-cant-sing.html. Accessed 1 April 2020.

[87] Susan G. Cole, 'Leonard Cohen Cannot Sing', *Now Toronto*, 30 December 2008. https://nowtoronto.com/music/leonard-cohen-cannot-sing/.) Accessed 1 April 2020.

[88] BBC News, 'Leonard Cohen: "I Never Thought I Could Sing" BBC News'. *YouTube* video, 0:02:30. 11 November 2016. https://www.youtube.com/watch?v=cMqtkyJeVwo.

[89] Interview with Steve Turner, 'Leonard Cohen: The Profits of Doom' (April 1988), reprinted in *Leonard Cohen on Leonard Cohen*, ed. Burger, p. 208.

When you're composing material and you know it's going to occupy an aural space, you can compose it with those inflections in mind . . . on the page you generally have a larger construction around the irony for it to come through . . . If you sing 'what's it to ya?' to some nice chords it really does sound like, 'Well, what's it to ya, baby?' But just to see it written, it would need a location.[90]

The uniqueness of his delivery, the almost chanted intonation of his lyrics contributed to the immense impact of his music. Cohen playfully told an interviewer that 'my voice just happens to be monotonous [and] I'm somewhat whiney so they are called sad songs. But you could sing them joyfully too'.[91] He puts it down to a 'complete biological accident'[92] that his songs are melancholic, but this downplays Cohen's conscious decision to sing his lyrics in a manner which enhances their effect.

Both Dylan and Cohen have demonstrated an awareness of the impact of their performance on the audience's understanding of their lyrics. It is not just the vocal performance and the tension between music and lyrics which gives the song its power, but the attitude and *persona* of the performer. We have already discussed Dylan's and Cohen's stage personas in an earlier chapter, but it is pertinent to remind ourselves of the *presence* that both men bring to their performances. The poet Simon Armitage believes that Dylan's 'virtue is in his style, his attitude, his disposition to the world and his delivery of the words'.[93] The idea of Cohen as a gloomy romantic and Dylan as a freewheelin' troubadour gives their songs an extratextual depth which informs our response. Seeing Cohen sing of lost loves and late nights in his tailored suits and latter day trademark fedora is akin to props used by screen actors, giving us a sense of their character, making the man on stage seem more 'real'. Watching Dylan perform in fringed leather jackets or Mississippi gambler knee-length jackets and cowboy hats lends an authenticity to folk ballads such as 'The Lonesome Death of Hattie Carrol' or the world weary 'Not Dark Yet'. As an audience we allow ourselves to believe that these men have lived the narratives of their songs.

[90] 'Interview with Robert Sward', *Malahat Review* (December 1986) reprinted in *Leonard Cohen on Leonard Cohen*, ed. Burger, p. 171.
[91] Tony Wilson, 'Behind the Enigma', *New Musical Express* (25 March 1972) reprinted in *Leonard Cohen on Leonard Cohen*, ed. Burger, p. 26.
[92] Wilson, 'Behind the Enigma', p. 26.
[93] Simon Armitage, 'Rock of Ages', *Do You, Mr Jones?* ed. Corcoran, p. 124.

Democratic poetry

We now want to go on to consider the idea of 'democratic' poetry – poetry for the people, and how the idea relates to Dylan and Cohen. In 2017 the Survey of Public Participation in the Arts found that only 11.7 per cent of adults in the United States had read a poem in that last year. This figure shows a rise from the paltry 6.7 per cent in 2012, but if we were to ask the same respondents how many had listened to a song, the numbers would be incomparable.[94] Poetry is not a part of people's everyday lives in the same way as music. It is prejudiced by the weight of assumptions about it, with most seeing it as difficult to understand without a formal training in the subject. Music, however, is woven into the tapestry of our lives. In some ways it is inescapable – from the supermarket radio station to the street corner busker. Songwriter Josh Ritter speaks for many when he claims, 'poetry has been turned into a lock-box which we can only write or read after we've been to graduate school'.[95]

This has not been the view of poets such as Allen Ginsberg, Federico García Lorca and Walt Whitman, but it is the consensus of many. The idea of poetry as the preserve of elites, whether aristocratic or intellectual, has been with us since it became a predominantly written form. Mass literacy did not develop in many Western countries until the late eighteenth and early nineteenth centuries and so vast swathes of the population were excluded from its enjoyment. Under the patronage system, poets composed their verse for the delight of monarchs and their courtiers, addressing issues of interest to the nobility, rather than the low-born.

The nineteenth-century French political philosopher and diplomat Alexis de Tocqueville saw the establishment of a new democracy in America as an opportunity for art to develop beyond its aristocratic confines. He argued that the increased wealth and leisure time of this independent nation would allow ordinary men to pursue both the production and consumption of art. He believed that in a democratic nation each generation began afresh, making it impossible for the strict conventions governing aristocratic art to arise.

[94] Colin Dwyer, 'Poetry Is Making a Big Comeback in the U.S., Survey Results Reveal', NPR.org. (8 June 2018). https://www.npr.org/2018/06/08/618386432/poetry-is-making-a-big-comeback-in-the-u-s-survey-results-reveal. Accessed 28 March 2020.

[95] Laura Barton, 'This Be the Verse', *The Guardian* (13 October 2006). https://www.theguardian.com/music/2006/oct/13/poetry.popandrock. Accessed 3 March 2020.

De Tocqueville drew clear distinctions between 'aristocratic' and 'democratic' literature, both in its production and its form. In a democratic society, though more men would be able write literature, they would be unable to devote themselves to it as fully as the aristocratic elite, needing to find other ways to generate income. He believed that for both readers and authors, 'the time they can devote to letters is very short . . . They prefer books which may be easily procured, quickly read, and which require no learned research to be understood . . . they require rapid emotions, startling passages.'[96] Democratic art, therefore, lacks the 'order, regularity, science'[97] of aristocratic writing whose practitioners could afford to devote their lives to studying their craft. De Tocqueville predicted that its authors would instead 'aim at rapidity of execution, more than at perfection of detail . . . literary performances will bear marks of an untutored and rude vigour of thought . . . to stir passions more than to charm the taste.'[98]

De Tocqueville believed that the subjects of aristocratic and democratic poetry would necessarily differ. While aristocracy was satisfied with the status quo and looked to the past for inspiration, the democratic artists would need to look to the future and would therefore create more innovative forms of art. In a democracy all men were equally 'insignificant', leaving no heroic figures to valorize through literature. Turning their backs on the old gods and masters, the democratic poets would fix their imagination 'on man alone'.[99] While de Tocqueville was yet to see the emergence of a true democratic voice in American art, the poet Walt Whitman was ready to declare himself so. Writing in a personal journal in 1851, he proclaimed, 'Comrades! I am the Bard of democracy'.[100] Whitman can be considered America's first democratic poet, breaking from the rarefied form of aristocratic writing, with its 'terror of vulgarity' and concern with decorum, and creating work which celebrated all men, from the high-born to the downtrodden.[101] The only men who did not interest Whitman were those

---

[96] Alexis de Tocqueville, *Democracy in America*, transl. Henry Reeve, ed. Henry Steele Commager (London: Oxford University Press, 1965), p. 330.

[97] De Tocqueville, *Democracy in America*, p. 331.

[98] De Tocqueville, *Democracy in America*, p. 331.

[99] De Tocqueville, *Democracy in America*, p. 342.

[100] 'Walt Whitman: Bard of Democracy', The Morgan Library and Museum (website). https://www .themorgan.org/exhibitions/walt-whitman#:~:text=I%20am%20the%20bard%20of,in%20a%20no tebook%20in%201859.&text=The%20exhibition%20explores%20Whitman's%20process,poetically %2C%20to%20his%20final%20years. Accessed 24 August 2020.

[101] Edward Dowden, 'The Poetry of Democracy: Walt Whitman', *The Westminster Review*, 96 (July 1871) *The Walt Whitman Archive*. Ed. Matt Cohen, Ed Folsom, and Kenneth M. Price. https://wh itmanarchive.org/criticism/reviews/tei/anc.00073.html. Accessed 24 August 2020.

'whose lives are spent among books'.[102] This is prescient of Dylan's own anti-intellectualism. Whitman had a profound influence on both Lorca and Ginsberg, who believed that poetry should reflect everyday life. It should be a form that spoke to the masses, not simply the upper classes. Both Lorca's and Ginsberg's ideas of democratic poetry would go on to influence Dylan and Cohen and perhaps contributed to their decision to choose music as their form of artistic expression.

Allen Ginsberg saw Dylan as the culmination of popular poetry. His songs had a far wider reach than the poet's own, but did not sacrifice their intelligence to appeal to a mass audience. Instead, Dylan's song lyrics introduced the listening public to poetry in a way that had never been done before. His quick wit and irony, his references and wordplay, and his fantastical imagery excited audiences because they were so far removed from the prosaic and banal lyrics of previous pop hits. Through the medium of popular song, Dylan became the bard of democracy of whom Whitman dreamt.

Dylan's and Cohen's songs are not just popularized poetry. Rather than reinventing the art form, we argue that their music takes poetry back to its oral roots. To reiterate, both Dylan and Cohen were influenced by traditional folk ballads and Jewish psalms and their work is the marrying together of folk arts with high culture.

Bob Dylan has often been accused of anti-intellectualism, doing little to dispel this impression with his laconic and often acerbic answers to journalists inquiring about the influence of poetry on his own work. In 'Ballad of a Thin Man', Dylan casts a withering eye over the culture of academia:

> You've been through all of / F. Scott Fitzgerald's books / You're very well read / It's well known / Because something is happening here / But you don't know what it is / Do you, Mister Jones?[103]

Dylan may not have much patience for the academics, but he is interested in literature and poetry. In his Nobel lecture he declared that the three novels that shaped him were from his high school days in Hibbing, Minnesota, from which he graduated in 1956 – *Moby Dick, All Quiet on the Western Front* and the *Odyssey*. The poetic language and universal themes of these works are repeated in Dylan's own oeuvre. He has also mentioned the poets Rimbaud, Verlaine

---

[102] Dowden, 'The Poetry of Democracy: Walt Whitman'.
[103] Bob Dylan, 'Ballad of a Thin Man', in *Lyrics 1962-1985* (London: Harper Collins, 1994), p. 303.

and Donne as impacting his appreciation of language. Alongside these high culture influences, Dylan cites Appalachian ballads, folk songs, the music of Buddy Holly and country and western singers such as Hank Williams. All these works combined to create his unique style as he 'pick[ed] up the vernacular. You internalise it . . . the devices, the techniques, the secrets, the mysteries'.[104]

This fusion of the folk and canonical is indicative of Dylan's own approach to songwriting and resembles Whitman's idea of democratic poetry. In the liner notes to Dylan's 1976 studio album *Desire*, Allen Ginsberg wrote that Bob Dylan was 'the culmination of poetry-music'.[105] This view has been echoed by critics and fans alike in their analysis of Dylan's poetic legacy. Aidan Day has argued that, 'his song poems . . . succeed in speaking as if there were no wall of poetic convention separating the statement from the listener' and declares this to be Dylan's 'major contribution to lyric poetry in English'.[106] Christopher Butler echoes this, claiming that the significance of Dylan's works lies in the fact that 'they are better memorised by the many than are the texts of many "canonical" poets by the minority'.[107]

The power of Dylan's lyric poetry is its ability to infiltrate people's everyday lives. It is not the preserve of the aristocracy nor only to be understood by an intellectual elite. In the true spirit of democratic art, it is accessible to all, without sacrificing its meaning. Dylan himself believed that music was the only democratic medium. In a 1965 interview, he declared that 'museums are cemeteries. Paintings should be on the walls of restaurants, in dime stores, in gas stations, in men's rooms . . . Music is the only thing that's in tune with what's happening.'[108]

Cohen is often cast as Dylan's antithesis – a refined urban intellectual to Dylan's swaggering cowboy. While Cohen resided adjacent to Ivory Tower as a scholar and writer of formalized poetry and celebrated literary star, he was also a believer in the democratization of art. Lorca, the poet who 'ruined' his life, was known in his native Spain as the 'Gypsy poet'. This epithet amused Lorca at first, who played up to the idea, but he later came to resent it for its implications of savagery and a lack of education.

---

[104] Dylan, *Nobel Lecture*, pp. 4–5.
[105] Ginsberg liner notes for Bob Dylan's *Desire* (1976).
[106] Aidan Day, 'Looking for Nothing: Dylan Now', *Do You, Mr Jones?* ed. Corcoran, p. 293.
[107] Christopher Butler, 'Dylan and the Academics', in *Do You, Mr Jones?* ed. Corcoran, p. 58.
[108] 'Interview with Nora Ephron and Susan Edmiston', *Positively Tie Dream*, (August, 1965) reprinted in *Dylan on Dylan*, ed. Cott, p. 54.

Cohen's music and poetry, as we will see in Chapter 8, reflects the themes and ideas woven throughout Lorca's New York poems, such as the degradation of poverty, human suffering, violence and disease. In this manner, Cohen follows the tradition of democratic art to address the plight of the common man, rather than focus on lofty ideals and depictions of nature. Indeed, Cohen's 1992 album *The Future* featured the single 'Democracy' and it was a subject that fascinated him throughout his life. 'Democracy is the great religion of the West,'[109] he told a reporter in 1993. He argued that 'it is important to experience yourself as a man, but also it's important to experience yourself as neither man nor woman'.[110] This sentiment speaks to the purpose of democratic art. In an equal society, art should be a platform for transcending our own physicalities and experiencing the lives and emotions of others. Through the universality of both Dylan's and Cohen's work we are granted access not only to our own innermost feelings, but those of others whose lived experiences elude us in everyday life. The flourishing of democratic art is not only a signifier of a strong democracy but acts as an equalizer within that society.

Leonard Cohen never believed himself to be 'a man of letters'.[111] He abhorred the idea of the lofty intellectual, cloistered away from his listeners, and this was perhaps one of the reasons he embraced the art of popular music as a form of immediate connection with his audience. In 1967, he declared that 'there was never any distance between myself and the reader'[112] when he wrote his novels and poetry, but he was aware that poetry did not have the same reach as a popular song. In 1993 he told an interviewer that he did not see any inherent distinctions between poetry and song as art forms but that '[there] still resides in a lot of poetry, that aspect of elitism where there's an assumption that there's a vast common culture and that we all participate in it. Unfortunately, things are a little more fragmented now and most people know Mr T and things like that'.[113] Cohen's analysis of modern poetry and the canonical knowledge of the everyman may sound bleak but is accurate. In an age of information overload, we no longer possess the cultural commons and shared knowledge of canonical texts that allow us to reach what Dante termed 'textual fruition'. In the medieval and early modern era, references to biblical allegories and ancient myths would

---

[109] Manzano, 'The Future', p. 320.
[110] Manzano, 'The Future', p. 325.
[111] Djwa, 'After the Wipeout, a Renewal', p. 12.
[112] Djwa, 'After the Wipeout, a Renewal', p. 12.
[113] Radio Interview with Vicki Gabereau, *Variety Tonight*, CBC Canada (6 September 1984) printed in *Leonard Cohen on Leonard Cohen*, ed. Burger, p. 153.

have been understood by their learned readers and contributed another layer of meaning to the text. In our era of democratized art, the old sources of knowledge have been flushed out by an overabundance of popular culture and mass media information.

Dylan and Cohen, though avoiding the trap of becoming obscure and esoteric in their lyrics, steep their work in allusions to the Talmud, the Bible, ancient writers and romantic poets. Returning to the principle of 'contrafact' as discussed earlier – the Jewish psalmist tradition of repurposing familiar melodies to deliver new messages – we contend that Dylan and Cohen use this principle to deliver both new and forgotten ideas. When Dylan arrived on the folk scene in the early 1960s, he set his lyrics to the tunes of well-known folk songs. Both men have played about with adhering to and diverging from the conventions that govern musical genres such as country, western, folk and pop. Contrafact makes new ideas easier to assimilate because they are presented to us in the familiar guise of a song we already know, or a genre we understand. In this way, both Dylan and Cohen have used the medium of popular song to create democratic poetry which reintroduces an art form which most people find alienating and exclusionary.

Conclusion

In this chapter we have examined the similarities between song lyrics and poetry, the historical links between the two forms, and the ways in which Dylan and Cohen may be considered popular poets in the bardic tradition. Song, as we have seen, is not poetry in its modern form. Lyrics must be sung, not read, to achieve their full impact. John Gibbens has stated that 'a metrical sequence that trips over itself on the page may be perfectly apt in its musical place . . . an emphasis that would be clumsy and false in a poetic line . . . can be spot on in a song'.[114] The 'song-text' needs to be placed in its musical context – it's 'texture' – it should not be isolated.

'Song-poems' are a form of poetry akin to the ancient tradition of oral poetry. This does not devalue the lyrics of Dylan and Cohen but instead prevents them from being compared unfavourably to the poets of the printed page whose work requires different techniques to achieve the same musical effect. Paul Williams

---

[114] Gibbens, *The Nightingale's Code*, p. 206.

has argued that when compared to Eliot or Pound, Dylan's isolated lyrics do not stand up – this is because he is first and foremost a songwriter. This is not a slight. The medium of popular song is as worthy of critical attention and praise as the Spenserian sonnet. Williams argues that Dylan's genius lies in knowing how to manipulate the interplay between his music and lyrics to maximum effect and that one day he will be celebrated alongside James Joyce for his contribution to the English language.

Performance is an integral component of the song. Instrumentation, cover versions, the singer's inflections and the 'grain' of their voice all affect the meaning of the lyrics. Poetry does not need to be performed to be appreciated. The reader's response is encoded into the framework of the text. The metre, rhyme scheme, line breaks and punctuation are dictated to the reader. Lyrics do not need this same framework; they have the 'texture' of instrumentation and performance to do this for them. Pat Kane has claimed, 'pop music is – popular poetry',[115] and the proof of this is in the work of both Cohen and Dylan. Their music takes poetry back to its ancient oral roots and democratizes the art form making it accessible and meaningful to everyone who wants to appreciate it.

[115] Troussé, 'Stupid and Contagious', in *The Message*, p. 47.

8

The spirit of duende

The duende, *on the other hand, does not appear if it sees no possibility of death, if it does not know it will haunt death's house.*

– Lorca[1]

Introduction

In this chapter we want to argue that appreciation of the lyrics, songs and poems of Leonard Cohen is greatly facilitated with reference to the reflections on poetry, dance, art and song by the poet who gave Cohen his voice and who inspired him from an early age, Federico García Lorca. We have already seen that Cohen was first and foremost a poet and a novelist. He is not always the most reliable source of opinion in assisting us in judging his significance as a poet and lyricist. He said that he aspired to be no more than a minor poet; indeed, he was humbled in kneeling at the feet of those who truly deserved the title of poet. In his most self-deprecating moments, he implied that he was no poet at all. He said, half seriously, 'I never did set poetry to music, I got stuck with that. It was a bum rap. I never set a poem to music. I'm not that hopeless. I know the difference between a poem and a song!'[2] He also believed, however, that poetry is a verdict made by a generation, the literary establishment. He asserted that one can't set out to be a poet, because it's what other people make of your expression. Whether his work is poetry or not, he maintained, 'doesn't really matter, it probably isn't.'[3]

In a reflective lecture entitled 'The Love Song', delivered by Nick Cave to the Vienna Poetry Festival, on 25 September 1998, at *atelierhaus der akademie der*

---

[1] Cited in Paul Binding, *Lorca: The Gay Imagination* (London: GMP Publishing, 1985), p. 161.

[2] Adrian Deevoy, 'All Good Things', *Q Magazine*, February 2017, p. 91.

[3] Jim Devlin, *Leonard Cohen in His Own Words* (London: Omnibus, 1998), p. 44.

bilden künste, the Antipodean told his audience that the love song is saturated with sadness.[4] It is the epitome of sorrow itself, an inexplicable yearning and longing of the soul that lives in the imagination and gives birth to the love song. It is a feeling that the Portuguese call *Suadade*, or the Welsh call *Hiraeth*, a bittersweet longing, both nostalgic and melancholic, with elements of hope. The Welsh term captures a bittersweet sadness, the nostalgic longing for someone or something lost.

Federico García Lorca, Cave maintained, tried to capture the essence of the power of this dark, eerie sadness that we all experience and which lives in the heart but which we may not all be able to express. In its expression it is what great poetry in its performance is made of. It is indescribable, ineffable and has the power to overwhelm us.[5] Lorca is emphatic that in their performance texts are profoundly affected by the presence or absence of duende, and we find it not only in poetry but also in 'deep song' which has its primitive musical roots in India, and from which flamenco emerged in the eighteenth century.[6] Cave makes the observation that duende is a thread that runs through Dylan's career and is specifically the hallmark that defines Cohen's.

There is a direct link between Cohen and Lorca, whereas the connection of Dylan and Lorca is more oblique, and therefore we will postpone our investigation into how duende manifests itself in Dylan's lyric poetry until Chapter 9. In this chapter we explore the profound influence that Lorca had on Cohen's poetic vision of the world and perhaps which explains the Canadian's considerable popularity in Spain, where in 2011 the Prince of Asturias Award was bestowed upon him for his contribution to literature, which had 'influenced three generations around the world'. The seventy-seven-year-old was congratulated by the jury for creating 'imagery in which poetry and music are melded into an unchanging worth'.[7]

In his acceptance speech on 21 October, Cohen expressed his gratitude to the soil and soul of the Spanish people that bequeathed him so much. It was through Lorca that he found his voice, after searching for it in vain among the great writers of English literature, and it was from a Spanish flamenco guitarist, a

[4]   Re-recorded and released on cd as 'The Secret Life of the Love Song', two lectures written and read by Nick Cave. Label: EMI Music UK; ASIN: B00002DDZG, 2000.

[5]   Lorca, 'Play and Theory of the Duende', *In Search of Duende*, prose selections edited and translated by Christopher Maurer (New York: New Directions Books, 2010), pp. 56–72.

[6]   Federico García Lorca, 'Deep Song', *In Search of Duende* (New York: New Directions Publishing, 1998), pp. 1–27.

[7]   'Leonard Cohen Wins Prince of Asturias Award', BBC News online, https://www.bbc.co.uk/news/entertainment-arts-13625379. Accessed 3 March 2020.

seventeen-year-old immigrant, that he learnt, in three lessons, to graduate from three- to a six-chord progression, upon which so much of flamenco music is based.[8]

This fascination with both Lorca and the guitar began when he was fourteen or fifteen years old. In 1949 or 1950 Cohen bought a second-hand guitar for purely mercenary reasons. He calculated that his chances of attracting girls playing the guitar were considerably better than playing the clarinet, piano or ukulele. In the same year, while browsing in a bookshop in Montreal, Cohen came across a book of poems by Federico García Lorca. He sometimes jokingly announced on stage that the collection ruined his life. It gave him licence to project his own voice. Nadel and, more recently, Simmons suggest that it was *Selected Poems*[9] and that the lines that particularly struck Cohen, Nadel suggests, were in a poem entitled 'The Diván at Tamarit'. *The Diván at Tamarit* was a collection of poems written between 1931 and 1934 and published in Spanish in 1936, after Lorca was assassinated by a republican firing squad. None of the *Diván at Tamarit* poems appeared in *Selected Poems*, first published in 1943 and translated by J. L. Gili and Stephen Spender. The words that made a profound impression on Cohen he read in translation: [10]

> Through the Arch of Elvira
> I want to see you go
> So that I can learn your name
> And break into tears

These are lines from 'Gacela: The Morning Market' which was published in the *Diván at Tamarit* and did not appear in translation until 1955.[11] Simmons identifies the poem correctly but neither she nor Nadel are aware that it wasn't in the collection available to Cohen in 1949 or 1950.

---

[8] Leonard Cohen, 'Acceptance Address for the Prince of Asturias Award', in Leonard Cohen, *The Flame: Poems Notebooks Lyrics Drawings* (New York: FSG Press, 2018), pp. 267–9. Tonal key: A Minor (C Major); D Minor (F Major); B Minor (D Major); E Minor (D Major); C# Minor (E Major); F# Minor (A Major).

[9] Federico García Lorca, *Selected Poems*, trans. Stephen Spender and J. L. Gili (London: Hogarth Press, 1943); Ira Nadel, *Various Positions: A Life of Leonard Cohen* (London: Bloomsbury, 1996), p. 23; Sylvie Simmons, *I'm Your Man: The Life of Leonard Cohen* (London: Jonathan Cape, 2012), pp. 28–9.

[10] https://www.youtube.com/watch?v=rAu4gp2iavY. Accessed 20 March 2020.

[11] *The Selected Poems of Federico García Lorca*, ed. Francisco García Lorca and Donald M. Allen (New York: New Directions Publishing, 1955). Spender and Gili translated the poem in this edition, but it differs from the one cited above: 'Through the Arch of Elvira/ I want to see you pass/ to know your name/ and begin weeping', p. 169.

The Spaniard, Cohen confessed, had 'been a man of extraordinary influence on both my political and personal work. I admire him. At fourteen years of age, I realized that to define the words "purity" and "poetry", I could go to Lorca.'[12] Such was the indelible mark he made on him that when Cohen's daughter was born in 1974 he named her Lorca. In an interview with Deborah Sprague in 1991 Cohen commented that his daughter 'wears the same name beautifully; she is a very strange and eccentric soul'.[13]

Cohen's first encounter with the poet Lorca was told in a story that he related relentlessly to express his gratitude to the Spaniard and by way of introduction to his own loose translation of 'Little Viennese Waltz' and 'Take This Waltz'. It is a free 'translation' from *A Poet in New York*. Cohen adds music and accentuates the surrealist and darker elements of love and death.[14] It was an immense achievement for someone whose Spanish was rudimentary, taking him '150 hours to translate and a nervous breakdown, so it's a very high price to pay for doing a translation'.[15] He did the translation as a contribution to the commemoration of the fiftieth anniversary of Lorca's untimely death at the hands of Franco's Granadian Falangists in 1936, during the Spanish Civil War. Cohen recorded the poem for a tribute compilation entitled *Poetas en Nueva York* and reworked it for his 1988 album, *I'm Your Man*. The enduring influence of Lorca on Cohen is evident in his 2008 *Book of Longing*, in which he publishes a poem 'The Faithless Wife', after a poem from *Gypsy Ballads* by Lorca, 'The Unfaithful Wife'.[16] Lorca begins the poem;

Y que you me la llevéal río	(I took her to the river),
Creyendo que era mozuela	(For I thought she was a maiden),
Pero tenía marido	(But she already had a husband),
Fue la noche de Santiago	(It was the night of Santiago)

[12] Interview with Jordi Sierra I Fabra, October 1978. Reprinted in *Leonard Cohen on Leonard Cohen: Interviews and Encounters*, ed. Jeff Burger (Chicago: Chicago Review Press, 2014), pp. 74–80, cited at p. 77.

[13] Reprinted in *Leonard Cohen on Leonard Cohen*, ed. Burger, pp. 249–55, cited at p. 251. Lorca Cohen and Rufus Wainwright had a daughter in 2011, Viva Katherine Wainwright Cohen. Cohen often talks about his daughter in introducing 'Take this Waltz' on stage. For numerous transcripts, see https://www.leonardcohenforum.com/viewtopic.php?t=4010. Accessed 3 March 2020.

[14] Federico García Lorca, *Poet in New York*, ed. with an intro. Christopher Maurer (London: Penguin, 1988).

[15] Interview with Alberto Manzano, his Spanish translator, May 1988, printed in *Leonard Cohen on Leonard Cohen*, ed. Burger, pp. 214–24, cited at 218.

[16] Leonard Cohen, *Book of Longing* (New York: Harper Collins, 2006), pp. 146–8. Federico García Lorca, *Gypsy Ballads*, trans. Laurent Paul Suer (no publication details recorded), poem 6.

Cohen's opening two verses play freely with Lorca's:

The Night of Santiago	She said she was a virgin
And I was passing through	That wasn't what I heard
So I took her to the river	But I'm not the Inquisition
As any man would do.	I took her at her word.

Cohen reworked the poem into a song that was released posthumously on *Thanks for the Dance,* in 2019. He transformed the first verse into the chorus, and the second verse into the first, changing the word 'virgin' to 'maiden' and replacing the line beginning 'But I'm not', with 'For the sake of conversation'. For dramatic effect he retitled it 'The Night of Santiago', but this time the reference to Lorca is omitted in the credits.

It was not only the poetry but also the Lorca persona that fascinated Cohen. Lorca's first foray outside of Spain was to study at Columbia University, New York (June 1929–March 1930), after which he visited Cuba for three months.

The allure of Columbia University and the newly liberated Cuba under Castro were irresistible for Cohen because of the association with Lorca. Columbia had the added attraction of being an Ivy League University where Cohen's mentor Louis Dudek earned his Ph.D. in 1951, just after Ginsberg obtained his degree in 1948. Ginsberg continued to be active on the New York scene with Kerouac, William Burroughs, Gregory Corso and Gary Snyder, while Cohen lived there. Cohen was bitterly disappointed with the curriculum at Columbia nor did he get beyond the fringes of the Beat culture that was emerging. The vibrancy of Greenwich Village with poetry recitals and jazz accompaniment and the anti-establishment radical individualism excited him. When he returned to Montreal, to perform his own poems to jazz, the city was devoid of the vibrancy he had experienced in New York. Writing in English was a minority activity in Montreal, attracting a limited circle of followers, in a city dominated by an exclusive French culture.

Undeterred by his first foray into Lorca territory, Cohen followed in his footsteps to Cuba. The revolution in Cuba was evocative of the Spanish Civil War in which Lorca fought and for which he was executed. For Cohen there was an affinity between Castro and Lorca, the fight for a just cause against corruption and injustice. There was an undeniable excitement about placing himself in harms way in order to experience the revolutionary fervour. Although the sleaze and debauchery were seriously curtailed, Cohen's long-standing nocturnal habits found him immersed in the sordidness that was left in the dying hours. The Bay of Pigs fiasco in April 1961, which humiliated the American counter-revolutionary invading forces, happened in the midst of Cohen's stay and led to a crackdown on freedom of movement, naturally generating a suspicion of foreigners. His paramilitary style of dress, unconventional behaviour and tendency to stray from the beaten track attracted the attention of the Cuban military who detained him on suspicion of being a spy. After hours of interrogation, he persuaded them that he was a tourist and fervent supporter of the revolution.[17] He endeared himself so thoroughly to his captors that they insisted he had his photograph taken with them.

With the political situation heightening in tension, Cohen decided to leave at the end of April, only to be detained at the airport after the discovery of the photo of him and the revolutionary guards on his person. He was accused of disguising himself as a tourist with a forged Canadian passport in order to defect. Amid a distracting commotion, Cohen fled and secreted himself on the plane which transported him to safety.

Lorca had travelled to Cuba in March 1930 where he gave a series of lectures, including one on *canto jondo* (deep song), a form of Andalusian music, which he illustrated by playing gramophone records.[18] He had first written and delivered it in 1922 in order to solicit support and prestige from Spanish intellectuals, for the Cante Jondo Festival. It had become unjustly associated in peoples' minds with immorality, taverns and late-night orgies, 'the dance floors of flamenco cafes, ridiculous whining – in short, all that is "typically Spanish".[19] Flamenco, he believed, had become popularized, commercialized and adulterated by pandering to the audiences in urban cafes and theatres. At this time, Lorca argued that *canto jondo* was a strictly rural phenomenon, which the gypsies had brought with them from the Orient, embodying intimate and anonymous cries of pain and longing, best expressed by amateurs. He maintained that 'it is song without landscape, withdrawn into itself and terrible in the dark. Deep song shoots its arrows of gold right into our heart. In the dark it is a terrifying blue archer whose quiver is never empty.'[20] Its sombre, melodic haunting style

[17] Tim Footman, *Leonard Cohen: Hallelujah* (New Malden, Surrey: Chrome Dreams, 2008), p. 36.
[18] Letter dated Havana, April 5, 1930 to his mother and father. Lorca, *Poet in New York*, pp. 254–6.
[19] Federico Garcia Lorca, 'Deep Song', in Lorca, *In Search of Duende* New York: New Directions Pearl, 1998), pp. 1–27. Cited at 1.
[20] Lorca, 'Deep Song', p. 16.

was an expression of collective consciousness. They were impersonal, vague, unconscious collective creations whose lyrics belonged to no one.[21]

In this 1922 formulation, Lorca emphasizes the creation of the text, rather than the creator; the performance, rather than the performer, with the implication that deep song intrinsically carries the qualities he identified independently of the artist performing it.

He was dissatisfied with having created a dichotomy between the performance and the individuality of the performer, probably prompted by becoming personally acquainted with professional singers (cantaores) and dancers (bailaores). In writing 'In Praise of Antonia Mercé, *La Argentina*' Lorca not only dwells on the creation of the work of art but quite emphatically also elevates the importance of the performer who contributes a 'very personal art' in its transmission. He contended, 'A Spanish dancer or singer or torero does not simply resuscitate, he invents and creates a unique, inimitable art, which disappears after death.'[22]

In coming to appreciate the works of Cohen and Dylan, Lorca's point reinforces our awareness of how integrally and inextricably entwined are the work of art and what is expressed in its performance by the artist. This is what Gregory Corso is getting at when he says: '*Howl* is essentially a poem to be read aloud, but only by the Howler. . . any other Howler would screw it up, thus for those unable to hear Ginsberg read his *Howl* will have to settle for its visuality.'[23] It's also what Bonnie 'Prince' Billy (Will Oldham) expressed when trying to sum up Cohen's greatness. It is, he argued, the 'very crucial co-dependent relationship between the presentation of the song vocally, the presentation of the song's arrangement and the lyric.'[24] No matter how many covers are produced of the songs of Dylan and Cohen, they are almost invariably disappointing. They lack something in their performance, with the few exceptions when the performer has invested the performance with his or her ineffable 'style', or duende, such as Jeff Buckley's version of Cohen's 'Hallelujah' or Jimi Hendrix's version of 'All Along the Watchtower'.

That duende is integral to the performance is, we think, undeniable. There is a danger, however, as we see with R. G. Collingwood's aesthetics and Yves Klein's International Blue, in the of eliminating form and content from art by

[21] Christopher Maurer, 'Preface', to Lorca, *In Search of Duende*, pp. viii–xii.
[22] Lorca, 'In Praise of Antonia Mercé, *La Argentina*', *In Search of Duende*, pp. 73–5. Cited at p. 74.
[23] Gregory Corso, *An Accidental Autobiography* (New York: New Directions Books, 2003), p. 10.
[24] Will Oldham, 'A Journey to Love', *Mojo*, March 2012, p. 79.

emphasizing, or over-emphasizing, the expression of emotion. Roberta Ann Quance is a little harsh contending that Lorca's representation of duende 'names an event and not a thing in the world' and thus fails to 'represent it in a text', suggesting only its effects.[25] Lorca confesses that duende is ineffable and elusive, it is almost indescribable, and 'there are no maps nor exercises to help us find the duende'.[26] It is something that everyone senses, but no one can describe. Cohen attests to this when he responds to variations of the question, 'How does anyone write a song this beautiful?' with his usual self-effacement: 'It is a miracle. I don't know where the good songs come from or else I'd go there more often'.[27]

Before we explore the concept of duende further in the writings of Lorca, in order to offer us an avenue into the poetic art of Leonard Cohen, it is revelatory and important to explore a little the ideas that led Lorca to revise and reformulate his views on 'Deep Song', leading to his mature reflections on duende. The reason for exploring Lorca's ideas is to suggest an alternative to the current popular, and somewhat superficial, approaches we will examine later. It is a path that points us in an interesting and intellectually stimulating direction to a deeper appreciation of the lyrics.

Lorca's *New York Poems* mark a significant development in Lorca's style from what he called the poetry of imagination to the poetry of inspiration associated with Lorca's attraction to surrealism and evasion. These distinctions are elaborated in a number of lectures variously reported in the press and collected under the title 'Imagination, Inspiration, Evasion'. They are different expressions of freedom, with evasion being the most unfettered.[28] Evasion is most closely associated with Lorca's attraction to surrealism and is equated with a dream world, which for him was nevertheless very real, in the requirement he had that mystery be visible and have form and sensuality. His rejection by his good friends and antagonists the surrealist artist Dalí and the surrealist sculptor Aladré, who accused Lorca of being a traditional bourgeois artist, led Lorca to abjure the idea of evasion as the principal aim of poetry.[29]

[25] Roberta Ann Quance, 'On the Way to "Duende" (through Lorca's *Elogio de Antonia Mercé, "la Argentina"*, 1930)', *Tesserae: Journal of Iberian and Latin American Studies*, vol. 17 (2011), pp. 181–94.

[26] Lorca, 'Play and Theory of the Duende', p. 60.

[27] Interview with Paul Zollo, 'Leonard Cohen: Inside the Tower of Song', *SongTalk* April 1993. Reprinted in *Leonard Cohen on Leonard Cohen: Interviews and Encounters*, ed. Burger, pp. 261–91. Cited at p. 285.

[28] Martha J. Nandorfy, *The Poetics of Apocalypse: Federico García Lorca's Poet of New York* (London: Associated University Press, 2003), p. 20.

[29] Nandorfy, *Poetics of Apocalypse*, p. 21.

Imagination, inspiration and evasion, nevertheless, remain important for our purposes. Imagination is synonymous with the aptitude we have for discovery. It enables us to illuminate what is hidden and to animate fragments of reality which have faded from the vision of humankind. Imaginative poetry, however, is bounded by horizons and is constrained by reality. Imaginative poetry has to conform to the laws of logic and reason, in that it is obliged to make connections within the architecture of the world. It aims to discover unexpected relations between objects and ideas in order to abate mystery. It is the poetry that explores and describes the universe. As Lorca suggests, 'One's imagination needs objects, landscapes, numbers and planets and the relationship between them within the purest form of logic is vital.'[30] It is the poetry that explores and describes the universe.

Lorca argues that imagination is located within human logic and controlled by reason. It is a special way of creating that requires order and boundaries. Imagination is the starting point in poetry, and the poet constructs a tower against the elements and against mystery. His voice is listened to because he creates order, but he finds it difficult to inspire intense emotions free from constraints. Poetic imagination, he contends,

> is the first step and the basis for all poetry. . . . With imagination the poet builds a tower against the elements and against mystery. He is unassailable, he creates order and is listened to. Almost always, however, the most beautiful birds and the most brilliant lights escape from him. It is difficult for a purely imaginative poet, if we can refer to him in this way, to produce intense emotions with his poetry.[31]

Ultimately imagination is impoverished, and poetic imagination even more so because it is impossible for imaginative poetry to create emotions, other than through a contrived formula related to its newly discovered or created laws of reality. The Spanish poet Góngora (1561–1627) is, for Lorca, a perfect representative of the poetry of imagination. His poetry is verbally balanced, has no mystery and 'knows no insomnia.'[32]

---

[30] Federico García Lorca, 'Imaginación, inspiración, evasión', in *Obras completas III: prosaed,* Miguel García-Posada (Barcelona: Galaxia Gutenberg, 1997). The text of the quotation comes from 'El Defensor de Grenada' Granada, 11 October 1928. We are indebted to Lisa Davies for translating the text. Unpublished manuscript, dated June 2001.

[31] Lorca, 'Imagination, Inspiration, Evasion', p. 3.

[32] Lorca, 'Three Types of Poetry', Text from 'La Prensa', New York, 10 February 1930. Translated by Lisa Davies, unpublished manuscript, p. 16.

In other words, poetic emotion is not contrived; it is a pure uncontrolled expression of emotion unfettered by constraints. Visible reality is more amorphous and nuanced than the poetry of imagination allows and intensely more poetic than imagination can comprehend. Lorca illustrates his contention by pointing to the conflict between scientific reality and imaginary myths. Imagination, for example, has attributed the construction of huge grottoes and cities of enchantment to giants. Scientific explanation, however, attributes their creation to continuous, patient, eternal drops of water seeping through crevasses, creating ravines, stalagmites and stalactites, testimony to the triumph of reality over imagination. Or more correctly, imagination becomes conscious of its shortcomings. Lorca argues that:

> Imagination seemed to be operating in a logical manner when it attributed to giants that which did, indeed, seem to be the work of giants. However, scientific reality, poetic to the extreme and beyond the logical field, showed us that the truth was to be found in eternal, crystal-clear water droplets. It is a great deal more beautiful to think that a grotto is the result of the mysterious caprice of water bound and governed by eternal laws, than the caprices of some giants which have no more meaning than that of an explanation.[33]

Lorca claims that poetic imagination is a fact of the soul, whereas poetic inspiration is a state of the soul which refers to a state of liberty devoid of boundaries and limits. The poetry of inspiration acknowledges and welcomes mystery. It moves in a world of poetic harmony and order that avoids imaginative reality with its conventionally perceived norms of beauty and ugliness. Inspiration enters instead into a poetic reality, which is characterized by astonishment, sometimes saturated with tenderness and at other times with immense, deep and dark cruelty. It is elusive and evades reality by following the pathway of dreams which subconsciously arrive at an unsuspected fact. The traditional metaphor and human logic in imaginative poetry give way to the poetic logic of inspiration.

Lorca contends that far from mystery requiring abatement by imagination, 'Only mystery enables us to live'.[34] The order and balance of imagination often gives way to the incongruity of inspiration. In this respect the poem is self-referential, pointing to nothing outside itself.[35] It is an evasion of reality. It follows

---

[33] Lorca, 'Imagination, Inspiration, Evasion', p. 4.
[34] Cited in Edward Hirsch, *The Demon and the Angel: Searching for the Source of Artistic Inspiration* (New York: Harcourt, 2002), p. 2.
[35] Derek Harris, cited by Maurer, p. xiv. In Lorca's *New York Poems*.

the path of dreams through the subconscious that arrives at poetic inspiration by breaking free from the control of human logic. It is a passionate rejection of the temptation to be understood. Lorca's enigmatic *Poet in New York* constitutes the point at which he attained the 'poetic fact' or 'poetic event', images that followed their own inner logic of poetic architecture and emotion.

In Lorca's view, poetry cannot be understood, it is received, not analysed. It is counter to intelligence and the received order of things. The poet of inspiration has to look at the world with the eyes of a child and, when asking for the moon, truly believe that someone will reach out and place it in his hands.[36] In sum, then, the poet of imagination is constrained by human logic and abates mystery by explaining the inexplicable, while the poet of inspiration is set free by poetic logic, acknowledging that not everything has a cause and effect and that pure reality evades explanation. The implication seems to be that imaginative poetry craves to be understood and makes propositions about reality which can be explored and refuted. Inspirational poetry delights in mystery, rejects the temptation to be understood and presents images to which truth and falsity are inapplicable.

The poetry of inspiration, on the other hand, acknowledges mystery; it is elusive and evades reality. The traditional metaphor in poetry gives way to the poetic fact which is tied to poetic logic. In this respect the poem is a 'self-sufficient entity without reference to any reality outside itself'.[37] Michael Oakeshott has something similar in mind when he characterizes poetic imagining as contemplative. You do not ask of the images whether they are fact or not fact. They are not propositions about the world to which truth and falsity are applicable; they are images to be delighted in.[38] This was what Lorca was suggesting in his lecture on 'The Mechanics of Poetry', delivered in Havana during the spring 1930.[39] It is pointless, he said, to ask him what constitutes truth or falsehood in poetry. Poetry is not something we seek to understand. It is received and not analysed. It is loved for its own sake. The Spanish poet San Juan de la Cruz (1542–91) most perfectly exemplifies poetic inspiration in his

[36] The text comes from 'El Sol', Madrid, 16 February 1929.
[37] Derek Harris, cited by Maurer, p. xiv. In Lorca's *New York Poems*.
[38] Michael Oakeshott, 'The Voice of Poetry in the Conversation of Mankind', in *Rationalism in Politics and Other Essays*, new and expanded edition (Indianapolis: Liberty Press, 1991), pp. 488–541.
[39] Lorca, 'The Mechanics of Poetry', text from 'Diaro de la Marina', Havana, Spring 1930. Translated by Lisa Davies, 2001, Unpublished MS.

yearning and desire for uncontrolled love, as his words soar above the elements with his toes grazing against the mountains.[40]

Lorca's distinction between the poetry of imagination and the poetry of inspiration, with the associated idea of evasion, enables us to make qualitative judgements about the aesthetic value of a poem or song. With the emphasis upon the 'work' itself, Lorca's concepts of imagination, inspiration and evasion complement the emphasis that duende places on the performance. In a lecture first delivered in March 1932, in which he introduced and read selections from his *New York Poems*, Lorca announced: 'before reading poems aloud to so many people, the first thing one must do is to invoke the *duende*'. He went on to say that 'poems like these are not likely to be understood without the cordial help of the *duende*'.[41] The concept of duende, although known to him in relation to flamenco, was not mentioned in his 1922 lecture on 'Deep Song' (*canto jondo*). Christopher Maurer points out that the revised lecture of 1930, 'The Architecture of Deep Song' (*Arquitectura del cante jondo*) introduces a criterion by which to judge the good artist from the bad. A *cantaor* can perform either with or without duende, distinguishing the mediocre from the truly great.[42]

Duende surges up from the inside in torrents of blood pumping through one's veins. It is an indescribable sadness or sorrow, a terrible deep harrowing question that has no answer: 'it burns the blood like powdered glass, that exhausts, rejects all sweet geometry we understand'.[43] Duende intimates the dark inexpressible sinister and unsettling undercurrents of all traditional societies. It is the mysterious, dark, black sounds buried in the mire of the fertile silt that gives rise to the 'very substance' of art. Lorca is emphatic that it is a power and a struggle, not a work or thought. Duende is not about ability, but of something much deeper, a true living style that generates spontaneous creation.[44] As Collingwood says of art proper, it is not a matter of first formulating an intention or plan to express a particular emotion but simultaneously to express the emotion in the act of the artistic creation itself, which until it is expressed is not consciously experienced.

---

[40] Lorca, 'Three Types of Poetry', p. 16.

[41] Lorca, 'Poet in New York' a lecture translated by Christopher Maurer in Lorca, *Poet in New York*, p. 184.

[42] Cited in Quance, 'On the Way to "Duende"' (through Lorca's *Elogio dAntonia Mercé*, "la Argentina" (1930)', p. 182.

[43] Lorca, Federico García (2004), 'Theory and Practice of the *Duende*', trans. A. S. Klein, http://www .tonykline.co.uk/PITBR/Spanish/LorcaDuende.htm, p. 3. Accessed 7 March 2020. The translation of this line is preferable to that of the Maurer translation: 'he burns the blood like a poultice of broken glass, that he exhausts, that he rejects all the sweet geometry we have learned', p. 60.

[44] Lorca, 'Play and Theory of the Duende', p. 57. Collingwood, *Principles of Art* (Oxford: Clarendon Press, 1938).

Lorca declares that all art forms are capable of duende, but it is most evident, and with the greatest range, in music, dance and spoken poetry, because their interpretation requires a living body.[45] Because it is a dark power summoned from the inner sanctums of the body, it is most at home when it senses the possibility of death and the opportunity to serenade at its door. In Lorca's view, all major Spanish art is the embodiment of duende in that it exhibits a sense of death as it struggles with mortality.[46] Quoting Goethe's reference to Paganini, Lorca maintains that duende is 'a mysterious power which everyone senses and no philosopher explains'.[47] The duende is the opening of a wound which cannot be healed. Poetry does not need followers, only lovers who become ensnared in, and wounded by, the blackberry branches with glass burrs that poetry plants.

Duende is not something that comes from outside of the artist like the angel which gives light and the muse which gives form. These are the three spirits that are at the centre of artistic creation. The angel, Lorca suggests, acts as a guide and defender. It looks forward, announcing and forewarning, dazzling as it soars high overhead clearing the path to an effortless realization, or manifestation, of charm in the work. The angel imposes a predestined order that is useless to resist. The nine muses are the daughters of Mnemosyne, the goddess of memory. Apollo, the god of beauty, poetry and music, is the half-brother of the muses. The muse moves in the artist the evocation of memory, based on emotional and cognitive experiences.[48] The muse is tired, dictating and prompting from afar, awakening intelligence, or intellect, which is the enemy of the poet, elevating him, or her, to lofty positions, forgetful of the calamities likely to befall him or her. The angel and the muse are external to the poet, bestowing their gifts, whereas duende is internal and must be awakened from 'the remotest mansions of the blood'.[49]

In other words, together, 'inspiration' and 'duende' intimate a challenge to the settled reality we know, a deep, dark overthrow of certainty, replaced by a disturbing, frightening mystery.

Lorca is consistent in his commitment to creating the poetic event and resisting the desire to be understood. Poetry is something that is received, rather

---

[45] Lorca, 'Play and Theory of the Duende', p. 63.
[46] Binding, *Lorca: The Gay Imagination*, p. 162.
[47] Lorca, 'Play and Theory of the Duende', 57.
[48] Edward Winters, 'Leonard and Lorca', in *Leonard Cohen and Philosophy: Various Positions,* ed. Jason Holt (Chicago: Open Court, 2014), pp. 75–85.
[49] Lorca, 'Play and Theory of the Duende', p. 59.

than explained and analysed.[50] In his lecture 'A Poet in New York', he effectively blames the reader, if he or she is unable to explain a poem or understand a poem. He declares: 'I can explain nothing, but stammer with the life that has been bestowed on me.'[51]

The intention of the author

There is a long tradition in literary interpretation, and in interpretation theory in general, for privileging the intention of the author in uncovering the meaning of a text, whether that be a poem, song or a work of fine art. In this respect, the claim is, whether explicit or implicit, that we have to go outside of the text itself in order to identify the referents in the text; that is, the people, places, things and events that serve to add significance to the words and reveal a greater depth of meaning than the 'work' projects independently of its context. For other interpreters, while acknowledging the place of authorial intention in shedding light on particular works, the meaning of a text is revealed by identifying its place in the great lexicon of artistic creations. In interpreting truly great poetry nothing less than the whole of the Western tradition, and beyond, will suffice. This search for meaning is characterized by the identification of echoes, influences and resemblances that need have no firmer evidential basis than that the connections are made in the mind of the interpreter whose contextual reference is the quasi-world of texts that constitute the 'canon'. Often it fails to rise above the level of a concordance mentality. James Abbott McNeill Whistler deprecates this method when he described it as 'collecting–comparing–compiling–classifying–contradicting', and for such people who engage in it 'a date is an accomplishment – a hall-mark, success'. In fact, they reduce 'art to statistics, they "file" the fifteenth century, and "pigeon-hole" the antique'.[52]

a) People places and objects

Cohen invites us to unravel the mystery of some of his songs and poems by describing them as reportage, or journalism, and offering us the external

---

[50] Nandorfy, *The Poetics of Apocalypse*, pp. 23–5.
[51] Lorca, 'A Poet in New York', a lecture translated by Christopher Maurer, in Lorca, *Poet in New York*, pp. 184–5.
[52] James Abbott McNeill Whistler, 'The Ten O'Clock Lecture' in *The New Oxford Book of English Prose* (Oxford: Oxford University Press, 1998), p. 532.

references which attach the events, characters and allusions to his songs or poems.[53] This is commonly acknowledged among songwriters. Bob Geldof, for example, contends that he is only able to write about those of his songs that are based on 'an empirical reality; those where I was referencing tangible things that had sparked a thought process and a song line'.[54] This is not to suggest that their meanings are self-evident or that they do not require interpretation, but instead there is an aspiration in them to make sense of a situation, an attempt to abate the mystery or make intelligible the world the writer inhabits, in what Lorca refers to as the poetry of imagination.

Within Cohen's repertoire, 'Suzanne', 'Sisters of Mercy' and 'Tower of Song' are probably the most celebrated, while 'On That Day', referring to the 9/11 Twin Towers attack, is less well known. From among the poems that were not translated into songs a few from *Flowers for Hitler, Book of Longing* and *The Flame* suffice. They are 'All There Is to Know about Adolph Eichmann', 'Roshi at 89' and 'Roshi Said'.

'Suzanne', which was first published as a poem 'Suzanne Takes You Down' in Cohen's *Parasites of Heaven*, is one of his best known songs, and he has freely pointed to the referents of the lyrics, and how the person, the place and the significance of the ambiguous relationship with Suzanne Verdal and her husband Arnand Vaillancourt. Cohen confesses that it is almost reportage. He suggests that when all of the pieces came together it was just a matter of 'really just being as accurate as I could about what she said'.[55] The song is intended to convey the purity of the occasion and deliberately evokes the area around the harbour before it was renovated, what is now called Old Montreal, with Our Lady of the Harbour, Notre Dame de Bonne Secours, towering over the port, with a statue of the Virgin, gilded and glistening in the sun that pours down like honey, with her arms open wide, welcoming the seafarers to a place of sanctity and solace. Cohen explains that it is a church for sailors, with models of ships decorating the interior. The church faces the river, and it is where sailors are blessed before embarking on their next voyage. This is why the flow of the lyrics

[53] 'All Good Things', interview with Adrian Deevo, *Q Magazine*.
[54] Bob Geldorf, *Tales of Boomtown Glory* (London: Faber Music, 2020), p. 17.
[55] Interview with Paul Zollo, 'Leonard Cohen: Inside the Tower of Song', Reprinted in *Leonard Cohen on Leonard Cohen*, ed. Burger, p. 286. There are, of course, many others, too numerous to recount, such as 'So Long Marianne' which has an added poignancy, of course, because of her very public death months before that of her eternal lover, Leonard Cohen. And, 'Chelsea Hotel #2', while an inadvertent indiscretion on Cohen's part, for which he expressed his deep regret, nevertheless, revealed the subject of the song was Janis Joplin; the force, despair, desperateness of their lives in New York at that time are brought jaggedly into focus.

moves effortlessly from immersion in Suzanne's presence to the introduction of Jesus Christ. Cohen explains: 'the next verse moves easily, you know onto the idea that Jesus was a sailor, sank beneath your wisdom like a stone. So you know you could establish a real coherence in the song if that was where you went . . . it hangs together very neatly.'[56]

On stage in Nuremburg in 1988 Cohen declared 'this is my story. It's a dismal story. It's a funny story. But it's my story.'[57] He was referring to 'Tower of Song'. Cohen was the most self-deprecating of men, and twenty years later, when inducted into the Rock and Roll Hall of Fame, 'not a distinction [he] coveted', he recited it as part of his acceptance speech. He often joked about his voice, most famously in 'Tower of Song', which sent his audience into spontaneous rapturous applause when he sang, 'I was born this way. I had no choice. I was born with the gift of a golden voice.' Cohen thought it one of his best two or three songs. His modesty shines through in placing Hank Williams a hundred floors above him in the 'Tower of Song'.

'On That Day', which appeared on *Dear Heather* (2004), was Cohen's and Anjani Thomas's immediate and poetic reaction to the atrocity that shocked the world and precipitated George W. Bush's war on the axis of evil, resulting in the intractable military intervention in Afghanistan and Iraq. Its lyric is morally ambivalent, regretting the occasion, but distancing himself from unequivocal condemnation. Once again, it is a piece of reportage, relaying what some people believe: that the attack on the Twin Towers was just desert, Divine punishment for crimes against God and the world. As if to presage 'The Night in Santiago', in which he opines, 'You were born to judge the world. Forgive me but I wasn't',[58] Cohen responds to the evangelists:

I wouldn't know
I'm just holding the fort
Since that day
They wounded New York

Turning to the listener he provokes a moment of self-reflection in asking: 'Did you go crazy or did you report, on that day they wounded New York?' On the

[56] Harry Rasky, *The Song of Leonard Cohen* (Oakville, ON: Mosaic Press, 2001), p. 99.
[57] Dorian Lynskey, 'Leonard Cohen in Twenty Songs, 1967–2016', *Q Magazine*, February 2017, p. 83.
[58] On *Thanks for the Dance*, 2019.

album's liner notes, he refers to *The American Heritage Dictionary* definition of 'report': 'To present oneself: report for duty'.[59]

On occasion a song may become inextricably associated with a referent that was not the original and devalues or demeans its subject, and to extricate it from its corrupting context may restore something of its purity. The association of 'Sisters of Mercy' with the 1971 film *McCabe and Mrs Miller*, directed by Robert Altman, who conceived the idea for the film while listening to *Songs of Leonard Cohen*, has indelibly stained the authenticity of the subject matter, in which Cohen himself was complicit.[60] Shane MacGowan, of the Pogues, is among many who, because of the film, believes that the song is 'about prostitution'.[61] Although there are some inconsistencies in detail, the song had its origins in Edmonton, Alberta, while Cohen was on tour around 1967. On a bitterly cold night during a snowstorm, knowing no one, he came across two women hitchhikers, Barbara and Lorraine, standing in a doorway. He invited them back to his hotel room, where he found their company comforting. While they slept in his double-bed, he occupied a chair, and by the light of the moon was inspired to write a song which he sang to them when they awoke.[62] Being aware of Cohen's gratitude for breaking the solitude and despair, his lyrics take on an added poignancy and depth of meaning.

> They were waiting for me
> When I thought that I just can't go on
> And they brought me their comfort
> And later they brought me this song

For two final examples we refer the reader to one poem each from *Flowers for Hitler* and *Book of Longing*.[63]

Karl Adolf Eichmann escaped justice at Nuremberg by fleeing Germany and remained in hiding in Europe until 1950, after which he escaped and lived under an assumed identity in Argentina.[64] He was illegally detained in Buenos Aires by Israeli Mossad operatives and flown to Israel nine days later on 20 May

---

[59] 9/11: Five Years later, Leonard Cohen's 'On That Day'. https://www.sfgate.com/entertainment/art icle/9-11-FIVE-YEARS-LATER-Leonard-Cohen-s-On-That-2488118.php.

[60] Nadel, *Various Positions*, pp. 170–1.

[61] 'Leonard Cohen 1934-2016: I'm Your Man, The Complete Story of Rock's Greatest Poet', *Uncut Magazine*, Uncut Ultimate Guide Series, 2017, issue 1, p. 115.

[62] Rasky, *The Song of Leonard Cohen*, pp. 103–4.

[63] London, Jonathan Cape, 1964; London, Bloomsbury, 2006; and New York, Farrar, Strauss, and Giroux.

[64] He obtained a passport from the International Red Cross in the name of Ricardo Klement, a native Italian without nationality, but went to no great lengths to suppress his identity while in Argentina,

1960 to face trial in the District Court in Jerusalem. Stripped of his authority, the Mossad operatives were surprised at how ordinary he looked, not at all imposing or sinister, as one would expect the incarnation of evil to be. The trial began on 11 April 1961 culminating in his execution on 31 May 1962. While not the architect of the 'final solution', nor among the highest ranking Nazis, Eichmann efficiently organized the transportation of its victims to the death camps, apparently without any qualms of conscience. He claimed he had not personally killed, nor ordered the killing, of any person.

In 1964 Leonard Cohen published 'All There Is to Know About Adolph Eichmann'. He described as medium the colour of Eichmann's hair and eyes, weight and height and intelligence. Eichmann had the normal number of fingers and toes and had no distinguishing features. Cohen ends: 'What did you expect? Talons? Oversize incisors? Green saliva? Madness?' In these few words he conveyed the extraordinary ordinariness that so unnerved the Mossad operatives and so struck Hannah Arendt in reporting the case for the *New York Times*.[65] She published a book based on the articles in 1963 and revised and expanded it in 1964. Arendt herself disavowed any suggestion that her book was a 'theoretical treatise on the nature of evil'.[66] Yet the subject matter of her book, the Holocaust and the Nazi desire to 'cleanse' the world of the mentally ill, gypsies and, above all, Jews, has become the epitome of evil, not only for the twentieth century but also for all time.

The book itself has become a touchstone for almost every attempt theoretically to understand the nature of evil, because it is so chilling in its conclusions. Arendt's article and subsequent book did not directly influence Cohen's poem, but he says:

> Hannah Arendt is somehow involved but I don't recall the circumstances. I didn't read the book, but I may have read a review of the book, or heard of the book. My old friend, Irving Layton and I were certainly discussing these matters, which hung heavy in the air at the time, and I guess the poem rose from those conversations. Irving most probably did read the book. I seem to remember that Hannah Arendt's position was unacceptable in some Jewish circles around Montreal.[67]

even registering his children, who joined him with his wife in 1952, under the name of Eichmann in a German school.

[65] Arendt's article and subsequent book did not directly influence Cohen's poem. Email to the author dated 30 January 2011.

[66] Hanna Arendt, *A Report on the Banality of Evil: Eichmann in Jerusalem* (London: Penguin, 1965), p. 285.

[67] Email to the author dated 30 January 2011.

Cohen's, or Jikan's (Ordinary Silence), long-standing relationship with his guru, master and confidante, Roshu Sasaki, better known as Roshi, is now legendary, and we have discussed the religious aspect of it in a previous chapter. There are many references to the relationship throughout Cohen's writings, which began in 1969 and continued intermittently for a few months a year until he withdrew to the monastery on Mount Baldy in 1993 for a period of over five years of intensive study and devotion, culminating in his ordination as a Buddhist monk, which because he was an assistant to Roshi, was a formal requirement of protocol. Roshi was an immensely influential and charismatic Zen master. He opened his Zen centre in Los Angeles and founded a Zen retreat in 1971 at Mount Baldy, located in San Bernardino County, California, and in 1972 he opened another in Jemez Springs, New Mexico. Cohen's relationship with Roshi was the subject of Armelle Brusq's documentary *Leonard Cohen: Spring 96*, which was filmed at the retreat at Mount Baldy. In the documentary Cohen describes his mentor as 'loving charming, deceptive – this guy is absolutely true. His love is a liberating sort of love.'[68] In his 1996 poem, 'Roshi at 89', published in *Book of Longing* in 2006, Cohen tenderly and mockingly characterized and caricatured him, commenting on his requiring another drink, 'will wonders never cease', to a stomach that is contented, facilitated by prunes that perform their function well. Roshu Sasaki died on 27 July at the age of 107 in 2014. Two years before his demise in 2012, a darker, sinister side of Sasaki emerged. For the whole of the period Cohen knew him, it was alleged that Roshi was a serial sexual abuser. A wave of former students and Buddhist nuns, on websites and discussion boards, related stories of Roshi's sexual predations and molestations during his one-to-one sessions at his Rinzai-ji Zen Centre in Los Angeles and at his retreat camps.[69] The investigation by an independent council of Buddhist leaders reported that Roshi probably abused hundreds of men and women over a long period of time. The report suggested that there were allegations of molestation and rape. A number of the incidents were reported to the Rinzai-ji board, which resulted in no disciplinary action. 'We see how, knowingly and unknowingly, the community was drawn into an open secret' the council wrote, adding: 'We have reports that those who chose to speak out were silenced, exiled, ridiculed

[68] Armelle Brusq's documentary *Leonard Cohen: Spring 96* Lieurac Productions, 1997.
[69] Paul Vitello, 'Joshu Sasaki, 107, Tainted Zen Master', *New York Times*, 4 August 2014. https://www.nytimes.com/2014/08/05/us/joshu-sasaki-a-zen-master-tarnished-by-abuse-claims-dies-at-107.html. Accessed 24 March 2020.

or otherwise punished.'[70] Newspaper articles frequently reported that Cohen was taught by Roshi and that their relationship was close and of long duration. He may have been unaware of Roshi's serial sex abuse, but they frequently drank together and discussed all sorts of issues. Cohen suggests in 1998 that he screened 'important sex videos' for Roshi to acclimatize him to North American culture. Roshi's response, in his usual broken English, was 'Study human love interesting, but not so interesting.'[71] Without trying to excuse his actions, Cohen issued the mildest of rebukes: 'Roshi,' he said, 'was a very naughty guy'.[72] This context is undoubtedly necessary for appreciating the poignancy of the poem 'Roshi said':

> During Roshi's sex scandal (he was 105)
> My association with Roshi
> Was often mentioned in the newspaper
> Reports.
> Roshi said:
> I give you lots of trouble.
> I said:
> Yes Roshi, you give me
> Lots of trouble.
> Roshi said:
> I should die.
> I said:
> It won't help.
> Roshi didn't laugh.[73]

We have argued that there are songs and poems that while it is not a necessary and sufficient condition for appreciating them, knowing their context, or referents, enhances our understanding by unravelling the mystery and allowing us a glimpse into the people and places to whom and to which the lyrics refer. Maurice Ratcliffe takes the same approach to all of Cohen's songs. While fully acknowledging that the poet trades in ambiguity, he implicitly conveys the view

---

[70] Cited in Corina Knoll, 'Sex Abuse Allegations Surround L.A. Buddhist Teacher', *Los Angeles Times*, 12 February 2013. https://www.latimes.com/local/la-xpm-2013-feb-12-la-me-zen-master-2013 0213-story.html. Accessed 25 March 2020.

[71] Leonard Cohen, 'Early Questions', *Book of Longing*, p. 45.

[72] David Remnick, 'Leonard Cohen Makes It Darker', *The New Yorker*, 17 October 2016. https://ww w.newyorker.com/magazine/2016/10/17/leonard-cohen-makes-it-darker. Page 13. Accessed 25 March 2020.

[73] Leonard Cohen, 'ROSHI SAID', *Book of Longing*, p. 21.

that we ought to be able to unravel what is ambiguous and indeed thinks that there are limits to ambiguity beyond which meaning is unintelligible or lost. In discussing 'The Old Revolution' (*Songs from a Room*), Ratcliffe asks: 'What is the protagonist talking about and why? Ambiguity is all very well, but it seems that here Cohen strayed over the boundary into impression.'[74] The assumption is that the song must have an authorial meaning and that it is a failure on the part of the poet if he or she does not convey it. Ratcliffe is much more in his comfort zone discussing 'Hey That's No Way to Say Goodbye' because he is able to disentangle the referents and discern the subject matter of the song. It was written in 1966 in Penn Terminal Hotel, New York. Contrary to the impression that the song gives, because it is similar in theme to 'So Long Marianne' on the same album, it is about a different but parallel relationship which had run its course. He was once again with the wrong woman! Ratcliffe does raise a note of caution when searching for referents to give a song meaning. He argues but does not heed the warning himself, that 'the story of the song's genesis underlines the perils of reading too much autobiography into a work of art'.[75] He even concedes that sometimes with poets who thrive on ambiguity the audience has to find the meaning for itself, and in certain songs, such as 'The Butcher' (*Songs from a Room*), the meaning is not easily yielded.

Persistently trying to tie meaning to outside referents, and tenaciously interrogating them mercilessly to yield authorial meaning, mistakes the part for the whole. With the poetry of imagination, where the author attempts to abate mystery, then one may confidently, but not invariably, assume that the words are designed to resolve the mysteries of life. Ratcliffe contends that 'First We Take Manhattan' (*I'm Your Man*) is an allegory for 'girding the loins for the rigours of his forthcoming tour, a call to arms directed at his band'.[76] The arduous schedule of touring may well suggest such imagery, but it does nothing to explain the song or help us appreciate it more. It is a song that is full of menace and threats and is not a political song because 'it neither identifies the causes of problems nor proposes solutions to them'.[77] He is quite right that this is not a finger-pointing song, but wrong to think it is not political because he cannot find the events or injustices to which it refers. Cohen once said that all his songs are political,

---

[74] Maurice Ratcliffe, *The Complete Guide to the Music of Leonard Cohen* (London: Omnibus, 1999), p. 29.
[75] Ratcliffe, *The Complete Guide to the Music of Leonard Cohen*, p. 19.
[76] Ratcliffe, *The Complete Guide to the Music of Leonard Cohen*, p. 80.
[77] Ratcliffe, *The Complete Guide to the Music of Leonard Cohen*, p. 45.

particularly 'A Singer Must Die' from *New Skin For the Old Ceremony*, in which the final verse is very strongly against a specific kind of authority.[78] The recorded version finishes with the penultimate verse of the printed version and substitutes 'I was just getting laid' for 'I was just getting home late'.

> it's their ways to disgrace, their knee in your balls and their fist in your face. *Yes and long live the state! By whoever its made! Sir I didn't see nothing, I was just getting laid.*

A poem or a song can be deeply political, representative of a counterculture, and unnervingly unsettling because of what it brings into question or because the mood is dark and threatening. The disturbing imagery may have no referent that we can identify, and language and meaning are inseparable, yet they may be profound in their impact upon the reader or hearer attuned to the duende. As for example, the menacing tone and allusions in the following lines:

> You loved me as a loser, but now you're worried that I just might win.
> You know the way to stop me, but you don't have the discipline
> How many nights I prayed for this, to let my work begin.
> First we take Manhattan, then we take Berlin.
> ('First We Take Manhattan', *The Future*)

Or the equally disturbing and apocalyptic, 'The Future':

> And now the wheels of heaven stop
> you feel the devil's riding crop
> Get ready for the future:
> it is murder

Believing that gathering new facts about a subject leads to cumulative understanding is simply a fallacy when it comes to appreciating the poetic fact of inspiration and its possession of duende. Mark Twain puts this eloquently in his *Life on the Mississippi*. He relates how he came to know every feature of the great river as well as he knew the letters of the alphabet. This in itself was an achievement: 'But I had lost something, too. I had lost something which could never be restored to me while I lived. All the grace, the beauty, the poetry had gone out of the majestic river.'[79]

---

[78] Devlin, *Leonard Cohen in His Own Words*, p. 59.
[79] From *The New Oxford Book of English Prose*, pp. 533–4.

Stephen Scobie strongly criticizes the approaches that search for referents outside the text. He comments that our appreciation of Cohen's 'Suzanne' is not enhanced by knowing the subject is Suzanne Vaillancourt. What is important is the song itself.[80] That, as we have argued, is not strictly true. Cohen freely talks about the contexts of his songs of reportage, and as we have seen this sheds light on, adds clarity and abates the mystery of obscure references in Cohen's songs of reportage.

b) Referents in poetic and musical sources

So the question remains, is the alternative nothing more than superficial influence hunting? Certainly, the method is one that could be affected by the use of a poetry, or blues, concordance.

Cohen's work has been approached in this way by, for example, Michael Ondaatje, George Woodcock, Desmond Pacey and Stephen Scobie. Ondaatje suggests that the poem 'Lovers', from *Let Us Compare Mythologies*, exhibits a bitter irony reminiscent of A. M. Klein. Both writers, he claims, employ similar poetic and rhetorical tricks: 'Apart from the obvious similarities – such as the exotic words and worlds, and a biblical style – there is the same gentle irony about oneself and about one's childhood heroism.'[81] In *Collected Poems* we find Dylan Thomas's 'tousled ghost', as well as some deft parodying of Eliot. We also find borrowings from and echoes of W. H. Auden and Edith Sitwell.[82] In *Recent Songs* 'The Gypsy Wife', for example, 'echoes, if it does not rely on, the *Blood Wedding* of Lorca, no less'.[83] The fact that Lorca wrote *Gypsy Ballads* is hardly sufficient grounds to link Lorca's relentlessly bleak play, with Cohen's lyrics which he says himself relate to the strained relationship he was in with Suzanne Elrod, the mother of his children, at the time it was breaking down. The emotion expressed is that of the conflicting feelings of wanting to break free, while at the same time jealously tortured by the thought that someone else may be in her arms.

Desmond Pacey juxtaposes Cohen with Wordsworth because the former resembles the latter in achieving magical clarity, not by looking at the world in generalities or through scientific concepts, but by close examination of detail,

---

[80] Stephen Scobie, *Leonard Cohen* (Vancouver: Douglas and McIntyre, 1978), p. xi.
[81] Michael Ondaatje, *Leonard Cohen* (Toronto: McClelland and Stewart, 1970), p. 6.
[82] George Woodcock, 'The Song of the Sirens: Reflections on Leonard Cohen', in *Leonard Cohen: The Artist and His Critics*, ed. Michael Gnarowski (Toronto: McGraw-Hill, 1976), pp. 155–6.
[83] L. S. Dormanand and C. L. Rawlins, *Leonard Cohen: Prophet of the Heart* (London: Onmibus, 1990), p. 306.

such as the streaks on a designated tulip. This juxtaposition is justified because at least once there is 'an obvious echo' of Wordsworth's 'Tintern Abbey' in *Beautiful Losers*.[84] Both poets exemplify a search for sensual exactitude. This is not to suggest, of course, that what is borrowed may occasionally be transformed into an original statement, as for example, in 'Travel' from *Spice-Box of Earth*, in which the lines, 'Horizons keep the soft line of your cheeks / The windy sky's a locket for your hair' follows lines that are no more than serviceable to Yeats, but with the word 'Horizons', 'a new spirit enters – that of a poet capable of an utterly individual statement within the convention, and from this point the resemblance to Yeats becomes ambivalent. These lines are no longer a good imitation of Yeats; they are lines which only Yeats could have imitated'.[85] Scobie, in reading *Let Us Compare Mythologies*, sees 'reminiscences of Eliot' in 'Rededication' and of Donne in 'The Fly'. He contends that Cohen's poem is a pale imitation of Donne's 'The Flea'.[86]

Inspiration and evasion

It has been suggested, then, that there are songs and poems in the body of work produced by Cohen that may appropriately be understood as poetry of the imagination and that in them the author attempts to unravel mystery or attain a heightened self-understanding revelatory of a clarity that serves to abate the mystery enveloping his life.

The second approach to appreciating the lyric poetry of Cohen is to understand it in terms of Lorca's idea of the poetic fact, the poetry of inspiration, evasion and duende, which revels in mystery, darkness, edginess and shocked sensibilities. It delights in flashing images.

For this type of song 'intention is a very, very small part of it'.[87] Cohen concedes that in some instances we may discard the poet's intention all together because the piece 'exists independently of his opinions about it'.[88] This isn't at all

---

[84] Desmond Pacey, 'The Phenomenon of Leonard Cohen', *Canadian Literature*, p. 34 (1967). In fairness, it must be added that Pacey's intention is to show how the book *Beautiful Losers* is the culmination of Cohen's own work and artistic development and not the intimation of that of others.
[85] Woodcock, 'The Song of the Sirens: Reflections on Leonard Cohen', pp. 156–7.
[86] Scobie, *Leonard Cohen*, p. 24.
[87] 'The Spin Doctor', interview with Mark Ellen, *The Word Magazine*, issue 53, July 2007, p. 90.
[88] 'Leonard Cohen: Inside the Tower of Song', interview with Paul Zollo, p. 285

a heretical or revolutionary idea. Cohen encountered it in an influential book written by William Empson, *Seven Types of Ambiguity,* when he was at school.[89] In this respect the words are not taken as statements. The words are indeed colours on the poet's palette that are used to paint and evoke powerful images which have the capacity to move us emotionally without having a determinate meaning. The immensely popular and enduring 1960s song 'A Whiter Shade of Pale', written by Keith Reid and performed by Procol Harem, is a perfect exemplification. In an interview with *Uncut* magazine, Reid rejects the idea that the lyrics have a meaning. He was trying to capture a mood, 'an image of a scene'.[90] More to the point, this is what Lorca meant by the poetic fact in the poetry of imagination, and in order to access it, the poet must feel the duende. Of his poem, 'Romance Sonámbulo' (The Somnambulant Lament), Lorca said: 'If you ask me why I wrote "a thousand glass tambourines/ were wounding the dawn", I will tell you I saw them, in the hands of angels and trees, but I will not be able to say more.'[91]

M. L. Rosenthal, the New York teacher and well-known critic, disparaged Cohen's lyric poetry for having little or no meaning. Paul Barrera at first glance seems to imply that the search for the author's meaning is futile, but then relents by suggesting that Cohen's ambiguities are something like cryptic crossword clues, and the reader must try to break the poetic code. There is a note of disappointment when he declares that the *Book of Mercy* (1984) is so personal that 'it is impossible to break through to the inner meanings'.[92] Doug Beardsley, a contemporary of Cohen in Montreal, appreciated that such comments, while literally true, miss the whole point of what some poets, at least, are doing. It was the aura and sense of the mysterious that the lyrics conjured and not their meaning that mattered.[93] Geldof articulates what all lyric poets possessive of duende experience. He says feelings, inchoate and unwanted, force themselves up from dark inaccessible recesses, demanding to be acknowledged. He maintains

---

[89] 'Leonard Cohen: Inside the Tower of Song', interview with Paul Zollo, p. 285. The book Cohen read at school was William Empson, *Seven Types of Ambiguity: A Study of Its Effects in English Verse,* third edition (London: Chatto and Windus, 1953).

[90] Jim Beviglia, 'Behind the Song: Procol Harum, "A Whiter Shade of Pale"', *American Songwriter,* 5 November 2019. https://americansongwriter.com/lyric-week-procol-harum-whiter-shade-pale/. Accessed 27 March 2020.

[91] Cited in Hirsch, *The Demon and the Angel,* p. 5.

[92] Paul Barrera, *Leonard Cohen: Came So Far for Love* (Andover, Hampshire: Agenda, 1997), pp. 17 and 57.

[93] Doug Beardsley, 'On First Looking into Leonard Cohen', in *Intricate Preparations: Writing Leonard Cohen,* ed. Stephen Scobie (Toronto, ON: ECW Press, 2000), p. 8.

that: 'often I have no idea what the lines "mean" or why these specific words occur, but upon writing them I know for absolute certain that they are true'.[94] Douglas Barbour contended, in reviewing Cohen's *Selected Poems* (1968), that poetry is neither right nor wrong. In conjures up images rather than propositions. Barbour talks of 'a poetry of enigma, where often it is impossible to know what is happening in the poem even while it exercises its charm upon you'.[95]

Lorca's understanding of the poetry of inspiration shows a sensitivity to the medium far more sophisticated than that of Rosenthal and is consistent with Cohen's own description of what it is appropriate and inappropriate to ask of a poem. In an interview with *New Musical Express,* Cohen argued that the poet is not absolved from clarity by immersing himself in ambiguity:

> there is a clarity that is perceived by the heart and clarity that is perceived by the mind. You know, clarity is not a fixed idea. Sometimes something that is clear to the heart needs quite complex expression. You just let the words or tune speak to you and it's very clear. You give yourself to the kiss or the embrace and while it is going on there's not any need to know what is going on. You just dissolve into it . . . But its there an obscurity in my work, it's something that no one can penetrate, not even me . . . You just try to be faithful to that interior landscape that has its own rules, its own mechanisms, and it's important to be faithful to them. If someone says 'I love the song, what the fuck does it mean?' the question is not as important as the declaration.[96]

The work itself, Cohen argued elsewhere, is beyond significance and meaning. Metaphorically the work is a diamond that the poet cuts and polishes, reflecting, refracting and amplifying light. Poetry is nevertheless an activity that is not merely summoned or invoked, it is not self-consciously premeditated, and the images present themselves as a consequence of the desperate and dismal lost battles of life.[97]

We think that we can detect in Cohen a self-conscious move from the poetry of imagination to the poetry of inspiration, from what he called reportage to what Lorca calls the poetry of imagination and evasion. We are not suggesting a discontinuity here because many of the themes are enduring, it is the imagery

---

[94] Geldof, *Tales of Boomtown Glory,* p. 17.

[95] Douglas Barbour, 'Canadian Books', *Dalhousie Review,* vol. XLVIII (1968), p. 568. Reprinted in *Leonard Cohen: The Artist and His Critics,* ed. Michael Gnarowski (Toronto: McGraw-Hill, 1976), p. 39.

[96] Biba Kopf, 'Jenny Sings Lenny', *The New Musical Express,* 14 March 1987.

[97] Cohen interviewed by Stephen Williams, 'The Confessions of Leonard Cohen', *Toronto Life,* February 1978, p. 48.

with which the themes are portrayed that become more surrealistic, sinister and even starkly frightening. *Flowers for Hitler* is the collection that manifests this completion of the transition that had already been taking place in individual poems previously. It is a book that is far less discerning than his previous books of poetry and which includes poems that are awkward and under-worked, many of which exhibit the philosophy of Irving Layton that the poet should just publish everything and that time will filter out the bad.

Cohen deliberately sets out to shock, by casting off an image that he misleadingly calls 'the golden boy', implying that his previous poetry did not contain similarly disturbing images. He wanted to move, he said, in the less socially acceptable dung-pile of the writer at the front line. The subjects he used for the poems were not addressed directly but tackled by employing symbolist and surrealist imagery. The book is, in a sense, a self-conscious revolt against style, a deliberate attempt to deny that the poems have any style. As Scobie points out, the pose of denying that they have style is itself a style. He recognizes that what Cohen is doing in much of the imagery is not to convey a literal or propositional meaning but instead to project the general atmosphere and tone of the book.[98] The content is political, not in any finger-pointing way, but in that it accentuates for view the most ugly, decadent, disjointed, sinister and threatening underlying realities, not as aspects of life, but present in all of life – the extraordinary in the ordinary, and what is worst, the ordinariness of the extraordinary.

After Cohen surfaced from the Monastery on Mount Baldly, he deliberately restricted the range and tone of his singing voice, reaching and conveying depths of emotion he had strived to accomplish all his life, to the point where critics attributed a deliberate religiosity or righteousness to the performances. Cohen himself dismissed the idea that his songs were self-consciously religious, declaring that it was part of the 'intentionalist fallacy'. He goes on to say, 'But when I see James Brown it has a religious feel. Anything deep does'.[99] *Ten New Songs*, in collaboration with Sharon Robinson, was hailed as his triumphant return, whereas, somewhat ironically, the succeeding albums were hailed as his long goodbye. John Lewis suggests that *Dear Heather*, for example, sounds like a man penning his own eulogy,[100] with the persistent, and not unprecedented,

[98] Scobie, *Leonard Cohen*, p. 46.
[99] Remnick, 'Leonard Cohen Makes It Darker', p. 16.
[100] John Lewis, '*Dear Heather*', in *Leonard Cohen 1943-2016, Uncut*, Ultimate Guide Series, 2007, Issue 1, p. 84.

but nevertheless accentuated, references to slipping away from the carnal into the ethereal, putting one's affairs in order by welcoming and celebrating the darkness, now more presciently revealed than the light the cracks let in. Having been dragged to the depths by depression and finally, in old age, breaking the chains that tethered him to despair, a new type of clarity and resignation broke through. The darkness of death is no longer as petrifying, but still feared, and menacing. It is there to be confronted and embraced, an unwelcome guest we are forced to entertain, and sometimes unexpectedly embrace.

Duende, darkness and death

The themes that Lorca impresses as characteristic of duende saturate Cohen's later lyric poetry. Fate and inevitability are intertwined by 'the pull of the moon and the thrust of the sun' ('Different Sides') in the imagery of a powerful undercurrent beneath and on top of the surface of the inhospitable 'dark infested sea' ('Banjo') 'so deep and blind' ('The Faith'). The darkness is a mysterious force that inverts experience, even sucking the sustaining properties of the past into its vortex. 'Oh see the Darkness yielding / That tore the light apart / Come healing of the reason / Come healing of the heart.'[101]

Throughout Cohen's long career, there have been many lyric poems that transcend reportage and which emerge from the inner depths from which duende emanates. Many of them reflect his struggle with depression and substance abuse. From his first album to the last despair, death, blood, humiliation and spiritual obsession are connecting threads, interwoven with contrasts between hope and despair, self-deprecation, irony and wit. The darkest track on his first album, *The Songs of Leonard Cohen*, comprises juxtaposed images of the idyllic and desperate, flashes of paradise with visions of hell. 'Stories of the Street' came from places within the deepest recesses of depression which dragged Cohen back from the glimmers of light that shine through. He never performed this offering on his touring sets nor was it reprinted in *Stranger Music*.[102] The night of poison gas is juxtaposed with

---

[101] 'Born in Chains', *Old Problems*; 'Different Sides' *Old Ideas*; 'Undertow', *Dear Heather*; 'Banjo', *Old Ideas*; 'The Faith' *Dear Heather*; 'Tennessee Waltz' *Dear Heather*; 'Darkness', *Old Ideas*; 'Come Healing', *Old Ideas*.

[102] Leonard Cohen, *Stranger Music: Selected Poems and Songs* (London: Jonathan Cape, 1993). This book was published when Cohen was at one of his all-time lows.

one hand on suicide and the other clutching a rose, while a rural idyllic scene of grass, apples and animals gently reared is broken by the thought of being taken to the slaughterhouse to lay with the lamb. The themes of slaughter and sacrifice continue with 'The Story of Isaac' and 'The Butcher' (*Songs from a Room*, 1969), another of Cohen's offerings that fail to surface on *Stranger Music*. They both have an underlying theme of the meek inheriting the earth, the child taking forward the baton and the sacrifice of innocence in the offering of the lamb. 'The Story of Isaac' is a retelling of the familiar biblical story of God's instruction to Abraham to sacrifice his son, an order with which he felt compelled to comply, 'when it all comes down to dust, I will kill you if I must'. 'The Butcher' begins with the gory image of the slaughtering of a lamb and ends with the exhortation, 'Lead on my son it is your world'.

Love and death, intertwined with the sacred and profane, are continuing themes: 'I'm almost alive, I'm almost at home; I'm blind with death / and anger / And that's no place for you / And death is old / But it's always new / I freeze with fear/ And I'm there for you' ('There For You', *Dear Heather*). 'So many graves to fill' unknowingly bestowed permission to 'murder and maim'; 'It's coming for me darling/ No matter where I go/ It's duty is to harm me / My duty is to know'. 'I have to die a little/ Between each murderous thought/ And when I'm finished thinking / I have to die a lot'. 'The party's over / But I landed on my feet/ I'll be standing on the corner / Where there used to be a street'.

Truth is elusive, evasive of certainty, and deceptive in its lies. Cohen once said that in order for him to feel comfortable in singing his songs they have to have a balance between 'truth and lies, light and dark'.[103] There is a difference between honesty and truth. Every writer strives to be honest, but no one knows the truth of the whole quest: 'Though all the maps of blood and flesh are posted on the door / There's no one who has told us yet what Boogie Street is for'.[104] There is a weary resignation to the transitory nature of truth: 'There's truth that lives / And truth that dies / I don't know which / So never mind'. 'Sounds like the Truth, but its not the truth today' 'Steer your heart past the Truth / you believed in yesterday' 'Come gather the pieces all scattered and lost / The lie in what's holy, the light in what's not'. Not even one's own inner feelings provide

---

[103] Interview with Paul Zollo, *Leonard Cohen on Leonard Cohen*, ed. Burger, p. 276.
[104] 'Boogie Street', *Ten New Songs*; 'Never Mind', *Popular Problems*; 'That Don't Make It Junk', *Ten New Songs*; 'It Seemed the Better Way', *You Want It Darker*; 'Steer Your Way', *You Want It Darker*; 'It's Torn', *Thanks for the Dance*.

an anchor for knowledge: 'I don't trust my inner feelings. Inner feelings come and go'.[105]

Even though there is darkness and death, humour and humility, optimism breaks through.

> You got me singing
> Even tho' it all looks grim
> You got me singing
> The Hallelujah hymn
> ('You Got Me Singing', *Popular Problems*).

'I don't need a pardon/ There's no one left to blame/ I'm leaving the table / I'm out of the game' ('Leaving the Table', *You Want It Darker*).

Lord Byron opens *Dear Heather*, lamenting the fading of love's pursuit, resigning himself to the soul's capacity to outlive the body, whose roaming has come to an end, a sentiment echoed by Cohen who is saved from the tiresomeness of choosing desire by a 'sweet fatigue', but nevertheless gratified by the exceptional kindness of women, who still have the power to take his breath away, and who implore him to gaze upon them 'one last time', as a man with no future whose days are few, embarking on his final journey home, unburdened of his sorrow and the public persona he wore, 'dying to get back home', travelling light and taking his leave with an au revoir.[106] The album he released weeks before his death rehearses his reconciliation with his G-d, but in no orthodox way. The profane shines through the sacred even at the dying of the light. 'As he died to make things holy / let us die to make thing cheap.' The imagery of life as a game of cards, and death as leaving the table, throwing down one's hand and declaring I'm out of the game.[107] In an interview, just before the release of *You Want It Darker*, Cohen declared that he had no spiritual strategy. He had some things to do and business to take care of but he was ready to die. He said: 'I hope it's not too uncomfortable. That's about it for me.'[108]

---

[105] Interview with Stina Lundberg Dabrowski, early 2001, Swedish National Television. Printed in *Leonard Cohen on Leonard Cohen*, ed. Burger, pp. 439-80, cited at p. 73.

[106] 'Go No More A-Roving' *Dear Heather* (2004); 'Come Healing', *Old Ideas* (2012); 'On the Level', 'You Want It Darker'; 'Because Of' on *Dear Heather* (2004); 'Darkness' 'Going Home' (*Old Ideas*); 'On the Level' (*You Want It Darker* 2016).

[107] 'The Goal', *Thanks for the Dance* (2019); 'Samson in New Orleans', *Popular Problems* (2014); 'The Faith', *Dear Heather*; 'You Want It Darker', *You Want It Darker*; 'Banjo' *Old Ideas*; 'Almost Like the Blues', *Popular Problems*; 'A Street' *Popular Problems*; 'Steer Your Way', *You Want It Darker*; 'Leaving the Table', *You Want It Darker*.

[108] Remnick, 'Leonard Cohen Makes It Darker', p. 18.

Conclusion

In this chapter we have used Lorca's distinctions to lay bare the different aspects of the poetic utterance in order to indicate our attitude and approach to appreciating a song such as 'Suzanne', which is undeniably reportage with its references to places and people who lived and breathed the air of Old Montreal, and 'First We Take Manhattan' or 'The Future', which revel in mystery and menace, invoking darkness and despair and surrendering to the abyss. The idea of duende indicates the inextricable relation between the poetry and the performance and enables us to capture the unique quality that Cohen the man invests in the poetic utterance, giving clear expression to what Gregory Corso recognized through intuition; the poem, especially the lyric poem, is dependent for its full force on the personality of the poet in the act of performance.

We will now show in the next chapter how Bob Dylan may be understood in similar terms by exploring his relation to Rimbaud and how he in turn gave inspiration not only to Cohen but also to Lorca himself,and to Dylan Thomas, the self-styled bohemian of the Uplands, Swansea, the Rimbaud of Cwmdonkin Drive.

9

Mine've been like Verlaine's and Rimbaud

Where do I begin . . . on the heels of Rimbaud moving like a dancing bullet thru the secret streets of a hot New Jersey night filled with venom and wonder.
– Bob Dylan[1]

Introduction

In this chapter we explore Dylan's alleged debt to Arthur Rimbaud and the conception of poetry he represented, demonstrating that both Lorca and Dylan Thomas are also exemplifications of what Rimbaud aspired to achieve. They did not offer a method for Bob Dylan to follow, but a vision of poetry to be emulated. We then consider different understandings of how we should appraise Dylan's lyrics, from those of the Dylanologists, who try to identify the people and places in songs, to literary critics, who search for literary allusions in the works of other poets, to those who think that the poetry or songs should be considered in their own right. The chapter continues with a consideration of Dylan's modus operandi in writing his songs and the charge of plagiarism often levelled against him. We conclude by briefly examining a few examples of the different genres that constitute Bob Dylan's oeuvre.

Rimbaud and Dylan Thomas

We have seen in Chapter 4 that Bob Dylan, Leonard Cohen and the Beat poets were attracted by Dylan Thomas's fame. As a bohemian performance poet, he had no contemporary rival, and his outrageous irresponsibility and his daring,

[1] Bob Dylan, liner notes to *Desire* (1975).

drinking and scandalous behaviour were legendary.[2] Given how much emphasis there has been on trying to establish a direct connection between the names of Dylan Thomas and Bob Dylan, which we argued earlier was more to do with Thomas as a person, his fame and lifestyle than his poetry, it is remarkable that almost no one attempts to attribute specific lyrical influence to Dylan Thomas upon Bob Dylan's work.

One of the few serious attempts is that of Christopher Ricks.[3] In reflecting upon the cruelty of blinding birds in order to make them sing better, Ricks claims that it is this very suffering to which Dylan Thomas alludes in the opening lines of one of his poems: 'Because the pleasure-bird whistles after the hot wires, / Shall the blind horse sing sweeter?'[4] Ricks speculates that these lines may have been combined by Bob Dylan with a nursery rhyme, 'My mother said that I never should / Play with gypsies in the wood', in which the little girl pays ten shillings for a blind white horse to take her across the sea.[5] The combination, as Ricks has it, prompts two moments in Dylan:

This is the blind horse that leads you around Let the bird sing, let the bird fly
    ('Under the Red Sky')

The Cuckoo is a pretty bird, she warbles as she files
I'm preachin' the word of God
I'm puttin'out your eyes
    ('High Water')

The attribution of some degree of inspiration, or influence, to the nursery rhyme upon the song, which is itself composed in the form of a macabre fairy tale, is entirely plausible. It was a song of English origin but widely sung by children in the United States. The young girl runs to the sea to escape the taunts of her parents, but she has no boat to take her across and secures her freedom by purchasing and riding away on a blind white horse vowing never to return. The ascent of the bird symbolizes the act of liberation.

The link with Dylan Thomas, however, is much less plausible. 'Because the Pleasure Bird Whistles' was written at the end of the year and looks back at the tension between how everything may be experienced clearer and sweeter

2   Dalrymple, 'The Rimbaud of Cwmdonkin Drive: Dylan Thomas the Last True Bohemian', *City Journal*, Winter, 2015.
3   Christopher Ricks, *Dylan's Visions of Sin* (London: Viking, 2003), pp. 77–8.
4   Dylan Thomas, 'Because the Pleasure-Bird Whistles', *The Collected Poems of Dylan Thomas*, ed. John Goodby (London: Weidenfeld and Nicolson, 2014), p. 108.
5   I. Opie and P. Opie, eds, *The Oxford Dictionary of Nursery Rhymes* (Oxford: Oxford University Press, 1951), pp. 315–16.

through incomprehensible or blind suffering. Even if we concede that Dylan Thomas was partly the inspiration for these two lines, the influence is both negligible and rather belated, and hardly constitutes any evidence at all for Bob Dylan's admiration of Dylan Thomas's poetry. Dylan's world-weary, harrowing 'Not Dark Yet', off *Time Out of Mind*, inspired Brian Hinton to remark that its 'railing against the mutability of life, [is] just like his namesake in "rage, rage against the dying of the light".[6] The difference is, of course, that Dylan Thomas was encouraging his dying father to rage against the dying of the light, whereas Bob Dylan is railing against his own imminent demise. 'Do Not Go Gentle' was one poem, however, that Bob Dylan selected and read on his Theme Time Radio Hour, taking as its subject 'Death and Taxes'.[7]

There is much more evidence to suggest that the French symbolist poet Jean-Nicolas Arthur Rimbaud (1854–91) was one of the major influences on Dylan's mental outlook in what the poet is aiming to achieve *in* writing. Even here, however, there are some connections with Dylan Thomas, the self-proclaimed 'Rimbaud of Cwmdonkin Drive',[8] who like Rimbaud gained both infamy and fame, but he was also often associated with surrealism, as Lorca had been. Thomas, like Rimbaud and Lorca, was conscious of his demons and aspired to afford them every opportunity for expression at the extremes of his consciousness. In a letter to Henry Trees, dated 16 May 1938, Thomas confessed:

> Very much of my poetry is, I know an enquiry and a terror of fearful expectation, a discovery and facing of fear. I hold a beast, an angel, and a madman in me, and my enquiry is as to their working, and my problem is their subjugation and victory, downthrow and upheaval, and my effort is their self-expression.[9]

Ralph Gleason argues that Dylan Thomas's characterization of poetry as requiring finding its own form, and never having it superimposed, relying on the structure of the poem to 'rise out of the words and the expression of them', is exemplified by Bob Dylan and the Band on *Planet Waves* (1974).[10]

---

[6]   Brian Hinton, *Bob Dylan Complete Discography* (New York: Universe, 2006), p. 309.
[7]   http://www.thebobdylanfanclub.com/theme/Death%20and%20Taxes. Accessed 3 May · 2020. It was broadcast on BBC Radio 6, Friday, 26 October 2007.
[8]   Letter from Dylan Thomas to Vernon Watkins, 28 May 1941, Dylan Thomas, *The Collected Letters*, new edition, ed. Paul Ferris (London: Dent, 2000), p. 548.
      John Goodby, 'The Rimbaud of Cwmdonkin Drive: Dylan Thomas and Surrealism', in *Dada and Beyond*, vol. 2, *Dada and Its Legacies* (New York: Brill, 2012), pp. 199–223. Both Lorca and Dylan Thomas had ambivalent relationships with surrealism, both exhibiting clear indications of influence, and both critical of it.
[9]   Thomas, *The Collected Letters*, pp. 343–4.
[10]   Ralph J. Gleason, 'Like a Rolling Stone', in *the authors of Rolling Stone Magazine, Knocking on Dylan's Door* (London: Dempsey, 1075), p. 92.

In a classic interview in San Francisco, in December 1965, Dylan, somewhat whimsically, listed a series of his favourite poets, two were singer-songwriters, Smokey Robinson and Charlie Rich; an inimitable comedy writer and performer, W. C. Fields; a circus trapeze and high-wire act, The Flying Wallandas; and two poets, Allen Ginsberg and Arthur Rimbaud.[11] Rimbaud was more than a throwaway name. On 3 September, at the Hollywood Bowl, he played 'From a Buick 6'. In the line which begins 'She walks like Bo Didley', he substituted Rimbaud.[12] In the 2016 Nobel Prize for Literature presentation speech Professor Horace Engdahl, in praise of Bob Dylan, argued that early in his career 'people stopped comparing him to Woody Guthrie and Hank Williams and turned instead to Blake, Rimbaud, Whitman, Shakespeare'.[13]

Rimbaud was for the Beat writers the exemplar of a visionary poet. John Lardas contended that Kerouac 'understood Rimbaud as celebrating the heightened sensitivity of the artist and calling for mental acuity through experience in order to have access to the realm of the universal'.[14] Bob Dylan invoked the name of Rimbaud and the tempestuous relationship he had with fellow poet Paul Verlaine (1844–96), in 'You're Gonna Make Me Lonesome when You Go' (*Blood on the Tracks*): 'Situations have ended sad / Relationships have all been bad / Mine've been like Verlaine's and Rimbaud'. On the surface the lines are self-explanatory and self-referential. They indicate that Verlaine and Rimbaud had a relationship that was certainly less than happy. At the level of particulars, outside the text, when we try to anchor the poem to the specifics of the actual relationship between Verlaine and Rimbaud the simple allusion becomes complicated. Questions arise such as who in this relationship does Dylan identify with – the older Verlaine or the younger dominant Rimbaud? Although neither admitted their relationship, they were lovers throughout their tempestuous intermittent periods together. The relationship was characterized by drunkenness, violent quarrels and Rimbaud's quest for power and its exercise through experiencing every type of debauchery, fuelled by Absinthe, morphine and hashish. The relationship in Paris, London and Brussels was sporadic between 1871 and 1873, at which time Verlaine was imprisoned for

[11] Bob Dylan, *Classic Interviews*, Chrome Dreams, 2003. ASIN B00008SHCN.

[12] C. P. Lee, 'Walking Like Rimbaud', *Isis: A Bob Dylan Anthology*, ed. Derek Barker (London: Helter Skelter, 2001), p. 79.

[13] 10 December 2016. http://www.thebobdylanfanclub.com/content/nobel-day-transcripts-banquet -speech-and-presentation-speech-©-nobel-foundation-2016. Accessed 27 April 2020.

[14] John Lardis, *The Bop Apocalypse: The Religious Vision of Kerouac, Ginsberg, and Burroughs* (Champaign, IL: Illinois University Press, 2001), p. 85.

attempted manslaughter after shooting Rimbaud in the wrist and trying to prevent him from leaving Brussels.[15]

Numerous Dylan interpreters have emphasized the importance of Rimbaud's symbolism to Dylan. Like so many of the claims about influences on Dylan there are competing versions of the 'truth'. Dave van Ronk, a close associate of Dylan's in Greenwich Village, contended that, although Dylan didn't speak of Rimbaud he was certainly interested in French symbolism because he owned a book of translations which van Ronk saw in Dylan's flat. Van Ronk suggests the influence can be seen in the later songs.[16] Both Dylan and Suze Rotolo concur that it was she who introduced him to Rimbaud.[17] Rotolo says she was reading Rimbaud, and it 'piqued his interest'.[18] Pete Karmen remembers Dylan saying to him in the Village, 'Rimbaud's where it's at. That's the kind of stuff means something. That's the kind of writing I'm gonna do'.[19]

What was it that Dylan got from Rimbaud? Ian Bell is quite dismissive of, and irritated by, the attribution of Rimbaud's influence. He says emphatically that 'What he got from the Frenchman was an idea about creativity, not a literary method'.[20] What he is particularly irritated by are those literary critics who seek to validate Dylan by reference to resemblances they find in lines of other poets. He does not say who he has in mind, but Michael Gray and Christopher Ricks pursue this line. Gray, for example, suggests that there may be a 'glancing allusion' to Rimbaud's 'The Drunken Boat' in 'Dignity' (*Oh Mercy*) when he sings 'I'm on the rollin' river in a jerkin' boat'. And similarly, 'True Love Tends to Forget' (*Street Legal*) has echoes of Rimbaud's 'Season in Hell', in the lines 'This weekend in hell / Is makin' me sweat'.[21]

Anthony Scaduto argued that Dylan wanted to write poetry for the people of the streets as Rimbaud had done. He maintains: 'There was much of Rimbaud in Dylan and his contemporaries: Rimbaud was an arrogant, rebellious young man, questioning the authority of government, church, educators, very much like a cat on the Village Streets or a Kerouac road bum.'[22] In *Chronicles* Dylan declares that his discovery of Rimbaud was 'a big deal'. He was particularly impressed by a letter in which Rimbaud said '*je est un autre*' – 'I Is Someone Else'. It resonated

---

[15] Wallace Fowlie, *Rimbaud and Jim Morrison* (Durham, NC: Duke University Press), pp. 43–4.

[16] Anthony Scaduto, *Bob Dylan* (London: Helter Skelter, 1998), p. 83.

[17] Dylan, *Chronicles, Volume One* (London: Simon & Schuster, 2004), p. 288.

[18] Suze Rotolo, *A Freewheelin' Time*, (London: Aurum Press, 2008), p. 199.

[19] Cited in Anthony Scaduto, *Bob Dylan* (London: Helter Skelter, 1996), p. 169.

[20] Ian Bell, *Once Upon a Time: The Lives of Bob Dylan* (London: Mainstream Publishers, 2013), p. 320.

[21] Michael Gray, *The Bob Dylan Encyclopedia* (London: Bloomsbury, 2006), pp. 576–7.

[22] Scaduto, *Bob Dylan*, p. 135. Also see, 179 and 221.

with him and corresponded with what he had found in 'Johnson's dark night of the soul and Woody's hopped-up union meeting sermons and the 'Pirate Jenny' framework'.[23] Rimbaud's letter also expressed the price of pushing the senses to the extreme, which Dylan himself had experienced immediately prior to his motorcycle accident. Rimbaud declared: 'The suffering is tremendous, but one must bear up against it, to be born a poet, and I know that's what I am. It's not all my fault. It's wrong to say *I think:* one should say *I am thought*.'[24] Rimbaud was to be a permanent inspiration to Dylan, not just during the 1960s when symbolism reigned supreme in many of his lyrics, but also to the present day. Patti Smith recognized she and Dylan had been working towards Rimbaud's 'derangement of the senses' to attain the knowledge that comes from 'pain, voyaging, searching'.[25] Smith, who wrote the preface to the 2011 edition of Rimbaud's *Season in Hell*,[26] met Dylan in 1975 for the first time and subsequently became a close friend. She accepted the Nobel Prize on his behalf at the 2016 ceremony in Stockholm, during which she performed 'A Hard Rain's a-Gonna Fall', a song associated with Dylan's fascination with Rimbaud.

This type of poem, Marjorie Perloff argues, stems from Rimbaud and is based on the principles of 'indeterminacy and undecidability', whose value resides in the fact that it is 'compositional rather than referential, and the focus shifts from signification to the play of signifiers'.[27] It has an internal dynamic that revels in, rather than resolves, mystery, requiring no external intelligible reality for its meaning. This is the tradition to which Lorca belonged, and it is also the conception of poetry that Dylan Thomas strived to achieve. Thomas argued that the poem is 'its own question and answer, its own contradiction, its own agreement . . . A poem moves only towards its own end, which is the last line. Anything further than that is the problematical stuff of poetry, not of the poem'.[28]

---

[23] Dylan, *Chronicles*, p. 289. The letter was written 13 May 1871 and was addressed to George Izambard, Rimbaud's teacher at the Collège de Charleville. Printed in Wyatt Mason, ed. *Rimbaud Complete* (New York: Modern Library, 2003), pp. 364–5.

[24] Rimbaud, letter to Izambard, p. 365.

[25] Robert Shelton, *No Direction Home*, Revised and updated edition, ed. Elizabeth Thomson and Patrick Humphreys (London: Omnibus Press, 2011), p. 299.

[26] Arthur Rimbaud, *A Season in Hell and the Drunken Boat*, translated by Louise Varèse, with a Preface by Patti Smith (New York: New Directions, 2011).

[27] Marjorie Perloff, *The Poetics of Indeterminacy: Rimbaud to Cage* (Evanston, IL: Northwestern University Press, 1999), p. 23.

[28] Letter from Thomas to Henry Treece, 16 May 1938, Thomas, *Collected Letters*, p. 344.

Lorca and Bob Dylan

Dylan has been far less explicit about his debt to Lorca than Cohen has been, but it extends beyond belonging to the same tradition as Rimbaud, although that in itself is not inconsequential. Christopher Rollason is in no doubt that the principal Spanish poet to invoke when discussing Bob Dylan is Lorca, who as we saw, was executed at the age of thirty-seven by Franco's fascists in 1936, just after the commencement of the Spanish Civil War. Lorca was an authority on duende in both 'Deep Song' and Flamenco. He played flamenco guitar and the piano, writing his own guitar compositions. In 1931 Lorca accompanied the singer 'La Argentinita' on piano, recording ten traditional Spanish songs, arranged and collected by him. Lorca had an abiding love of the guitar and wrote many poems in its praise and of its umbilical relation to deep song.[29] His poem, 'The six strings', compares a guitar to a tarantula that weaves a great star![30] Dylan's *Tarantula* mentions 'Lorca graves', evoking the Spaniard's horrific death. When Dylan is wracked with the pain of his acrimonious divorce from Sara Lownds, it is the unrelentingly despairing imagery of Lorca's *Blood Wedding* he evokes. On the much underrated album *Planet Waves* (1974), there is a pervading air of desperation. It was the first album since *John Wesley Harding* to express an emotional depth and commitment. There is an intensity of anger and frustration that had not been as evident since the classic albums of the mid-1960s. In 'Wedding Song', he declares he loves his wife more than 'blood', confessing in 'Going, Going, Gone', that he cares little for what happens to him next, but he's pulling back from the ledge and hating himself for being weak and 'on a trip down suicide road' ('Dirge'). There is a hectoring tone to the pronouncement: 'Go sing your praise of progress and of the Doom Machine, the naked truth is still taboo whenever it can be seen' ('Dirge'). It is an album tinged with nostalgia for Duluth and the cemetery in which he played as a child ('Something There Is About You' and 'Nobody 'Cept You'), where the joy turns to mournfulness at the image of 'the bones of life' piled high, in the town where he has become a stranger. The bittersweet nostalgia for Duluth is reflected in the notes on the back cover, written in a childish scrawl and supressed on subsequent pressings of the album. Dylan wrote: 'Duluth – where Baudelaire Lived & Goya cashed in his

---

[29] See Federico García Lorca, *In Search of Duende* (New York: New Directs Pearl, 1998). It includes 'A Note on the Guitar' (pp. 28–30); 'The Guitar' (pp. 31–3); and 'The Riddle of the Guitar' (p. 33).

[30] Christopher Rollason, '"Sólo Soy Un Guitarista": Bob Dylan in the Spanish-Speaking World – Influences, Parallels, Reception, and Translation', *Oral Tradition*, vol. 22 (2007), see pp. 124–8.

Chips, where Joshua brought the house down!' Unlike *Blood Wedding*, however, rays of optimism break through *Planet Waves* in such songs as 'You Angel You' and 'Forever Young'. Rollason suggests that both Lorca and Dylan share an emotive identification of places with music, with strong affinities between southern Spain with its deep song and flamenco traditions, and blues music of America's South, Dylan's 'Blind Willie McTell', invoking the familiar imagery of the gypsy so emblematic of Lorca: 'The charcoal Gypsy maidens / Can strut theirs well / But nobody can sing the blues / Like Blind Willie McTell.'[31]

Demystifying Dylan

A growth industry has sprung up around the analysis of Dylan's lyrics. Scholars declaring themselves 'Dylanologists' have devoted their intellectual lives to deciphering cryptic lyrics and obscure references.[32] These are people Michael Gray refers to as Dylan interpreters 'whose mutton headed aim is to say what Dylan's songs are "about".'[33]

With reference to Dylan's finger-pointing, or protest songs, what Cohen refers to as 'reportage', this may be perfectly legitimate. Knowing who Davey Moore was and how he died is essential to getting the point of Dylan's 'Who Killed Davey Moore' (*The Bootleg Series* 1–3, cd 1), just as asking who the pawn was in 'Only a Pawn in Their Game' (*The Times They Are a-Changin'*) is more than idle curiosity. To extend this approach to all his songs, however, is ill-conceived. As Peddie maintains

> Dylan's protest songs are his least procedurally Rimbaldian. Take, for example, the line 'William Zanzinger killed poor Hattie Carroll' despite the missing 't' in Zantzinger's name, and biographical fact, its power lies in word pointing directly to referent – that could in fact, be the definition of what Dylan termed, a 'finger-pointing song'. And, in a finger-pointing song, you need to know where to direct your finger'.[34]

[31] Bob Dylan, *1962-2001 Lyrics* (London: Simon and Schuster, 2004), p. 478.
[32] For some comprehensive examples see: Oliver Trager, *Keys to the Rain: the Definitive Bob Dylan Encyclopedia* (New York: Billboard Books, 2004); Hinton, *Bob Dylan Complete Discography*; Michael Karwowski, *Bob Dylan: What the Songs Mean*; (Kibworth, Lancashire: Matador, 2019); Scott P. Livingston, *Blonde on the Tracks:Dylan's Discography Re-imagined and Re-examined* (Amazon Platform, CreateSpace Indepednent Publishing, 2019); and, Philippe Margotin Jean-Michel Guesdon, *Bob Dylan: All the Songs, the Story Behind Every Track* (New York: Black Dog and Leventhal, n.d.).
[33] Gray, *The Bob Dylan Encyclopedia*, p. 196.
[34] Kat Peddie, 'I Is Somebody Else', *Popular Music History*, vol. 8, No. 2 (2013): p. 185.

Authors such as Christopher Ricks, Keith Negus and John Gibbens, whom Gray would consider engaged in the much more worthy occupation of 'critic', have published volumes which claim to deconstruct Dylan's words to arrive at their ultimate meaning – but this negates the idea that the song speaks in a different voice to each individual listener. Bob Dylan has often dismissed theories surrounding his work, declaring that even he doesn't know what he was trying to say. This does not invalidate various interpretations of his lyrics, but it does raise the question as to whether it is authorial intention, the listener's response, or both, that gives the song its meaning.

In 1967, French literary theorist Roland Barthes published his infamous essay, 'Death of the Author', in which he posited an end to the 'tyranny' of the author and a restoration of the reader to his or her rightful place of power over the text. Barthes argued that the reader's interpretation usurps the author's intention. In Barthes' model, the author should be altogether disregarded when examining a text, advocating a closed circuit of analysis between the reader and the work.[35]

The role of the reader, Barthes suggested, is to construct meaning from the text and the author's intentions aren't the ultimate arbiter of the text's 'truth' for the individual. The artist does not need to be conscious of what is being expressed. Biographies should not be considered when discussing the text. The reader is the ultimate arbiter of the text's meaning. This leaves the text in an essentially nebulous form, its message changing from one reader to the next.

Stephen Scobie, however, has argued that Barthes's theory of reader-reception does not necessarily dismiss the author from the text but instead intimates that the author should not dictate it. It is not the author who dies, but his authority or privileged access to the meaning of the text. Therefore, biographical details of the lives of both Bob Dylan and Leonard Cohen may be used to decode their messages, rather than dismissing without consideration any influence the writer may have had on the meaning of the song. In Scobie's view, key events in the artists' lives will undoubtedly have shaped their songs, albeit without their awareness.

Paul Williams believes that it is not biographical details or obscure inferences that make Bob Dylan's music resonate so profoundly with people, but the universality of his work. Williams argues that the song means 'exactly what the person who's listening to it hears and feels in it'.[36] Sustained analysis

---

[35] R. Barthes, 'Death of the Author', reprinted in Barthes, *Image, Music, Text* (London: Fontana, 1977), pp. 142–8.
[36] Paul Williams, *Bob Dylan Performing Artist* (London: Omnibus, 1994), p. 58.

of the song presents problems because each individual projects his or her own listening experience onto the song, making it difficult to arrive at a consensus. Williams compares discussing Dylan's music in critical terms as trying to give 'a liner description of a multi-dimensional experience'.[37] That is not to say that a critical analysis of his work is to be dismissed. Reading other responses to Dylan's and Cohen's work can enhance our own enjoyment of them and add another layer of meaning to the song, but we must be aware that ultimately the song is a profoundly personal experience and its meaning cannot be proclaimed as fixed or definitive. Art is important because it unlocks thoughts and feelings which lay dormant in its audience in everyday life. Encounters with art allow the individual to see the world differently to explore ideas they had not previously considered and to connect with their own emotional core. As Greil Marcus has declared, 'I was never interested in figuring out what the songs meant. I was interested in figuring out my response to them'.[38] The songs of Dylan and Cohen, he suggested, are so effective and loved by their audiences precisely because they do not premeditate their messages but allow each individual listener to experience it for themselves, without the safety-rails and signposting of authorial intent.

Dylan is far less reticent to take liberties with the music than he is with the words, and on this basis we can give more weight to his emphasis on the primacy of the words. In an interview with Richard Farina, Joan Baez's brother-in-law, Dylan contended that 'It ain't the melodies that're important, man, it's the words. I don't give a damn 'bout melodies.'[39] To Robert Shelton, Dylan confessed that 'I consider myself a poet first and a musician second'.[40] The vast amount of commentary, when it is not obsessively biographical, concentrates not upon the music as such, except to explain the different styles, but upon the words that, when at their best, for many commentators attain the level of poetry. Both Michael Gray and Christopher Ricks take Dylan's words very seriously, analysing them as works of poetry in themselves or as having broader biographical, historical or literary/poetic referents. Gray is much harsher on the later material, although the greater part of his major book on Dylan is devoted to it. Ricks extends more or less equal weight to the whole

---

[37] Williams, *Performing Artist*, p. 59.

[38] Greil Marcus, *Bob Dylan: Writings 1968-2010* (London: Faber and Faber, 2011), Introduction.

[39] Anthony Scaduto, *Bob Dylan* (London: Helter Skelter, 1973). Revised edition, p. 135. For Dylan's relationship with Farina see David Hajdu, *Positively 4th Street* (London: Bloomsbury, 2003).

[40] Cited in Ricks, *Dylan's Visions of Sin*, p. 11.

of Dylan's output.[41] Generally, interpretation of Dylan's lyrics takes the form of decoding the apparent or hidden meaning embedded in the songs, as, for example, the late Mike Marqusee, who acknowledged Dylan's work as art and viewed it as a personal take on, rather than a reflection of, the times.[42]

We now want to look at how commentators have interpreted Dylan and highlight what seems to us some obvious flaws in their methods. As R. G. Collingwood long ago recognized, asking the right questions is a prerequisite to arriving at the right answers.[43] When faced with different views about the appropriate way to 'read' Dylan's lyric poetry, how do we differentiate between the validity of the claims, if indeed we can? How should we read Dylan? And if we are to read different types of poem differently in what ways are the types to be helpfully distinguished?

Christopher Ricks, for example, distinguishes between songs that are about matters of historical fact, what Cohen called reportage, such as 'The Lonesome Death of Hattie Carroll' and 'Only a Pawn in Their Game' and songs that inhabit the world of myth and consequently whose 'Truth is to be tested and manifested otherwise than in history'.[44] Variations on, modifications of, and refusals to acknowledge this distinction abound in the commentaries and critical analyses of Dylan.

The first claim we want to examine is widespread in the literature and internet discussions of Dylan. This is what Gray called 'mutton headed'. Its distinctive feature is the search for references in the songs or poems to places, peoples and objects however oblique they may be outside of the poem itself, in the 'real' world. The second interpretative approach is the search for references or influences, whether they are musical or poetic. This, for Gray, is the only legitimate form of literary criticism.[45]

The first approach, searching for references in people, places and objects, assumes that the more you know about the things and people to which the song alludes, the better appreciation you have of it. Take, for example, 'Positively 4th Street', the single that immediately followed 'Like a Rolling Stone' and was recorded four days after the 1965 Newport Folk Festival. It is often interpreted

---

[41] Michael Gray, *Song and Dance Man III* (London: Cassell, 2000) and Ricks, *Dylan's Visions of Sin*.

[42] Mike Marqusee, *Chimes of Freedom: The Politics of Bob Dylan's Art* (New York: The New Press, 2003).

[43] The classic formulation is to be found in R. G. Collingwood, *An Autobiography: and Other Writings*, ed. David Boucher and Teresa Smith (Oxford: Oxford University Press, 2013: first published 1939), chapter V.

[44] Ricks, *Dylan's Visions of Sin*, p. 234.

[45] Gray, *A Bob Dylan Encyclopedia*, p. 196.

as a bitter attack by Dylan on his friends and critics in the folk movement, and whose title refers to where he was living on West 4th Street in Greenwich Village at the time. Indeed, in *Chronicles* Dylan tells us that he and Suze Rotolo had spent a lot of time together in the apartment on West 4th Street before they went in different directions. The fact that Dylan denies his estrangement from his folk community and friends was the subject matter of the song seems to make no difference to its interpreters. It would be legitimate to respond that Dylan and the truth have never been the most intimate of acquaintances.[46]

Alternatively, Minneapolis has been identified as the location because Dylan went to university there, and Minneapolis happens to have a 4th Street. He dropped out of the University of Minnesota, which might account for the vitriol and indicate that his former friends and students around Dinkytown were the target. Toby Thompson, in tracing the footsteps of Dylan through Minnesota, suggests that everyone around Dinkytown in Minneapolis, the student area, believed that 'Positively 4th Street' is about its namesake there; the area where Dylan hung around, socialized and sang in the 'The Scholar' and 'Bastille' coffee houses. Thompson says, 'Fourth Street would represent all of that to Bob, the social scene, the university crud . . . the old folk people'.[47]

For another example, take 'Just Like a Women' (*Blonde on Blonde*) and the usual story that accompanies it.[48] The song appears on the soundtrack of *Ciao Manhattan,* starring Edie Sedgwick. She died a few days after filming ended in 1970. She was from a wealthy family, and was both a fashion model and actress, a resident at the Chelsea Hotel at the same time as Dylan in 1965. She is the star of many of Andy Warhol's films and was to be seen more often than not hanging around with Warhol's Factory friends. Sedgwick and Dylan were briefly in a relationship in early 1966, which ended when Warhol told her that Dylan had married Sara. It was during the period when Dylan was in his 'transition from folk purity to the rock insanity'.[49] Sedgwick poured various cocktails of drugs into her body, living life to its extremes, experiencing violent swings of mood induced by a vicious circle of amphetamines and barbiturates to keep pace with her frenetic lifestyle. She was self-destructive. Her flamboyant and confident exterior disguised a deep inner fragility. Understood in this way the lines in

---

[46] Booklet accompanying *Biograph,* p. 52.

[47] Toby Thompson, *Positively Main Street,* revised edition (Minneapolis and London: University of Minnesota Press, 2008), p. 114.

[48] Trager, *Keys to the Rain,* pp. 347–9.

[49] In *Edie: An American Biography* by George Stein, ed. George Plimpton (New York: Dell, 1983), p. 228.

the song are propositions about an identifiable woman, which many feminists believed to be patronizing and sexist.[50] If this is the case, it is legitimate to ask whether the statements are true or false:

> Nobody has to guess
> That Baby can't be blessed
> Till she sees finally that she's like all the rest
> With her fog, her amphetamines and her pearls

Such an approach has a tendency to prioritize the detail over the song – the external referents of the song become more important than the song itself. But does the gathering of new facts about a subject lead to understanding its meaning better?

The author may appear to invite us to make the link with outside references, but the referents may serve intentionally to obscure rather than illuminate and complicate rather than elucidate. Endless speculation has surrounded the subject of 'Ballad of a Thin Man' (*Highway 61 Revisited*). It is a song, Mark Polizzotti suggests, that continues the prosecutorial vein of 'Like a Rolling Stone' (*Highway 61 Revisited*) and 'Positively 4th Street' (*Biograph* and released as a single in 1965).[51] Phil Ochs maintained that coming across Dylan at that point 'was like walking into a threshing machine'.[52] It was generally believed that the subject was Brian Jones of The Rolling Stones, who was a close friend. Dylan was always evasive about the target of his ire in this song. Brian Jones is also believed to be referenced in 'I Want You' in the lines: 'Now your dancing child with his Chinese suit / He spoke to me, I took his flute', and 'because time was on his side'. Jones wore satin Chinese styled jackets, played a flute and The Rolling Stones reached the top ten for the first time in the United States with 'Time Is On My Side' in 1964.[53]

Polizzotti concludes that with 'Ballad of a Thin Man', as 'with "Rolling Stone" and any other such lyric, trying to assign a specific individual to the character is ultimately a fool's game, and it is just as valid to say that Mr Jones is all of us – as Oliver Trager calls him, a "composite irritant"'.[54] This song is one of the few which Dylan performs regularly that has not undergone a radical rearrangement and which retains its original lacerating tempo and tone.

50 Marion Meade, 'Does Rock Degrade Women?' *New York Times*, 14 March 1971.
51 Mark Polizzotti, *Highway 61 Revisited* (London: Bloomsbury, 2006), p. 106.
52 Hinton, *Bob Dylan: The Complete Discography*, p. 51.
53 Philippe Margotin and Jean-Michel Guesdon, *Bob Dylan All the Songs: The Story Behind Every Track* (New York: Black Dog and Leventhal, 2015), p. 227.
54 Polizzotti, *Highway 61*, p. 109.

Let's take two further examples: first, the title song to the album that made Dylan a star, 'Highway 61 Revisited'. 'Highway 61' is, of course, an old blues song recorded in various versions and under various titles by many of Dylan's early exemplars, in which the route and towns through which it winds are not always faithfully rendered. Both Michael Gray and John Gibbens trace the blues and geographical associations of Highway 61. The term 'revisited' is seen to refer to both the bluesmen and the music that influenced Dylan's youth and to the highway that passed through his hometown of Duluth, Minnesota. Gibbens devotes twenty-six pages discussing the route of the highway and the places where famous bluesmen were born or lived.[55] This information says nothing about the song itself nor the fact that the song mentions no places or blues singers but instead capitalizes upon the symbolism of the road as the site of discrete and unconnected narrative sketches, ranging from the biblical story of Abraham relocated to Highway 61 to the possible location of the Third World War. In other words, Highway 61 is an image on which other images are placed and connected to each by the common site of their occurrence. Nothing we know about the real Highway 61 adds to our understanding of the lyrics of the song. Had the subject matter been 'Route 66', stretching from Chicago to Los Angeles, the subject of Chuck Berry's classic song, doing something of a travel guide might have been relevant. The song highlights and recommends towns and cities along the way for those planning to travel West, with the incentive that they can get their kicks on Route 66.

On Highway 61 you get more than you bargain for, a thousand useless telephones; a man whose application for clothing was turned down by the welfare department; a second mother with a seventh son; a fifth daughter on the twelfth night; and cheap seating in a temporary grandstand for viewing the next world war.

What then is the sense of meaning sought by those who anchor the song to the highway itself? Is it Frege's correlation of the sense and reference of a sentence in the use of language? Frege added an additional distinction which he deemed irrelevant to the meaning of an expression, what he called its colour. Thus, the use of guy, chap or man as synonyms in a sentence is a matter of colouration rather than offering propositions. The sense of a sentence has to do with the dictionary definition of the words in the context of the sentence, or at least those

---

[55] John Gibbens, *A Nightingale's Code* (London: Touched Press, 2001), pp. 66–92.

that are relevant to the truth value of an expression, and those things to which they refer, the referents of the words.

Basically, by identifying Edie Sedgwick as the subject of 'Just Like a Woman' we are able to determine the truth value of the statements in the song. In this respect we understand poetry just as we would understand any other sentence as a statement about the world. In this approach relating to the search for referents, meaning is equated with the psychology of the author, that is, with authorial intention, and building up the context assists us in retrieving the intention.

However, even in cases where we may with some degree of accuracy determine the subject of the song, its meaning may not always correlate with an author's intention. In the booklet that accompanied *Biograph* (1–3 in the bootleg series), Dylan reveals the process that sometimes happens even with songs that may conform to 'fact' or 'reportage', such as 'Forever Young':

> The lines came to me, they were done in a minute. I don't know. Sometimes that's what you're given. You're given something like that. You don't know exactly what it is you want but this is what comes. That's how that song came about. I certainly didn't intend to write it.[56]

The second approach is similarly a search for referents, allusions and resemblances, but instead of in places and people, or events, in the identification of influences in poetic and musical sources. This approach is exemplified by John Gray, Christopher Ricks (both with strong leanings towards F. R. Leavis) and Greil Marcus. The assumption is that if we can discover that someone wrote or sang something similar elsewhere this adds to our understanding of what Dylan has wrote and sung. All three are dismissive of what Gray calls 'superficial message hunting'.[57]

So the question remains, is this alternative simply another version of superficial influence hunting, something that the clever use of an encyclopaedic knowledge of poetry, or of blues lyrics, that enables the critic to match words and phrases with similar words and phrases in Dylan's songs? Such resemblances are almost invariably linked together not by evidence but by subjective intuition and flashes of inspiration. The connections are impressionistic and tenuous and

---

[56] Cameron Crowe with Bob Dylan, in Bob Dylan *Biography*, Sony Music Entertainment, 1985, p. 62.
[57] Gray, *Song and Dance Man III*, p. 1. Christopher Ricks, in distinguishing songs on their basis in historical fact and those that have their basis in myth, often talks of the latter category in terms of poetic influences particularly in Keats, Andrew Marvell, Shakespeare, Tennyson and, more recently, Philip Larkin.

expressed in deliberately imprecise language, as the example of a resemblance with Dylan Thomas's poetry indicated at the beginning of this chapter.

When linking Bob Dylan's work with other poets, Gray uses connecting lines such as, 'it seems to me to contain many recollections of major English poets'; it 'sometimes calls John Donne to mind'; 'the techniques resemble each other'; 'seems to remind one vaguely'; 'there is a keen correspondence'; a 'minor correspondence'; and even 'an exact echo'. We are also told that 'Dylan inherits ideas from Patchen too, I think – or again, perhaps just from the milieu that Patchen was a creative part of'.[58]

Ricks is largely sympathetic with Gray's manner of interpretation, while he nevertheless disagrees on the substance of some of the interpretations themselves.[59] Ricks is equally, if not more, imaginative in the links that he makes between the lyrics of Dylan and the poems of the great canon of poets, using similarly impressionistic, imprecise and deliberately vague words and phrases to make the connections. When Ricks discusses 'Sad Eyed Lady of the Lowlands' as an example of the sin of covetousness, he makes comparisons with Algernon Charles Swinburne. He maintains that Swinburne's 'Dolores' need not be the source of 'Sad Eyed Lady for the Lowlands' nor would Dylan have to be alluding to the poem for it to 'illuminate' the song's art. Ricks suggests that Dylan's use of the word 'outguess' in 'Sad Eyed Lady of the Lowlands' 'is in *tune* [our emphasis] with Swinburne's "outsizing", 'outlove', 'outface and outlove us'.[60] Ricks goes on to make the claim that *Dolores* 'may be heard as a prophecy of the Dylan song, a song that has been sensed, in its turn, as blandishingly hypnotic'.[61] In discussing Dylan's 'Day of the Locusts' Ricks asserts that in the use of the word 'birdies' Dylan is 'calling up the songs of Robert Burns'.[62] In other words, Dylan is doing all sorts of things with words without intention, agency or design, and Swinburne displays a remarkable talent for clairvoyance in foreseeing the shape of things to come.

The problem with the search for influence and origins, however, is the tendency for infinite regress. To say 'Dylan shares with Eliot the use of urban imagery and the expression of urban disillusionment'[63] is to invite the process of

---

[58] See pages 54, 65, 70, 76 and 77.
[59] While acknowledging the bracing discipline of Leavis's approach, Ricks nevertheless finds it too constraining. *Dylan's Visions of Sin*, p. 103.
[60] Ricks, *Dylan's Visions of Sin*, p. 100.
[61] Ricks, *Dylan's Visions of Sin*, p. 100.
[62] Ricks, *Dylan's Visions of Sin*, p. 195.
[63] Gray, *Song and Dance Man III*, p. 72.

infinite regress. Dylan shares this with a whole range of other poets, including Baudelaire, Rimbaud and Lorca.

Marcus follows a more subtle, sophisticated, authentically appropriate line of reasoning, evocative of the American landscape with which Dylan connected. In exploring the breadth and depth of the 'Basement Tapes', he tries to capture what Dylan and the Band 'took out of the air' and what in their songs resonated with it. They captured not abstractions but the ghosts of the real sons and daughters of American history, manifest for a moment in the *Anthology of American Folk Music*, 'the founding document of the American folk revival' compiled and produced by Harry Smith.[64] The anthology comprises eighty-four songs recorded between 1927 and 1932 when the Great Depression devastated folk music sales. This five-year period captured the diversity of regional music in the United States in the era before the 'phonograph, radio and talking picture had tended to integrate local types'.[65] For Marcus, *The Basement Tapes* were in fact a 'shambling' version of this anthology.

The past is another country

The third approach to appreciating the lyric poetry of a song is to abandon the thought that understanding its meaning has to be achieved by reuniting it with the external references to which it alludes, or to the resemblances it may evoke between it and other poems or songs, and adopt Dylan Thomas's attitude that the poem is self-contained and ends at the last line. The words are not taken as statements, or propositions that can be 'fact checked', or propositions that can be verified by confirming their 'correspondence' with other poems or songs. The words are more like pigments on the artist's palette, used to paint powerful images with the capacity to move us emotionally without having a determinate meaning or propositional value. Paul Williams agrees when he writes that asking who the real Bob Dylan is and what he is really trying to say are not strictly speaking answerable questions. Williams argues that he can listen to 'Sad Eyed Lady of the Lowlands' and feel empathy with the song and, become absorbed in its imagery, because the composer has successfully communicated an emotion despite the fact that the line 'My warehouse eyes

---

[64]　Greil Marcus, *Invisible Republic: Bob Dylan's Basement Tapes* (London: Picador, 1998), p. 87.
[65]　Harry Smith, 'American Folk Music', booklet introducing the *Anthology of American Folk Music*, p. 2.

and my Arabian drum' have no clear meaning to him or even to the writer of the words. Nevertheless, they have a relevance to him in the process of appreciating the song. Art, for Williams, is not interpreted but experienced.[66] In his view *Basement Tapes* signify the point at which Dylan purposely goes beyond the conscious statement.

John Harris, after quoting the first four lines of 'I Want You' exclaims: 'What is all that about? It probably doesn't matter. It sounds beautiful . . . .'[67] There are certain types of poetry, such as those that fall under the banner of symbolism, abstract expressionism, surrealism and what Perloff included within the categories of 'indeterminacy and undecidability', which do not lend themselves to over analysis and interrogation to reveal their meaning: 'The beauty of form and the music of speech which criticism destroys, and to which philosophy is, at best, indifferent, are elements essential to poetry.'[68] It should come as no surprise that poets, artists and philosophers share things with others of their kind. Indeed, Picasso made no apology for his pillaging of past art, which he nevertheless transformed and made his own. One of his most famous and politically powerful paintings, *Guernica*, is a pastiche of different styles and influences, including medieval Spanish iconography.

From his first album Dylan was not averse to pillaging the past and transforming songs – and folk standards – to suit his inimitable affected styles. He was more reticent, however, than he was subsequently to become, about claiming authorship. *Bob Dylan* includes songs which are traditional, such as 'Freight Train Blues' and 'House of the Rising Sun', whose arrangement he 'borrowed' from Dave van Ronk; songs which are written by Dylan such as 'Song to Woody' and 'Talkin' New York'; songs that are arranged by Bob Dylan such as 'Gospel Plough' and 'Man of Constant Sorrow'; and songs by well-known bluesmen such as 'She's No Good' (Jesse Fuller), 'Fixin' to Die Blues' (Bukka White) and 'See That My Grave Is Kept Clean' (Blind Lemon Jefferson). There is very little resemblance between any of the songs he did not compose and the originals. On *The Freewheelin' Bob Dylan*, it is well known that Dylan pillaged the melodies of the English and Irish folk traditions, having visited Britain in December 1962 to January 1963 to appear as Bobby in the Evan Jones play, 'Madhouse on Castle Street' for the BBC. He 'borrowed' the melodies, for

---

[66] Paul Williams, *Bob Dylan: Watching the River Flow* (London: Omnibus, 1996), p. 19.
[67] John Harris, 'In Praise of Bob Dylan', *Q Dylan, Maximum Bob*, 1 January 2000, p. 12.
[68] Henry Jones, *Browning as a Philosophical and Religious Teacher* (Glasgow: Maclehose, 1892), 2nd edition, p. 3.

example, from Martin Carthy's arrangements of 'Lord Franklin' ('Bob Dylan's Dream') and 'Scarborough Fair' ('Girl from the North Country'). The borrowing of melodies continues in 'The Times They Are a-Changin''. 'With God on Our Side' is sung to the melody of the Irish folk song 'The Merry Month of May' which Dominic Behan, the brother of Brendan, used for his 'Patriot Game', sung around Greenwich Village at the time by the Clancy Brothers. They also sang the traditional Irish song 'The Parting Glass' which Dylan used for the melody of 'Restless Farewell'.

Plagiarism or borrowing?

Throughout the whole, but particularly in the second half, of his career Bob Dylan used a songwriting method that was similar to that of David Bowie and of the writer William Burroughs. A precursor of it is to be found in Johnathan Swift's *Gulliver's Travels* (1726). The Engine at the Academy of Projectors in Lagado housed a huge frame which included all of the words and sounds of the Laputan language. When manipulated it generated random patterns of words, sometimes making parts of sentences. When perfected it would replace the usual laborious methods for producing works in the arts and sciences. The professor told Gulliver, 'by his contrivance, the most ignorant person at a reasonable charge, and with a little bodily labour, may write books in philosophy, poetry, politics, law, mathematics, and theology, without the least assistance from genius or study'.[69] When Kat Peddie described *Tarantula* as not 'fully symbolically integrated – it seems to act more like a collaged poem of spliced scenes that only start to generate possible meaning in relation to each other',[70] she is closer to the truth of its creation than she realizes.

In an interview with Paul J. Robbins, referring to writing a book which he tentatively called 'Bob Dylan Off the Record', and was published the following year as *Tarantula*,[71] Dylan gave an indication that he was experimenting with the method. He asked Robbins: 'Hey, you dig something like cut-ups? I mean, like William Burroughs?' He went on to say, 'Yeah that's where it's at'. He maintained that he was not able to sing what was in the book because it was 'all collages' that

---

[69] Jonathan Swift, *Gulliver's Travels* Book 3, Chapter 5.
[70] Kat Peddie, 'I Is Somebody Else', *Popular Music Hisory*, vo. 8, No. 2 (2013), p. 174.
[71] Bob Dylan, *Tarantula* (London: MacGibbon and Kee, 1971). First Published in 1966.

'had no rhyme, all cut up, no nothing, except something happening, which is words'.[72]

William Burroughs's method of writing was to cut up texts in random patterns and paste them together to create a text. Bowie used a computer to achieve the same effect in order to provoke and generate new images or a novel way of looking at something familiar.[73] The lyric content of Bowie's *Outside* (2003) was produced in this way. Bowie claims that he is not alone in using this method. It is common to many poets.

Dylan once confided in Joni Mitchell that sometime from the middle of his career that the 'box' wrote his songs. He explained that he constantly wrote things down from films and from things he heard people say. He put all the pieces in a box which he used to compose his lyrics. This did not, in her eyes, diminish the quality of the songs because Dylan still put the pieces together.[74] This explains the appearance of lines of dialogue from Hammet's *The Maltese Falcon* on Dylan's *Empire Burlesque*,[75] and the ten or more lines from seven poems by the obscure American Civil War poet Henry Timrod on *Modern Times*, justified on the grounds that Dylan was 'sampling' and not plagiarizing. Although specific attention has been paid to the use of Timrod, the album 'samples' numerous other sources including from the great blues singers Robert Johnson, Muddy Waters, Memphis Mini, Sonny Boy Williamson and Blind Lemon Jefferson, as well as Cole Porter, Hoagy Carmichael and Jerome Kern among the great American song writers. Robert Polito contends that 'So pervasive and crafty are Dylan's recastings for *Love and Theft* that I wouldn't be surprised if someday we learn that every bit of speech on the album – no matter how intimate or Dylanesque – can be tracked back to another song, poem, movie, or novel'.[76]

[72] Interview with Paul Robbins, Los Angeles Free Press, 17 and 24 September 1965. Printed in Carl Benson, ed., *The Bob Dylan Companion: Four Decades of Commentary* (New York: Schirmer Books, 1998), pp. 56–7.
[73] Bill De Main, 'David Bowie on Song Writing', *Classic Rock*, 28 May 2014. https://www.loudersound.com/features/david-bowie-on-songwriting. Accessed 21 April 2020.
[74] David Kinney, *The Dylanologists: Adventures in the Land of Bob* (New York: Simon & Schuster, 2014), pp.172–3.
[75] Doc Pasquale, *Back in the Rain: The Making and Unmaking of Bob Dylan's Blood on the Tracks*, self-published Amazon platform Book, no date, ISBN 36626914R00066.
[76] Robert Polito, 'Bob Dylan: Henry Timrod Revisited', https://www.poetryfoundation.org/articles/68697/bob-dylan-henry-timrod-revisited. Accessed 23 April 2020.

Back to Rimbaud

Encouraged by Charles Bretagne, Arthur Rimbaud studied Oriental and Kabbalah philosophies, in their mystical and occult dimensions, culminating in his idea of the poet as *voyant*, a visionary or seer. In 1871 he wrote that he was striving towards becoming a seer, by which he meant taking the path 'towards the unknown by a derangement of *all the senses*. The suffering is tremendous, but one must bear up against it to be born a poet, and I know that's what I am.'[77] Rimbaud did not have one style of poetry that unites his oeuvre, rather he develops styles that he employs very briefly. In 1873 he published the only work he considered finished, *A Season in Hell*.[78] The last of Rimbaud's major works was put together by Paul Verlaine and comprised mostly prose poems with some verse. The prose poems for Rimbaud constituted a liberation from the constricting forms of established verse. Wyatt Mason suggests that the *Illuminations* contains the most direct and vivid imagery Rimbaud ever produced in which each image stands almost completely alone, existing in its own right.[79] Take, for example, 'Barbarian', from the *Illuminations*, in which each word, series of words and sentences are separate brush strokes, and swathes of the palette knife, composing a picture in which each object is disconnected, creating flashing animated, disturbing and picturesque juxtaposed images which assault the senses and unsettle the equilibrium of place and time:

> Long after the seasons and days, the living and land,
> A flag of flesh, bleeding over silken seas and arctic flowers (they do not exist),
> Surviving old heroic fanfares still assaulting hearts and heads, far from
> earlier assassins . . .
> Infernos hailing frosty gusts – such sweetness! Fires in a rain of diamond
> wind, tossed by an earthly heart, endlessly burned to black, for us. . .

Rimbaud was a poet who, for Lorca, possessed duende dressed 'in the green suit of a saltimbanque'.[80] In Lorca's view, this rational derangement is integral to Rimbaud's notion of disorienting the senses in order to transform the soul into a monstrosity, by unhinging the intelligence. Herman Melville, whom Dylan cites as a major influence upon him in his Nobel lecture, also possessed

---

[77] Letter to George Izambard, Charleville, 31 May 1871. In Mason, ed., *Rimbaud Complete*, p. 365.
[78] Rimbaud, *A Season in Hell*.
[79] Mason, 'Introduction', *Rimbaud Complete*, p. xxxvi.
[80] Cited in Edward Hirsch, *The Demon and the Angel* (New York: Harcourt, 2002), p. 36.

the darkened energy characteristic of duende. Melville wrote out of what he called the instinctive 'knowledge of the demonism in the world'. Melville said of his masterpiece, *Moby Dick*, 'I have written a wicked book, and feel spotless as a lamb.'[81] Edward Hirsch argues that *Poet in New York* is Lorca's *Season in Hell* [Rimbaud]. It is the *Waste Land* [T. S. Eliot], his *Residence on Earth* [Pablo Neruda], his *Orphic Songs* [Dino Campana]. It is the book that 'concretized his idea of the demonic, the apotheosis of his duende'.[82]

The idea that art is the expression of emotion, while it is contested, nevertheless has widespread support. Paul Williams, in discussing Dylan's artistic performance, describes it as the expression of emotion and gives emphasis to what the performer is feeling at that particular time.[83] This relates to the emphasis that Lorca gives to the performative element in duende. We saw that with too great an emphasis on duende, there is danger of separating style from substance, that is, dissociating the performance from the song. In the art world take, for example, International Klein Blue, a colour developed by Yves Klein in collaboration with Edouard Adam; the intensity of the colour, preserved in a polyvinyl acetate binder, is so powerful that it has become the work of art itself, superseding form and content. See, for example, *Untitled Blue Monochrome* (IK74), 1958, in the San Francisco Museum of Modern Art. Michael Oakeshott emphasized the self-referential and non-propositional character of art, that is, art for arts' sake. Michael Oakeshott understood poetry to be a particular way of imagining, distinct from practical, scientific or historical images. He argued that what distinguished the voice of poetry in the conversation of mankind from the other voices is its manner of being active, or what Heidegger calls *Dasein* – being in the world. Artistic, or poetic, activity is contemplating or delighting in the making of images for their own sake. They are, as opposed to the images in other idioms of discourse, such as practical life, science and history, 'mere' images. They are not facts about the world because they are not propositions, and therefore truth and falsity are inappropriate terms in which to appreciate them. You do not ask of the images, could this have happened, is it possible or probable or just an illusion or make-believe, because to ask these questions assumes the distinction between fact and not fact which is out of place in poetic contemplative imagining. When Kate Melua sings Mike Batt's song 'Nine Million Bicycles', it makes no difference to the appreciation of the song whether

[81] Cited in Hirsch, *Demon and the Angel*, p. 85.
[82] Edward Hirsch, *Demon and the Angel*, (New York: Harcourt, 2002), p. 229. We have added the authors in square parentheses.
[83] Williams, *Performing Artist*, p. 3.

there are, or are not, nine million bicycles in Beijing. This, of course, doesn't deter curious people from wondering whether the figure is accurate! The website 'Song Meanings + Facts' is devoted to unravelling the 'truth' of the lyrics of songs and concludes that it was reasonable to assume in 2005 that there were about nine million bicycles in Beijing![84]

Furthermore, the images are present images, and they have no past or future. They are delighted in for what they are, rather than for what they are related to, that is, the occasions that may have inspired them. A photograph may lie if it purports to be a genuine likeness of its subject, but a poetic image cannot lie because it neither affirms nor denies anything. It is irrelevant to the work of art that it does not faithfully represent the subject.

Cézanne's *Rocky Scenery of Provence* is a composition of irregular coloured shapes, which together comprise an image whose artistic quality does not depend on whether it is a faithful representation of Provence. The same may be said of Picasso's *Demoiselles d'Avignon*, whose angular geometrical juxtaposed blocks of colour are not representative of, nor related to, an external reality which it purports to represent. To go to Avignon in search of demoiselles resembling those of Picasso's is bound to result in disappointment. The appeal of van Gogh's *Starry Night* is not to be judged on its practical or scientific use to a traveller without a map wishing to navigate from one place to another with the aid of the sky at night. Cézanne's, Van Gogh's and Picasso's paintings exist only as the poetic images they created. The arrangement and diction of the contemplative images are what distinguishes one poet or artist from another, the symbols are not interchangeable; to substitute one as a synonym for another destroys the image.

Oakeshott maintains that poetic images are mere images because the relation between symbol (language) and meaning (thought) differs in poetry from the relation between symbol and meaning in non-poetic ways of thinking. R. G. Collingwood agrees with Oakeshott in this respect. In *Speculum Mentis*,[85] Collingwood distinguishes art, religion, science, history and philosophy from each other in terms of the different relations they posit between symbol and meaning. In our everyday practical lives, for example, each symbol, or word, has a determinate referent or signification. In Oakeshott's view, the more determinate, the better the communication. If I ask for a loaf of bread in order

---

[84] https://www.songmeaningsandfacts.com/meaning-of-nine-million-bicycles-by-katie-melua/. Accessed 4 August 2020.
[85] R. G. Collingwood, *Speculum Mentis or the Map of Knowledge* (Oxford: Oxford University Press, 1924).

to purchase it, I am using a symbol to invoke an image, not to create one. I am not trying to give a novel nuance to the symbol. I merely wish to be understood in a shared settled language. In other words, meaning and symbol are distinct but not radically separable because in this respect 'every word has its proper reference or signification'.[86] The symbol is separable from and the means by which we convey meaning. The reason why art or poetry is different is because there is no separation of symbol and meaning: A poetic image is its meaning, it symbolizes nothing outside of itself.[87]

Lorca enables us to refine this understanding of poetry a little further. Lorca's *New York Poems* reflect his unease with the landscape of a vast impersonal city, with its poverty, degradation, segregation and violence – a suffering which seems to defy explanation. These poems mark a significant development in Lorca's style, from the poetry of imagination to the poetry of inspiration. This distinction was elaborated in Chapter 8 and resonates just as aptly with Dylan's lyrics as they do with Cohen's.

Bob Dylan's development falls into three overlapping and concurrent phases which correspond to the three types of poetry identified by Rimbaud, Collingwood, Oakeshott and Lorca. First, art as magic, where an emotion is deliberately aroused in order to achieve a particular practical effect, is represented by the topical songs of both the 'finger-pointing' and 'protest' varieties. Examples in the genre of finger-pointing would include, 'Let Me Die in My Footsteps', 'Who Killed Davey Moore', 'Lonesome Death of Hattie Carroll', 'Only a Pawn in Their Game', 'George Jackson' and 'Hurricane'. In these songs the crime and its perpetrators are clearly identified; sometimes the whole of society may be guilty.

The early protest songs are clearly injunctive in their intent. They are preconceived both in purpose and practical effect. Most even draw the moral for the listener. These songs are meant to charge the audience emotionally, channelling this emotion into active support for political causes. Some are direct exhortations to act, in other words calling upon the audience to do something about a particular situation or injustice. 'Let Me Die in My Footsteps' is a representative example:

If I had rubies and riches and crowns
I'd buy the whole world and change things around

---

[86] Michael Oakeshott, 'Poetry in the Conversation of Mankind', *Rationalism in Politics*, new and expanded edition (Indianapolis: Liberty Press, 1991), p. 503.

[87] Oakeshott, 'Poetry in the Conversation of Mankind', p. 527.

I'd throw all the guns and the tanks in the sea
For they are mistakes of past history.

In an interview in 1963 Dylan is explicit about his intent: 'What comes out in my music is a call to action.'[88]

The protest songs are in principle distinguishable from the finger-pointing songs because they are more subtle and expressive of exasperation at structural or economic injustices and of degenerative elements, or trends, in society. Here injustices are explored, the unexpected connections exposed, and the imagery embedded in occasions or situations which project a political point, often more subtle than the finger-pointing songs. These include 'Subterranean Homesick Blues', 'Chimes of Freedom', 'Union Sundown', 'Neighborhood Bully', 'It's All Good' and 'Murder Most Foul'.

Take the following two examples, which are 'topical' songs, but do not directly point the finger at anyone nor offer a solution, but they are 'protest' songs. In 'Its All Good' (*Together Through Life*, 2009), Dylan uses irony to maximum effect, as he does throughout his career. The title of the song raises expectations of optimism, whereas this sentiment is undermined by the lyrical and musical content. It is a portrayal of a world in disintegration, on the verge of collapse in an apocalyptic atmosphere of lying politicians, marital collapse, catastrophic sickness and accusations of murder. It is a mocking belittlement of the deceitful narcissists and privileged elites who flippantly retort, despite the litany of failures, it's all good.

The murder in Dylan's 'Murder Most Foul' refers to the assassination of John F. Kennedy in 1963, and as it transpires, the first single to presage *Rough and Rowdy Ways*, released in June 2020. 'Murder Most Foul', remarkably Dylan's first Billboard singles chart topper, is not in the mode of songs from his principal protest era. It is recited, rather than sung, has little vocal melody, and no chorus, just a repetition of 'murder most foul'. The song is a retrospect on contemporary American history, with periodic forays into literature and more distant pasts providing the imagery, held together by the continuous thread of Kennedy's demise.

It was the event that is often invoked as the turning point in Dylan's career when he stepped back from the centre stage of the protest movement and into the arms of the counterculture of the Beat generation. He had a morbid

---

[88] Cited in Clinton Heylin, *Dylan the Biography: Behind the Shades* (London: IT books, 2003, first published 1991), p. 77.

curiosity with the assassination of Kennedy. He visited the site and purportedly wrote about it in a typescript which was auctioned in the 1990s, which Dylan has disclaimed as a forgery. He did, nevertheless, have sufficient fascination to paint portraits of Lee Harvey Oswald and Jack Ruby, Oswald's killer.[89] The song is not merely a pastiche of images and cultural references but also a political intervention. Dylan comes down squarely on the side of those who claim that Kennedy was assassinated by a clandestine company of conspirators intent on seizing power and of deflecting the true intent by attributing the killing to a rogue gunman, Lee Harvey Oswald. It was the perpetration of a major con that fooled Dylan's generation and undermined democracy.

Second, we may further distinguish Dylan's poetry by referring to a category expressive of his personal deeper emotional feelings and turmoil, what still may be called 'reportage', but resembles more like Lorca's poetry of the imagination, in which the chaos of the moment is crystalized in a series of images that try to make sense of a time, place, person or event, such as 'My Back Pages', 'Ballad in Plain D', 'You're a Big Girl Now', 'If You See Her Say Hello', 'Shot of Love', 'Most of the Time', 'Ain't Dark Yet', 'I Contain Multitudes' and 'I've Made up my Mind To Give Myself to You'.

Take, for example, 'My Back Pages'. It is a lyric poem that on the surface could be taken to be a series of images: 'Crimson flames tied through my ears / Rolling high and mighty traps.' But if taken merely as images, the import of the song is lost. Knowing its referents makes a difference to our appreciation, despite the fact that it does not take a narrative form. It is a song of self-criticism, criticism of talking in certainties and absolutes and of being too arrogant and sanctimonious to realize it. It is a thinly veiled criticism of those whom he felt had used and tried to control him and of himself for being so easily fooled:

'Equality', I spoke the word
As if a wedding vow.
Ah, but I was so much older then,
I'm younger than that now.

One of Dylan's most intense songs is 'A Hard Rain's a-Gonna Fall'. In it Dylan expresses his emotions not in any literal, narrative or descriptive way, but abstractly, often through disconnected images, not through a story or a portrayal of a situation, and it is doubtful that he had any intention to arouse any particular emotions in

---

[89] See https://whowhatwhy.org/2020/05/09/what-everybody-is-missing-about-bob-dylans-jfk-song/. Accessed 16 June 2020.

his audience to any practical effect. The singer responds to a series of questions posed by an interested, non-judgemental, caring parent figure. The questions are simple: Where have you been? What have you seen? What have you heard? Who have you met? What will you do now? The answers are a series of evocative images, mostly disconnected, but in the first three verses the number 10,000 is repeated. He has been '10,000 miles in the mouth of a graveyard'; saw '10,000 talkers whose tongues were all broken'; heard '10,000 whispering and nobody listening'. The notes to *Freewheelin'* suggest that this song was written during the Cuban Missile Crisis (although there is some doubt about this)[90] and represents an expression of what feelings the crisis generated in Dylan. Scaduto is sensitive to what Dylan is doing when he writes: 'Hard Rain is filled with spare, sparkling images that evoke the terrors of national injustice and of international-insanity-diplomacy. Never mentioning nuclear war or fallout, the evils of segregation or man's inhumanity to his own kind, but forcing the listener to conjure with such terror out of his own emotions.'[91] It is not a polemical protest song, but as Nat Hentoff says in the notes, it is a transmutation of Dylan's 'fierce convictions into what can only be called art'. Tom Paxton, one of the first to hear it, said that it very quickly became acclaimed by Dylan's fans as his greatest work to date, and Dave van Ronk maintained that everyone became intensely aware that it heralded an artistic revolution.[92] Paul Williams suggests that Dylan wrote this song with no preconceived idea of what it should mean, nor with a calculated intent in what it should evoke in his audience, but nevertheless with a sensitivity to the effect upon the listener.[93] And this is the point that Bob Dylan is making when in talking of the film *Renaldo and Clara*, he says, 'When you go to a movie, do you ask what does that person do in real life?'[94]

These types of song are what Lorca called poetry of the imagination, the exploration of the interconnectedness of reality, the unravelling of its contradictions in order to make sense of them. As Dylan himself commented, he wanted to write songs that worked on many different levels. The same words with an interchanging subject may be both sincere and ironic when approached from different perspectives.

[90] See Marqusee, *Chimes of Freedom*, p. 60.
[91] Scaduto, *Bob Dylan*, p. 127.
[92] Andy Gill, *My Back Pages* (London: Carlton Books, 1999), p. 30.
[93] He says that the poet, in whose company he includes Dylan at this point, 'does not premeditate, and in a real sense is inspired, and yet at the same time must work very hard and have a talent that is uniquely his own, in order to seize the moment and be the voice of his times, his generation'. Williams, *Performing Artist*, p. 60.
[94] Cited by Allen Ginsberg, 'Bob Dylan and Renaldo and Clara', in *Wanted Man: In Search of Bob Dylan*, ed. John Bauldie (New York: Citadel Underground Press, 1991), p. 122.

Third, there is a point at which Dylan ceases to be a craftsman, ceases to have a preconceived idea with a determinate purpose, ceases to express his emotion, which was largely anger, *by* writing songs, and came to express his emotion instead *in* writing them. This is what he is trying to say in October 1965 when he comments that 'I don't write now unless it just happens'.[95] The process by which 'Like a Rolling Stone' became a song confirms this. His diversions into free form prose and poetry, and even playwriting, were an expression of his frustration at the restrictions of the medium of the song in which to express himself. 'Like a Rolling Stone' was a spontaneous expression of the anger and frustration he felt at the sterility of his art. He was bored with what he was doing and dissatisfied with what he had produced. On the plane home from London after his short 1965 acoustic tour, he vented his anger in a flow of consciousness with no preconceived subject and at an abstract focal point. At this stage 'it was ten pages long, it wasn't called anything, just a rhythm thing on paper all about my steady hatred directed at some point that was honest'.[96]

The absence of intention also characterizes the film project of 1966. ABC commissioned a one-hour television special based upon the tour of 1966. D. A. Pennebaker, the specialist in cinéma-vérité, was hired once again after the successful collaboration on *Don't Look Back*. Harry Rasky the serious film and documentary maker was recruited to produce the special using Pennebaker's crew. After thirty-five years, Rasky published his account of the unfortunate collaboration. He asked Dylan what he thought the film should say. Dylan answered: 'Say, man. It doesn't have to say anything.' Dylan went on to suggest that the film had to be something, but when asked what, he answered: 'I don't know. How can I know now?'[97] In other words, whatever was going to be expressed in that abortive film, was not going to be formulated beforehand, but instead would be expressed *in* the making of it.

The third category, what Lorca called inspirational and characterized in their performance by duende, Bob Dylan calls 'hallucination . . . atery' songs. Essentially, he is talking about an abstract song, not necessarily drug-induced, whose lyrics conjure up images with scattered referents, with no particular story, but which may have a point or many points, without needing to be stated. Dylan maintained in the mid-1960s that 'I've stopped composing and singing anything that has either a reason to be written or a motive to be sung . . . .

[95] Cited in Heylin, *Dylan: Behind the Shades* (Harmondsworth: Penguin, 1992), p. 125.
[96] Cited in Heylin, *Dylan: Behind the Shades*, p. 129.
[97] Harry Rasky, *The Song of Leonard Cohen* (Oakville, ON: Mosaic Press, 2001), p. 146.

The word "message" strikes me as having a hernia-like sound.[98] The songs are often dark, disturbing, disjointed and disorienting, even disfiguring, having only tenuous connections with the material and temporal world. They are the stuff of nightmares, dreaming we are awake in a world gone wrong. They are the type of poems that Lorca referred to as abandoning the quest for meaning and making sense of the world's confusions and conundrums, and abandoning oneself to oblivion, going where the images take you, and surrendering to the feeling of ground-glass coursing through your veins.

These songs are most strongly influenced by Rimbaud. As we saw, he was a rebel who wanted to reach a wider popular audience with his poetry in which he questioned all types of establishment authority, including church and state. Like Woody Guthrie he almost lived the life of a vagrant and drank very heavily. In addition, Rimbaud indulged excessively in marijuana and opium. Rimbaud claimed that in order to transform the poet into a seer or visionary the senses must become disordered or disturbed by a prolonged process of disorientation. Dylan's own well-documented drunkenness and excessive abuse of drugs coincides with the development of his abstract, almost surreal, poetic phase. Here art is no longer representational, but fragmentation, a series of abstract images, emotionally demanding, but having no direct intent. It is the world around him that provides the inspiration, often a specific incident or event, which stimulates his creative talent resulting in a series of images, mostly abstract, evocative of a mood or feeling, but you could not say that the songs were about the particular situations that proved inspirational. Even though the Vietnam War weighed heavily on Dylan's mind when he wrote 'Tombstone Blues' (*Highway 61 Revisited*), and the poetic images are inspired by it, the song is not a narrative but instead a series of metaphors whose inspiration happens to be the Vietnam War:

> The king of the Philistines his soldiers to save
> Put jawbones on their tombstones and flatters their graves
> Puts the pied piper in prison and fattens the slaves
> Then sends them out to the jungle.

President Lyndon Johnson is the Philistine leader who throws the draft dodgers in prison, has a programme of inner-city rejuvenation meant to improve the condition of the blacks, who are disproportionately represented in the battalions

[98] Cited in Paul Williams, *Bob Dylan: Watching the River Flow. Observations on His Art in Progress 1966-1995* (London: Omnibus, 1996), pp. 16–17.

in Vietnam. These may or may not be the referents to the images, but the images are meant to stand alone. In other words, a song can evoke the mood of an era, without having specific referents within it. Jon Landau realizes this in his review of *John Wesley Harding*. He contends that Dylan exhibits a profound awareness of the war and the effect that it is having upon everyone, just as the country is about to split apart over the assassinations of Martin Luther King and Robert Kennedy, over race, political and police riots, the presidential election and the carnage in Vietnam. Landau does not claim that any of the songs are about Vietnam or a protest against it: 'All I mean to say is that Dylan has felt the war, and there is an awareness of it contained within the mood of the album as a whole.'[99]

The songs that most epitomize this genre of Dylan's output are, for example, 'Desolation Row', 'Stuck Inside of Mobile with the Memphis Blues Again', 'Sad Eyed Lady of the Lowlands' and 'Visions of Johanna'. They are not confined, however, to the mid-1960s and feature prominently throughout his career: among them are 'One More Cup of Coffee' (*Desire*, 1976), 'Dignity' (*Bob Dylan's Greatest Hits*, vol. 3, 1994, *Bootleg*, vol. 8, 2008), 'Thunder on the Mountain' (*Modern Times* 2006), 'Pay in Blood' (*Tempest*, 2012), 'My Own Version of You' and 'False Prophet' (*Rough and Rowdy Ways*, 2020). In these songs many names are mentioned, some quite familiar, such as John the Baptist, Casanova, Galileo, Einstein, T. S. Eliot, Cecil B. De Mille, Shakespeare, Mona Lisa, The Madonna, Ezra Pound, and more recently Alicia Keys, Ginsberg, Corso Kerouac, Leon Russell, Liberace and Al Pacino. Other names have no apparent obvious referent, such as 'Brother Bill', 'Dr Filth', 'Louise' and 'Ruthie'. What all the names have in common is that they are contemplative images, not persons: the situations they are in, the roles they play, are flashing images, brush strokes on a canvas, that together comprise a populated landscape, whose reality is irrelevant.

By the mid-1960s Dylan had come to see his songs as experiences, and comprehending the meaning of the words was not necessary to understanding the experience, indeed, too much intellectualizing could destroy the experience.

Even though *John Wesley Harding* signalled a musical transformation, it did not herald a transformation in Dylan's poetry, but instead a steadier control of the imagery. The songs are still characterized by the presentation of images unfolding as narratives in dramatic form, but at the same time the songs elude those who seek to discern a meaning by appearing to have a direction and point,

---

[99]   Cited in Greil Marcus, *Invisible Republic* (London: Picador, 1998), p. 55

but suddenly veer off in a different direction, or unexpected turn. One reviewer, commenting on 'The Ballad of Frankie Lee and Judas Priest', asserted that 'There is a frightening delight in meaningless: drawled words. . . . irrelevant details and non-sequiturs'.[100]

'One More Cup of Coffee' (*Desire*, 1976), for example, was inspired by a gypsy festival in the South of France, but the landscape in which it is set has no place and time. Dylan says that the song wasn't about anything; that the verses came from some other place, and the 'valley below' was just a fixture to hang the verses on. 'Valley below', he added, 'could mean anything'.[101] Dylan tries to sing it with a flamenco inflection, with Scarlet Rivera on violin, evocative of both Lorca's obsession with gypsies and flamenco.

More recently, 'Thunder on the Mountain' (*Modern Times*, 2006) certainly contains biblical allusions and moral judgements about good and evil, truth and reality, and this is not surprising given the world of imaginings he inhabits, and how deeply affected he once was by both Jewish and Christian fundamentalist doctrines. It is, therefore, a temptation to find hidden meanings or injunctive messages in the lyrics. Starting from the assumption that appreciating a Dylan song necessarily entails deciphering its lyrics, Margotin and Guesdon speculate that 'Thunder on the Mountain' may refer to the exodus of the Jewish people from Egypt, or it may even allude to the Sermon on the Mount, or it may just possibly refer to his comeback post-religious conversion. And if all this fails, maybe it's about his divorce from Sara Lownds?[102] For Michael Karwowski, the title of the song definitely refers to Moses receiving the Ten Commandments from God on Mount Sinai, and he reads the meaning of the lyrics as a re-interpretation of God's descent in flames. Furthermore, Dylan's reference to 'Today's the day, gonna grab my trombone and blow', is a statement of his vocation as an artist in response to the words from Exodus, 'trumpet exceeding loud', abjuring it as biblical nonsense. As an added afterthought, 'The "blowing" in turn conjures the idea of the wind of truth, the inspiration for his vocation'.[103] Both interpretations presuppose that Dylan is engaged in creating what Lorca called poetry of the imagination. In it, they think, he is trying to make sense of the inexplicable by attributing some logic or meaning to the world and

---

[100] Jean Strouse, 'Bob Dylan's Gentle Anarchy', *Commonweal*, 1968. Reprinted in *The Bob Dylan Companion*, ed. Carl Benson (New York: Schirmer, 1998), p. 87.

[101] Paul Zollo, *Song-Writers on Song-Writing*, fourth expanded edition (Cambridge, MA: Da Capo, 2003), p. 84.

[102] Margotin and Guesdon, *Bob Dylan All the Songs*, p. 647.

[103] Karwowski, *Bob Dylan What the Songs Mean*, pp. 458–9.

Dylan's place in it.[104] The process by which Dylan 'compiled' the lyrics to his songs do not lend themselves consciously to present, or even allude to, deeper meanings than the disconnected juxtaposition of images would imply. Dylan's previous album *Love and Theft* (2001) had elicited a torrent of accusations of plagiarism, blaming him of appropriating fragments from Junichi Saga, the writer of a book about a Japanese gangster; Henry Timrod, the Civil War poet; and Ovid. In the interpretations of 'Thunder on the Mountain', a great deal of weight is placed on the first four lines, and particularly, on the voice of God in the book of Exodus. The fifth line, however, immediately diverts the listeners' attention away from Exodus and to a contemporary phenomenon, a female singer by whom Dylan had been captivated at the Grammy Awards, Alicia Keys. He says: 'I was thinking 'bout Alicia Keys, couldn't keep from crying.'[105] The first part of the line is taken from line one, and the second from line nine of Memphis Minnie's 1940 'Ma Rainey': 'I was thinking about Ma Rainy . . . I just couldn't stop crying.'[106]

'False Prophet', the third song to precede *Rough and Rowdy Ways*, announced on 8 May 2020 was illustrated with a skeleton, dressed in top hat and tails from the era to which the title track of the album belongs, the 1920s, holding a gift box tied with a ribbon and carrying a hypodermic syringe, not a scythe, in his right hand under the shadow of a hanged man: The Grim Reaper, bearing gifts and dressed to kill, the dispenser of justice and punishment. On 'Black Rider', Dylan comes face to face with death itself, alluding to Four Horsemen of the Apocalypse from the Book of Revelations (6. 1-8). The voice speaking in the first person tries to bargain for his life, menacingly threatening to hack off the Grim Reaper's arm, before submitting to his fate. In 'Crossing the Rubicon', the narrator, possessed by the holy spirit, guided by the light that freedom brings, takes charge, self-righteously threatening to cut up the addressee with a 'crooked knife', and terminating his prospects of reaching 'old age'.[107]

These are songs whose lyrics disorient the senses and defy narrative logic. They do not abate mystery by imposing some rationality or explanatory framework but instead surrender themselves to that mystery, inviting the hearer

[104] Karwowski, *Bob Dylan: What the Songs Mean*, pp. 458–9.
[105] Sean Wilentz, *Bob Dylan in America* (London: Bodley Head), pp. 308–9.
[106] See https://www.youtube.com/watch?v=0iyiJCfhDsQ. Accessed 8 August 2020, to hear her sing 'Ma Rainey'.
[107] Mark Beaumont, 'False Prophet', says 'the new song from Bob Dylan, suggests his upcoming album will be a late-career high point', *New Musical Express*, 8 May 2020. https://www.nme.com/reviews/false-prophet-bob-dylan-new-album-2020-rough-and-rowdy-ways-2662401. Accessed 17 June 2020.

to delight in it. We argue that the protest song phase in Dylan's early career may best be understood as pseudo art, or what Collingwood called art as magic. The songs are not only faithful in many respects to the form of the genre but also unique in the subtlety of the message, portraying the murderers and murdered as victims of a sick society. He is not offering a structural analysis of society in which the forces at work are impersonal. Instead he attributes agency to the officers of the institutions who have vested interests in perpetuating racism, the arms race or the running down of traditional industries. These songs, we suggested, are quite different from those which are expressive of personal rather than collective emotion and whose referents are still anchored in the logic of everyday reality, what Lorca called imaginative poetry. Finally, both forms of lyric are to be distinguished from the abstract expressionism of the overlapping 'inspirational' phase. Here we are presented with a parallel universe made up of the accentuated absurdities of our own, a series of images, but not propositions, about which it makes no sense to ask whether they are right or wrong, and whose images, to use Oakeshott's words, are to be delighted in, but in a macabre sort of way, with imagery inspired by the disorienting words of Rimbaud who 'contrived to purge' his mind of hope and joy by strangling it 'with the stealth of a wild beast'.[108]

Conclusion

We have shown that in at least some moods Bob Dylan should be considered to be emulating the type of poetry that Rimbaud, Lorca and Dylan Thomas aspired to write, where the imagery is self-referential within the poem, needing nothing outside itself for further illumination or elucidation. Namely, the poetry of inspiration possessive of duende. Whereas these poets did not provide Bob Dylan with a method, they presented him with a vision, an aspiration to be attained, not a formula to be followed. We then examine two orders of inquiry that purport to elucidate Dylan's work. The first takes each song to be presenting us with a series of propositions that can be 'tested' by discovering the people, places and things to which they refer. The second admits the futility of this endeavour to find the 'real' meaning of the text and instead follows the allusions by the author to other poets or songs and informs

[108] Rimbaud, *A Season in Hell*, p. 3.

the reader of how certain lyrics remind them of other words, ideas or lines found in other poets and writers of songs. Following from this we demonstrate that many interpreters take Dylan's songs, or lyric poetry, to exemplify the type of self-contained, self-referential imagery that characterizes the works of Rimbaud, Lorca and Thomas.

Conclusion

We began this book by suggesting that both Dylan and Cohen became inducted into the great American folk tradition and its immensely important revival through a familiarity with the inspirational *People's Songbook* and *Anthology of American Folk Music*. The deep convictions of Dylan and Cohen were initiated by a common immersion in traditional folk and contemporary music, with each adding his own nuance: Dylan the rich English and Irish melodies, and Cohen the European heritage of Spanish Flamenco and French chanson. That great virtuoso of the guitar, John Fahey, described Smith's project as a work of genius and an immensely important compilation of American folk songs. He credits Smith with having created the folk canon of America. 'Make no mistake: there was no "folk canon" before Smith's work.'[1]

Van Morrison once said that he always felt a considerable degree of trepidation about putting his songs out there. Writing them was comparatively easy in comparison with the scrutiny and analysis to which they were subjected by critics attempting to discover their true meaning. He said that not even he knew what they meant. They came from somewhere in the subconscious.[2] Among those songwriters who produce quite complex, elliptical and imaginative lyrics, this is a common refrain. We have argued that certain songs, those that conform to the kind of poetry that Rimbaud, Lorca and Thomas exemplified in their best moments, do not bear the type of analysis that tries to excavate a deep meaning. The imagery itself carries all that is necessary within it. What we have tried to do is to construct and explore the various contexts and contours in which Dylan and Cohen are reflected in order to indicate from where the songs emanate and have not endowed them with meanings that the authors themselves have not directed us towards, such as those that Cohen refers to as reportage and Dylan's topical songs.

---

[1] John Fahey in 'A Booklet of Essays, Appreciations, and Annotations Pertaining to the *Anthology of American Folk Music*', ed. Harry Smith, Smithsonian Folkways Recordings, Washington, DC, 1997, p. 8.
[2] 'Van Morrison at the BBC', broadcast on BBC4, 30 August 2020.

Their deeply spiritual natures and perpetual quests for religious fulfilment, whether in Christianity, Judaism, Buddhism or Hinduism, provided the sources for much of the imagery reflected in their compositions. We have not tried to suggest that there is a golden thread that runs through their lives nor have we tried to condemn them for the many contradictions between what they say and what they practice. One of the reasons for the remarkable longevity of their careers has been their openness to change, to take on new mantles and express themselves in different vernaculars. They projected many selves by wearing different masks that at once defined them, at least their public selves, while attempting, not always successfully, to preserve and protect the private selves they thought themselves to be, and often this was incompatible with the religious doctrines they were imbibing, which taught that the self is insignificant in the great scheme of things, absorbed into an eternal consciousness in which there is not I and thou. Remorse and redemption, guilt and salvation, envelop and saturate their constant struggles with keeping faith with themselves and with their changing audiences. The price of fame for them, as it was for the Beats and Dylan Thomas, whom they tried to emulate, was mental torture, and like Thomas they longed for a mask to shield them from the outside world.

Dylan remained much more publicly visible through the astute orchestration of his management whose sustained past and present images in sound and vision populated the consciousness of his insatiable audience, while at the same time The Never Ending Tour provided the opportunities to see him 'Live and in Person', without, as an audience member, having any real connection with him. Cohen's visibility has been less sustained, and because of the relatively small output of studio albums, there have been fewer opportunities for originality in recreating past images without constant repetition of the same songs whose arrangements became more sophisticated but remained instantly recognizable. Nevertheless, this millennium has not been bereft of resurrections with the release of *Field Commander Cohen* (2001), which reprised his 1979 tour, and *Live at the Isle of Wight 1970* (2009), capturing one of his legendary and most notorious performances in sound and vision.

The music is a vital element in encapsulating the power of the lyrics of popular songs and integral to this is the singer's voice. Dylan and Cohen have been persistently ridiculed for their vocal performances and styles, but the uniqueness of their voice is what captivated so many of their listeners. Afficionados of Dylan and Cohen ruminate on, what Barthes termed, the 'grain' of the singers' voices. The 'grain' is the *timbre* or body of the voice, what Lorca termed 'duende'.[3] The song, in Barthes's opinion, may be divided into the *pheno-song* which includes everything encapsulated in the lyrics, which serves the purpose of communication. The *geno-song* signifies how the melody works upon the sounds, focusing not on the words, but on their expression, that is *how* the voice and diction are used to express the words. When applied to the work of Dylan and Cohen, it is widely acknowledged that the performance is essential to their artistic content.

So many recording artists have 'covered' Dylan and Cohen songs, often in tribute to the legends whom they admire so greatly, but few have emulated the beauty and power of the original, and that is because they lack the 'duende', the depth of feeling that came from the innermost, and often darkest, recesses of the minds of their composers.[4]

---

[3] Roland Barthes, 'The Grain of the Voice', In Image, Music, Text, ed. and trans. Stephen Heath (London: Fontana, 1977), p. 189.
[4] As this book goes to press Universal Music has acquired Dylan's entire back catalogue of about 600 songs for an undisclosed sum reputed to be between $300-$400 million. Lucien Graige, Chairman and Chief Executive of Universal Music Group commented: 'I have no doubt that decades, even centuries from now, the words and music of Bob Dylan will continue to be sung and played – and cherished – everywhere'.

Acknowledgements

A good deal of this book has been written during the Covid-19 pandemic with restricted access to libraries. Where we did not already have the materials at hand, Camilla Boisen of the New York University, Abu Dhabi, came to the rescue, tracking down and obtaining electronic copies of the most obscure publications. We are deeply indebted to her.

During the period 2012–14, the years surrounding Dylan Thomas's centenary, David Boucher and Jeff Towns gave audiovisual talks at numerous venues and festivals. They were joined on stage at different times, discussing the 'Two Dylans', by Michael Gray, Michael L. Jones and Daniel Williams. Huw Davie adeptly provided the engineering skills throughout those performances. It was a privilege to have worked with such knowledgeable and convivial colleagues.

Leonard Cohen has been most helpful over the years in graciously, and swiftly, answering any queries we had concerning his views on various issues, such as on Hannah Arendt and her book on Adolf Eichmann. Although Kelley Lynch was superseded by the management of Robert Kory and Michelle Rice, she was extremely helpful in the early years of research for this book. Bob Dylan's manager, Jeff Rosen, was always quick to respond to queries and has been encouraging throughout.

Leah Babb-Rosenfeld, our commissioning editor at Bloomsbury, has been encouraging, patient and understanding during the writing process, and we are grateful for her kindness. We would also like to thank Rachel Moore and Mohammed Raffi for their efficiency and professionalism.

David Boucher and Lucy Boucher

Index